S0-AYC-608

Child Welfare Revisited

Child Welfare Revisited

An Africentric Perspective

EDITED BY

JOYCE E. EVERETT

SANDRA P. CHIPUNGU

BOGART R. LEASHORE

RUTGERS UNIVERSITY PRESS

NEW BRUNSWICK, NEW JERSEY, AND LONDON

LIBRARY OF CONGRESS CATALOGING-IN-PUBLICATION DATA

Child welfare revisited : an Africentric perspective / edited by Joyce E. Everett,
  Sandra P. Chipungu, and Bogart R. Leashore.
      p.   cm.
  Includes bibliographical references and index.
  ISBN 0-8135-3462-3 (hardcover : alk. paper) — ISBN 0-8135-3463-1 (pbk. : alk. paper)
    1. Social work with African American children.   2. Social work with African
  Americans.   3. Child welfare—United States.   I. Everett, Joyce.   II. Chipungu,
  Sandra P., 1950–   III. Leashore, Bogart R.
  HV3181.C485 2004
  362.7′089′96073—dc22   2004000748

A British Cataloging-in-Publication record is available for this book
from the British Library

This collection copyright © 2004 by Rutgers, The State University

Individual chapters copyright © 2004 in the names of their authors

All rights reserved

No part of this book may be reproduced or utilized in any form or by any means,
electronic or mechanical, or by any information storage and retrieval system, without
written permission from the publisher. Please contact Rutgers University Press,
100 Joyce Kilmer Avenue, Piscataway, NJ 08854–8099. The only exception to this
prohibition is "fair use" as defined by U.S. copyright law.

The publication program of Rutgers University is supported by the Board
of Governors of Rutgers, The State University of New Jersey.

Manufactured in the United States of America

To our siblings and extended families

CONTENTS

PART THREE

Using an Africentric Perspective
for Practice and Service Delivery

LIST OF FIGURES

LIST OF TABLES

Child Welfare Revisited

Introduction

JOYCE E. EVERETT

Our first book, *Child Welfare: An Africentric Perspective*, was prompted by concerns about the overrepresentation of African American children in foster care and the lack of recognition that their overrepresentation was a problem. It seemed to us that there was within the field a denial of the existence of a problem. Why were there proportionally more African American children in foster care than white children? Was this an indication of institutional racism, simply a chance occurrence, or the result of the interaction among a combination of situational, environmental, and personal factors that lead to child placement? Like Billingsley and Giovannoni (1972) and Close (1983), we wondered why many members of the child welfare field treated race as if it were invisible and/or they appeared to be insensitive to the effects race and racism had on the lives of thousands of children of color. Double standards seemed to have been applied in the interpretation of the experiences of foster children who were African American and those who were white. In short, the foster care experience was interpreted differently for white children and African American children. White children were readily adoptable, while African American children were hard to place. Overgeneralizations about these experiences were also fairly common in that placement and adoption practices that were successful for white children were assumed to work similarly for African American children in foster care.

Our first book was an attempt to call attention to racial differences and to elevate the importance of race in child welfare by arguing that race must be considered in child welfare practice and in the development of policies that enhance and support children of different races. After twelve years, we wanted to examine the changes that have occurred in child welfare practices and policies with regard to African American families and children, using an Africentric perspective. While a flurry of national activities and other efforts suggest that researchers, policy makers, administrators, child advocacy groups, and interest

groups are currently debating the issue of racial disproportionality, the conclusions are the same—disproportionality appears to exist, but its causes are complex and require continuous study.

Despite these conclusions, the editors of this book are quite taken with the
fact that at least twice in the past two years, maybe more, stories about children
living in foster care have appeared as headlines in the national news. One such
story focused on the disappearance of a young ward of the state of Florida who
had been missing for more than a year after being taken by her caseworker from
the home of a relative with whom the child had been placed (Canedy 2002). The
other headline story described the discovery of the dead body of a young male
child found in a trash can in the basement of the foster home in which the New
Jersey Division of Youth and Family Services had placed him (Jones 2003). In
both cases, the children involved were African American, a fact that few find
surprising and few, if any, news reporters highlight. Upon reading these headlines one wonders whether anyone ever cared about these children. Stories of
this type leave lasting impressions of a system in disarray and disorder. And
while stories of this nature are far from commonplace, they dramatize some of
the persistent flaws within the child welfare system. These flaws range from an
inaccurate accounting of the numbers and types of placement of children in
care, to an inability to closely and regularly monitor the placement of children
in the state's custody, to the inadequacy of investigations of alleged abuse and
neglect by foster parents as well as birth parents.

For the brief amount of time these stories are the focus of media coverage,
the plight of these scorned children is the subject of widespread discussion in
governors' offices, departments of children and families, states' attorneys general offices, child welfare advocacy organizations, and among child welfare workers. Most of these discussions are aimed at determining who is to be blamed and
what can be done to correct the situation, while others concentrate on damage
control and reorganization. These discussions are likely to be limited to the specific circumstances pertaining to the case and to the operations of the state
agencies implicated in the news story. Few of these initial discussions will be ele-
vated to a consideration of the flaws in national policy, and all of these discussions will be framed within the context of the state budgetary constraints. None
of the discussions will stress the issue of race or the implications of administrative or policy changes for minority children and their families. Yet, it would be
difficult to understand the current crisis in child welfare without reflecting upon
the role that segregation and racism have played in shaping the development of
child welfare policies across time (Rosner & Markowitz 1997).

African American Children and Child Welfare through Time

African American families and children have long experienced discrimination
in the child welfare system. As a group, African Americans were virtually

excluded from any meaningful and structured governmental services prior to World War II (Billingsley & Giovannoni 1972; Roberts 2002). Rather, African American families and children relied upon themselves and their churches for mutual aid and support. As White and Hampton (1995) note, "Before the American Revolution, African American churches were established as centers for social welfare, antislavery activity and leadership development" (115–116). These authors indicate that Richard Allen and Absolom Jones at the end of the Revolutionary War established the first formal social welfare agency in Philadelphia. For many African American slaves and freedmen, their extended families, kin networks, and churches became the only means for assuring many displaced African American children a home during the pre-emancipated period. Church congregations, according to Billingsley and Giovannoni (1972), helped to develop orphanages, kindergartens, and schools for children. Only a few private orphanages offered in-home services to former slave families, while the orphanages established by the Bureau of Refugees, Freedmen, and Abandoned Lands, commonly known as the Freedmen's Bureau, were short-lived. However brief its existence, the Freedmen's Bureau was instrumental in establishing hospitals, orphan asylums for children, and schools for African American children, and in distributing rations to both blacks and whites in the post–Civil War period.

By far the dominant forms of care for African American children following the Civil War were developed through the self-help efforts of churches, mutual aid organizations, and voluntary associations. As O'Donnell (1994) indicates, "Black self-help philanthropy flourished into the Progressive Era" (763). Nevertheless, African Americans were denied access to orphanages, settlement houses, and clinics serving whites. For example, "in 1883 78 percent of the 353 orphanages across the country excluded black children, 68 mostly public institutions admitted a tiny number and only nine orphanages exclusively sheltered black children" (Morton 2000, 141). Most of these all–African American orphanages were overcrowded and understaffed. Between 1890 and 1933, the number of orphanages for white and nonwhite children increased; however, there was a notable decrease in racially integrated institutions. At the time the prevailing philosophy governing child welfare services was one of child rescue, with little recognition or regard for the role and value of the family as a unit (Stadum as cited in Hodges 2001).

Despite the denial of access to most child welfare services, African American charities sponsored by churches, social clubs, lodges, and secret organizations were established in northern cities and throughout the South. W.E.B. DuBois documented the hundreds of African American charities in northern cities and in the South by the turn of the nineteenth century (O'Donnell 1994, 764). Day nurseries, educational programs, orphanages, "old people's" homes, and recreation and settlement houses were prominent among African American benevolent institutions. Organizations that were primarily limited to men, such as the Masons and the Knights of Pythias, sponsored activities and fund-raising for benevolent causes (Hodges 2001). Often poorly funded and without a stable source of funding, these charities were far less regimented than government-sponsored programs, and they emphasized industrial training for the jobs available to African Americans. Some scholars (Gordon 1994; Ross 1978) note that in the African American self-help tradition, there was less of a status distinction between helper and the helped and greater emphasis on community development and the group as a whole. Of particular note were the child welfare efforts sponsored by the African American women's clubs before and after the turn of the nineteenth century. All of the self-help efforts sponsored by these black women's clubs were aimed toward the "social uplifting of the race," in the form of charity, self-improvement through education, and campaigns for more respect for the African American race (Gordon 1994). The forms of social uplift divided along social class lines, with middle-class African American women organizing clubs, the black working class relying on mutual benefit programs that offered insurance for illness, burial, or other misfortunes, and poor women relying on church organizations (Gordon 1994). For the black women's club members, greater priority was given to the establishment of schools ranging from kindergartens to colleges, health programs, and "old people's" homes.

In spite of these self-help efforts, needy African American children were more likely to be labeled and treated as delinquent and sent to adult prisons between the Progressive Era and the 1920s. They were excluded from child welfare institutions and received fewer in-home services before being labeled delinquent rather than dependent children. Once labeled as delinquent, African American children, especially males, were sent to adult prison (Billingsley & Giovannoni 1972, 80). As a result of these practices, African American children were virtually invisible to the child welfare system. Billingsley and Giovannoni (1972) draw two generalizations about the child welfare system's response to the needs of African American children during the early 1900s; first, that the array of services was inaccessible to African American children, and second, that the intersection between agency auspices and racial patterning adversely affected African American children. In northern cities like New York, sectarian agencies controlled the care of dependent children, even though they were not funded by public agencies. Consequently, African American dependent children in these cities were either denied service or were underserved through the child welfare system. Private sectarian agencies refused to serve them, offered segregated services to only a select few, or served a limited quota of African American children. Still, the number of orphaned African American children within the public sector rose, while the number of institutional facilities capable of providing services to them declined. Billingsley and Giovannoni (1972) note that in New York, for example, all services were provided through sectarian agencies that were partially or totally segregated, and adoption services for African American children were nonexistent.

The situation grew bleaker for African American children following World War II as more African Americans migrated from southern to northern and midwestern states at an accelerated rate. Poverty among these recent migrants who lived in geographically concentrated areas was relatively high, yet the number and range of services to address their needs did not rise. In fact, greater emphasis was placed on the integration of African American children into existing facilities that were designed for white children. And sectarian agencies in northern cities continued to openly discriminate against African Americans, as exemplified by the *Wilder v. Sugarman* lawsuit filed in New York in the 1960s and settled some twenty years later in 1984 (see Bernstein 2001). There were continued self-help efforts on the part of African Americans through such organizations as the National Urban League and the National Association for the Advancement of Colored People. Notable among the efforts sponsored by the National Urban League was its success in encouraging African Americans to obtain social work degrees in the early 1900s and through its local affiliates, the Foster Care and Adoption Projects that began in the 1950s. The latter successfully demonstrated that African American "children could and would be adopted" (Billingsley & Giovannoni 1972, 171), ushering a new service option for many.

As the reliance upon public agencies increased, many of the services and agencies established through African American self-help efforts were extinguished due to the increasing professionalization of social work with its emphasis on social diagnosis and treatment and the increasing difficulty in raising the necessary funds to support them. Historical accounts of the treatment of African American children by the child welfare system following World War II are, to say the least, sketchy. What is fairly clear is that there was a dramatic rise in the number of dependent African American children, their placement history was lengthy and frequently geographically distant from their ethnic communities, access to mental health and other services was restricted, and the likelihood of their return to birth parents was limited. Given a history of segregation and discriminatory treatment, is there any reason to assume that things have markedly changed?

Overview of the Book

Rather than engaging in a lengthy discussion in response to the aforementioned question, we prefer instead to change the lens through which child welfare practices and policies might be viewed. By using an Africentric perspective to examine child welfare policies and practices, we are asserting the importance of a cultural perspective. Taking a culturally based perspective can serve as a catalyst for creativity and innovation in the formulation of policies and practices used to secure safety and permanency for African American children. From such a lens, the parallels between the qualities of the previously described self-help efforts of African Americans and their current strengths and resilience can be drawn. The Africentric perspective "is used to describe the social context, value base, attitudes and behaviors that shape the belief systems, coping strategies, defensive styles, help-seeking behaviors, and treatment responses of African American families and children" (Everett, Chipungu & Leashore 1997, 11). It stresses the importance of kinship ties, collective identity, spirituality, the oneness of body, mind, and spirit, and harmony between nature and humanity. Twelve years ago, the idea of taking an Africentric perspective was a major departure from the norm. We were surprised by the positive reception the first book received from child welfare workers and students who witness differential treatment daily and struggle to maintain their capacity to deliver services to and engage with clients from a culturally responsive perspective. We do not, however, assume that our readers or the contributors to this book assume an Africentric perspective. Many will dismiss its relevance. Others will consider its import and some will reject it completely. Yet, it is a perspective that is gaining interest as an interpretative framework, and one that we think remains useful in the delivery of child welfare services to African American families and children.

Like our previous book, this one is organized into three parts, designed to establish the societal, cultural, and policy context in which African American families and their children function, a knowledge base for working with African American families, the social problems they confront, and descriptions of some innovative practice strategies for delivering child welfare services. Greater emphasis is placed in this book on child welfare practices. In chapter 1, Jacqueline Marie Smith provides a demographic profile of African American families and children drawn from a variety of databases and discusses the implications of this profile for social policy. Robert Hill, in chapter 2, directly examines the extent to which institutional racism plays a role in child welfare. He carefully and systematically reviews and assesses recent studies that have investigated the issue of racial disproportionality in child welfare decision making. Sandra Chipungu in chapter 3 summarizes the major policy developments in child welfare since 1991 and assesses their impact on African American children.

The second part of the book is designed to increase the reader's understanding of the inner workings of African American families. It begins, in chapter 4, with a description of a creative practice model for working with African American families. Joyce Beckett and Nicole Lee's model integrates the strengths, empowerment, resiliency, and ecological perspectives to create an ecological Africentric model to guide practice with African American families. In chapter 5, Melvin Wilson, LaKeesha Woods, and Gina Hijjawi describe the context within which African American families function, including the internal challenges affecting the roles assumed by family members and their impact on their ability to parent healthy children. Parental absence, poverty and unemployment, incarceration, health, and child welfare represent external challenges to family functioning and are also described. Chapter 6 by Carmen Moten provides a selective review of the literature on parenting styles within African American families by focusing on parental expectations, child-rearing practices, and parent training interventions. An understanding of African American child-rearing practices is essential for making assessments of the inherent strengths of extended families. The next two chapters specifically focus on birth mothers and birth fathers. Marian Harris in chapter 7 focuses on the historical relationship between African American birth mothers and their children. Based on this historical assessment, she offers guidelines for assessment and intervention with birth mothers whose children are placed with kin. Waldo Johnson and Vaughn Bryant's research examines caseworkers' perceptions and their capacity to engage unwed fathers in permanency planning. It is fairly common to ignore unwed fathers in permanency planning; however, paternal involvement can be a viable alternative for securing a safe, secure, and nurturing home for dependent children.

In the third part of the book we turn to an examination of the shift in child welfare practices that emphasize holistic interventions, client involvement, community-based services, systems of care, and adoption practices. In chapter 9, Joshua Okundaye, Claudia Lawrence-Webb, and Pamela Smith describe the interrelationship between substance abuse, homelessness, HIV/AIDS, and child welfare. Given the interrelatedness of these problems, these authors call for more holistic intervention strategies. Crystal Mills and Debra Usher in chapter 10 describe an innovative model of intervention, family group decision making. This model was instituted by law in New Zealand in 1989 in response to certain concerns about the alienation of children in foster care from their ethnic, racial, and tribal heritage; a failure to involve family members in decisions about placement; and instability of placements. The model has been adapted in several communities in the United States, England, and Canada and has been found to reduce out-of-home placement and to increase the likelihood that children are placed within their own ethnic, racial, or religious group (Samantrai 2004). Alma Carten and James Dumpson in chapter 11 describe legislative trends that support the development of neighborhood-based services and family preservation interventions, which they argue is a universal and enduring theme of the black experience. Shifting the location of child welfare services reduces the distance between the helper and the helpee and reduces the alienation between the child and his or her ethnic, racial roots. In chapter 12, Maxwell Manning calls attention to the problems of integrating mental health services with child welfare. African American children in out-of-home placements are at greater risk of experiencing mental health disorders, yet they have far less access to mental health services and lower utilization rates. Manning advocates for a culturally competent systems of care model. Systems of care models are child-centered, family-focused, family driven, and community-based, and are culturally competent and responsive. In the final chapter adoption practices are considered. Ruth McRoy identifies service delivery issues in adoption practices, describes informal adoption practices among African Americans, and identifies the barriers faced by African Americans who wish to adopt. Specialized recruitment and retention programs for African American adopting families are described and best practices in adoption are illustrated.

Child welfare services were never developed to serve primarily African American children. Structural discrimination as Hill (chapter 2) describes it is simply an insidious artifact of child welfare history that has resulted in what is now recognized as racial disproportionality. Recognizing the historical antecedents to the current overrepresentation of African American children in the child welfare system is one of the first steps toward rectifying the problem. Using a culturally based perspective such as the Africentric perspective to assess the underlying factors influencing child welfare decision making constitutes yet another step. "Admittedly, the Africentric perspective is evolving. However, when it is juxtaposed with the Eurocentric and American philosophies, the contrast in the value base, in ways of knowing and doing, reveals the incongruencies and inconsistencies in current practice and its effects on ethnically and racially different groups" (Everett 1997, 11). The next step is action in the form of developing responsive service delivery systems and culturally responsive policies. The following chapters are informed by and illustrate the use of a cultural perspective on child welfare.

REFERENCES

Bernstein, N. 2001. *The Lost Children of Wilder: The Epic Struggle to Change Foster Care*. New York: Pantheon.

Billingsley, A., & J. Giovannoni. 1972. *Children of the Storm: Black Children and American Child Welfare*. Atlanta: Harcourt Brace Jovanovich.

Canedy, D. May 25, 2002. "Urgent Plea Made for Data on Lost Girl, Papers Show." *New York Times*, 14.

Close, M. 1983. "Child Welfare and People of Color: Denial of Equal Access." *Social Work Research Abstracts* 19/4:13–20.

Everett, J. 1997. Introduction to *Child Welfare: An Africentric Perspective*, edited by J. Everett, S. Chipungu & B. Leashore. New Brunswick, NJ: Rutgers University Press.

Everett, J., S. Chipungu & B. Leashore. 1997. *Child Welfare: An Africentric Perspective*. New Brunswick, NJ: Rutgers University Press.

Gordon, L. 1994. *Pitied But Not Entitled: Single Mothers and the History of Welfare, 1890–1935*. New York: The Free Press.

Hodges, V. 2001. "Historical Development of African American Child Welfare Services." In *African American Leadership*, edited by I. Carlton-LaNey, 203–213. Washington, DC: NASW Press.

Jones, R. L. March 9, 2003. "Two Brothers Found in Newark Basement Are Placed in Foster Care." *New York Times*, 35.

Morton, M. 2000. "Institutionalizing Inequalities: Black Children and Child Welfare in Cleveland, 1859–1998." *Journal of Social History* 34/1:141–162.

O'Donnell, S. 1994. "The Care of Dependent African American Children in Chicago: The Struggle between Black Self-Help and Professionalism." *Journal of Social History* 27:736–776.

Roberts, D. 2002. *Shattered Bonds: The Color of Child Welfare*. New York: Basic Books.

Rosner, D., & G. Markowitz. 1997. "Race, Foster Care, and the Politics of Abandonment in New York City." *American Journal of Public Health* 87/11:1844–1849.

Ross, E. 1978. *Black Heritage in Social Welfare, 1860–1930*. Metuchen, NJ: Scarecrow Press.

Samantrai, K. 2004. *Culturally Competent Public Child Welfare Practice*. Pacific Grove, CA: Brooks Cole.

White, B., & D. Hampton. 1995. "African American Pioneers in Social Work." In *Encyclopedia of Social Work*. 19th ed. Edited by R. Edwards & J. Hopps, 115–120. Washington, DC: NASW Press.

PART ONE

Societal and Cultural Context

The first three chapters in this book provide an overview of the current status of African Americans in the United States, African American children in child welfare, and the trends and impact of child welfare policies on African American families and children. These chapters set the stage for discussing some of the critical theoretical, practice, policy, and empirical issues that still need to be addressed.

The first chapter provides a comprehensive and critical analysis of the current status of African American families in the United States using census data and archived national samples and longitudinal surveys to describe the types of African American family structures and rates of formation and disruption. This chapter also provides an overview of the household living arrangements of African American children and their parents, along with their geographic distribution in the United States. The analysis of the distribution of extended households and the living arrangements of African American children in families with relatives is timely. The update on the characteristics of family households and the marital status of parents is useful for policy makers and planners. The characteristics of households including the age of household members and children help one understand potential needs. The analysis of poverty status by households is particularly insightful as poverty rates have declined for children of color who have higher rates of poverty than other groups.

The analysis of African American family formation, structural changes in the rates of family disruption, and the numbers of children in nonfamily settings and institutional arrangements are very relevant for foster care, group home care, and juvenile justice. These analyses, among other things, point to the disproportionate representation of African American children in institutions. Finally, these analyses indicate that families have to cope with the staggering effects of child homicides and the mortality of children under the age of one.

The implications of these demographic analyses for child welfare suggest that in order to serve African American families effectively, work with extended family members such as grandmothers be expanded and that increasingly fathers should be involved. Additionally attention must be paid to the high death rates of African American male children under the age of one.

Chapter 2 thoroughly examines trends for African American children in the child welfare system (e.g., they are more likely than white children to be placed in foster care; they are less likely to be adopted and to remain in care for longer periods; and they are more highly concentrated in foster care than white children). That these trends have existed for the past forty years suggests historic discrimination and institutional racism in child welfare.

Chapter 2 also discusses the various arguments about why African American children are overrepresented in child welfare. First, they have higher maltreatment rates, which is supported by some research; other research contradicts this finding. Second, class bias has been offered as an argument for overrepresentation due to the higher percentages of low-income children in child welfare and higher percentages of African American children who are poor. The third argument attributes overrepresentation to racial bias at various stages of the decision-making process within the child welfare system.

Finally, in chapter 2 Hill examines "structural discrimination," which refers to the disparate adverse consequences of societal trends and institutional policies on racial minorities that may not have been explicitly designed to have racially discriminatory effects. Structural discrimination is examined in mental health, schools, and juvenile justice. Analyses of the child welfare system's decision-making processes are presented, as are foster care placements and kinship care. The chapter ends by recommending how institutional racism can be addressed by the child welfare system.

Chapter 3 provides an analysis of the current status of African American children in foster care and examines the disproportionality of African American children in foster care. Major child welfare policies of the 1990s that have important implications for African American children are examined. The Adoption and Safe Families Act of 1997 (PL 105-89), the Multiethnic Placement Act of 1994 (PL 103-382), the Interethnic Placement Act of 1996 (PL 104-193), sections of the Personal Responsibility and Work Opportunity Reconciliation Act of 1996, and the Adoption Initiative of 2002 are discussed and examined using the criteria of equity, equality, and adequacy. Implications of these federal policies for African American families and children are presented.

1

The Demography of African American Families and Children at the End of the Twentieth Century

JACQUELINE MARIE SMITH

Introduction

A once popular public service announcement on network television began with a scene of almost total darkness. Neither the sun nor the moon shone in a vast expanse of the blackness of the night. The environment seemed to bristle with the tension of the unknown. As television viewers metaphorically stood at brink of this unknown abyss, a narrator's voice poignantly asked, "Do you know where your children are?" The atmosphere almost crackled with fear for their safety and well-being.

Similarly, in the context of changed social policies, and political and cultural strife, the twenty-first century looms before us like a deep chasm. As the century begins, the world as we have known it is filled with the tension of the unknown fates of African American children and families. Do we know where African American children are today? Where have they been? Are they safe and secure within their families?

In the context of social science conceptualizations of family structure and family functioning, these questions can be answered by examining the demography of the African American family at the beginning of the twenty-first century. What types of family structures (with and without children) were present in African American communities across the United States? How did African American family structures vary across age cohorts (family life cycle) and regions of the country? What were the rates at which various types of families formed? What were the rates at which various types of families were disrupted? What are the types of living arrangements of African American children? How do they vary across states and smaller geographical areas?

This chapter uses public data from Census 2000, as well as data from archived national samples and longitudinal surveys to describe the types of African American family structures and their rates of formation and disruption. To better describe the status of children in the context of development across the family life cycle, special attention is given to age and gender variations of household members. The social, political, and economic environment is critical to family life. Geographical differences in this environment are used as gross indicators of the social environment. Where feasible, the analysis highlights state- and county-level differences in rates of family formation and disruption.

The data presented here have several critical limitations. Generally, estimates of the numbers of the poorest and most vulnerable African Americans are likely to be underreported in the Census and Census of the Population surveys. For example, estimates of smaller geographical areas (e.g., counties) presented here are not as accurate as estimates of larger areas, such as states. Because the United States no longer requires states to collect and publish data on marriage, or marriage by race, it is not possible to examine trends over time or to calculate rates for the varying geographical areas of the United States over time. Finally, point-in-time data limit generalizations about trends.

Definitions of Family

Definitions of family tend to emphasize its structure and functioning. For example, sociological theorists like Parsons (1951) have defined the family as a primary group structure with a system of statuses, associated roles, and processes that function to meet basic social needs (socialization, reproduction, etc.). Parsons emphasizes marital/conjugal relationships and the superiority of such relationships in social functioning. Early family demographers have also defined the family as a structure with a system of statuses, associated roles, and processes, but they tended to analytically concentrate on events within households that expand and contract the structure (Coale 1971; Teachman, Polonko & Scanzoni 1987). However, the definitions by family historians have ranged from that of a household unit with an isolated nuclear structure (Laslett & Wall 1972) to dynamic structures that transcend the boundaries of households in order to interact with networks of kin (e.g., Hareven 1974). Still other family scholars, using comparative methodology, have implicitly defined the family as a primary group whose degree of structural differentiation varies with the systems and systemic forces with which it interacts (e.g., Goode 1963). Thus, the definitions vary in the degree of emphasis given to the system, culture, and time frame when the family is studied.

The African American Family

Scholars of law, religion, social science, medicine, and therapy "have used definitions of family . . . to label, diagnose, treat, harass, reward, and separate" (Settles 1987, 157). Scholars who have examined African American family life have focused attention on the structural variations in families that are associated with performance of family roles and family/society exchanges. When family functioning is placed on a continuum, there are many studies at either end. At one end of the continuum are a significant number of studies that have associated the structure and functioning of African American families with pathology, ineffective role performance, and exchanges that threaten the well-being of African American children and families (e.g., Moynihan 1965). At the other end of the continuum are scholars who have documented the diverse family structures and processes that have contributed to the well-being of African American children and families in the midst of oppressive political, social, and economic conditions (Billingsley 1968, 1992; Gibson 1972; Hill 1971).

Study Rationale

The analysis presented here is eclectic, as it draws from many perspectives on families. The conscious selection of these perspectives and the empirical data on family demography presented here are based on an appreciation of the rich diversity of form and function of families in African American communities. Here, family is defined as a primary group of persons whose members are embedded in a complex web of social, psychological, and legal relationships. Members of the family protect, provide, and enhance each other by meeting biopsychosocial needs. Family relationships examined in this analysis are defined as more inclusive than simple blood ties and/or legal relationships. Legal family relationships are based on marriage, birth, or adoption. In the absence of legal relationships, social relationships are most often initiated by affective/emotional bonding, sexual unions, and sometimes, economic unions of persons who share living arrangements. The demography presented here is placed at the end of the continuum of family studies that document the diversity of family structures and processes, and that capture the richness of life for African Americans.

Household Living Arrangements: Children and Their Parents

At the beginning of this decade, there were approximately 36,179,355 persons who reported African American ancestry (U.S. Census Bureau, table QT-P4). Households headed by persons with African American ancestry constituted about 12 percent of all the households in the United States (U.S. Census Bureau, table H8). African Americans were more likely to live in family households (83 percent) with spouses, relatives, or their own children than alone (9 percent), with nonrelatives (3 percent), or in institutional settings (3 percent) (see figure 1.1).

Children under the age of eighteen made up a little more than 31 percent of the total African American population (see figure 1.1). At the time of Census

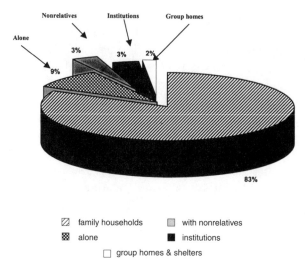

FIGURE 1.1 African American population by living arrangements, 2000

Source: Census 2000 SF1, table P27B.

2000, there were more than ten million African American children. At the start of this century, most African American children under age eighteen (80 percent) lived in families with one or both of their biological parents. However, Survey of Income and Program Participation (SIPP) data suggest that mid-decade a "smaller proportion of all Black children lived in traditional nuclear families (26%) than children in other racial/ethnic groups (65% of White non-Hispanic children, 58% of Asian and Pacific Islander children, and 48% of Hispanic children)" (Fields 2001, P70-74:4).

There are clear geographic patterns in the types of households in which African American children under eighteen live. Figure 1.2 shows the geographic distribution of African American family households with children under age eighteen across the United States. The map shades represent the number of families with children under eighteen in each state.

In figure 1.2, the smaller the number of families with children under age eighteen, the lighter the area that appears on the map. Conversely, the darker the shade of an area, the greater the number of families with children under age eighteen. The lighter shades in figure 1.2 indicate that, at the time of Census 2000, central, northwestern, and southwestern states tended to have fewer African American families with children. Figure 1.2 also shows that the greatest numbers of African American families with children under age eighteen are located on the Eastern Seaboard, on the Gulf Coast, and in California.

African American children are slightly more likely to live with a single mother than with married parents (50 percent vs. 42 percent; see figure 1.3). Figure 1.4

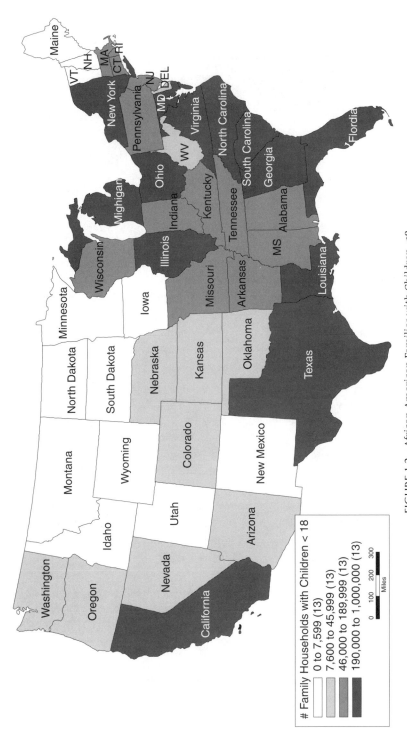

FIGURE 1.2   African American Families with Children <18
Source: Census 2000 SF1, table 35B.

Family Households with Children < 18
  0 to 7,599 (13)
  7,600 to 45,999 (13)
  46,000 to 189,999 (13)
  190,000 to 1,000,000 (13)

0 100 200 300
Miles

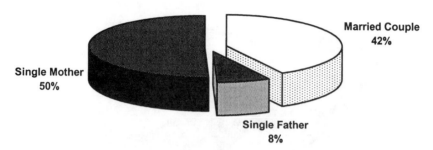

FIGURE 1.3   Families with Children <18 (%) by Parental Marital Status
Source: Census 2000 SFI, table P35B.

shows the relationship between density of the population of families with children
and the type of family for the geographical areas of the United States at the time of
Census 2000. In figure 1.4, the greater the number of African American households with children under eighteen in a state, the darker the color of the geographical area shown. Also in figure 1.4, vertical bars in each state represent the
percentage of married-couple families in all family households with children
under the age of eighteen. The greater the height of the vertical bars, the greater
the proportion of married-couple families. Somewhat surprisingly, figure 1.4 shows
that relatively high proportions of married-couple families with children are
found in the areas with relatively smaller numbers of African American families
with children under eighteen.

Figure 1.5 efficiently illustrates this tendency by focusing on the sorted
rankings of the percentage of married couples for geographical areas. Figure 1.5
shows that the top ten areas (i.e., areas with the highest percentage of married-
couple families) are states with relatively small numbers of African American
families with children (e.g., Idaho, Hawaii, North Dakota). Figure 1.5 shows the
states with the lowest percentages of married-couple families. Note that for
these states, the percentages ranged in the twenties and thirties. Figure 1.5
shows that areas like Washington, DC, and Pennsylvania, with relatively high
numbers of African Americans, had the lowest percentage of married-couple
African American families at the end of the last decade.

This pattern is somewhat counterintuitive. Generally, environments that
are relatively rich in resources are better able to support large population sizes.
Further, a relatively resource-rich environment is probably more likely to sustain a greater variety or diversity of types of subpopulations. Within this context, it is somewhat reasonable to assume that greater numbers of African
Americans are likely to reside in states and areas with relatively rich economic
opportunities. Furthermore, the relative richness of the economic environment
(i.e., opportunities for employment and training) would probably enhance the
formation and incidence of two-parent or married-couple African American
families.

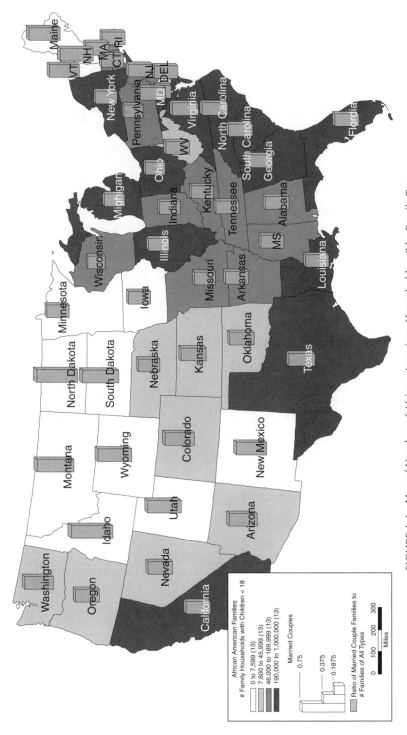

FIGURE 1.4   Map of Number of African American Households <18 by Family Type

Source: SF1, 100 percent data table 35B.

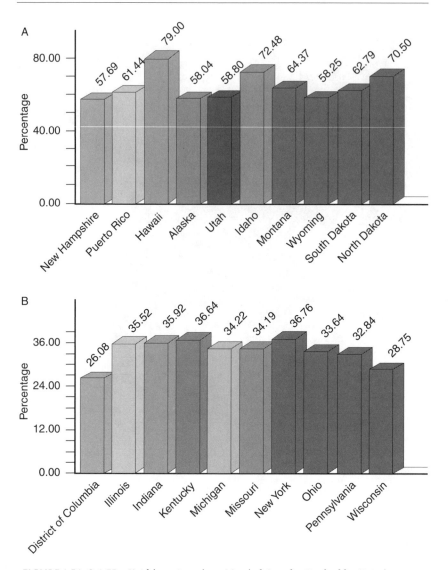

FIGURE 1.5A & 1.5B   % African American Married Couples Ranked by State in 2000
Source: Census 2000 SFī.

Yet, this pattern was not observed. One possible explanation is that public policies create and contribute to the resource richness of family and community environments. Consequently, public policies affect the geographical distribution of the types of families. Thus, public policies may serve as forms of environmental supports or stressors for the formation and functioning of families. Variations in the richness of environments may serve as push or pull factors for the migration and settlement patterns of families within geographical areas. This pattern suggests that future research that examines intragroup variation in the African American population should focus on state policies and regional socioenvironmental policies that act as stressors and supports for African American families with children.

Extended Household Living Arrangements: Children in Families with Relatives

For purposes of this analysis, family structures that have expanded beyond parent-child dyads and/or nucleus of biological parents and children are defined as extended families (Fields 2001). Data from Census 2000 provide, at best, crude or gross estimates of extended family relationships among African American families at the start of the twenty-first century, because it does not capture informal relationships not based on blood or marriage ties. However, scholars have described the social significance of fictive kin relationships in African American communities (Billingsley 1992; Hill 1971). Thus, census data may undercount the numbers of extended families among African Americans. Nevertheless, using Census 2000 data, the estimated number of children in extended families has increased over the last decade. In 1991, there were approximately 8.0 million children in extended families. By 1996, there were approximately 10.3 million children in extended families (Fields 2001).

Racial and ethnic groups vary considerably in the extent to which children live in extended families. For example, figure 1.6 shows that in 1996, children of color—Native American (24 percent), Asian and Pacific Islander (24 percent), Hispanic (22 percent), and African American (23 percent)—were much more

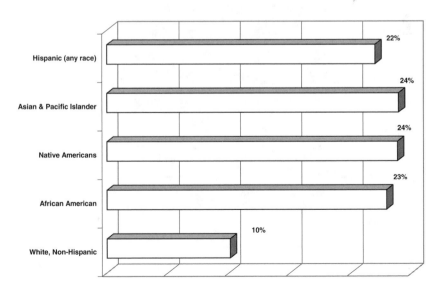

FIGURE 1.6   Percent of Children Living in Extended Households by Race, 1996

Source: Fields 2001, Current Population Reports, Series P70-74, table 7.

likely to live in extended family households than white (10 percent) children. Furthermore, the composition of extended families also varies by race and ethnicity. Generally, "extended households are formed by the presence of an additional relative" rather than a nonrelative (Fields 2001, figure 1.5). Figure 1.7 shows for each racial/ethnic group the presence of relatives and nonrelatives in extended families. In extended families, children of color were much more likely than white children to live with relatives. Asians were much more likely than other groups to live in extended households with relatives. Figure 1.7 shows that 91 percent of Asians who lived in extended families lived with relatives. Figure 1.7 also shows that for African Americans (79 percent), Hispanics of any race (78 percent), and Native Americans (75 percent), the tendency to live in extended households with relatives is similar.

The opposite pattern is observed when the tendency to live in extended families composed only of nonrelatives is examined within each racial/ethnic group. Thirty-seven percent of white non-Hispanic children who lived in extended families lived with nonrelatives. However, 23 percent of Native Americans, 18 percent of African Americans, and 16 percent of Hispanics of any race lived in extended families with nonrelatives only (see figure 1.7).

In summary, a careful analysis of the patterns revealed by figures 1.6 and 1.7 suggests that in the mid-nineties, children of color were more likely than white non-Hispanics to live in extended families, and that children of color, including African Americans who lived in extended households, were most likely to live

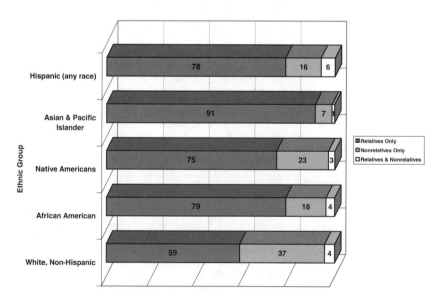

FIGURE 1.7   Percent of Children Living in Extended Families by Race and Presence of Relative, 1996

Source: Fields 2000, Current Population Reports, Series P70-74, table 7.

with relatives only, rather than nonrelatives. This tendency persisted until the end of the decade. Census 2000 data also show that when African American children do not live in households headed by biological parents, they are more likely to live with relatives than with nonrelatives (Census 2000, Summary Tape 1, table P28B).

Census data presented here captured the presence of individuals under the age of eighteen in extended families in which the designated household head is related to children in the household. In Census 2000, relationship to household head refers to either parent, grandparent of a child, or some other relative (i.e., in-law, nephew, niece) related to the designated head of household in which there are children under the age of eighteen.

Interestingly, grandparents and other blood relations are resident in the homes of considerable numbers of African American children under the age of eighteen. Figure 1.8 illustrates the frequency with which African American children under the age of eighteen live with relatives. The figure only includes data for African Americans rather than for the entire population of the United States. In the map, the darker the shade, the greater the percentage of African American children who live in households in which the designated head is a relative who is not their biological parent. The visual pattern of dark shades in the map for African Americans is very similar to the visual pattern for the general population of the United States.

When African American children under age eighteen do live with relatives, they are most likely to live in a household headed by a grandparent rather than an aunt, uncle, cousin, and so on (U.S. Census Bureau, table P28B). This tendency is consistent with national trends. In 1970, about 3.2 percent (2.2 million) of all American children lived in grandparent maintained households. By 1997, this figure had risen to 5.5 percent (3.9 million) (Casper & Bryson 1998). Estimates in the mid-1990s suggested that the proportion of African American children (62 percent) who live with their grandparents is higher than the proportion of white non-Hispanic (42 percent) or Hispanic (32 percent) children (Fields 2001, 2).

In figure 1.8, vertical bars represent the proportion of African American children under eighteen who live with their grandparents and other relatives. The greater the height of the vertical bars, the greater the proportion of children who live with their grandparent or other relative who is household head. Note that in figure 1.8, the states with proportionately more children living with their relatives (states that have the darkest coloration) also tend to be states in which proportionately more children under age eighteen live with their grandparents (i.e., states with the highest vertical bars on the map). But figure 1.8 shows that states in the West, in which there are relatively high percentages of children living with their relatives, do not also have relatively high percentages of African American children living with their parents. Rather, figure 1.8 shows

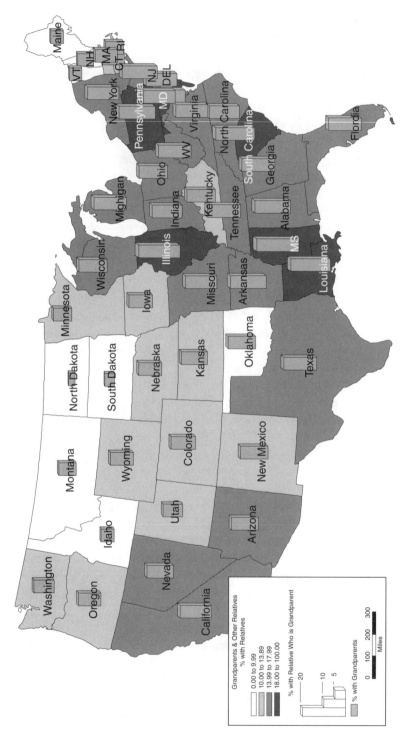

FIGURE 1.8   Map of Proportion of Households with African American Children <18 Who Live with Relatives

Source: U.S. Census 2000, table 28B.

that the concentration of grandparent households tends to be in the states that are on the East Coast.

In summary, figure 1.8 shows that the percentage of African American children who live with their grandparents appears to vary somewhat by region. The possible regional variations may be responsive to state, county, and city differences in practices and services for relatives of African American children and families involved with the child welfare system.

Characteristics of Family Households: Marital Status of Parents

In addition to the observed pattern of grandparents as household heads with children under eighteen, some evidence suggests the presence of households with grandparents designated as household heads may vary with the marital status of biological parents. For example, data show that about mid-decade, an estimated 6.6 million African American children lived with unmarried parent(s) (Fields 2001, P70-74, table 3).

It is possible that parents who are not married may be in cohabitating relationships with a partner. Furthermore, census data show an increase in cohabitation among adults over several decades (Fields 2001, 70-74:5). But there are racial/ethnic differences in patterns of cohabitation. Data for 1996 show that African American children living with unmarried parents are the least likely of all racial/ethnic groups to live with cohabiting parents. Greater proportions of white non-Hispanic (20.1 percent) and Native Americans and Alaskan Natives (25.6 percent) lived with cohabiting unmarried parents than African Americans (Fields 2001, P70-74, table 3). Only 9 percent of African American children with an unmarried parent(s) lived with cohabitating parent(s). Furthermore, most children who do not live in married-couple families live with their mothers (Fields 2001, P70-74, table 3).

Single parents who are not cohabitating may be more likely to live with adult relatives. Kamo (2000) suggests that extended families may extend downward for the inclusion of younger members, or upward for the inclusion of older members (parents, grandparents, mother-in-law, etc.). Kamo argues that African American families are more likely to extend downward. Kamo also found that even after controlling for different levels of economic variables, African American single mothers were more likely than ethnic counterparts to live with their parents. This suggests that housing services provided to single mothers might need to take into consideration the nature of the extended family household.

For single African American mothers, Census 2000 data suggest that the tendency to live with relatives and/or nonrelatives has been relatively stable. Further, the gap between single mothers who live on their own and single mothers who lived with others in extended households has been fairly stable over time (see figure 1.9). In contrast, the tendency for African American fathers to live on their own versus with others has fluctuated more frequently than for single mothers. Indeed, the tendency for single fathers to live with relatives appears to be much closer to convergence than for single mothers (see figures 1.9 and 1.10). Overall, when the patterns for single parents shown in figures 1.9 and 1.10 are compared with the pattern for married couples who live with others (see figure 1.11), the pattern for married couples who live in extended households has generally shown the greatest stability over time. The convergence of the living arrangements for single fathers suggests that social workers who seek to involve the biological father's family in permanency planning for children may find these family networks more accessible than in the past.

These patterns have several possible implications. African American family support systems may be less frequently utilized by single mothers because family systems that are accessible to women may be structurally different from those available to men. Or single African American mothers who are not cohabiting may use family support systems differently from men because public poli-

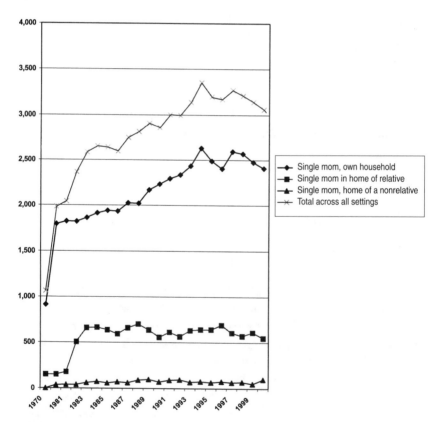

FIGURE 1.9   Living Arrangement Patterns Among African American Single Mothers

Source: U.S. Census Bureau 2001, table FM-2.

cies may provide greater support via social services for women than for men. However, as the number of African American males who live with their children as single fathers has increased over time, single fathers may have relied more on relatives for support because of relatively less access to social services.

It is also possible that single fathers who live with their children may be cohabiting with partners in shorter, sequential, relatively transient cohabitating relationships that are missed by most data collection methods used in censuses and panel studies like the Survey of Income and Program Participation (SIPP). Shorter, sequential, relatively transient cohabitating relationships may provide different cohabitation premiums to black men and black women because social services guaranteed by public policies may be more supportive of motherhood than fatherhood. If unmarried fathers who live with their children cohabit with partners who are not the biological mother of their children, the relationship may be transitory and highly responsive to labor market expansions and contractions. Because men may have relatively less access to social services than women as the labor market contracts, unmarried fathers who live

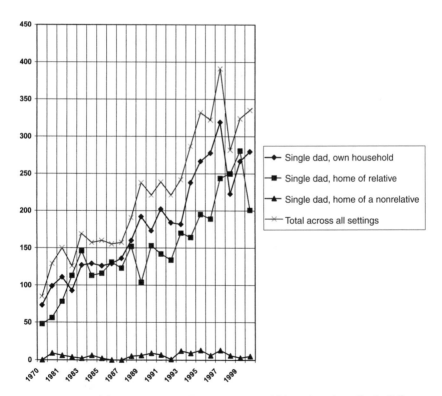

FIGURE 1.10   Living Arrangement Patterns Among African American Single Fathers

Source: U.S. Census Bureau 2001, table FM-2.

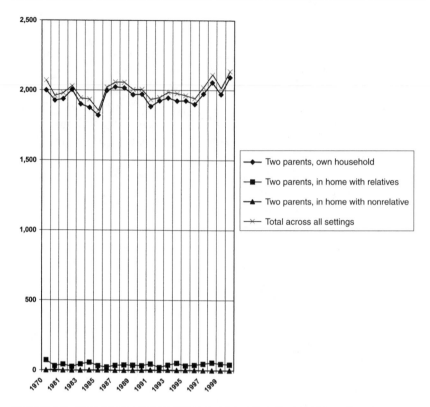

FIGURE 1.11   Living Arrangement Patterns Among Two-Parent African American
Families

Source: U.S. Census Bureau 2001, table FM-2.

with their children may transition more frequently than women in their living
arrangements between relatives and cohabitation partners. The underestima-
tion of cohabitation for African American single fathers also has implications
for the accuracy of estimates of family formation and disruption discussed in
later sections of this chapter.

Characteristics of Households: Age of Household Members

Children

The age of children in families is significant as family members attempt to acquire
resources linked to the effective mastery of developmental challenges associated
with infancy, early childhood, and adolescence. Households are more likely to
have children under the age of eighteen (36 percent) than they are to have individuals who are age sixty-five and older (23 percent) (U.S. Census Bureau, table 1).
About one out of every four children under the age of eighteen is preschool age.

The age of children in families, as well as the age of their caregivers, is of critical importance as family members attempt to master their own developmental challenges, and function in order to meet basic survival needs of family members.

Figure 1.12 shows the covariation of the age of children in families and the marital status of the designated household head. There are virtually no differences between single parents and married couples in the presence of school-age children in families. Possibly somewhat more challenging for families is (1) the presence of preschool children and (2) the mix of developmental needs of preschool children in the same household with children who are school age.

The chronological and developmental age of children affects the extent and level of child care needs for employed parents. For example, infants require more intense care than toddlers, and toddlers require more intense care than school-age children. Furthermore, the cost of care may reflect the level of care that is provided. Thus, child care may cost more financially for very young children. Child care for very young children may also cost parents more in terms of time. Transportation to and from child care is carried out most often prior to and after work hours. Thus, transportation to and from child care for preschool children may also add substantial time costs to parenting.

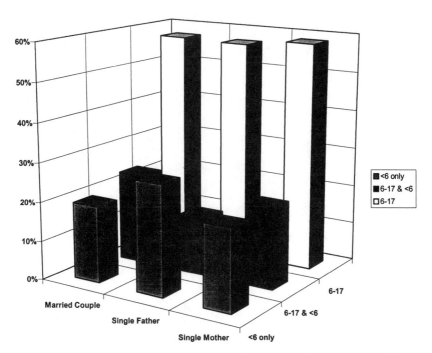

FIGURE 1.12   Bar Graph of African American Children in Families by Age of Children and Marital Status of Household Head

Source: Census 2000 SF1, table P34B.

Employed parents of children with a mix of ages (i.e., preschool and school age) may expend more time in transportation to child care, and expend more money for child care than parents with school-age children. Thus, families with a mix of children with varying ages may have greater need for time and child care monies than families with children who are school age. Further, the greater needs of these types of families may interact with gender associated family and work roles.

Single-parent fathers are the least likely family type to have this type of age mix when they are designated as household head. However, African American single fathers are noticeably more likely to have families in which the child is preschool age (see figure 1.12). In figure 1.12, the height of the vertical bars indicates the extent to which children of varying ages are present in the homes of different types of parents. The higher the vertical bars, the greater the occurrence of children in the specified age group. In the first row of bars, which illustrates the tendency of parents to have households with children under the age of six, the slightly higher bar for single fathers shows that they are more likely than married couples and single mothers to live in a household in which the children are under the age of six. This data also suggest that some services may be needed to stabilize the households of African American men who are single parents.

Characteristics of Households: Poverty Status

Child and Family Poverty

The age of household members is also important because of the interrelationship of age and poverty. Census data show that children under age eighteen have a higher rate of poverty than other age groups. In 2000, the poverty rate (16.2 percent) for children was the lowest that it has ever been since 1979. Thus, a considerable number of children still live in poverty, but the proportion that lives in poverty has declined.

Census data indicate that about 19 percent of African American families lived below the official government poverty level in 2000 (Dalaker 2001, table A). African American and Hispanic families of any race are about three times as likely as whites to live below poverty level. African Americans and Hispanic families of any race were about twice as likely as Asian and Pacific Islanders to live below poverty level.

When gender and marital status are disaggregated from these rates, the picture becomes even bleaker for some types of families. For example, African American married couples are less likely to fall below poverty level than single male and female heads of households. The disparities between types of families are particularly evident when attention is focused on families with children under the age of eighteen. In 2000, about 6 percent of married-couple African

American families with children under age eighteen were below poverty level. In contrast, about 41 percent of single female-headed households with children under age eighteen were below poverty level (U.S. Census Bureau, table 4).

The dramatically higher rate of poverty for all African American families is a long-standing and persistent pattern for African American families with children. While rates are still relatively high, they have declined over time (i.e., the poverty rate for African American families with children under eighteen has decreased). In 1990, the poverty rate for all African American families was 29.9. By 2000, the rate had fallen to 19.1.

There is also a long-standing pattern of disproportionately high numbers of African American families with children under age eighteen headed by single mothers falling below poverty level. Figure 1.13 shows the poverty rates for each of the types of families with children under the age of eighteen, and illustrates the disparities between family types. Figure 1.13 also illustrates the relatively recent decline in the proportion of families below poverty level by family type.

From 1970 until 1997, the percentage of single female-headed African American households below poverty level was never less than 50 percent. While rates for these families did drop somewhat during periods of economic boom between 1993 and 1997, the poverty rates have never dropped to the levels for whites. The

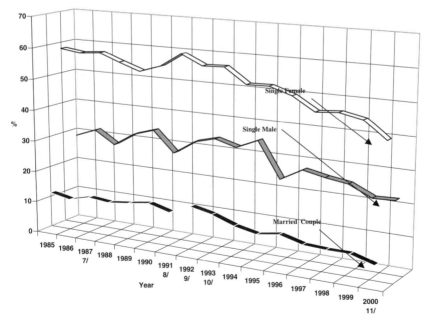

FIGURE 1.13   % Below Poverty Level of African American Families with Related Children <18

Source: Data from Dalaker 2001, table A-3, Poverty Status of Families by Type of Family: 1959 to 2000.

poverty rates for single male-headed households with children under age eighteen are also high. In 2000, about 22 percent were below poverty level. However, the proportions of single male heads of African American households below poverty level have never been as high as the proportions of single women with children under age eighteen. Between 1974 and 2000, the percentage of households with children under eighteen headed by males ranged from a low of 15 percent to a high of 34 percent (Historical Poverty Tables, table 4).

When gender and marital status are disaggregated for poverty rates, the decline becomes more dramatic. Census data show that black female heads of households never experienced a poverty rate significantly below 40 percent until 1989 (see figure 1.13). Blacks and Hispanics both experienced drops in rates by 2000 (Dalaker 2001). But as data presented here clearly show, record lows in rates have not eliminated either race/ethnic or intragroup variation in poverty status of families with children under age eighteen.

Family Formation

The demography of the African American family is also indicated by changes in diverse family structures. Structural changes in family forms reflect the contraction and expansion of roles in the system of positions within the family. Contractions occur with the loss of roles because of involuntary (death, out-of-home placement, institutionalization) and voluntary terminations of relationships (divorce, separation). The expansion of family systems occurs with the addition of new roles because of birth and adoptions, as well as legal guardianships and informal arrangements for caregiving of the young, the old, and the disabled. Both contractions and expansions also represent adaptive responses to the external social environment.

The description of household composition presented thus far does not capture the rate of formation for the different types of families. Rates of marriage and adoption are two indicators of family formation. The detailed data on marriage for racial/ethnic groups in the United States population needed for the calculation of African American marriage rates are not available because the federal government no longer collects or publishes this information since 1995 (Federal Register 1995). Furthermore, marriage rates are not indicators of the rate of formation of families with children or the various types of extended families.

Even though there are no data available to estimate marriage rates for the African American population, retrospective data from the SIPP provide some information about the formation of married-couple families. For example, Kreider and Fields (2002) report that greater proportions of African Americans are never marrying for the younger age cohorts. Most black men and women age twenty-five to twenty-nine in 1996 had never married. Sixty-two percent of black men age twenty-five to twenty-nine in 1996 had never married, and 58 percent of black women age twenty-five to twenty-nine were never married. While most African Americans age twenty-five to twenty-nine have never married, less than half of white American men (45 percent) have never been married at age twenty-five to twenty-nine. But by the age of forty-five, most African Americans, like most other persons forty-five and older in other racial/ethnic groups, have married. Thus, African Americans tend to postpone married-couple family formation until older ages.

The pattern is less evident for other racial/ethnic groups among whom about one-third of the population age twenty-five to twenty-nine has never been married, compared with white non- Hispanic and Hispanic women (Kreider & Fields 2002, 70–80). The Kreider and Fields study showed that by age forty-five, about 90 percent of African Americans had married.

When African Americans do marry for the first time, retrospective data suggest that first marriages that end in divorce tend to last about eight years. This suggests that if children are born during the marriage and divorce occurs, the marriages generally do not last long enough for children to reach adolescence. Interestingly, African Americans whose first marriage ends in divorce tend to be married just a little longer than other racial/ethnic groups whose first marriage ends in divorce. Furthermore, the marriages of African Americans who marry a second time tend to last longer than the marriages of other racial/ethnic groups (Kreider & Fields 2002).

Rather than focus on the formation of two-parent families, many researchers have focused on the formation of single-parent families because of the relatively high proportions of unwed teen mothers (Taylor, Tucker, Chatters & Jayakody 1997). Between 1990 and 1998 the percentage of single-headed African American families rose slightly from 54.6 percent to 54.8 percent. The amount of increase (3.6 percent) was higher for European Americans (McLoyd et al. 2000, 1071–1072). McLoyd et al. indicate that between 1990 and 1998, households headed by single African American fathers increased 2 percent. These writers point out that structural changes occurred with greater rapidity in African American families than with the general population. Between 1990 and 1998, there were greater declines in the proportion of African Americans who were married. Furthermore, the proportion of African Americans who were never married increased more for African Americans than for the general population (McLoyd et al. 2000, 1072).

Census data also suggest that families headed by grandparents have formed at an increased rate. In the general population, substantial increases occurred among all types of households maintained by grandparents regardless of the presence or absence of the grandchildren's parents (Casper & Bryson 1998, 2). "In the general population families with children's parents absent . . . grew rapidly: both grandparents, no parents present families grew by 31 percent and grandmother only, no parents present families grew by 27 percent. Families with children's parents present grew only 13 percent" (Casper & Bryson 1998, 7).

Some evidence suggests that this trend may hold for African Americans. Children in single female-headed households and children living in grandmother-only, no parent present households are more likely to be poor and to be African American. If this trend holds for the African American population, then the rate of this type of family formation has implications for the well-being of African American children (Chalfie 1994; Hardin, Clark & Maguire 1997; Rutrough & Ofstedal 1997). Family type has been shown to have a statistically significant effect on whether a child will live in poverty. Casper and Bryson (1998, 15) argue that "the family structure disadvantage for grandchildren does not stem solely from the marital status of household heads, nor from the number of adult family members, nor even from the gender of the householder, but rather from a combination of the three."

Changes in Family Structure

Structural changes in African American families reflect not only the expansion of roles in the family system, but also the contractions. Unlike the expansions that occur with birth, marriage, adoption, and informal adoption, contractions occur with the loss of roles in the system of positions because of voluntary and involuntary termination of relationships. Death, out-of-home placement of children neglected or abused by their parents, divorce, and separations are examples of contractions. McLoyd et al. (2000) suggest that structural changes in African American families were more rapid during the last decade when they are compared with the general population. During the 1990 through 1998 period, the proportion of African Americans never married increased. During the same period the rate of divorce for African Americans increased faster than the rate in the general population.

In summary, there has been, in the last decade, a decline in the proportion of African Americans who were married. For many African American children, family life involves a single, unmarried parent. Increasingly, single unmarried fathers care for children, particularly children age six and younger. But many more African American children tend to live in households with single unmarried mothers. African American children also are more likely to live in extended family households, particularly in households with relatives. Even after economic factors are controlled, single African American mothers are more likely than their ethnic counterparts to live in extended households. Furthermore, more grandparent(s) head families with children when biological parents are not caregivers.

Structural Changes and Rates of Family Disruption

It is debatable whether the structural changes that derive from family formation (i.e., marriage, cohabitation, grandparent-headed households) and discussed thus far are disruptive to family well-being. Less debatable are changes in family functioning when children are placed in foster care. Clearly, court-ordered removal of children from families serves to interrupt family relationships.

Courts order the removal of children from families because the safety and well-being of children are jeopardized by abuse or neglect. Courts also order the removal of children from homes because of delinquency or criminal acts of children. Very few African American children are removed from their families because of sexual abuse (4.7 percent) or physical abuse (13 percent) (USDHHS 1998). An overwhelming majority (57 percent) of African American children are placed in the care of the child welfare system because of neglect.

In 1998, approximately 260,491 African American children were removed from their families and placed in other settings. The placement of African American children by the child welfare system is disproportionate, relative to the proportion of African American children in the population (see figure 1.14). African American children made up about 47 percent of all children placed by the child welfare system. But children constitute only 31 percent of the population of all African Americans. Furthermore, African American children constitute only 17 percent of all children estimated to be under the age of eighteen in 1998 (see figure 1.14). Thus, disproportionate numbers of children show up in the child welfare system.

Figure 1.15 shows the frequency of out-of-home placements for African American children by state. The map is based on 1998 data from the Adoption and Foster Care Analysis and Reporting System and Census estimates (USDHHS 1998). AFCARS data are based on case-level data for children. Data were aggregated to the state level for this analysis. Data in this map are missing for some states. Still other states had very small numbers of African American children in their system.

The darker the area in the map, the greater the frequency of out-of-home placements for African American children. The darkest areas in figure 1.15 indicate that in 1998, the greatest number of African American children were in foster care systems in California, Texas, Missouri, Illinois, Florida, Pennsylvania, North Carolina, and New York.

The likelihood that an African American child under the age of eighteen will become involved with the child welfare system and placed away from his or her biological parents varies by state. In figure 1.16, the darker the area, the greater the risk of out-of-home placement. The risk of out-of-home placement was calculated as the ratio of the total number of African American children placed in 1998 to the census estimate of the total number of African American children age eighteen and under at mid-year 1998. In figure 1.16, the states with the greatest risk of out-of-home placement are California, Oregon, Washington, Minnesota, Wisconsin, Illinois, Pennsylvania, New York, and Maine. But a comparison of areas of figure 1.15 and figure 1.16 suggests that most of the states with relatively high risk of out-of-home placement (California, Illinois, Minnesota,

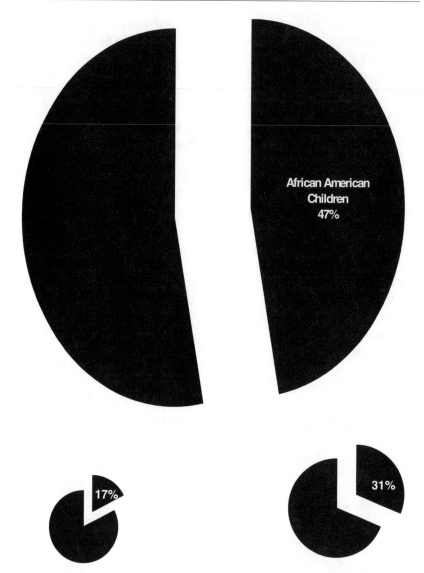

FIGURE 1.14 Disproportionality of African American Children in the Child Welfare System

Source: AFCARS 1998 and U.S. Census Population Estimates.

Illinois, Pennsylvania, Wisconsin, and New York) are states with a large number of African American children in the foster care system. There are notable exceptions. Figure 1.16 shows that Oregon, Washington, Montana, and Maine do not have particularly large numbers of children in care, but children who live in these states face relatively high risks of disruption of family functioning by placement away from their biological parent(s).

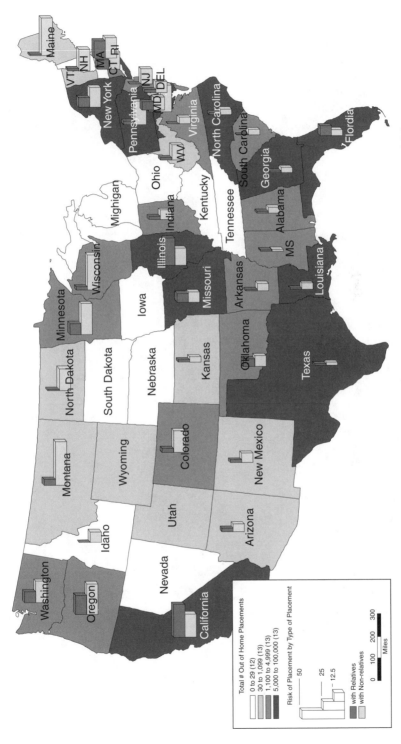

FIGURE 1.15   Frequency of Out of Home Placements by Risk of Type of Placement for African American Children, 1998

Source: AFCARS 1998 and U.S. Census Time Series Population Estimates.

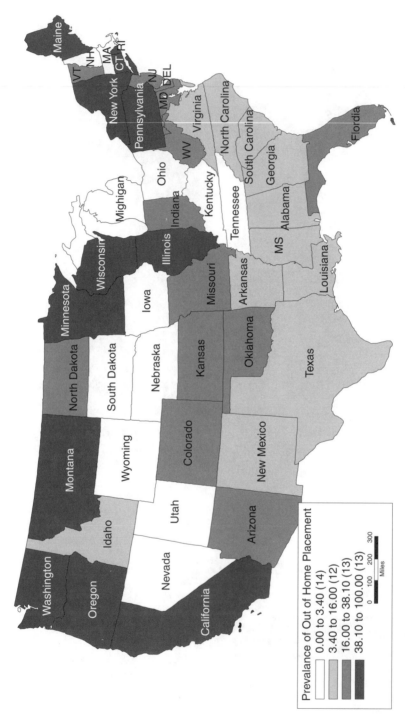

Prevalence of Out of Home Placement
☐ 0.00 to 3.40 (14)
▨ 3.40 to 16.00 (12)
▨ 16.00 to 38.10 (13)
■ 38.10 to 100.00 (13)

0   100 200 300
Miles

FIGURE 1.16 Prevalence of Out of Home Placements by State

Source: AFCARS 1998 and U.S. Census Population Estimates.

There is a statistically significant relationship between the numbers of children placed out of home by the child welfare system and the occurrence of out-of-home placement with relatives. As the number of African American children placed out of their homes increases, so does the frequency of placement with relatives (Pearsons $r = .702$). Further, the size of the correlation coefficient indicates that this is a very strong relationship.

Table 1.1 shows that there is also a statistically significant positive correlation between frequency of placement with relatives and placement with nonrelatives. These interrelationships are also graphically illustrated in figure 1.15. In figure 1.15 the length of the horizontal bar indicates for each state the relative risk of placement with relatives and nonrelatives. The risk of placement in a particular type of setting was calculated as the ratio of the number of African American children age eighteen and younger placed in a type of setting, to the estimated number of all African American children age eighteen and under in each state.

When African American children live in a state with relatively large numbers of children in out-of-home placements, they are more likely to be placed

TABLE 1.1

Pearson Correlation Coefficients for Mean Age of Children, System Size, and Risk of Specific Types of Out-of-Home Placements for African American Children Age Eighteen and Under, 1998

			Risk of Out-of-Home Placement		
	Average Age	*System Size*	*Relatives*	*Nonrelatives*	*Group Home*
Average Age	1	−.079	−.158	−.145	.243
System Size	−.079	1	.701[b]	.065	.014
Relatives			1	.321[a]	.287
Nonrelatives				1	.321[a]
Group Home					1

Note: System size was measured as the total number of children formally involved with the child welfare system or placed by child welfare officials. Risk of placement was calculated as the ratio of type of out-of-home placement to total number of African American children age eighteen and under. Estimates of children in the general population were taken from U.S. census estimates of population by age, race, and sex.

[a]Two-tailed statistical significance level of .05.

[b]Two-tailed statistical significance level of .01.

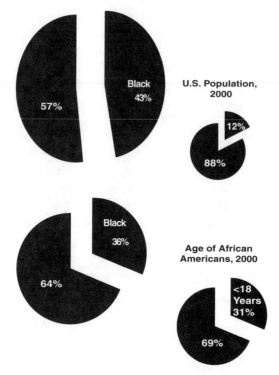

FIGURE 1.17   Population in Corrections/Juvenile Institutions, 2000
Source: U.S. Census SF1, tables PC and 17B.

with nonrelatives than with relatives. This relationship is illustrated in figure 1.15, which indicates that for most of the states with the largest numbers of African American children (Texas, Louisiana, Georgia, Pennsylvania, New York, and North Carolina), the risk of placements with nonrelatives is almost equal to or greater than the risk of placement with relatives. The exceptions are California, Illinois, and Florida, for which the length of the horizontal bar representing placement with relatives is substantially longer than the length of the bar representing the risk of placement with nonrelatives. The correlation of the risk of placement with relatives and the risk of placement with nonrelatives is statistically significant; however, the relationship is not as strong ($r = .32$).

Analysis of AFCARS and census data demonstrates that about seventy-six out of every one thousand African American children in California and Minnesota are removed from their biological families and placed elsewhere by the child welfare system. In contrast, about seven out of every one thousand children in Mississippi and about nine out of every one hundred in Texas are placed by the child welfare system. In Louisiana and Alabama about ten out of every one thousand African American children are placed out of home. Thus, south-

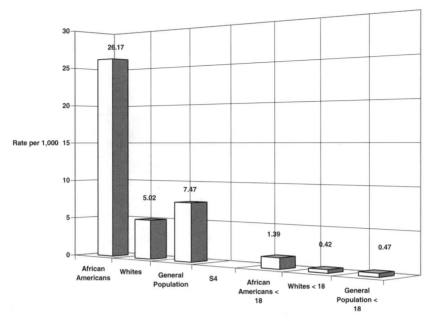

FIGURE 1.18   Incidence of Institutionalization in Corrections & Juvenile Facilities, 2000
Source: U.S. Census, tables PCT 17, PCT 17A, PCT 17B.

ern states appear to utilize out-of-home placement less frequently than other regions.

Children in Nonfamily Settings: Institutional Living Arrangements

Thus far, this chapter has described the households of African American families and children. Children who do not live in family settings tend to live in institutional settings. The rate of placement of children in institutional settings serves as an indicator of family disruption. Disproportionate numbers of African American children under age eighteen live in institutional settings away from family life. Figure 1.17 shows that the proportion of African Americans who are institutionalized in correctional and juvenile institutions is higher than the proportion of African Americans in the population. Indeed, the proportion of African American children under eighteen who are institutionalized in correctional and juvenile institutions is slightly higher than the proportion of African American youth under eighteen in the African American population as a whole (see figure 1.17). Further, the incidence of institutionalization in correctional institutions is three times greater for African American children than for whites (see figure 1.18).

African American children are also placed by the child welfare system in group homes. Table 1.2 uses AFCARS data to show the average age of African American children under eighteen for each state. The mean age is a measure of the relative age of a system's foster care population. Table 1.2 shows that some states have a relatively young African American population in their overall foster care system. For example, New Mexico ($Y = 7.06$), New Jersey ($Y = 8.14$), and Montana ($Y = 8.06$) have relatively young children in their foster care system. Others have relatively older populations. For example, Kansas ($Y = 11.82$), Delaware ($Y = 10.88$), and West Virginia ($Y = 10.66$) have somewhat older foster care populations. But there is no statistically significant correlation between the average age of children in foster care and the risk of placement of African American children in a group home (see table 1.2). In other words, the risk of placement in a group home does not go up and down with the changes in the age of children in the foster care system.

The likelihood of the disruption of African American family functioning by placement of children in group homes is generally lower than the risk of placement in family settings with relatives and nonrelatives. In table 1.2, there are three states with noticeably higher risks for placement in group homes; the risk of placement is highest in Minnesota (9.52), California (7.09), and Vermont (9.82).

Child Mortality and Homicide Rates

As indicated earlier, family functioning can be disrupted by deaths of family members, particularly the death of children. Figure 1.19 shows the death rates by homicide and other causes for African American children under the age of fourteen for the 1993–1998 period. Figure 1.19A shows that the death rates are highest for black males under age one. The mortality of children is also illustrated by homicide rates (fig. 1.19B). The highest homicide rates for African American children occurred in 1996 for African American males under one year of age. These data are alarming because they suggest that African American males are most vulnerable at the youngest ages. Given the relatively high rates of incarceration for black males of all ages, the disruption of the functioning of male roles is quite disturbing. The high rates also suggest that child welfare services are particularly ineffective in protecting the safety and well-being of African American male children.

Poverty, Public Assistance, and Child Welfare Policies at the End of the Decade

How has public policy figured in the demographic patterns presented here? One of the most compelling findings of the analysis presented here is that in the last decade a sizable proportion of African American children and their families

TABLE 1.2

Average Age of African American Children Age Eighteen and Under and Risk of Placement in Group Home by State, 1998

Name	Average Age	Placement in Group Home per 1,000 Children
Alabama	9.52	0.32
Alaska	Data not available	Data not available
Arizona	9.25	4.50
Arkansas	9.58	Data not available
California	9.17	7.09
Colorado	10.14	2.10
Connecticut	8.78	0.91
Delaware	10.88	0.89
District of Columbia	8.91	5.58
Florida	8.47	0.88
Georgia	9.06	0.72
Hawaii	9.55	1.89
Idaho	8.00	Data not available
Illinois	8.78	0.69
Indiana	9.07	0.40
Iowa	Data not available	Data not available
Kansas	11.82	2.95
Kentucky	Data not available	Data not available
Louisiana	9.95	0.68
Maine	8.26	0.59
Maryland	9.25	1.76
Massachusetts	Data not available	Data not available
Michigan	Data not available	Data not available
Minnesota	9.60	9.52
Mississippi	9.08	0.82
Missouri	9.23	0.34
Montana	8.06	3.50
Nebraska	Data not available	Data not available
Nevada	Data not available	Data not available

(continued)

TABLE 1.2 Average Age of African American Children Age Eighteen and Under and Risk of Placement in Group Home by State, 1998 *(continued)*

Name	Average Age	Placement in Group Home per 1,000 Children
New Hampshire	Data not available	Data not available
New Jersey	8.14	1.80
New Mexico	7.06	1.20
New York	8.96	0.86
North Carolina	9.04	0.80
North Dakota	9.76	1.64
Ohio	Data not available	Data not available
Oklahoma	9.27	6.75
Oregon	8.90	0.56
Pennsylvania	10.10	3.93
Rhode Island	9.18	12.44
South Carolina	9.24	3.85
South Dakota	Data not available	Data not available
Tennessee	Data not available	Data not available
Texas	8.43	0.40
Utah	8.96	Data not available
Vermont	10.77	9.82
Virginia	10.44	1.73
Washington	8.60	1.68
West Virginia	10.66	4.65
Wisconsin	9.53	1.52
Wyoming	8.56	Data not available

Source: Adoption and Foster Care Analysis and Reporting System (AFCARS) [MRDF]. Ithaca, New York: National Data Archive on Child Abuse and Neglect. Family Life Development Center. Cornell University (producer) (1997). Washington, DC: Children's Bureau. Administration on Children, Youth, and Families. Administration for Children and Families. U.S. Department of Health and Human Services.

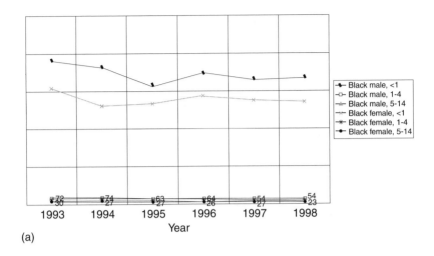

(a)

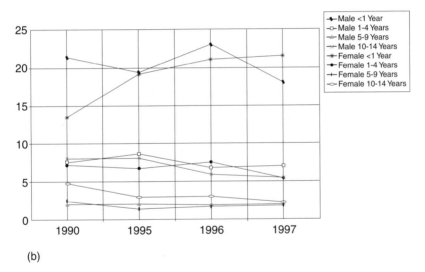

(b)

FIGURE 1.19   Mortality Rates for African American Children <14 by Gender, 1990–1997

Source: Table 121, Statistical Abstract of the United States, 1997; table 118, Statistical Abstract of the United States, 1995; table 95, Statistical Abstract of the United States, 2002.

continue to experience the harshest poverty. The poorest were also most likely to be members of families that departed from the socially acceptable nuclear family in which parents are married and live separate and apart from their families of origin. Historically, public welfare policies have regulated family formation, composition, and functioning by specifying residency and financial criteria for program eligibility. For example, early policies like Aid for Dependent Children (ADC) and Aid to Families with Dependent Children (AFDC) provided disincentives for married and cohabitating two-parent families and were unfriendly to nuclear families (Bell 1965). Some suggest that welfare benefits during these policy eras were associated with the growth of female-headed families and discouraged fatherhood (Ellwood & Bane 1985; Moffit 1998).

Historically, public welfare policies and programs have also been far from family friendly to the poorest African American children and families. Some states instituted stringent "suitable home" requirements during the ADC/AFDC era (Bell 1965; Curran 2002). During this policy era, unsuitable homes were defined as homes in which there was evidence of sexual behavior or relationships outside of marriage. In the context of "suitable home" policies, children born outside of marriage indicated sexual behavior and relationships outside of marriage that were regarded as promiscuous and indicative of a mother's low moral character (Bell 1965).

"Suitable home" requirements were exceptionally harsh to the poorest African American children and families (Levenstein 2000). In the 1960s disproportionate numbers of African American mothers were on ADC rolls. In 1960, for example, African Americans made up 66 percent of the Louisiana ADC caseload, but African American children born outside of marriage made up 98 percent of the state's overall ADC caseload (Levenstein 2000, 13). In July 1960, during the "suitable home" policy era, more than twenty-three thousand African American mothers were cut from Louisiana's Aid for Dependent Children rolls (Levenstein 2000).

In her analysis of public discourse in this era, Levenstein suggests that welfare cuts were racialized and that they were regarded by some as retribution for civil rights gains in voting and school desegregation. Levenstein reports that black journalists consistently maintained this position (Levenstein 2000, 12). Thus, early welfare policies were not family friendly to African American children and families, particularly to poor, single unwed African American mothers. Furthermore, changes in the welfare system's response to poor African American families may reflect multisystem linkages associated with changes in relationships between racial and economic groups in the larger political and social system. Thus, the interaction of race and class weaves across multiple interlinked systems.

Welfare policies in the 1980s slightly shifted the public welfare focus from the moral character and suitability of mothers to economic parenthood. With the implementation of the Child Support Act (1984), emphasis was placed on the establishment of paternity and economic fatherhood for nonresidential fathers. As federal and state governments downsized their caseloads and reduced their ever-expanding costs, public debate was much less focused on the morality of poor African American women and much more attentive to the establishment of paternity because the government's economic fatherhood could be carried out by the biological father. During the 1980s, states established administrative procedures that resulted in greater regularity in establishing paternity and in determining the amount and the manner of distribution of child support for nonresidential fathers (Garfinkel 2001).

Despite these efforts, child support collections decreased in the eighties. In 1989, less than 40 percent of all families eligible for child support actually received any (Hanson, Garfinkel & McIanahan 1996). Analysis of Current Population Survey Child Support Supplement (CPS-CSS) data show that the proportion of African American mothers with child support awards did indeed increase during the eighties (Hanson, Garfinkel & McIanahan 1996, table 1). However, African Americans were less likely than whites to be awarded child support, and when support was awarded, African Americans tended to be awarded lower amounts (Hanson, Garfinkel & McIanahan 1996, table 2). Furthermore, African Americans were less likely than whites to actually receive child support that had been awarded (Hanson, Garfinkel & McIanahan 1996, table 2). Possible explanations for the limited scope of the benefits of child support policies and the differential effects of race on child support awards include the relatively low wage earnings of unwed African American fathers, and the relatively higher levels of unemployed African American men compared with whites, even during periods of economic boom. Generally, then, the family functioning of a sizable proportion of African American single parents relied on the state for economic support.

In the 1990s, with the passage of the Personal Responsibility and Work Opportunity Reconciliation Act (PRWORA), the attention of public welfare policy remained focused on child support. PRWORA requires states to give administrative agencies authority to establish paternity without court orders. PRWORA also requires all states to establish central state registries of child support orders and centralize collection and disbursement units (Garfinkel 2001, 445). In addition, PRWORA expanded the federal role in child support payment by requiring that all states adopt the Uniform Interstate Family Support Act (UNIFSA) and participate in a federal/state directory. UNIFSA allows the direct withholding of wages obligated to child support between states (Garfinkel 2001). Thus, PRWORA reconfigured federal/state relationships by expanding the federal role in child support, and restructuring federal/state and state relationships in child support.

PRWORA is unique when compared with earlier policies like AFDC and ADC because it eliminated entitlement to financial assistance, imposed lifetime caps on assistance, and gave states permission to establish family caps that denied cash benefits to children born into families already receiving assistance (McGowan & Walsh 2000). Despite the reconfiguration of federal/state relationships that characterize PRWORA, this legislation is also consistent with earlier public assistance policies. PRWORA, like ADC and AFDC, regulates and controls family formation, composition, and functioning. For example,

PRWORA requires that states eliminate cash benefits to teens under age eighteen who do not live with their parents. However, PRWORA abolished AFDC and replaced it with Temporary Assistance to Needy Families (TANF).

TANF is a work-based welfare assistance policy. As a policy it consists of a mixed bag of incentives, sanctions, diversions, and time limits centered on the employment of adults within families that receive temporary assistance. Some suggest this focus, along with changes in the configuration of the service delivery system, have contributed to a culture change for the public welfare service delivery system (Corcoran et al. 2000). The infrastructure of public welfare service delivery systems is now more vested in employment preparation than in eligibility criteria (Brodkin 1995; Corcoran et al. 2000). The boundaries between the public and the private sectors are more easily permeated as public services are contracted out (Osborne & Gaebler 1992).

Like public welfare policy, child welfare policy has also shifted its focus and priorities during the last decade. In a response to foster care drift in 1980, the Adoption Assistance and Child Welfare Act was enacted. This law (PL 96-272) required permanency planning and reasonable efforts to reunify children with their biological parents. The provisions of this legislation attempted to reduce foster care drift. When the problems of drift did not diminish with the enactment of Public Law 90-272, the Adoption and Safe Families Act (ASFA) became one of the most critical child welfare policies of the last decade of the twentieth century.

While ASFA reaffirmed permanency planning, it also established concurrent planning for termination of parental rights for parents whose children had been abandoned infants, or had been in foster care for fifteen of the most recent twenty-two months. Underlying concurrency planning is a shift in priorities. With the 1980 legislation, family reunification was the ultimate priority. To ensure the effectiveness of concurrency planning and the adherence to the timelines, states were given a variety of incentives and disincentives (McGowan & Walsh 2000). By establishing and rigorously monitoring timelines for permanency outcomes, AFSA in effect gave child development greater priority than family reunification. Some analysts also suggest that AFSA prioritized adoption as a permanency outcome of greater importance than reunification and family preservation (McGowan & Walsh 2000).

Policy Implications of African American Family Demography

At the historical moment that almost half of African American children under age eighteen live with a single parent, child welfare and public assistance policies neglect, ignore, or acknowledge in a very limited manner the nonresidential father. In this sense, public policy lags behind the social concern regarding this issue. In the print and visual media, there are ferocious debates over quality time, effective parenting, and emotional responsibility for divorced fathers. Researchers, talk show hosts, the children of the divorced, and divorced parents look for answers to forestall possible tragedies and problems that may derive from single parenthood. The frequency, intensity, and persistence of such public debates indicate considerable social angst regarding this issue.

The social anguish also suggests that there is some degree of ambiguity regarding the noneconomic role of the nonresidential divorced father in single-parent families. There are many questions to be answered. How does the nonresidential father participate in the socialization of children? How does the nonresidential father maintain emotional attachment to children when physical contact with his children is limited to visitation? To what extent should social and psychological fatherhood be contingent upon economic fatherhood? What is the role of the nonresidential father in decision making for the family with whom he does not live?

While much of the public debate currently focuses on divorced fathers, it is very likely that the same role ambiguity occurs for the nonresidential unmarried father. Furthermore, for the unwed, nonresidential father, role ambiguity is probably further complicated by ethnicity and income. For the unwed or divorced African American father who does not live with his children, how should the father participate in the socialization of children? How do ethnic communities in which occupational mobility is blocked by discrimination and race define the economic and noneconomic roles of fatherhood? If fathers have never had an emotional or legal attachment to the mother, how does the father function in the roles of social and psychological fatherhood? Finally, how do social institutions and the communities in which single-parent African Americans live support not only the single-parent family, but also the other types of families as well?

Recommendations

It is likely that in the context of past and current policies, the persistent demographic trends described in this chapter indicate a substantial need for services currently not available. Some research suggests that men who become parents outside of marriage are younger, less likely to have a high school diploma, more frequently depressed, and more frequently report drug and alcohol use than men who father children within marriages (Garfinkel et al. 1998; McLanahan et al. 2001). These characteristics suggest barriers to the role of economic fatherhood as well as noneconomic fatherhood.

Should public policy and social services support strengthening the bonds between the substantial numbers of unwed African American parents? A recent study (the Fragile Families and Child Well-Being Study) provides evidence about the nature of the bonds between unwed single parents that can inform the answer to this question. Researchers in the study report that of the 1,238 black unwed mothers who made up their sample, 39 percent were living with the father of their child, and 44 percent had a "romantic" or "steady" relationship at the time their child was born (McLanahan et al. 2001). In the context of the romantic relationships between these unwed parents, researchers suggest that the bonds between many unwed parents represent the early family formation of family relationships that are highly vulnerable to disruption because of low earning capacity, unemployment, drug and alcohol use, and general poverty.

In this context, if before and at a child's birth unwed fathers and mothers were involved and targeted for employment, as well as any needed drug and alcohol services, the reconfigured social services delivered to fragile families might support increased formation of married-couple families in African American communities. Thus, study findings seem to suggest the practicality and feasibility of the early support of fragile families at the time of the birth of children. However, the data presented here also show increased numbers of persons with marriages ending in divorce. Particularly for teen parents, marriage may not always be the best solution regarding family formation. However, social services that provide mediation or increase communication and conflict resolution skills of unwed parents are likely to enhance the attachment of nonresidential fathers to children with whom there is no romantic relationships with their mothers.

Data and the analysis presented in this chapter also suggest that as the government has withdrawn from economic involvement in the poorest families, roles for organizations and institutions within African American communities should expand. The ambiguity associated with the role of nonresidential father should be publicly discussed and debated in the African American print and visual media, so that community expectations emerge. Schools, churches, sororities, fraternities, and so on should serve as forums for such discussions. In addition, churches and other organizations can support family formation and functioning by pooling resources and engaging in mutual support. For example, some churches already have an Adopt a Family program in which relatively self-sufficient, stable families adopt the poorest, most vulnerable families. In addition, the child welfare system's use of family conferencing techniques and collaboration with community organizations during the family conference can promote family formation and functioning. Ultimately, the empowerment of stable, functioning families will enhance the well-being of African American communities.

In conclusion, this chapter began with questions about African American children in the context of changed social policies and political and social strife as the twenty-first century loomed before us. Do we know where our children are? Yes, we have data that begin to answer this question. At the start of the twenty-first century, most African American children were either living at home with both of their parents or living at home with a single unmarried mother. When single mothers headed the households in which they lived, the family lived below poverty level. Increasingly, the rate at which families are formed by marriage is dwarfed by the rate of formation for single-headed households and grandparent households. Disproportionately high numbers of African American families experience disruptions to family functioning because of the child welfare system's placement of children outside their homes. In addition, a disproportionately high number of African American families experience the disruption of family functioning because of the institutionalization of children in correctional centers. Finally, families have to function with the staggering effects of child homicides and the mortality of children under the age of one year.

NOTE

The 1998 data from Adoption and Foster Care Analysis and Reporting System (AFCARS) on out-of-home placements by the foster care system were made available by the National Data Archive on Child Abuse and Neglect, Cornell University, Ithaca, NY, and have been used by permission. AFCARS data were originally collected by the Children's Bureau. Funding was provided by the Children's Bureau, Administration on Children, Youth, and Families, Administration for Children and Families, U.S. Department of Health and Human Services. Neither the collector of the original data, the funder, the Archive, Cornell University, or its agents or employees bear any responsibility for the analyses or interpretations presented here.

REFERENCES

Adoption and Safe Families Act of 1997. Public Law No. 105-89, III Stat. 2115.

Bell, W. 1965. *Aid to Dependent Children.* New York: Columbia University Press.

Billingsley, A. 1968. *Black Families in White America.* Englewood Cliffs, NJ: Prentice-Hall.

Billingsley, A. 1992. *Climbing Jacob's Ladder: The Enduring Legacy of African American Families.* New York: Simon & Schuster.

Brodkin, E. 1995. "Administrative Capacity and Welfare Reform." In *Looking Before We Leap: Social Science and Welfare Reform,* edited by W. Weaver & W. Dickens, 75–90. Washington, DC: Brookings Institution.

Casper, L., & K. R. Bryson. March 1998. *Co-resident Grandparents and Their Grandchildren: Grandparent Maintained Families.* Population Division Working Paper no. 26. Washington, DC: U.S. Bureau of the Census.

Census Data Information. 2001. In "American Factfinder Help." Retrieved 11/26/01 from http://factfinder.census.gov/servl.

Chalfie, D. 1994. *Going It Alone: A Closer Look at Grandparents Rearing Grandchildren.* Washington, DC: American Association of Retired Persons.

Child Support Act of 1984. Public Law No. 98-378, Stat. 26842.

Coale, A. 1971. "Age Patterns of Marriage." *Population Studies.* 25:193–214.

Corcoran, M., S. K. Danziger, A. Kalil & K. S. Seefeldt. 2000. "How Welfare Reform Is Affecting Women's Work." *Annual Review of Sociology.* 26:241–69.

Curran. L. September 2002. "The Psychology of Poverty: Professional Social Work and Aid to Dependent Children in Postwar America, 1946–1963. *Social Service Review* 76/3: 365–86.

Dalaker, J. 2001. *Poverty in the United States 2000: Consumer Income.* Current Population Reports, Series P60-214. U.S. Census Bureau. Washington, DC.

Ellwood, D., & M. J. Bane. 1985. "The Impact of AFDC on Family Structure and Living

Arrangements." In *Research in Labor Economics*, edited by R. Ehrenberg, 137–207. Greenwich, CT: JAI Press.

Federal Register 24. December 5, 1995. Vol. 60:64437–64438.

Fields, J. April 2001. *Living Arrangements of Children: 1996*. Current Population Reports, Household Economic Studies. Series P70-74. U.S. Census Bureau. Washington, DC.

Fields, J., & L. M. Casper. 2001. *America's Families and Living Arrangements: 2000*. Current Population Reports, Series P20-537. U.S. Census Bureau. Washington, DC.

Garfinkel, I. 2001. "Child Support in the New World of Welfare Reform." In *The New World of Welfare Reform*, edited by R. M. Blank & R. Haskins, 442–460. Washington, DC: Brookings Institution.

Garfinkel, I., S. McLanahan & T. Hanson. 1998. "A Patchwork Portrait of Nonresident Fathers." In *Fathers under Fire: The Revolution in Child Support Enforcement*, edited by I. Garfinkel, S. McLanahan, D. R. Meyer & J. Selzer. New York: Russell Sage Foundation.

Gibson, R. 1972. "Kin Family Network: Overheralded Structure in Past Conceptualization of Family Functioning." *Journal of Marriage and the Family* 34:13–23.

Goode, W. 1963. *World Revolution and Family Patterns*. Glencoe, IL: Free Press.

Hanson, T. L., I. Garfinkel & S. S. McIanahan. November 1996. "Trends in Child Support Outcomes." *Demography*. 33/4:483–496.

Harden, A. W., R. L. Clark, & K. Maguire. 1997. *Informal and Formal Kinship Care*. Washington, DC: U.S. Department of Health and Human Services.

Hareven, T. 1974. "The Family as Process: The Historical Study of the Family Cycle." *Journal of Social History* 7:322–329.

Hill, R. 1971. *The Strengths of Black families*. New York: Emerson Hall.

Kamo, Y. 2000. "Racial and Ethnic Differences in Extended Family Households." *Sociological Perspectives* 43/2:211–229.

Kreider, R., & J. Fields. 2002. *Number, Timing, and Duration of Marriages and Divorces: Fall 1996*. Current Population Reports, Series P70-80. U.S. Census Bureau. Washington, DC.

Laslett, P., & R. Wall. 1972. *Household and Family in Past Time*. Cambridge: Cambridge University Press.

Levenstein, L. Winter 2000. "From Innocent Children to Unwanted Migrants and Unwed Moms: Two Chapters in the Public Disclosure on Welfare in The United States, 1960–1961." *Journal of Women's History* 11/4:10–33.

Masur, D., M. Silwinski, R. Lipton, A. D. Blau & H. A. Crystal. 1994. "Neuropsychological Prediction of Dementia and the Absence of Dementia in Healthy Elderly Persons." *Neurology* 44:427–432.

McGowan, B., & E. M. Walsh. January/February 2000. "Policy Challenges for Child Welfare in the New Century." *Child Welfare* 79/1:11–27.

McLanahan, S., I. Garfinkel, N. Reichman & J. Teitler. 2001. "Unwed Parents or Fragile Families? Implications for Welfare and Child Support Policy." In *Out of Wedlock: Causes and Consequences of Nonmarital Fertility*, edited by L. L. Wu & B. Wolfe, 202–228. New York: Russell Sage Foundation.

McLoyd, V. C., A. M. Cauce, D. Takeuchi & L. Wilson. November 2000. "Marital Process and Parental Socialization in Families of Color: A Decade Review of Research." *Journal of Marriage and the Family* 62:1070–1093.

Moffit, R. A., R. Reville & A. E. Winkler. 1998. "Beyond Single Mothers: Cohabitation and Marriage in the AFDC Program." *Demography* 35/3:259–278.

Moynihan, D. 1965. *The Negro Family: The Case for National Action*. Washington, DC: U.S. Government Printing Office.

Ofstedal, M. B., G. McAuley & A. R. Herzog. 2002. *HRS/AHEAD Documentation Report*. Docu-

mentation of Cognitive Functioning Measures in the Health and Retirement Study. Ann Arbor, MI: University of Michigan, Survey Research Center.

Osborne, D., & T. Gaebler. 1992. *Reinventing Government: How the Entrepreneurial Spirit Is Transforming the Public Sector.* New York: Plume Books.

Parsons, T. 1951. *The Social System.* Glencoe, IL: Free Press.

Personal Responsibility and Work Opportunity Reconciliation Act. Public Law 104–193.

Rutrough, T. S., & M. Ofstedal. 1997. *Grandparents Living with Grandchildren: A Metropolitan-Nonmetropolitan Comparison.* Presented at the Population Association of America Annual Meeting. Washington, DC.

Settles, B. 1987. "A Perspective on Tomorrow's Families." In *Handbook of Marriage and the Family,* edited by M. B. Sussman & S. K. Steinmetz, 157–180. New York: Plenum Press.

Taylor, R. J., B. Tucker, L. M. Chatters & R. Jayakody. 1997. "Recent Demographic Trends in African American Family Structure." In *Family Life in Black America,* edited by R. Taylor, J. S. Jackson & L. Chatters, 14–62. Thousand Oaks, CA: Sage Publications.

Teachman, J., K. A. Polonko, & J. Scanzoni. 1987. "Demography of the Family." In *Handbook of Marriage and the Family,* edited by M. B. Sussman & S. Steinmetz, 3–36. New York: Plenum Press.

U.S. Census Bureau. 1998. "No. 151. Homicide Rates by Race, Sex, and Age: 1990 to 1995." In *Statistical Abstract of the United States, 1998.* Washington, DC: U.S. Government Printing Office.

———. 2000. "No. 139. Homicide Rates by Race, Sex, and Age: 1996 and 1997." In *Statistical Abstract of the United States, 2000.* Washington, DC: U.S. Government Printing Office.

———. "Table 4. Poverty Status of Families, by Type of Family, Presence of Related Children, Race, and Hispanic Origin: 1959 to 2002." Retrieved 1/6/04 from http://www.census .gov/hhes/poverty/histpov/hstpov4.html.

———. "PCT17. Group Quarters Population by Sex by Age by Group Quarters Type." Retrieved 11/11/03 from http:factfinder.census.gov/servlet/DTTable?_ts=91737731499.

———. "PCT17A. Group Quarters Population by Sex by Age by Group Quarters Type." Retrieved 11/11/03 from http:factfinder.census.gov/servlet/DTTable?_ts=91738762151.

———. "PCT17B. Group Quarters Population by Sex by Age by Group Quarters Type." Retrieved 11/11/03 from http:factfinder.census.gov/servlet/DTTable?_ts=91675020297.

———. 2002. "No. 95. Death Rates by Age: 1940 to 2000." In *Statistical Abstract of the United States, 2000.* Washington, DC: U.S. Government Printing Office.

———. 1997. "No. 121. Death Rates, by Age, Sex, and Race: 1970 to 1995." In *Statistical Abstract of the United States, 1997.* Washington, DC: U.S. Government Printing Office.

———. 1995. "No. 118. Death Rates, by Age, Sex, and Race: 1970 to 1993." In *Statistical Abstract of the United States, 1995.* Washington, DC: U.S. Government Printing Office.

———. "Table P27B. Population by Age, Race, and Hispanic or Latino Origin for the United States: 2000 (PHC-T-9)." Retrieved from http://factfinder.census.gov/servlet/ DTTable_ts=91541153755.

———. "1990 to 1999 Annual Time Series of State Population Estimates by Age, Sex, Race, and Hispanic Origin." Retrieved 11/02/2003 from http://eire.census.gov/popest/ archives/state/st_sasrh.php.

———. "Table FM-2. All Parent/Child Situations, by Type, Race, and Hispanic Origin of Householder or Reference Persons: 1970 to Present." In *Current Population Survey Reports. Historical Time Series. Families.* Retrieved 11/03/2002, from http://www .census.gov/population/socdemo/hh-fam/tabFM-2.pdf.

———. "P35B Family Type by Presence and Age of Related Children." Retrieved 11/11/03 from http://factfinder.census.gov/servlet/DTTable?_ts=91740631059.

————. "Table I. Population by Age, Race and Hispanic or Latino Origin for the United States: 2000 (PHC-T-9)." Retrieved 11/2/02 from http://landview.census,gov/population/www/sen2000/phc-t9.html.

————. "Table P28B. Relationship by Household Type for the Population under Eighteen Years (Black Alone)." Retrieved 11/1/02 from http://factfinder.census.gov/servlet/DTTable?_ts=7152215280.

————. "Table P34B. Family Type by Presence and Age of Own Children (Black Alone Householder)." Retrieved 11/2/02 from http://factfinder.census.gov/servlet/DTTable?_ts=71525626790.

————. "Table QT-P4. Race, Combination of Two Races and Not Hispanic or Latino: 2000." Retrieved 5/21/03 from http://factfinder.census.gov/servlet/DTTable?_ts=71542404220.

————. "Table H8. Total Races Tallied for Householders." Retrieved 5/21/03 from http://factfinder.census.gov/servlet/DTTable?_ts=71542404220.

U.S. Department of Health and Human Services. 1998. Adoption and Foster Care Analysis and Reporting System public use data files. In National Data Archive on Child Abuse and Neglect [MRDF]. Dataset #86. Ithaca, NY: Cornell University (producer). Children's Bureau. Administration on Children, Youth, and Families. Administration for Children and Families.

Welsh, K. A., N. Buters, J. P. Hughes, R. C. Mohs & A. Haymana. 1992. "Detection and Staging for Alzheimer's Disease: Use of the Neuropsychological Measures Developed for the Consortium to Establish a Registry for Alzheimer's Disease." Archives of Neurology 49:448–452.

2

Institutional Racism in Child Welfare

ROBERT B. HILL

Introduction

The status of African American children in the child welfare system is generally characterized by the following racial patterns: (1) they are more likely than white children to be placed in foster care, (2) they are less likely to be adopted and to remain in foster care for longer periods, and (3) they are more highly concentrated in foster care than white children. Yet, the data for these observations are based on a national study of child welfare programs conducted by Helen Jeter (1963) almost forty years ago. Why have African American children continued to be overrepresented in the child welfare system over the past half century?

One explanation describes this overrepresentation as appropriate, since African Americans are believed to have higher rates of child maltreatment than whites and to be more tolerant of abuse than whites. Indeed, several national and state studies have found higher rates of child abuse and neglect among African Americans than whites (Cappelleri, Eckenrode & Powers 1993; Gil 1970; Jason, Andereck, Marks & Tyler 1982; Spearly & Lauderdale 1983). According to the National Child Abuse and Neglect Data System (NCANDS) data for 1999, the victimization rate (per 1,000) for African American children (25.2) was two and one-half times higher than the victimization rate (per 1,000) for white children (10.6). However, such findings are contradicted by more comprehensive national surveys (Gelles & Straus 1979; Sedlak & Broadhurst 1996). All three waves of the National Incidence Studies (NIS)—1979, 1986, and 1993—found no overall differences in child maltreatment rates between African Americans and whites (Sedlak & Broadhurst 1996). Research also reveals that African Americans have less tolerant attitudes about child abuse and neglect than whites (Giovannoni & Becerra 1979; Rose & Meezan 1996).

Another reason offered to account for this overrepresentation is class bias. African Americans account for 2 out of 5 of the 588,000 children who were in foster care in 2000, which is comparable to the proportion (40 percent) of all poor children who are African American. The National Incidence Surveys found the highest rates of child maltreatment among low socioeconomic status (SES) groups. Since African Americans are more highly concentrated among low-income families, it is their class status—not their race—that contributes to their higher representation (Gelles 1982; Pelton 1978). Or, African American children are represented in child welfare in similar proportion to their distribution among low-income families.

A third explanation attributes this overrepresentation to racial bias at various stages of the decision-making processes within the child welfare system (Morton 1999). African Americans are more often reported to child protection agencies for child maltreatment and placed in foster care than whites (Courtney et al. 1996; Hampton 1986; Holton 1990; Stehno 1982). Andrew Billingsley and Jeanne Giovannoni examined the impact of racism in 1972 in their seminal work on African American children and child welfare, *Children of the Storm*. The authors characterize America's child welfare system as manifesting institutional racism in its treatment of African American children and their families. They cite three forms of this racism: devaluing the culture and functioning of African American children and their families, providing inadequate and inequitable services, and excluding members of the African American community from participating in the decision-making processes and the control of agencies that affect their children and families.

Before proceeding with this assessment of institutional racism, it is necessary to operationally define the concept. Billingsley and Giovannoni (1972) provide an appropriate definition: "It is the systematic oppression, subjugation, and control of one racial group by another dominant or more powerful racial group, made possible by the manner in which the society is structured. In this society, racism emanates from white institutions, white cultural values, and white people. The victims of racism in this society are Black people and other oppressed racial and ethnic minorities" (8).

Other important characteristics of institutional racism are that it can be covert or overt, unconscious or conscious, and unintentional or intentional. In other words, for this form of racism to occur, it is not necessary for a group of people to assemble in a back room to consciously conspire against another group. They must only internalize the operating norms and values of the agency, institution, or society in which they are situated (Day 1979). As Downs (1970) observes, institutional racism can result from people with good intentions, and who are without malice:

> Racism can occur even if the people causing it have no intention of subordinating others because of color, or are totally unaware of doing so. Admittedly, this implication is sure to be extremely controversial. Most

Americans believe racism is bad. But how can anyone be "guilty" of doing something bad when he does not realize he is doing it? Racism can be a matter of result rather than intention because many institutional structures in America that most whites do not recognize as subordinating others because of color, actually injure minority group members far more than deliberate racism (78).

An important premise of this assessment is that persons and groups with good intentions who are genuinely concerned about the "best interests" of children developed most policies in child welfare. This is a major reason why the policies have endured so long. Nevertheless, many of these well-meaning policies continue to have adverse effects on poor children in general, and disproportionately on African American and other children of color, because of the influence of institutional racism. This racism is also strongly correlated with classism and sexism. Thus, some of the most severe manifestations of institutional racism can be found among poor children who live in families headed by women who are members of a racial minority. It should also be noted that members of minority groups who conform to the norms of racist institutions might be institutionally racist. For example, an African American police officer who frequently is more aggressive with African American than white suspects, or an African American social worker who often sanctions poor African American families more harshly than poor white families could both be exhibiting institutional racism (Day 1979).

This discussion focuses on a form of institutional racism that is known as "structural discrimination." Structural (or unintentional) discrimination refers to the disparate adverse consequences of societal trends and institutional policies on racial minorities that may not have been explicitly designed to have racially discriminatory effects (Hill 1990). It seeks to build on the notion of "disparate adverse impact" in the legal field. Several Supreme Court decisions (notably, the 1971 *Griggs v. Duke Power* edict) have held that policies in the areas of employment, housing, and voting rights that have disproportionate adverse impact on minorities can be declared racially discriminatory or unconstitutional, even if those policies were not originally designed to have negative effects on those groups (Calmore 1989). In short, structural discrimination shifts the focus from the prejudiced attitudes or malevolent intentions of individuals to the consequences or effects of systems or institutions.

Advocates in the child welfare field might find it useful to review legal precedents relating to disparate adverse impact to determine whether they might be applied to reduce disproportionate adverse effects of policies and practices in child welfare on children of color. An example of such a strategy are the lawsuits that have been instituted by Children's Rights Inc. in about ten states in which state officials have been charged with violating the rights of

foster children under Title VI of the Civil Rights Act of 1964. In an unprece-
dented court-ordered settlement in Tennessee on May 15, 2001, for example, the
state agreed to have an independent expert conduct statewide evaluations to
identify disparities in order to reduce disparate treatment of African American
children in foster care. A major purpose of this essay is to describe how African
American children and their families have received disproportionate adverse
treatment in the child welfare system in the past and present.

This chapter describes how institutional racism influences the operation of
the child welfare system and how this results in disparate adverse effects on the
development and functioning of African American children and their families.
First, it views institutional racism from a historical perspective to understand
how it affected the evolution of child welfare policies regarding African American children and families. Second, the extent to which institutional racism may
affect the decision-making processes at various stages of the current child welfare system is assessed. Third, the chapter offers recommendations to reduce
the impact of institutional racism on children of color and their families in the
future.

Historical View

One of the earliest indictments of the inequitable treatment of African American children by child welfare services was at the 1930 White House Conference
on Child Health and Protection of Dependent and Neglected Children. Dr. Ira
Reid, director of research at the National Urban League, presented a paper that
described the discriminatory treatment of African American children in four
areas: welfare assistance, foster care, health services, and child care (Billingsley
& Giovannoni 1972). His data revealed that African American families were
sharply underrepresented or largely excluded from participating in the Mother's Aid program (the forerunner of Aid to Families with Dependent Children
(AFDC) in both the North and South. Despite the much higher illegitimacy rates
among African Americans, the existing facilities that cared for unmarried
mothers or their out-of-wedlock children were almost exclusively for whites.
Furthermore, despite the alarmingly higher rates of infant mortality among
African Americans, medical and health care services that existed were mainly
for whites. Similarly, although African American mothers were more likely to
work than white mothers, the day care services that were available were mostly
for whites (Billingsley & Giovannoni 1972). These inequities persist today.
Although much higher proportions of African American children and families
are currently represented in each of these programs, the services are still inaccessible or inadequate for the large numbers of low-income families that need
them (Pear 1998; Revkin 1999).

It is important to note, at the outset, that the child welfare system was not originally designed to serve African Americans. It developed toward the end of the nineteenth century along with the settlement house movement to serve the needs of thousands of poor and working-class white families who had emigrated from Europe. Initially, most child welfare services were provided in large residential institutions. However, by 1900, the child welfare system (i.e., the foster boarding homes and orphanages) had acquired its major function—to provide services to children out of their homes—and had split from agencies that provided services to poor families in their homes.

Consequently, the African American community had to develop its own social welfare agencies to care for the poor, aged, and dependent. Since its inception in the 1700s, the Black Church, through its mutual aid and fraternal societies, was the major catalyst for the creation of numerous institutions, such as credit unions, banks, orphanages, homes for the elderly, homes for unmarried mothers, hospitals, schools, and colleges (among free blacks during slavery and after slavery ended) (Curry 1981; Ross 1978). Because of entrenched segregation, many of these institutions survived over long periods of time. Indeed, many African American banks and colleges continue to exist today. However, some of these organizations were destroyed as a result of race riots and other racial conflicts. The advent of integration during the 1950s and 1960s contributed to the demise of many social welfare agencies in the African American community.

Moreover, over the years, the African American community began to place more pressure on federal and local governments to provide services to African Americans, since their taxes were being used to fund those programs. As a result, increasing numbers of African American children and families were served by public agencies and, to a much lesser extent, by private agencies. The shift to foster homes during the 1930s and 1940s had positive consequences for African American families, since it meant an increased involvement of the African American community in caring for its own children. Yet, higher participation of African Americans did not similarly occur regarding adoption, which had a different function from foster care. Unlike foster care, adoption was a service to be provided for the benefit of adults, not children. It was designed to meet the needs of middle-class parents who could not have children. Until the 1960s, most of the children adopted through agencies were not poor, but were out-of-wedlock children born to middle- and upper-income white women. Since African American children were less likely to be adopted than white children, African American children were more likely to remain in the system for longer periods of time, and to age out of it. Thus, African American children continued to be more highly represented in foster care than white children (Day 1979).

In order to make a proper assessment of the impact of institutional racism, it is necessary to adopt a broader view of child welfare. Indeed, Billingsley and Giovannoni (1972) argued that child welfare services should also include "child-oriented" services in the areas of public assistance, child care, health insurance, child support, juvenile justice, education, and mental health. Institutions in these different areas have a major impact on foster care and adoption, the two traditional areas of child welfare (Stehno 1982). The impact of other "child-serving" institutions will now be described.

Mental Health

Mental health institutions play an important role in the development of children in the child welfare system. Research on "modern racism" has shown that institutional racism is often manifested in inequitable mental health treatment of racial minorities through "aversive racism" (Whaley 1998). Aversive racism is a form of structural discrimination that refers to prejudicial attitudes and discriminatory behavior that may be exhibited unconsciously or unintentionally by persons with liberal views and tolerant predispositions. Aversive racists often rationalize or justify their negative stereotypes, uncomfortable feelings, or differential treatment of minorities on nonracial grounds (such as poverty, parental absence or inadequacy, and perceived aggressive behavior).

Several studies have revealed that mental health professionals, who had internalized stereotypes of African Americans as being more violent or aggressive, more often diagnosed African American patients as schizophrenic than white patients (Whaley 1998). African American youth are more likely than white youth to be prescribed psychiatric medications (especially Ritalin) in order to control their "aggressive" behavior. African American students are also more likely than white youth to be labeled as "mentally or educationally retarded" and assigned to special education (Smith & Chunn 1989). African American adolescents are more often referred to secure correctional facilities, while white youth with the same violent behavior and psychopathology are more often referred to mental health services as outpatients. In short, diagnoses based on racial prototypes by well-meaning clinicians are more likely to result in higher rates of placement of African American children in foster care than white children (Stenho 1982; Whaley 1998). Moreover, while most African American children have few mental health problems when they enter foster care, their mental health deteriorates markedly by the time they leave or age out of the system as a result of continual shifts from home to home and inadequate social and psychological services (Curtis, Dale & Kendall 1999).

Schools

Educational institutions are another important source for identifying children in need of protective services. Members of the teaching profession also exhibit aversive racism in their differential perception and treatment of students. Educators who may unconsciously perceive African American students to be more belligerent than white students are more likely to recommend African Americans for detention, suspension, or expulsion. African American youth are more likely to be suspended or expelled than white youth who are responsible for the same infractions of school regulations (Smith & Chunn 1989). School officials may recommend that these "incorrigible" young people be placed in foster care because of truancy, aggressiveness, or as persons in need of services (PINS). These examples of institutional racism do not only apply only to the behavior of white educators. African American teachers who subscribe to stereotypes about African Americans may also exhibit aversively racist behavior that results in double standards in the differential treatment of African American and white students.

Juvenile Justice

An important source for recruiting African American youth into the child welfare system is the juvenile justice system. About 15 percent of children in foster care were placed because of delinquent behavior or status offenses. Numerous studies have found that minority youth are markedly overrepresented in juvenile correctional institutions. For example, among youth with no prior admissions, African American youth are six times more likely than white youth to be sent to state public correctional facilities (Youth Law Center 2000). The racial disparity reached such alarming levels that Congress amended the Juvenile Justice and Delinquency Prevention Act (PL 93-415) in 1988 to require all states to monitor and reduce the extent of disproportionate minority confinement (DMC) by identifying the amount of racial overrepresentation at each stage of the decision-making processes of the juvenile justice system.

Studies consistently show that racially disparate treatment occurs at various stages by justice personnel. African American youth are more likely than white youth, with the same offenses, to be referred to juvenile court, to be detained prior to trial in secure facilities, to be formally charged in juvenile court, to be waived for disposition in adult courts, and to be committed to a juvenile or adult correctional institution (Youth Law Center 2000). It is also interesting to note that, while government data reveal regularly that white youth use and sell more drugs than African American youth, African Americans are more likely to be charged with drug offenses than whites at each stage of criminal processing (US-OJJDP 1999). Furthermore, African Americans charged with possession of crack cocaine receive more severe sentences than whites charged with similar amounts of powder cocaine. Clearly, institutional racism pervades all stages of the juvenile justice (and adult criminal justice) system. It is also important to observe that the correctional institutions receive many youth who leave the child welfare system without being adopted or reunited with their parents. Research has revealed that youth who age out of foster care (who are disproportionately children of color) often become homeless, or turn to prostitution and crime (Jonson-Reid & Barth 2000). Many studies have also found that maltreated children are more likely than non-maltreated children to engage in delinquent or criminal behavior as youth or adults that eventually leads to incarceration (Wiebush, Freitag & Baird 2001). Once again, this leads to the overrepresentation of African American youth and the underrepresentation of white youth in correctional institutions (Mauer 1999).

Decision-Making Processes

To what extent do decisions made at various stages of child welfare processes contribute to the concentration of African American children? A brief overview of research findings will be provided that focuses on the following stages: reporting, referrals, investigation, substantiation, and placement in foster care. Which families are more likely to be reported to child protective services (CPS)? Most research suggests a strong correlation between social class and child abuse and neglect. Government reports and research studies have found that child maltreatment is reported more for low-income than middle- and upper-income families (Gelles 1982; O'Toole, Turbett & Nalepka 1983). Research has revealed that doctors are more likely to diagnose physical injuries as "abuse" among poor families and as "accidents" among affluent families (Katz et al. 1986; McPherson & Garcia 1983). Similarly, some researchers have concluded that child maltreatment is reported more for African Americans than whites. For example, Hampton and Newberger (1985) found that hospitals overreported abuse and neglect among African Americans and underreported among whites. Three-fourths of African Americans were reported for maltreatment by the hospitals, compared with 60 percent of whites. Several studies revealed that African American women were more likely than white women to be reported for child abuse, when their newborns had tested positive for drug use (Chasnoff, Landress & Barrett 1990; Neuspiel et al. 1993). On the other hand, many studies do not find strong racial differentials in the reporting of child maltreatment. These studies have concluded that the strongest predictors of reporting are severity of injury, cases with prior reports, and history of family problems (Hampton 1991; Newberger et al. 1977; Wolock et al. 2001).

After receiving reports on alleged child maltreatment, child welfare agencies routinely screen them to decide which ones would be referred for investigation. Sizable numbers of cases that are reported for child maltreatment are not referred for investigation. According to NCANDS data, 40 percent of the three million referrals to Child Protective Services (CPS) in 1999 were screened out, while 60 percent were screened in and investigated. Similarly, a nationwide survey of child welfare agencies by the Urban Institute revealed that 36 percent of the cases that had been reported to child protection agencies in 1996 were screened out prior to investigation (Tumin & Green 2000).

During the screening process, a decision is made about whether or not some cases will be investigated. An in-depth longitudinal study of child maltreatment reports in New Jersey found that African Americans (20 percent) and whites (23 percent) had similar rates of investigation (Wolock et al. 2001). Although a reanalysis of NIS-3 data did not find that race alone had any effects on investigation, it found strong interactions between race and severity and type of maltreatment on the probability of investigation (Sedlak & Schultz 2004). For example, the NIS-3 reanalysis found higher rates of investigation for African Americans than whites (1) among children who were emotionally maltreated or physically neglected, and (2) among children whose parents were substance abusers.

At the conclusion of the investigation, a decision is made whether or not to confirm or substantiate the allegation. Only a fraction of child abuse reports are substantiated. According to 1999 NCANDS data, only 29 percent of the cases investigated were substantiated, while 55 percent were not substantiated. Similarly, the Urban Institute survey revealed that only 38 percent of the cases investigated for child maltreatment in 1996 were substantiated, and only one-fourth (27 percent) of all reports for maltreatment were substantiated (Tumin & Green 2000).

Are there racial differentials in substantiation? A comprehensive review of studies of the substantiation of child maltreatment reports identified four key predictors: status of reporter, prior reports of maltreatment, race or ethnicity of victim or family, and type of maltreatment (Zuravin, Orme & Hegar 1995). Substantiation was more likely when the reports were made by professionals, when there had been prior reports of abuse or neglect, when the report was for physical abuse rather than neglect, and when the victim or family was a member of a minority group (i.e., African American or Hispanic). This review also found that workers had greater confidence in substantiating a report when it was a professional reporter, a severe injury or allegation, a male perpetrator, and the victim or family was African American. Furthermore, while most risk assessment studies reveal greater substantiation for African Americans than whites, they found similar recurrence rates of substantiation among racial groups (Baird, Ereth & Wagner 1999; Eckenrode et al. 1988).

But the evidence on racial differentials in substantiation decisions is mixed. For example, the New Jersey study of child maltreatment did not find racial differences regarding substantiation rates. When race/ethnicity was included in regression models to estimate the probability of substantiation, it had no significant effects (Wolock et al. 2001). But it revealed three strong predictors of substantiation: parental substance abuse, number of children, and family functioning. On the other hand, based on an analysis of NCANDS data for selected states, Morton (1999) found the rates of substantiation for African American children were consistently higher than the rates for white children, while the substantiation rates for Latino children were comparable to those of white children. Clearly, decisions about substantiation might be operating differently for African American and Latino children.

In sum, the data are contradictory about whether there are racial differences at various stages of the child welfare system. A major reason for these mixed results is the paucity of research studies and data by race at the different stages. However, as there are many studies of racial patterns regarding placement in foster care, it will now be examined in greater detail.

Foster Care Placement

To what extent is race a determinant of placement into foster care? One of the most comprehensive analyses of the role of race in the child welfare system was based on the National Study of Protective, Preventive, and Reunification Services (NSPPRS) Delivered to Children and Families, which was conducted by Westat in 1994 to update the findings of the 1977 National Study of Social Services to Children and Their Families. A major objective of the NSPPRS was to document the number and characteristics of children and families based on a nationally representative sample of 2,109 children who received in-home or out-of-home child welfare services between March 1, 1993, and March 1, 1994.

Although the NSPPRS is primarily a cross-sectional survey, it has a longitudinal component, since it obtains outcome data on the subgroup of children who were discharged during the six-month period after February 28, 1994. Another advantage of the NSPPRS is that, since it is based on interviews with caseworkers who provided information from case records about specific children and their parents, the survey was able to include many variables that are usually not found in studies that rely solely on administrative records.

Since the NSPPRS has data on all children who received child welfare services, it is possible to determine whether there are racial differentials between foster care placement and in-home services. African American children are more likely than whites to be placed in foster care and less likely to receive services in the home. In fact, African American children were twice as likely as white children to be placed in foster care (56 percent vs. 28 percent). Or, 72 percent of white children received services in the home, compared with only 44 percent of African American children (U.S. Children's Bureau 1997).

The researchers compared children who received services in-home with those who were placed in foster care on a number of social and economic characteristics. In general, they found that children who were more likely to receive in-home services were older when entering the child welfare system, lived in two-parent families, had at least one employed parent, no parent abused drugs, the family relied on earnings and not on AFDC, they lived in neighborhoods with low levels of crimes and drugs, and had no prior case openings. Racial comparisons revealed, as expected, that African American children were less likely than white children to have these advantaged characteristics that were positively correlated with receiving child welfare services at home.

The analysts then addressed the question "If African American children had the same advantaged characteristics as white children, would they have the same likelihood of receiving services in-home or of being placed in foster care?" The data revealed that African American children whose parents were employed, not drug abusers, relied on earnings income, lived in neighborhoods with low levels of crime and drugs, and had no prior case openings were still significantly more likely than comparable white children to be placed in foster care. These results strongly suggest that it is not decisions based on the disadvantaged social and economic characteristics of African Americans that explain their greater propensity to be placed in foster care, or not to receive in-home services (U.S. Children's Bureau 1997).

In order to assess whether race continued to be a significant predictor of foster care placement, when combined with other important social and economic variables, it was necessary to conduct multivariate analyses of the NSPPRS data. Hill (2004) tested various logistic regression models to determine the set of variables that were the strongest predictors of placement in foster care. His analysis identified five strong predictors: race of child (i.e., African American), substance-abusing parents, children with disabilities, Medicaid recipients, and cases with abuse allegations. Further analyses revealed that, even when African American children had a combination of advantaged characteristics (such as no child disability, no receipt of Medicaid, no substance-abusing parent, and no abuse allegation), they were still significantly more likely to be placed in foster care compared with white children with more disadvantaged characteristics.

Consequently, the study concluded that race remained a strong predictor of foster care placement, even when combined with the other four strong determinants. On the other hand, several other variables in the study were no longer significantly related to foster care placement when combined with the strong five predictors. These variables included family structure, parental employment status, parental educational status, whether the family received AFDC, and whether there was a prior case opening (Hill 2004).

The NSPPRS study identified other racial differentials in the child welfare system (i.e., among children who were placed in foster care and among those not placed in foster care but who received services at home). African American children (four years) enter the child welfare system at younger ages than white children (eight years). African American children have more disadvantaged characteristics than white children, such as single parents, parents who are unemployed, parents with substance abuse problems, government income, recipients of AFDC and Medicaid, and residents of neighborhoods with crime and drug problems. African American children remain in the system for longer periods of time and experience more placements in different settings while in the system. Yet, no racial differences between African Americans and whites were found regarding some attributes, such as children with disabilities, in poor physical health, and with no prior case openings (U.S. Children's Bureau 1997). Other studies have found that the parental rights of African American children are terminated at much younger ages than white children, resulting in higher proportions of African American children who are freed for adoption (Pinder-hughes 1991). Although African American children are more likely than white children to be freed for adoption, they are still less likely to be adopted than white children. Thus, African American children are more likely to be "legal orphans" in child welfare than white children. Yet, contrary to the widespread belief that African American families are not interested in formal adoption, the National Urban League Black Pulse Survey revealed that one-third (or three million) of all African American households said they were interested in formally adopting children. Government data also reveal that the adoption rates among African American families are often the same as, and sometimes higher than, the rates among white families (Hill 1999; Mason & Williams 1985; U.S. Children's Bureau 1984).

To what extent are there racial differentials in the delivery of services? Racial differences were found in the NSPPRS study in three areas: parenting skills, caretaker substance abuse problems, and housing problems. White families with housing problems were offered housing services more than African American families with housing problems. On the other hand, African American caretakers with substance abuse problems were more likely to be offered substance abuse services than white caretakers with substance abuse problems. Similar patterns held among African American and white caretakers with parenting problems. Thus, these findings are mixed, since African Americans were offered more services than whites regarding parenting and substance abuse problems, while whites were offered more services than African Americans with regard to housing problems (U.S. Children's Bureau 1997). But the National Black Child Development Institute (NBCDI) survey revealed that drug-abusing parents received more inadequate services than parents whose children were placed in foster care for other reasons (Walker, Zangrillo & Smith 1994).

Moreover, a comprehensive review of child welfare research found that nonwhite children generally received fewer or more inadequate services in the child welfare system than white children (Courtney et al. 1996). A secondary analysis by Close (1983) of the 1977 national survey of social services revealed that African American and Latino children had fewer visits with their families, less contact with workers, and fewer services overall than white children. A study of the foster care system in New York found that African American and Latino children were less likely than white children to be placed in agencies that had superior outcome records, irrespective of their entry-level characteristics (Gurak, Smith & Goldsen 1982). The researchers concluded that their literature review suggests "a pattern of inequity, if not discrimination, based on race and ethnicity in the provision of child welfare services" (Courtney et al. 1996, 112).

Kinship Care

One foster care arrangement in which researchers have found the inequity of services to be most evident is among children who had been placed with relatives. The differential treatment of kin caregivers and their children is a blatant manifestation of institutional racism in the child welfare system. Since African American children are overrepresented in kinship care families, this type of foster care placement will now be examined in greater detail.

"Informal adoption," or the rearing of African American children by kin, is a long-standing cultural tradition that is a survival of the African heritage (Hill 1977). Consequently, prior to the 1980s, very few African American children who lived in households headed by relatives were in the child welfare system. However, with the advent of crack cocaine and HIV/AIDS in inner cities in the mid-1980s, the number of children in need of protective services increased sharply. Yet, as the survey by the NBCDI revealed, most of the children of drug-abusing parents were placed for neglect, not abuse (Walker, Zangrillo & Smith 1994). Since fewer (traditional) nonrelated foster parents were available, child welfare agencies began to aggressively recruit relatives as foster parents. The number of children placed with kin soared to such an extent that a new type of foster placement was created: "kinship care." In fact, in many large cities today, such as Baltimore, Los Angeles, and Chicago, the majority of the children in foster care are placed with relatives. But the kin families in the child welfare system make up only a small fraction of all African American children who are living with relatives. Eighty percent (or eight hundred thousand) of the one million African American children not living with either parent are informally adopted by relatives, while only the remaining 20 percent (or two hundred thousand) are in the foster care system (Hill 1999).

What are the characteristics of kinship care families? About two-thirds are headed by grandmothers, while the remaining one-third are headed by aunts, uncles, or older sisters and brothers. Kin caretakers usually have no spouse, are older (with a median age of fifty years), have less education, and tend to have low or fixed income. A national survey of children in kinship care reveals that over half (55 percent) of the kin caregivers had no spouse, 36 percent had less than a high school degree, and 41 percent had incomes below the poverty level (Ehrle, Green & Clark 2001). Most kin caregivers receive the inadequate Temporary

Assistance for Needy Families payment that averages about $200 per month, depending on the number of children, and are not able to receive much higher foster board payments for nonrelatives that range from $356 to $431 per month, depending on the age of the child. Moreover, despite their eligibility, the majority of kinship care families do not receive important government benefits: 72 percent received no AFDC assistance, about half (47 percent) received no Medicaid assistance, and 40 percent did not receive any food stamps (Ehrle, Green & Clark 2001). These differential government benefits structurally discriminate against kin families, since it does not cost less to care for a child because it is with a relative than it would if the child were with a nonrelative.

What other differences are there between kinship care and nonrelated foster families? Children in kinship care are in more stable living arrangements than children in traditional foster care. Children in nonrelated foster care were three times more likely to be moved to different homes or settings than children in kinship care (33 percent vs. 10 percent). Moreover, children in nonrelated foster care are likely to experience more episodes of foster care placement than children in kinship care (30 percent vs. 14 percent) (U.S. Children's Bureau 1997). Children in kinship care are at higher risk of poor physical and mental health than children with non-kin as a result of their greater likelihood of having parents who were drug addicted or HIV/AIDS-infected. Despite the high risk factors among kinship families, research has also revealed differences in services provided to kin and non-kin caregivers. Studies have found that kin caregivers are less likely to receive foster parent training, respite care, educational or mental health assessments, individual or group counseling, or tutoring for their children than non-kin foster parents (Chipungu et al. 1998; Iglehart 1994).

What racial differences exist regarding kinship care families? Indeed, African American children are twice as likely to be placed with kin than white children (29 percent vs. 14 percent). Some observers assert that African American children are staying longer in foster care because they are more often placed with relatives. The NSPPRS data strongly contradict such beliefs. African American children spent about the same time in foster care whether they were with kin (32.9 months) or non-kin (27.2 months). Similarly, white children spent the same time in foster care whether they were with kin (18.1 months) or non-kin (19.1 months). But, African American children remained in foster care much longer than white children, whether or not they were with kin. These findings suggest that factors other than kinship placement account for the longer time that African American children spend in foster care (U.S. Children's Bureau 1997). Furthermore, studies have found the lowest levels of child abuse to be among African American children who live with relatives. Thus, children are safest when living with or in regular contact with extended family members (Cazenave & Straus 1979; Hill 1999).

Conclusions

What conclusions can be drawn as a result of an examination of the different decision-making points in the child welfare system? It is important to acknowledge that this assessment has not "proven" that institutional racism is pervasive in the child welfare system. It is difficult to prove the existence of racism in any form, since appropriate qualitative and quantitative data at both the individual and institutional levels do not currently exist. Moreover, many research studies in child welfare have data on race or ethnicity, but the analysts do not use them to determine whether any racial differences or similarities exist. Consequently, this chapter has focused on racial differentials and inequities. It is based on the premise that the preponderance of data demonstrating racial inequities in different areas strongly suggests patterns of discrimination—whether conscious or not. This is why special emphasis was placed on structural or unintentional discrimination. Given these caveats, conclusions and implications for policy and practice will now be discussed.

This chapter focused on various explanations for the higher concentration of African American children in the child welfare system than white children. National surveys and, especially, the National Incidence Studies on Child Abuse and Neglect, suggest that this overrepresentation is not due to inherently higher rates of child maltreatment in African American families. Another possible explanation was that African American families have more class-related problems (such as single-parent families, unemployment, poverty, substance abuse, drug addiction, incarceration, inadequate housing, etc.) that might place children at greater risk of abuse and neglect. Indeed, most studies reveal that African Americans have a higher incidence of these problems than whites. Yet, when these disadvantages are removed, the analyses reveal that African American children continue to be more likely than white children to be placed in foster care.

Consequently, this assessment described how other institutions—mental health, schools, and juvenile justice—contributed to the concentration of children of color in the child welfare system. In addition, this examination sought to identify racial differentials at various stages of the decision-making processes in the child welfare system: reporting, investigation, substantiation, and placement in foster care. With regard to reporting, the research findings were contradictory. Some studies found African Americans more likely to be reported than whites, while other research found no such differences. Yet, there was some consensus regarding findings that African American women were more likely to be reported for maltreatment than white women, when their newborns tested positive for substance use. Most studies did not find racial differentials regarding investigations; whites were just as likely to be screened in for investigations as

African Americans. On the other hand, there was evidence that African Americans were more likely to be substantiated than whites. In fact, several risk assessment studies found substantiation rates to be higher among African Americans than whites.

The research shows that racial differences continue after children are placed in foster care. African American children remain for longer periods than white children. African American children are more likely to have the rights of their parents terminated than white children. Although African American children are more likely to be freed for adoption than white children, they are less likely to be adopted. African American children are more likely than white children to be placed with relatives—where they are likely to experience the lowest levels of abuse, which should be an advantage. But kin caregivers (who are often old and poor) receive less government income, benefits, and services than non-related foster parents (Iglehart 1994). In short, children who are placed with kin experience structural discrimination by being denied equitable support and services. It is ironic that, while many social workers state that African American children are often placed in foster care to provide them with vital services, many studies have found that they often receive fewer benefits and services than white children, especially when they are living with relatives.

Why are African American children treated more inequitably than white children? One answer is provided by Billingsley and Giovannoni (1972)—the devaluing of the culture and functioning of African American families. Since African American families are overrepresented among the poor, they are often perceived and treated differently because of class-related characteristics. Yet, many African American families who do not have those disadvantaged attributes are also assumed to be dysfunctional. Apparently, many social work professionals still agree with Glazer and Moynihan (1963, 51) that African Americans have "no values and culture to guard and protect." Although informal adoption by relatives is viewed by the African American community as a long-enduring cultural strength that promotes family preservation and reunification, large segments of the child welfare community devalue this form of child rearing. Many disparaging epithets are often made about kin caregivers, such as the "apple does not fall far from the tree," "they are only doing it for the money," or "they are too old to care for children." Such expressions are recurring examples of cultural insensitivity in current child welfare practice.

In order to reduce the likelihood of individual or institutional racism, child welfare professionals must enhance their sensitivity toward and appreciation of diverse cultural beliefs and practices (Altstein & McRoy 2000; Holton 1990; McPhatter 1997). They must disavow the belief that "different" cultural values or practices are inherently "inferior" to theirs. Self-assessments might increase awareness of stereotypes about different classes, races, or ethnic groups. All families should be viewed and treated as partners or consumers, and not as adversaries or clients (Curtis, Dale & Kendall 1999; Pinderhughes 1991). One should also realize that it is possible to discriminate against people of color without consciously intending such outcomes. Examples of culturally sensitive policies are the Title IV-E waiver experiments to test the feasibility of extending subsidies to kin caregivers who want to become guardians, but not adoptive parents, of their minor relatives. Federal policies provide subsidies to parents who want to adopt, but offer no funds to caretakers who want to become guardians—regardless of their inadequate income. The five-year Subsidized Guardianship Demonstration in Illinois is innovative, since it provides equitable financial support to related and nonrelated foster parents. Preliminary results from a comprehensive evaluation reveal that giving financial subsidies to kin guardians achieves comparable levels of child permanency, stability, and safety as children in adoptive homes (Westat 1999). Furthermore, various states are experimenting with providing their own funds and additional services to enhance the social and economic well-being of children and their kin caregivers.

Another strategy for reducing institutional racism is for the child welfare system to become more racially and ethnically inclusive regarding the governance and control of agencies. African American–controlled organizations have shown repeatedly that it is easy to recruit African American families, but it is very difficult to ensure that they become adoptive parents (Day 1979). For example, only two of the eight hundred African American families that were recruited in an Urban League campaign were eventually able to adopt a child (McRoy, Ogelsby & Grape 1997). There is a vital need for broader participation in decision making at all stages of child welfare processes to achieve more culturally diverse and sensitive policies and practices. For example, illustrative is the racial disparity in New York—a state with one of the largest number of foster children in the nation. Although African Americans make up over 60 percent of the children in foster care in New York, they control only about 10 percent of the private agencies that are licensed to provide adoption and foster care services in the state (National Adoption Information Clearinghouse 2001). Moreover, contrary to the widespread belief that African American families cannot be found for placing African American children, many African American–controlled (and other progressive) agencies are demonstrating that permanent and safe homes can be found in the African American community. These agencies have also proven that permanent homes for children of color can be found by implementing both culturally sensitive and cost-effective strategies (Day 1979; McRoy, Ogelsby & Grape 1997). The federal government should provide financial and other incentives to states that take aggressive actions to increase the racial and ethnic diversity of the governance and staffing of their child welfare agencies. If genuine steps are taken to implement some of these suggestions, children of color would receive more equitable treatment and exhibit more positive outcomes from the child welfare system.

REFERENCES

Altstein, H., & R. McRoy. 2000. *Does Family Preservation Serve a Child's Best Interest?* Washington, DC: Georgetown University Press.

Baird, C., J. Ereth, & D. Wagner. June 1999. *Research-Based Risk Assessment: Adding Equity to CPD Decision-Making.* Madison, WI: Children's Research Center.

Billingsley, A., & J. Giovannoni. 1972. *Children of the Storm: Black Children and American Child Welfare.* New York: Harcourt Brace Jovanovich.

Calmore, J. 1989. "To Make Wrong Right: The Necessary and Proper Aspirations of Fair Housing." In *The State of Black America: 1989*, edited by J. Dewart, 77–109. New York: National Urban League.

Cappelleri, J., J. Eckenrode, & J. Powers. 1993. "The Epidemiology of Child Abuse: Findings from the Second National Incidence and Prevalence Study of Child Abuse and Neglect." *American Journal of Public Health* 83/11:1622–1624.

Cazenave, N., & M. Straus. 1979. "Race, Class, and Network Embeddedness and Family Violence." *Journal of Comparative Families Studies* 10/3:281–300.

Chasnoff, I., H. Landress, & M. Barrett. 1990. "The Prevalence of Illicit-Drug or Alcohol Use During Pregnancy and Discrepancies in Mandatory Reporting in Pinellas County, Florida." *New England Journal of Medicine* 332/17:1202–1206.

Chipungu, S., J. Everett, J. Verdick, & J. Jones. 1998. *Children Placed in Foster Care with Relatives.* Washington, DC: Administration on Children, Youth, and Families.

Close, M. M. 1983. "Child Welfare and People of Color: Denial of Equal Access." *Social Work Research and Abstracts* 19/4:13–20.

Courtney, M., R. Barth, J. Berrick, D. Brooks, B. Needell, & L. Park. 1996. "Race and Child Welfare Services: Past Research and Future Directions." *Child Welfare* 75/2:99–137.

Curry, L. 1981. *The Free Black in Urban America: 1800–1850.* Chicago: University of Chicago Press.

Curtis, P., G. Dale, & J. Kendall, eds. 1999. *The Foster Care Crisis: Translating Research into Policy and Practice.* Lincoln: University of Nebraska Press.

Day, D. 1979. *The Adoption of Black Children: Counteracting Institutional Discrimination.* Lexington, MA: D. C. Heath.

Downs, A. 1970. "Racism in America and How to Combat It." In *Urban Problems and Prospects*, edited by A. Downs, 5–114. Chicago: Markham.

Eckenrode, J., J. Powers, J. Doris, J. Munsch, & N. Bolger. 1988. "Substantiation of Child Abuse and Neglect Reports." *Journal of Consulting and Clinical Psychology* 56/1: 9–16.

Ehrle, J., R. Green, & R. Clark. February 2001. "Children Cared for by Relatives: Who Are They and How Are They Faring?" *Urban Institute New Federalism Report.* Series B-28.

Gelles, R. 1982. "Child Abuse and Family Violence: Implications for Medical Professionals." In *Child Abuse*, edited by E. Newberger, 25–41. Boston: Little, Brown.

Gelles, R., & M. Straus. 1979. "Determinants of Violence in the Family." In *Contemporary Theories about the Family.* Vol. 1. Edited by W. R. Burr, R. Hill, F. I. Nye & I. L. Reiss, 549–581. New York: Free Press.

Gil, D. 1970. *Violence against Children in the United States.* Cambridge: Harvard University Press.

Giovannoni, J., & R. Becerra. 1979. *Defining Child Abuse.* New York: Free Press.

Glazer, N., & D. Moynihan. 1963. *Beyond the Melting Pot.* Cambridge, MA: MIT Press.

Gurak, D., D. Smith, & M. Goldsen. 1982. *The Minority Foster Child.* New York: Hispanic Research Center, Fordham University.

Hampton, R. L. 1986. "Race, Ethnicity, and Child Maltreatment. In *The Black Family*, edited by R. Staples, 172–185. Belmont, CA: Wadsworth Publishing.

———. 1991. "Child Abuse in The African American Community." In *Child Abuse: An Afri-centric Perspective*, edited by J. Everett, S. Chipungu & B. Leashore, 220–246. New Brunswick, NJ: Rutgers University Press.

Hampton, R. L, & E. Newberger. 1985. "Child Abuse Incidence and Reporting by Hospitals: Significance of Severity, Class, and Race." *American Journal of Public Health* 75/1:56–60.

Hill, R. B. 1977. *Informal Adoption among Black Families.* Washington, DC: National Urban League Research Department.

———. 1990. "Economic Forces, Structural Discrimination, and Black Family Instability." In *Black Families*, edited by H. B. Cheatham & J. B. Stewart, 87–105. New Brunswick, NJ: Transaction Publishers.

———. 1999. *The Strengths of African American Families: Twenty-Five Years Later.* Lanham, MD: University Press of America.

———. 2004. "The Role of Race in Foster Care Placements." In *Race Matters in Child Welfare: The Overrepresentation of African American Children in the System.* Edited by M. Testa & J. Poertner. Washington, DC: Children Welfare League of America.

Holton, J. K. 1990. *Black Families and Child Abuse Prevention: An African-American Perspective and Approach.* Chicago: National Committee to Prevent Child Abuse.

Iglehart, A. P. 1994. "Kinship Foster Care: Placement, Service, and Outcome Issues." *Children and Youth Services Review* 16/1–2:107–122.

Jason, J., N. Andereck, J. Marks, & C. Tyler Jr. 1982. "Child Abuse in Georgia: A Method to Evaluate Risk Factors and Reporting Bias." *American Journal of Public Health* 72/12: 1353–1358.

Jeter, H. 1963. *Children, Problems, and Services in Child Welfare Programs.* Washington, DC: U.S. Department of Health, Education, and Welfare.

Jonson-Reid, M., & R. Barth. 2000. "From Placement to Prison: The Path to Adolescent Incarceration from Child Welfare Supervised Foster or Group Care." *Children and Youth Services Review* 22/7:493–516.

Katz, M., R. Hampton, E. Newberger, R. Bowles & J. Snyder, J. 1986. "Returning Children Home: Clinical Decision-Making in Cases of Child Abuse and Neglect." *American Journal of Orthopsychiatry* 56/2:253–262.

Mason, J., & C. Williams. 1985. "The Adoption of Minority Children." In *Adoption of Children with Special Needs*, edited by E. Segal & M. Hardin, 81–93. Washington, DC: American Bar Association.

Mauer, M. 1999. *Race to Incarcerate.* New York: New Press.

McPhatter, A. R. 1997. "Cultural Competence in Child Welfare." *Child Welfare* 76/1:255–278.

McPherson, K., & L. Garcia. 1983. "Effects of Social Class and Familiarity on Pediatricians' Responses to Child Abuse." *Child Welfare* 62/5:387–393.

McRoy, R., Z. Ogelsby & H. Grape. 1997. "Achieving Same-Race Adoptive Placements for African American Children." *Child Welfare* 76/1:85–104.

Morton, T. 1999. "The Increasing Colorization of America's Child Welfare System: The Overrepresentation of African American Children." *Policy and Practice*, 23–30.

National Adoption Information Clearinghouse. 2001. *National Adoption Directory: 2001.* Washington, DC: National Adoption Information Clearinghouse.

Neuspiel, D., T. Zingman, V. Templeton, P. DiStabile & E. Drucker. 1993. "Custody of Cocaine-Exposed Newborns: Determinants of Discharge Decisions." *American Journal of Public Health* 83/12:1726–1729.

Newberger, E., R. Reed, J. Daniel, J. Hyde & M. Kotelchuck. 1977. "Pediatric Social Illness: Toward an Etiologic Classification." *Pediatrics* 60/2:178–185.

O'Toole, R., P. Turbett & C. Nalepka. 1983. "Theories, Professional Knowledge, and Diagnosis of Child Abuse." In *The Dark Side of Families: Current Family Violence Research*, edited by D. Finkelhor, R. Gelles, G. Hotaling & M. Straus, 349–362. Newbury Park, CA: Sage.

Pear, R. February 28, 1998. "More Children Go Uninsured Despite Status for Medicaid." *New York Times,* C:1.

Pelton, L. 1978. "Child Abuse and Neglect: The Myth of Classlessness." *American Journal of Orthopsychiatry* 48/4:608–617.

Pinderhughes, E. 1991. "The Delivery of Child Welfare Services to African American Clients." *American Journal of Orthopsychiatry* 61/4:599–605.

Revkin, A. February 24, 1999. "Plunge in Use of Food Stamps Causes Concern." *New York Times,* 1:17.

Rose, S., & W. Meezan. 1996. "Variations in Perceptions of Child Neglect." *Child Welfare* 75/2:139–160.

Ross, E. L. 1978. *Black Heritage in Social Welfare.* Metuchen, NJ: Scarecrow Press.

Sedlak, A., & D. Broadhurst. 1996. "Executive Summary of the Third National Incidence Study of Child Abuse and Neglect." Washington, DC: U.S. Department of Health and Human Services.

Sedlak, A., & D. Schultz. 2004. "Race Differences in Child Protective Services Investigation of Abuse and Neglected Children." In *Race Matters in Child Welfare: The Overrepresentation of African American Children in the System.* Edited by T. Testa & J. Poertner. Washington, DC: Child Welfare League of America.

Smith, W., & E. Chunn, eds. 1989. *Black Education.* New Brunswick, NJ: Transaction Publishers.

Spearly, J., & M. Lauderdale. 1983. "Community Characteristics and Ethnicity in the Prediction of Child Maltreatment Rates." *Child Abuse and Neglect* 7/1:91–103.

Stehno, S. 1982. "Differential Treatment of Minority Children." *Social Work* 27/1:39–45.

Tumin, K., & R. Green. 2000. "The Decision to Investigate: Understanding State Child Welfare Screening Policies and Practices." *Urban Institute Report,* Series A, No-38.

U.S. Children's Bureau. 1984. *Child Welfare Notes #3.* Washington, DC: U.S. Department of Health and Human Services.

———. 1997. *National Study of Protective, Preventive, and Reunification Services Delivered to Children and Their Families.* Washington, DC: U.S. Department of Health and Human Services.

U.S. Office of Juvenile Justice and Delinquency Prevention. 1999. *Juvenile Offenders and Victims: 1999 National Report.* Washington, DC: U.S. Department of Justice.

Walker, C. D., P. Zangrillo & J. Smith. 1994. "Parental Drug Abuse and African American Children in Foster Care." In *Child Welfare Research Review.* Vol. 1. Edited by R. Barth, J. Berrick & N. Gilbert, 109–122. New York: Columbia University Press.

Westat. December 1999. *Evaluation of the Illinois Subsidized Guardianship Waiver Demonstration: Preliminary Findings.* Rockville, MD: Westat.

Whaley, A. L. 1998. "Racism in the Provision of Mental Health Services." *American Journal of Orthopsychiatry* 68/1:47–57.

Wiebush, R., R. Freitag & C. Baird. July 2001. "Preventing Delinquency through Improved Child Protection Services." *OJJDP Juvenile Justice Bulletin.*

Wolock, I., P. Sherman, L. Feldman & B. Metzger. 2001. "Child Abuse and Neglect Referral Patterns: A Longitudinal Study." *Children and Youth Services Review* 23/1:21–47.

Youth Law Center. 2000. *And Justice for Some: Differential Treatment of Minority Youth in the Justice System.* Washington, DC: Youth Law Center.

Zuravin, S., J. Orme & R. Hegar. 1995. "Disposition of Child Physical Abuse Reports: Review of the Literature and Test of a Predictive Model." *Children and Youth Services Review* 17/4:547–566.

3

The Impact of Child Welfare Policies on African American Families

A Decade Later

SANDRA P. CHIPUNGU

Twelve years ago in our first book on African American children in child welfare, we hoped to elevate the importance of race in child welfare and argued that race must be considered in child welfare practice and in the development of policies that enhance and support racial differences. Our arguments were made against a context in which African American children were overrepresented in the child welfare system in foster homes, group homes, and institutions. These trends still persist over a decade later. Higher percentages of African American children compared with other racial and ethnic groups are in the child welfare system. Furthermore, this pattern has persisted for forty years (Jeter 1963). Unlike twelve years ago, the debate over racial disproportionality has now risen to the national level. Researchers, policy makers, administrators, child advocacy, and interest groups are currently debating the issue of racial disproportionality (Race Matters Forum I 2001; Race Matters Forum II 2002; Research Roundtable on Children of Color in Child Welfare 2002).

In our first book, we also argued that the public foster care system could not replace African American families and urged that child welfare services consider the Africentric values of extended family systems, communalism, collective identity, and spirituality in placement decisions for African American children. The percentages of African American children placed with relatives have indeed increased in the past decade. These placements with relatives have resulted from an increase in entries of African American children, a decrease in available nonrelative foster care homes, and policy changes encouraging relative placements. But what else has happened to African American children in the child welfare system since 1990? We will examine the current status of African American children and the changes in federal policies since our first book was published.

Current Status of African American Children in Child Welfare

According to the Adoption and Foster Care Analysis and Reporting System (AFCARS) Report #8 (USDHHS 2003), there were 542,000 children in foster care as of September 2001. That number represents a decrease of less than 2 percent from September 2000. The mean age of these children was ten years. The race/ethnicity of children in foster care was as follows: 35 percent were white, 38 percent were African American, 15 percent were Hispanic, 2 percent were American Indian/Alaskan Native, 1 percent were Asian/Pacific Islander, and 8 percent were of unknown race/ethnicity or the information was not determined. Fifty-two percent of the children were male and 48 percent were female. The types of foster homes were as follows: 48 percent of these foster children live in the home of a nonrelative, 25 percent live in the home of a relative, 10 percent were in institutions, 8 percent were in group homes, 4 percent were in preadoptive homes and 3 percent were on trial home visits with their parents, 1 percent were in supervised independent living arrangements, and approximately 2 percent were runaways.

Current demographic trends indicate that the number of children in foster care appears to be declining. In FY 1998, there were 558,000 children in foster care compared with 556,00 in FY 2000 and 542,000 in FY 2001. The numbers of entries and waiting children has been flat (Maza 2003). While the number of children in foster care appears to be declining, the cost of foster care is increasing. In FY 2000, states spent $20 billion on child welfare services including $9.9 billion in federal funds, $7.9 billion in state funds, and $2.2 billion in local funds (Geen 2003). Federal funds account for approximately 49 percent of all child welfare expenditures, but states' reliance on federal funds vary greatly. Of the forty-five states that provided adequate data, thirty-nine spent more on child welfare services in FY 2000 than they did in FY 1998 (Geen 2003). Others have estimated the total costs of child abuse and neglect, including hospitalization, chronic health problems, mental health system, child welfare system, law enforcement, and the judicial system, as $24,384,347,302 (Fromm 2001). One of the challenges to the child welfare system today is addressing why costs are increasing at the same time that caseloads are decreasing. Yet the percentages of African American children are increasing. Why is there a disproportionate representation of African American children in foster care?

Disproportionality of African American Children in Foster Care

Since 1990, the discourse on disproportionality of African American children has risen to national debate among researchers, administrators, and policy makers. An increasing number of national forums have examined the disproportionality of minority children in child welfare: Race Matters Forum I (2001),

Race Matters Forum II (2002), and Research Roundtable (2002). Researchers, academicians, policy makers, administrators, and interest groups have held national meetings to examine the issue of overrepresentation of African American children in foster care, utilizing available data to determine what factors contribute to the persistence of overrepresentation of African American children in child welfare.

Research findings presented at these forums identified the following factors as being associated with the overrepresentation of African American children: (1) urban versus rural differences, (2) county differences within states, (3) TANF participation, (4) prior child welfare history, (5) child behavior problems, (6) mental health of children, (7) poverty, (8) discrimination in worker decision making, and (9) parental risk factors (Derezotes & Poertner 2001). Thus far, researchers agree that the causes and correlates of overrepresentation of African American children are complex yet compelling.

Demographic Trends during the 1990s

What were the trends during the preceding decade? Goerge, Wulczyn, and Allen (1994) identified several trends in foster care placement, using individual administrative data on children in foster care. Among the trends noted in their analysis of substitute care rates were the following:

1. Foster care caseloads had doubled over ten years (1984–1994).
2. First-time admission patterns in foster care placements were more dynamic than were exit patterns.
3. Overall, infants and young children were the fastest growing age groups in the foster care population; they were entering care in greater numbers than other groups and tended to remain in foster care longer.
4. Much of the recent growth in foster care had involved the placement of children with relatives. Children in kinship placements tended to stay in care longer than children in nonrelative placements; when they did exit, kinship foster children were less likely than others to reenter care.
5. Almost two-thirds of the children who left the child welfare system were reunified with their own families; most reunifications occurred within two years of the child's initial removal from home and entry to care.
6. Approximately 10 percent to 15 percent of foster children in the Multi-State Archive database left care to adoption. (The Archive is a multistate database that contains foster care histories for all children who have been placed in a state-supervised substitute care living arrangement. The data for the archive are extracted directly from the administrative data systems operated by each state's child welfare agency.) Children who entered care as infants were much more likely to be adopted than children who entered

at older ages. Most adoptions occurred within three to five years from the time of entry into care.

7. While most children who entered foster care exited in a relatively timely basis, a substantial share of these children became long-term clients of the child welfare system. Over one-third of Archive children stayed in care over thirty months.

Based on AFCARS data, these trends persist. The average length of time in care identified in AFCARS data was thirty-three months. The mean length of stay was thirty-three months (just short of three years). Close to one-fifth (17 percent) of the children in foster care in March 2000, however, had been in foster care five years or more. The permanency planning goals for these children were as follows: reunification (43 percent), other relatives (4 percent), adoption (20 percent), long-term foster care (8 percent), emancipation (5 percent), guardianship (3 percent), and case plan not yet established (17 percent) (USDHHS 2003). In FY 2000, 146,000 children entered foster care, while 124,000 exited foster care. The number entering foster care continues to outnumber the children exiting foster care. Of those exiting foster care, 60 percent were reunited with their birth parents or primary caretaker, 15 percent were adopted, 11 percent were living with relatives, 6 percent were emancipated, 3 percent exited to guardianship, 3 percent were transferred to another agency, and 2 percent ran away.

Major Federal Policy Changes Since 1990

In the past decade, several major federal policies have been passed that have tremendous implications for African American children in the child welfare system. Some of these federal policies recognized the importance of race and ethnicity in child welfare (MEPA 1994; ASFA 1997; TANF 1997), while another (IEPA 1996) explicitly states that "race does not matter." Policy efforts have been made to ensure safety and well-being of children while speeding up the process of terminating parental rights if reunification is not possible (USDHHS 2000a).

Five major federal child welfare policies have been passed and implemented since 1991. They are the Multiethnic Placement Act of 1994 (MEPA) (PL 103-382), the Interethnic Placement Act of 1996 (IEPA) (PL 104-88), sections of the Personal Responsibility and Work Opportunity Reconciliation Act of 1996 (PL 104-193), the Adoption and Safe Families Act of 1997 (ASFA) (PL 105-89), and the Adoption Initiative of 2002. All of these policies directly affect the child welfare practices and permanency outcomes for African American children. ASFA will be discussed first.

Adoption and Safe Families Act of 1997

The Adoption and Safe Families Act of 1997 (PL 105-89) made changes and clarified the policies established under the Adoption Assistance and Child Welfare

Act of 1980 to help states protect and care for children in the child welfare system (USDHHS 2000a). ASFA is the major federal policy that sets the standards for child welfare in this country. ASFA promotes adoption and other permanent placements for abused and neglected children who cannot be returned safely to their families. ASFA requires that the child's health and safety is the primary concern in making service provisions, placement, and permanency planning (USDHHS 2000a). The key provisions of ASFA are as follows: (1) the safety of children is the paramount concern that must guide all child welfare services, (2) foster care is a temporary setting and not a place for children to grow up, (3) permanency planning efforts should begin as soon as a child enters the child welfare system, (4) the child welfare system must focus on results and accountability, (5) innovative approaches are needed to achieve the goals of safety, permanency, and well-being (USDHHS 2000a).

The mandatory changes under ASFA 1997 are as follows: first, the focus on safety; second, the twelve-month timeline for permanency hearings; third, the requirement for initiating termination of parental rights if a child is in state custody for fifteen of the most recent twenty-two months, unless the exceptions apply; fourth, health insurance for children with special needs for whom there is an adoption assistance agreement; fifth, an expanded focus on family preservation and support programs to include time-limited family reunification and adoption promotion and support services; and sixth, reports to Congress on selected issues (USDHHS 2000a).

The implications of ASFA for African American children are manifold. First, the policy emphasis of ASFA has shifted from reunification to adoption. Second, the time limits for reunification with birth parents have been shortened, so parents with chronic problems may lose legal custody of their children. Third, relatives are being pressured to adopt or assume legal guardianship of related children in order to move them out of the system legally. Fourth, the current funding system does not allow foster care maintenance payment for legal guardianship, but does provide funding for adoption subsidies.

Multiethnic Placement Act of 1994 (MEPA)
and Interethnic Placement Act of 1996 (IEPA)

The Multiethnic Placement Act of 1994 (PL 103-382) was passed to allow more whites to adopt more African American children from the foster care system. The manifest function of MEPA is to address perceived discrimination in adoptive and foster placements and increase the likelihood that children of color would have a fairer chance at adoption (Barth, Goodhand & Dickinson 1999). MEPA prohibited federally funded agencies and entities from denying anyone the opportunity to become a foster parent or adoptive parent due to the race of either the parent or the child, and denying a child the opportunity to be placed due to the race of either the parent or the child. In addition, the legislation required states to develop plans for the diligent recruitment of potential foster

and adoptive families who reflect the diversity of children in need of placement
(Barth, Goodhand & Dickinson 1999). Congress assumed that there were willing
white parents waiting to adopt African American children who were being
denied the opportunity to do so. However, by 1996, Congress determined that
the act was not facilitating the adoption of children of color, so MEPA was
revised two years later to further limit the extent to which race could be considered in adoptive and foster placements. IEPA prohibits federally funded
agencies and entities denying placement "on the basis of race" rather than
"solely on the basis of race." In addition, agencies may not "deny to any person
the opportunity to become an adoptive or foster parent" (Barth, Goodhand &
Dickinson 1999). Although child welfare has had a long commitment to MEPA's
value of equity, many practitioners believe that MEPA/IEPA ignores the value of
providing culturally competent services to clients (Brooks et al. 1999, as cited in
Barth, Goodhand & Dickinson 1999).

Both MEPA and IEPA federal laws are based on the assumption that African
Americans are not interested in becoming adoptive parents. These assumptions
are being challenged by past and current research. A study by the Urban Institute showed that African Americans were interested in adoptions, but were
being denied approval by agencies (Hill 1999). Results to the Multistate Archive
data show that adoption is a reasonable outcome for African American children
in foster care, but that it takes longer for this outcome to be achieved (Wulczyn
2003). Utilizing Archive data for 1990, Wulczyn found that the likelihood of
adoption among African American children (19 percent) was clearly greater
than the comparable figure reported for Caucasian children (13 percent). The
average time required to complete an adoption does, in fact, differ depending
on the child's race and ethnicity. The median duration reported for Caucasian
children adopted from the 1990 admission cohort was approximately thirty-six
months. For all other children the median duration was more than fifty-eight
months, or more than 50 percent longer. Wulczyn argues, "These data represent
something of a conundrum in that adoptions among African American children
are more likely, but the adoptions take longer" (Wulczyn 2003).

Recent adoption statistics show increases in adoption rates. The number of
adoptions finalized in FY 1998 was 37,000, FY 1999 was 47,000, FY 2000 was
51,000, and FY 2001 was 50,000. The trend in public agency adoption rates
ranged from 7.8 percent in 1998 to 8.9 percent in 2001 (Maza 2003). The majority of the adoptions were by former foster parents. In 1998–1999, 64 percent of
adoptions were by former foster parents, while relatives did 15 percent to 16 percent. In 2000–2001, foster parents completed 61 percent and 59 percent of the
adoptions. In contrast, in 2001–2002, relatives completed 21 percent to 24 percent of the adoptions. It was expected that white parents would adopt more
African American children; however, it appears that current foster parents and
relatives are doing most of the adoptions. In FY 2001, 59 percent of adoptions

were by foster parents—24 percent were by relatives and 17 percent were by non-relatives (Maza 2003).

The United States has no national database on adoptions. However, there is a requirement that the number of children adopted from the public be documented by AFCARS. An estimated 15 percent (fifty-four hundred) of the thirty-six thousand foster children adopted in FY 1998 were transracial or transcultural adoptions (USDHHS 2000b). The concern that the passage of MEPA would lead to an increase in transracial adoptions appears to be unwarranted, or at least cannot be documented. Transracial adoptions remain a controversial issue in child welfare.

Adoption Initiative of 1996

President Clinton established "Adoption 2002" in 1996, with the goal each year of doubling the number of children adopted or placed in permanent homes by 2002 (USDHHS 1997). To meet this goal, states will have to modify their current procedures for moving children through the foster care system and into adoption. This goal translates into an increase in adoptions and permanent placements from twenty-seven thousand in 1996 to fifty-four thousand in 2002. This goal has been met based on statistics cited earlier in this document. The Department of Health and Human Services proposed a financial bonus to states for children adopted from the public foster care system. For each child adopted over the base number for that year, a bonus would be awarded to the state. States have been receiving these financial bonuses.

Personal Responsibility and Work Opportunity Reconciliation Act of 1996 (PRWORA)

In 1996, Congress passed the Personal Responsibility and Work Opportunity Reconciliation Act (PL 104-193) (PRWORA). PRWORA repealed Aid to Families with Dependent Children (AFDC) and replaced it with Temporary Assistance to Needy Families (TANF). States have much of the responsibility for the design and administration of the TANF programs. The legislation also includes child welfare provisions. PRWORA directs states to "consider giving preference to an adult relative over a nonrelated caregiver when determining a placement for a child" (Geen & Waters 1997, 3). Children in formal kinship relationships remain in the state's custody after placement; these kinship care providers generally received some type of financial assistance for caring for a related child under AFDC. Depending upon the state policies and the specific case, formal kinship care providers receive an AFDC child-only grant, an AFDC family grant, a foster care maintenance payment, or an alternate type of grant paid by child welfare (Geen & Waters 1997). AFDC child-only grants offered states as well as the federal government a cheaper alternative than foster care payment for formal kinship care providers.

There are various types of relative placements and different funding mechanisms used for relative placements. First, some related children are in the legal custody of the state but the physical custody of relatives. Second, some children's relatives have assumed legal guardianship of their related children, with and without subsidy, and are no longer considered part of the public child welfare system. Third, an increasing number of relatives are now adopting their related children with subsidies. Fourth, a number of relatives are adopting related children without subsidies (USDHHS 2003).

Evaluation of the Federal Policies Using Selected Criteria

In our first book, we argued that policies needed to be evaluated using the criteria of equity, equality, and adequacy, and the values of extendedness, communalism, and spirituality. Equity is defined as the extent to which "situations in similar circumstances are dealt with similarly (Flynn 1985). Equality refers to "the same treatment of everyone—to all an equal share" (Gilbert & Specht 1986). Adequacy is defined as the degree to which benefits provided meet some predetermined level. How do African American children fare under the federal policies MEPA, IEPA, ASFA, and the Adoption Initiative of 2002 using these criteria? Let's examine each of them.

Some argue that the values underlying MEPA and IEPA were equity for potential adoptive parents, and for children of color, unmet permanency needs. So, one could argue that MEPA meets the equity needs of potential adoptive parents and gives some consideration to the cultural needs of African American children. Parents interested in adopting African American children would be allowed to do so based on their civil rights. However, MEPA did allow that workers could consider race and culture in placement and adoption decisions. Later, this protection was removed under IEPA, which does not allow race to be considered in placement and adoption. Agencies are still expected to recruit foster parents and adoptive parents similar to their foster care population. This legislation implies that children can be reared by anyone, regardless of race, but it was really passed with the expectation that whites would adopt African American children because African Americans were unwilling to do so. IEPA discounts the need for culturally appropriate foster homes and adoptive parents. The provisions of IEPA do not support the criteria of adequacy for African American children, because it denies the opportunity for them to grow up in cultural appropriate homes.

ASFA does take culture into consideration based on the provisions on kinship care. ASFA allows termination of parental rights to be "exempted" if the child is placed with a relative. However, it is unclear if states are implementing the law as written, or if workers are interpreting ASFA to mean that relatives must assume guardianship or adoption within the time limits. Some relatives may be threatened that the related child will be removed from their home, parental rights will be terminated, and the child will be placed for adoption in order to achieve legal permanency. ASFA does not meet the criteria of adequacy under the time limits imposed to achieve permanency. The AFCARS report (USDHHS 2003) shows that the average length of time it takes to achieve reunification is thirty-three months, the average length of time it takes to achieve adoption is sixty months, and the average length of time it takes to finalize adoption after parental rights have been terminated is twenty-eight months. Thus, utilizing the figures provided by the federal government demonstrates that ASFA time limits are unreasonable and unrealistic for some birth parents with chronic problems.

The underlying assumption of ASFA is that the needs of all families and children entering the foster care system can be resolved in one year. However, the last National Study on Protective, Preventive, Reunification Services Delivered to Children and Their Families found that children who experience foster care placement are more likely than children who receive in-home services to remain in the system for over eighteen months and to have services provided to them and their families (USDHHS 1994). African American children are not treated equally in the provision of in-home services. Minority children, and in particular African American children, are more likely to be in foster care placement than receive in-home services, even when they have the same problems and characteristics as white children (USDHHS 1994).

TANF gives priority to placing children with relatives. Thus, it meets the criteria of equity and cultural competency. However, TANF funding may also be used by states as an alternative funding source for foster care maintenance payments rather than Title IV-E foster care maintenance payments. These practices result in unequal treatment of poor children in the foster care system, because some receive higher maintenance rates on Title IV-E contrasted to those receiving minimal rates on TANF.

The Adoption Initiative of 2002 had good intentions—to increase the number of adoptions by rewarding the states that achieved this outcome. Adoptions have increased from thirty-seven thousand in 1998 to fifty thousand in 2001. However, the majority of these adoptions have been by foster parents and relatives. There are several unintended consequences of this presidential adoption initiative. First, a large number of foster homes have been converted into adoptive homes, thereby further reducing the number of temporary foster homes available for future children in need. Second, state child welfare agencies do not have financial incentives to reunify families, but have more incentives to work toward the adoption. Guardianship is still not a subsidized federally funded outcome except in federally funded demonstration projects (Illinois, Maryland). Third, the majority of the adoptions have been subsidized. Subsidized adoptions cost less than regular foster care due to savings in administrative costs;

however, they will contribute to an increase in regular foster care expenditures over time.

Summary

Trends in child welfare policy have shifted to adoption as a priority in contrast to reunification with birth parents. Financial incentives for states to increase adoptions have resulted in increased adoptions by foster parents and relatives. Most of these adoptions are subsidized. The latent or unintended consequences of these changes are that foster care caseloads are decreasing while the cost of foster care is increasing. The foci on preventive services and reunification services have decreased, as states now have a shorter timeline to work with birth parents. Additionally, regular nonrelated foster homes will decrease as they have been converted into adoptive homes. Furthermore, it appears that adoptions of African American children are possible, but it takes longer to achieve, certainly longer than ASFA allows. These contradictions in child welfare policies will be the challenge of the next decade. So far, African American children are not treated equitably in prevention services, reunification services, or adoption services. They are less likely to receive in-home preventive services, less likely to be reunified than whites, and require longer time frames to achieve adoption. Improvements in the current child welfare policies need to be made. MEPA and IEPA need to be repealed, though it is unlikely under the current conservative administration. ASFA timelines need to be lengthened, when necessary, to achieve stable reunifications. Financial incentives need to be attached to reunification as well as adoption, because child welfare practices tend to follow the federal financial incentives. The child welfare system cannot replace families, and legal permanency outcomes are not necessarily permanent. Former foster care children will need postadoption services in order to remain stable. These challenges and trends will be discussed throughout the remainder of this book. The challenge of the twenty-first century will be: What will happen to the least of these—our children?

REFERENCES

Barth, R. P., J. Goodhand & N. Dickinson. June 1999. "Reconciling Competing Values in the Delivery of Child Welfare Services Under ASFA, MEPA, and Community-Based Child Protection. Changing Paradigms of Child Welfare Practice: Responding to Opportunities and Challenges." U.S. Department of Health and Human Services, Administration for Children and Families, Administration on Children, Youth and Families, Children's Bureau.

Barth, R. P., R. L. Geen & J. M. Miller. January 2001. "Toward Understanding Racial Disproportionality in Child Welfare Services Receipt." Paper presented at the *Race Matters Forum I: Examining the Overrepresentation of African American Children in the Child Wel-*

fare System. Chevy Chase, MD: Children and Family Research Center, School of Social Work, University of Illinois at Urbana-Champaign.

Derezotes, D. M., & J. Poertner. January 2001. "Toward Understanding Racial Disproportionality in Child Welfare Services Receipt." Paper presented at the *Race Matters Forum I: Examining the Overrepresentation of African American Children in the Child Welfare System.* Chevy Chase, MD: Children and Family Research Center, School of Social Work, University of Illinois at Urbana-Champaign.

Flynn, J. P. 1985. *Social Policy: Analysis and Presentation for Community Practice.* Chicago: Nelson-Hall.

Fromm, S. 2001. "Total Estimated Cost of Child Abuse and Neglect in the United States: Statistical Evidence." Report of Prevent Child Abuse America. Retrieved from www.preventchildabuse.org.

Geen, R. March 2003. "Improving Child Welfare Agency Performance through Fiscal Reform: An Assessment of Recent Proposals." Presented at the Joint Center for Poverty Research: Child Welfare Services Research and Its Policy Implications. Washington, DC: Northwestern University/University of Chicago.

Geen, R., & S. Waters. November 1997. *The Impact of Welfare Reform on Child Welfare Financing* Series A/A-16. Washington, DC: Urban Institute.

Gilbert, N., and J. Specht. 1986. *Dimensions of Social Welfare Policy.* 2d ed. Englewood Cliffs, NJ: Prentice-Hall.

Goerge, R. M., F. H. Wulczyn & W. Allen. 1994. *Foster Care Dynamics, 1983–1992. A Report from the Multistate Foster Care Data Archive.* The Chapin Hall Center for Children at the University of Chicago.

Hill, R. B. 1999. *The Strengths of African American Families: Twenty-five Years Later.* Lanham, MD: University Press of America, Inc.

Jeter, H. 1963. *Children, Problems, and Services in Child Welfare Programs.* Washington, DC: U.S. Department of Health, Education, and Welfare.

Maza, P. April 2003. "Adoption Data Update based on AFCARS." Presentation at Howard University School of Social Work.

Race Matters Forum I. January 2001. *Examining the Overrepresentation of African Americans in the Child Welfare System.* Chevy Chase, MD: Children and Family Research Center, School of Social Work, University of Illinois at Urbana-Champaign.

Race Matters Forum II. March 2002. *Examining the Overrepresentation of African Americans in the Child Welfare System.* Chicago: Children and Family Research Center, School of Social Work, University of Illinois at Urbana-Champaign.

Research Roundtable on Children of Color in Child Welfare. September 2002. Washington, DC.

USDHHS. 1994. "National Study on Protective, Preventive, Reunification Services Delivered to Children and Their Families."

———. February 1997. "Adoption 2002: A Response to the Presidential Executive Memorandum on Adoption Issued December 14, 1996."

———. 2000a. "Rethinking Child Welfare Practice under the Adoption and Safe Families Act of 1997: Resource Guide." Washington, DC: U.S. Government Printing Office.

———. 2000b. *Transracial Adoption* (Report of the National Adoption Information Clearinghouse). Retrieved from www.calib.com/naic/pubs/s_trans.cfm.

———. 2003. *The AFCARS Report (#8).* Retrieved from www.acf.hhs.gov/programs/cb/publications/afcars/report8.htm.

Wulczyn, F. March 2003. "Leaving Foster Care: Old Myths and New Realities." Presented at the Joint Center for Poverty Research: Child Welfare Services Research and Its Policy Implications. Washington, DC: Northwestern University/University of Chicago.

Wulczyn, F., A. Harden & R. Goerge. 1993. *The Multi-State Foster Care Data Archive Year One Results: Foster Care Dynamics in Five States.* U.S. Department of Health and Human Services, Administration for Children and Families. The Chapin Hall Center for Children at the University of Chicago.

PART TWO

Understanding African American Families and Children

There is wide variation in the types of families who come to the attention of child welfare workers. No two families are alike, whether within a particular racial or cultural group or across racial and cultural groups. Certainly child welfare workers, which in countless studies have been reported to be predominantly white, are increasingly working with a greater number of children and families of African American or Latino descent. And the recent influx of families from diverse parts of world including Southeast Asia, the Middle East, Africa, and the Soviet Union suggests that workers will confront and are likely to misinterpret child-rearing practices among such diverse groups. Although child welfare practice has been driven by Eurocentric norms and standards for years, the changing demographic composition of child welfare caseloads requires further training in delivering culturally competent services. To be culturally competent means that one accepts and respects differences, and is willing to adapt one's practice approaches in such a way as to make them culturally appropriate and relevant to one's clients.

Cultural competence is "the ability to transform knowledge and cultural awareness into health and/or psychosocial interventions that support and sustain healthy client system functioning within the appropriate cultural context" (McPhatter 1997, 261). Becoming culturally competent involves (1) developing self-awareness–learning more about one's own culture and how it has affected one's values, beliefs, and behaviors–(2) developing knowledge about one's own culture, the culture of the client, and "understanding the dynamics of 'difference,' 'power,' and 'authority' in worker-client relationships" (Samantrai 2004, 33), and (3) developing and/or adapting practice skills to the cultural context of the client. Self-awareness particularly for social workers is a continuous and lifelong pursuit. It is a process that both white and African American workers go through. Neither is exempt from gaining perspectives about how their respective cultural backgrounds are likely to affect behaviors and decision making.

The five chapters in the second part of this book examine the cultural heritage of African American families, providing a basic knowledge base for working with these families. Although each chapter describes the unique characteristics of African American families, they do not claim that these are monolithic characterizations. Variations do exist among African American families due to differences in social environments, cultural experiences, and lifestyles. Regional, geographic, ethnocultural, socioeconomic, and personality differences account for many of the variations in African American families. In spite of this diversity, "some cultural similarities do prevail" (Everett, Chipungu & Leashore 1997, 80). These similarities include the cultural views of children, cultural communication styles, family structure and roles, prescribed and proscribed behavior in formal and informal relationships, norms regarding interdependency and obligation within kinship networks, religious and spiritual orientations, and views of change and intervention (Samantrai 2004).

Beckett and Lee introduce an innovative practice model, the ecological Africentric model for practice with African American families in child welfare. The model synthesizes from the strengths, empowerment, resiliency, ecological, and Africentric perspectives to introduce an integrative approach for work with African American families. Comparisons between Eurocentric and Africentric assessments are illustrated, as are the premises of multicultural communication practice. Suggestions for practitioner activities and case vignettes illustrate how the model might be applied in everyday practice situations. Wilson, Woods, and Hijjawi in chapter 5 describe and update the social context in which African American families function. Internal challenges such as changes in family formation and structure since 1990 are described, including the rise in single-parent households and intergenerational households (grandmother-only families), and their effects on parenting and child outcomes. External factors affecting the functioning of African American families are also discussed. The authors argue that African American families, although a part of the dominant culture, function in distinct ways as a result of the external factors they face and the cultural values they embrace. Consequently, the Eurocentric assumptions about family practices, family structure, and parenting styles may not realistically correspond to the realities of African American life. Moten in chapter 6 examines child-rearing practices among African American families. Studies of the parenting styles of African American families have classified them as authoritative–high on control, clarity of communication, maturity demands, and warmth and nurturance. At issue is the extent to which authoritative parenting styles affect academic performance. Like Taylor (1997), Moten concludes that parenting styles function within a specific context and are a function of available resources including social relationships of the parents, as well as socioeconomic and compositional variations in family structure. Much more research is needed about parenting styles across racial and ethnic groups and about the impact of parental training programs on child outcomes. Mothers and fathers play a significant role in the development of children. Consequently, Harris in chapter 7 examines the significance of collective identity, motherhood, and intergenerational parenting among African American birth mothers. She then offers best practice guidelines for assessment of and intervention with African American birth mothers whose children are placed in kinship care. Johnson and Bryant, in chapter 8, examine caseworkers' perceptions of the participation of unwed fathers in the permanency planning process. African American paternal involvement, according to recent research, tends to be relatively high irrespective of socioeconomic status, which suggests that unwed fathers might play a significant role in permanency planning if provided with support. These authors argue that one of the major challenges facing child welfare is the development of practice-based knowledge for working with resident and nonresident fathers.

REFERENCES

Everett, J., S. Chipungu & B. Leashore. 1997. "Understanding Families and Child Rearing." In *Child Welfare: An Africentric Perspective*. Edited by J. E. Everett, S. S. Chipungu & B. R. Leashore, 79–83. New Brunswick, NJ: Rutgers University Press.

McPhatter, A. 1997. "Cultural Competence in Child Welfare: What Is It? How Do We Achieve It? What Happens Without It?" *Child Welfare* 76/1:255–78.

Samantrai, K. 2004. *Culturally Competent Public Child Welfare Practice.* Pacific Grove, CA: Brooks/Cole.

Taylor, R. 1997. "Child Rearing in African American Families." In *Child Welfare: An Africentric Perspective.* Edited by J. E. Everett, S. S. Chipungu & B. R. Leashore, 119–155. New Brunswick, NJ: Rutgers University Press.

4

Informing the Future of Child Welfare Practices with African American Families

JOYCE O. BECKETT
NICOLE LYNN LEE

As a group, African American children and families face significant challenges in today's society. Each day, 114 African American children are born to mothers who did not receive prenatal care; 500 African American children drop out of school; 1,426 African American children are arrested; and 5,725 African American children are suspended from public schools. Further, every day, 723 African American children are born into poverty, 5 African American children die from firearms, and 1 child commits suicide (Children's Defense Fund 2001). The plight of African American children is clearer if one examines the representation of African American children in the child welfare system. African American children comprise 15 percent of the U.S. population, yet represent 44 percent of children in the foster care system (Child Welfare League of America 1998). Of the 117,000 children who are waiting to be adopted, 51 percent of them are African American. For all children, the average length of time spent in foster care is thirty-three months (USDHHS 2002). However, African American children remain part of the child welfare system an average of two years longer (Courtney et al. 1996). During their involvement in the child welfare system, these children are more likely than other children to have emotional, behavioral, and developmental problems (Kortenkamp & Ehrle 2002), and are at increased risk for unintended pregnancy, substance abuse, lower educational achievement, and involvement in the criminal, welfare, and mental health systems (Child Welfare League of America 1998; Yancy 1998).

African American children and families face inequalities and cultural insensitivity inherent within the child welfare system (Denby, Curtis & Alford 1998; Morton 2000). This is evident in the way in which the current child welfare system addresses the needs of African American children and their families who participate in kinship care. Kinship care is a form of foster care in which children are reared by relatives other than the biological mother or father

(Danzy & Jackson 1997; O'Donnell 1999). Historically, this type of arrangement protected African American children who lived in unsafe or unstable environments (Brown & Bailey-Etta 1997) and provided a practical response to the African American's community needs. Current child welfare policies are insensitive to alternative family functioning patterns and are not congruent with a kinship care model (Danzy & Jackson 1997). For example, child welfare policies treat families involved in kinship care arrangements differently from licensed foster families, with the former not eligible for respite services or financial support (Davidson 1997). Further, there is a lack of knowledge concerning the complexity of kinship care (Gleeson, O'Donnell & Bonecutter 1997).

In order to assist African American children and their families, practitioners must disavow a traditional Eurocentric worldview that espouses a deficit model of practice. Instead, practitioners must employ practice models that consider African American families and their functioning in the context of an Africentric worldview. Practitioners must be willing to examine traditional theories or perspectives and determine how or if they can be adapted for use with African American families. This may require combining elements from several theories or models to create practice approaches that are culturally sensitive and effective for working with African American families who are involved with the child welfare system. In essence, working with African American families requires an eclectic, holistic approach.

This chapter introduces such an approach by discussing how integrating and synthesizing the strengths, empowerment, resiliency, and ecological perspectives in the context of the Africentric perspective is an innovative, appropriate, and culturally sensitive way to work with African American children and families. It begins with an explication of each of these perspectives, beginning with the ecological perspective, followed by the empowerment, strengths, and resiliency perspectives. Finally, this chapter suggests an ecological, Africentric model for practice with African American children and families who are involved with the child welfare system.

Ecological Systems Perspective

Connectedness is a major concept of the ecological systems perspective that dates back at least to Mary Richmond (1917), who emphasized the importance of both the client and the environment in which the client interacted. In 1937, Ludwig von Bertalanffy introduced general systems theory (GST), a precursor to the ecological systems perspective, as a conceptual model that organizes diverse theories and facilitates communication and cooperation among practitioners of the applied sciences. He proposed a holistic approach that focused on the entire entity as a social system (Anderson, Carter & Lowe 1999; von Bertalanffy 1968), a structure composed of interdependent units (Green & Ephross 1991). Von Bertalanffy conceived of the individual as one type of social system with ultimate and unique expression of both organized complexity and creativity. GST reduces highly complex phenomena and interactions into manageable constructs by integrating a range of disciplines including philosophy, psychology, organizational theory, economics, and others. It uses concepts such as structure, boundary, equilibrium, entropy, equifinality, homeostasis, input, and output to describe the functioning of systems. GST is a model that is useful for understanding any social system, not just individuals (Shaw & Constanzo 1982, 12).

When GST is used to describe and analyze persons and other living systems and their transactions, it is referred to as the ecological systems perspective (ESP) (Miller 1978; Zastrow & Kirst-Ashman 1990). Ecology focuses on "how things fit together, how they adapt to one another" (Greif 1986, 225). One principle of the ESP is that a change that occurs at one system level affects and changes the entire network of interrelated systems. The definitive work on living systems (Miller 1978) points to the interrelations among all levels of living and nonliving systems from atoms through cells, families, communities, cultures, macroeconomic forces, international political and economic phenomena, and ultimately the universe. Thus, practitioners no longer need to focus solely or primarily on helping individuals and families adapt to their environmental systems, but can and should address helping societal systems, such as child welfare services, better adapt to their clients.

Urie Bronfenbrenner (1979), a developmental psychologist, made major contributions to the ecological systems perspective, especially in the areas of cross-cultural perspectives and specification of hypotheses to be tested using rigorous scientific methods. While Kagan (1984), another developmental psychologist, does not explicitly use GST terminology, he significantly contributed to the ecological systems perspective by integrating biology, culture, macro system forces (e.g., economic, political), and chance events into his understanding of behavior, utilizing research-based evidence.

Several African Americans were prominent in the development of this approach as well (Beckett & Coley 1987; Billingsley 1968; Chestang 1976; Dodson & Ross 1977; Hill 1972; Norton 1976). For example, Billingsley and Giovannoni (1972) related the ESP specifically to African American children in the child welfare system. However, to date, there has been little meaningful integration into human services of biological or spiritual information on the "person" side, nor of larger societal forces (e.g., discrimination, economic, political, religious, and physical/environment) on the "environment" side. Diversity theory has provided an understanding of the effects of economic power (e.g., unequally distributed according to race and other cultural variables) on human development and functioning, but practice in general has not incorporated this context or theory. Beckett (1976, 1988, 1994), Beckett and Dungee-Anderson (1996, 1998), and Beckett and Johnson (1995) have contributed to efforts to relate behavior and development to macro forces such as corporate, employment and government policies. Practitioners, regardless of preferences for other intervention frameworks, usually view ESP as an organizing framework rather than an intervention perspective (for example, see DuBois & Miley 2002).

In 1973, Billingsley addressed the neglect of African American families in the social science literature, including information that propagated stereotypes and myths. This neglect of African Americans, Billingsley indicated, enhanced the status of social science, encouraged ignorance and misinformation, misguided policy makers, and perpetuated the depressed status of African Americans. A decade later, the results of Hartman's national survey (National Child Welfare Training Center 1983), and three decades later, a major report of the Children's Defense Fund (2001) indicated little progress.

Hartman's survey (National Child Welfare Training Center 1983) showed that 80 percent of both child welfare workers and supervisors were Euro-Americans, while 37 to 55 percent of the children in the foster care system were children of color. Furthermore, only 25 percent of state agencies had training programs to prepare staff to intervene with these children and families. Hartman reasoned that "the results of these circumstances may be stereotyped knowledge and preconceptions that impede delivering culturally sensitive services to minority children and families" (National Child Welfare Training Center 1982, p. i) When these findings are compared with those from the Children's Defense Fund discussed in the introduction to this chapter, the situation has changed little over the last three decades.

Two tools that Hartman (1978) developed in response to challenges in providing child welfare services are particularly useful for intervention with African American families: the eco-map and the genogram. Both are helpful in graphically understanding the client's situation and in planning and evaluating interventions. In this chapter, attention will focus on the first tool, the eco-map, because of its comprehensiveness. The eco-map helps the practitioner order an often overwhelming amount of data, including biological, physical, psychological, social, and spiritual variables, about the client in his or her total life space (Germain 1979; Hartman & Laird 1983). The eco-map includes the major formal and informal systems that are presently and potentially a part of the individual's life. The informal or primary and intimate relationships include family, friends, ethnic culture, self-help groups, and so on; while the formal or secondary relationships consist of formal, larger organizations and institutions, such as employment, education, and social service agencies, and the physical environment.

The practitioner can use the eco-map in the assessment, planning, intervention, and evaluation processes of intervention. In assessment, the eco-map helps to identify problems and strengths, and provides an understanding for the client and practitioner of the interactions, or lack of them, that influence the challenges and strengths. It also points to areas for intervention and can be adapted to a particular intervention focus (see, for example, O'Miley, Melia & DuBois 2002). There are usually five intervention foci: (1) the client's relationships with formal service organizations such as school, department of social services, employment, recreation, or the church; (2) the client's relationship with the informal network, such as the extended family, friends, neighbors, and fictive kin; (3) the relationships between formal organizations and informal networks that have consequences for the client; (4) the relationships between formal organizations that influence the client; and (5) the relationships between informal systems that influence the client. For example, the social worker may find that the medical system is not effectively communicating with the mental health system about the medication that could interact with a child's psychotropic drugs (relationships between two formal systems), or that a grandmother needs information about adoption that would allow her to receive social security benefits for the grandchild in her care (relationships among informal and formal systems).

Finally, practitioners can employ the eco-map to evaluate outcomes and measure changes. A comparison of eco-maps during the initial phase and at termination or periodic evaluation points can help clients and practitioners measure the change. Hartman (1978) states: "No matter how the eco-map is used, its primary value is in its visual impact and its ability to organize and present concurrently not only a great deal of factual information, but also the relationships between variables in a situation."

Although the ecological systems perspective and the eco-map are helpful, they are not a panacea. They do well by focusing explicitly on the client's physical and social life space and incorporating this information into the intervention process. However, they do not explicitly address the often needed, more detailed assessments. For example, the eco-map does not incorporate behavior indicators for attention deficit hyperactivity disorder, agency bureaucracy, oppression, alienation, ethical practice, and so on. The eco-map, however, can point to areas that require more careful assessment. For example, the practitioner may notice that African Americans prematurely terminate from groups for prospective adoptive parents. More careful attention to this agency-level issue might indicate that African Americans are hesitant to discuss issues in mixed racial groups (Davis 1979). In this situation, the agency may need to decide if it should have separate groups for African Americans and, if so, how to handle staff and clients who might view this decision as reverse racism.

As illustrated in the last example, this perspective does not indicate the specific techniques needed to accomplish the goals. The practitioner, using his or her professional expertise, decides what techniques are necessary. This model, nevertheless, encourages the social worker to consider such techniques as advocacy and brokerage, which are often more effective in child welfare than the traditional techniques of elaboration, clarification, and confrontation. This is because environmental issues are often an integral part of the issues that social workers and clients face in child welfare.

Lastly, this approach requires the social worker to be able to evaluate and intervene with numerous social systems, from the individual to the family, to the community, to the universe. Few schools of social work provide such comprehensive training. This usually means that the social worker must (1) conceive of education as a lifelong process; (2) rely on others, including the client, who have expertise; (3) coordinate services with other agencies and professionals, such as members of the clergy; and (4) be creative. The ESP does not guarantee successful intervention with African American clients in child welfare or any other service system. It nevertheless can be an excellent supplement to other necessary conditions for effective intervention. These conditions include the social worker's (1) sensitivity to and understanding of African Americans; (2) desire to understand the client's views of the concerns and strengths; (3) participation with the client and his or her family to jointly develop intervention goals; (4) willingness to view systems in the environment as targets for change; and (5) attention to the client's strengths as well as challenges. The ESP can facilitate the acquisition of each of these characteristics.

Empowerment Perspective

Research conducted by Ackerson and Harrison (2000) documented that, among human service practitioners, empowerment as a concept is difficult to identify and define. Practitioners define empowerment based on the needs of their client populations. Further, for some practitioners, empowerment is a goal, a process, or both. Regardless of the ambiguity inherent in its definition, empowerment practice is utilized in organizations as small as neighborhood voluntary associations (e.g., crime prevention programs) and as large as community management organizations (e.g., local and national governments) (Perkins 1995). In addition, practitioners continue to view the empowerment perspective as important for, and relevant to, work with oppressed persons (Carter 1999; Gibbs & Fuery 1994; Gutierrez, GlenMaye & DeLois 1995; West Stevens 1998).

Solomon (1976) conceptualized empowerment and demonstrated its relevance to African American communities. Other scholars (e.g., Carter 1999; Gutierrez 1990; Gutierrez, GlenMaye & DeLois 1995; Perkins 1995) have expanded the conceptual framework for empowerment practice. More recently, scholars (e.g., Ackerson & Harrison 2000; Gutierrez, Oh & Gillmore 2000) have devoted substantial effort to defining and conducting research on empowerment practice and its relevance to oppressed persons and communities.

Gutierrez (1990) defined empowerment as "a process of increasing personal, interpersonal, or political power so that individuals can take action to improve their life situations" (149). Gutierrez, Oh, and Gillmore (2000) define several kinds of power. "Personal power involves experiencing oneself as an effective and capable person. . . . Interpersonal power is the ability to influence others with social power" (586). Political power, according to Gutierrez, Oh, and Gillmore, "is the ability to influence the allocation of resources in an organization or community through formal or informal means" (586).

Empowerment practice encourages marginalized individuals and groups to cultivate their strengths and talents to use for liberation from their oppressive situations. Marginalized groups are those groups that are systematically denied power or access to resources by those who own or control these resources. Embedded within this proposition is the belief that the individual has a responsibility to improve the larger society. This belief is consistent with traditional African values that emphasize collective action and system-level change. For example, during the Civil Rights movement in the 1960s, African American communities throughout the United States used the church as a mobilizing agent to fight for civil rights for themselves and future generations. Consequently, African Americans "built a coalition of strength, courage, and progress" (Raider & Pauline Morand 1998, 58). This demonstrates the power that individuals can wield when they work together and are motivated by their responsibility to the larger society. In essence, the individuals become change agents.

The empowerment perspective posits that the practitioner must analyze the individual within the context of his or her environment (Lee 1996). Thus, the empowerment perspective "requires both a macro as well as a micro approach to work with clients" (Ackerson & Harrison 2000). Instead of "blaming the victim" for his or her deficiencies, the empowerment perspective seeks to understand how the individual's environment contributes to specific circumstances (239).

Lee (1996) discusses two methods (i.e., consciousness raising and critical analysis) that are central to the empowerment process. The term "consciousness raising" is somewhat misleading; the practitioner does not raise the client's consciousness. Rather, the practitioner uses tools, such as reframing and feedback, to help the client raise his or her own level of knowledge concerning a situation or issue. For example, an African American child who does not attend school regularly may not understand the value and importance of education to his or her future. Instead, the child may identify other children who attend school regularly as trying to "act white." A practitioner working from an empowerment perspective would engage the child in a discussion about the history of education for African Americans in America. The goal would be to provide knowledge to the child so that he or she would have additional information to make an informed decision of what education could mean personally.

Critical analysis involves asking the client questions concerning his or her beliefs. The practitioner designs the questions in ways that permit the client to view the situation from multiple perspectives. A client may begin to detect factors that he or she had not noticed before, and these revelations may stimulate a heightened level of awareness of the complexity of the situation as well as multiple potential solutions. For example, an African American single mother may identify herself as "poor." However, a practitioner working from the empowerment perspective may ask a beginning question such as: What does it mean to be poor? The practitioner would continue to ask questions with increasing specificity such as: How do you get food for your family? How do people in your neighborhood handle their economic situation? What creative resources do you use to increase your income? These additional questions would provide an opportunity for the mother to question what being poor means for her and her family. Additionally, critical questioning may provide an opportunity for the mother to identify multiple ways of viewing her situation. Thus, the mother may recognize new solutions to her challenges.

Finally, a practitioner using an empowerment approach needs interpersonal communication skills (Lee 1996), especially those of active listening. Active listening is "a process of sending back to the speaker what the listener thinks the speaker meant, both literally and emotionally" (e.g., see Hecht, Collier & Ribeau 1993). Active listening lets the client know that the practitioner is attentive to his or her situation. For example, when families meet with child welfare practitioners, it is important to provide nonverbal cues such as appropriate eye contact or head nodding to indicate that the practitioner is focused on what the family is saying. Additionally, the child welfare practitioner should disclose when he or she does not understand words or statements used by clients, should ask questions to clarify information, and should then paraphrase the answers so that clients have opportunities to verify that the practitioner understands. Active listening requires time, skill, and willingness to suspend expectations, assumptions, judgments, self-assertiveness, and defensiveness. The goal of active listening is to understand, not to agree with, what the client says. Lindahl (2002) states that when people experience the depth of active listening, they also begin to listen to others in the same way. Active listening, then, results in changes that can reverberate throughout the systems in which the client and practitioner interact.

These are not the only skills required for practitioners operating from an empowerment approach. However, consciousness raising, critical analysis, and good interpersonal communication skills facilitate the client's ability to achieve empowerment. In summary, these skills increase the likelihood that communication will promote an environment of client empowerment.

Strengths and Resiliency Perspectives

It is important to preface this chapter with a note about the complementary nature of the strengths and resiliency perspectives. In the literature, scholars define strengths and resiliency perspectives as distinctive perspectives (DeVito 2001, 127). However, one may identify the development of resiliency as a cultivation and practical use of strengths that have developed during challenging situations (Fraser 1997; Saleebey 1997). Combining the strengths and resiliency perspectives allows practitioners to investigate specific strengths within a family unit, as well as understand how these strengths are constantly evolving, especially in the face of adversity.

Saleebey (1997) conceptualizes strengths-based practice and provides practitioners with a set of propositions that form the nexus of strength-based work. In addition, scholars (e.g., Blundo 2001; Graybeal 2001; Laursen 2000; Rapp 1997; West Stevens 1998) have expanded Saleebey's work and applied the strengths perspective to specific populations (e.g., African American girls, older persons, and substance abusers) and to specific client systems (e.g., individuals, groups, and communities). Similarly, Fraser (1997) conceptualizes resiliency-based practice with children and additional scholars (Fraser, Richman & Galinsky 1999; Palmer 1997; Polk 1997) have applied resiliency-based work to specific populations (e.g., adult children of alcoholics and health care clients).

The strengths and resiliency perspectives have several central propositions; however, only a few essential propositions of each perspective will be discussed here. First, both perspectives are predicated on the belief that humans have strengths that may emerge, or may be cultivated, during times of adversity (Fraser 1997; Saleebey 1997). Sometimes, both practitioners and clients have difficulty defining strengths. Instead, they use a deficit model that obscures strengths and even labels them as "problems." For example, an African American child who moves from foster home to foster home may develop an ability to care for her- or himself with limited adult supervision. In response to increased adult supervision, the child may reject authority and actually challenge it. Traditional practice may identify this phenomenon as pathological and label the child as "oppositional" without considering how the child's behaviors have helped her or him to adapt to a changing environment. Instead of immediately labeling the child as "defiant" or "oppositional," the practitioner and foster family may explore ways in which the child's ability to adapt and be self-sufficient can be helpful in his or her current situation. In this manner, the practitioner demonstrates sensitivity to "difference" and an ability to understand the strengths inherent in humans.

The strengths and resiliency perspectives posit that negative life situations are not immediately correlated with poor outcomes for individuals or families. Rather, the resiliency perspective theorizes that humans can and do develop strategies that enable them to endure and gain insight from difficult situations (Fraser 1997). For instance, a child who resides in a crime-ridden area may have limited outside experiences due to safety concerns. A practitioner examining this situation from a deficit model may identify the child's primary caregiver as overprotective and suspicious of others. However, this situation does not mean that the child will have poor social skills or maladaptive behaviors. The child may use the time inside to develop close family relationships and a strong sense of responsibility toward the family unit. A practitioner operating from the strengths or resiliency perspective may identify the child's "lack of trust for outsiders" as an effort to protect the family unit from externally derived harm. The practitioner can then begin to determine how to use the child's strong family identity to strengthen the family's functioning and extend its social relationships, if necessary.

The strengths and resiliency perspectives advocate understanding the importance of relationships and human interactions. This proposition is important to the African American community because African Americans have created communal relationships that are different from traditional Eurocentric norms (Hill-Collins 2000). For instance, the African American community has "othermothers" and "fictive kin" (Hill-Collins 2000). Othermothers are persons other than the biological mother who are involved in the direct rearing of children. These othermothers may exert more authority over children than the biological mother. Further, these relationships exist for a variety of reasons, not always the "pathological" reasons identified by practitioners operating from a Eurocentric perspective. Othermothering may be a way for the community to respond to the biological mother's need for child care and support. The strengths and resiliency perspectives underscore the importance of understanding these relationships and not pathologizing them.

The strengths perspective specifies the importance of a positive therapeutic relationship between the client and practitioner (Goldstein 1997). Laursen (2000) identifies this relationship as a partnership that builds "authentic relationships with children and families" (71). An authentic relationship involves the practitioner understanding that the client's thoughts and views are accurate reflections of the client's reality (Early & GlenMaye 2000); thus, the client's goals for treatment should be considered valuable, at least initially, rooted in the client's experiences and views. The client's goals, then, should become the main goals of the intervention (Cowger 1997). This proposition underscores the importance of client self-determination in the strengths perspective (Laursen 2000; West Stevens 1998). Consequently, a strengths-based practitioner respects the client's right to craft his or her reality based on personal experiences.

Those who wish to be effective strengths and resiliency practitioners should master several skills. First, the practitioner must have active listening skills, to clearly hear and believe how the client perceives the situation. The discussion about the empowerment perspective included active listening. Next, the ability to reframe "problems" into "potentials" is necessary. Practitioners must be able to view the strengths inherent in seemingly negative situations. The ability to use strengths-based language, as well as language that the client understands (Cowger 1997), is important in strengths and resiliency perspectives. For example, African American families may not respond to practitioners who introduce themselves as "therapists." However, they may respond to practitioners who introduce themselves as "people who will listen and provide support." In this way, the immediate relationship is not defined with the practitioner as the "expert."

Finally, the practitioner must be able to view the assessment process as part of the intervention. A practitioner who truly listens to a client and provides opportunities for the client to acknowledge strengths and resiliency can assist in the empowerment process. In this respect, the assessment phase is the beginning of the intervention because changes begin in this phase, even if it is only the client gaining a more powerful view of him- or herself.

Relevance of Perspectives to Africentric Worldview

The Africentric worldview or perspective posits that (1) individuals and groups have strengths, and these strengths can be cultivated and enhanced; (2) there is a connection between individual difficulties and societal oppression; (3) differences between groups and individuals are assumed and accepted; and (4) the individual is important, but the collective identity is even more so (Schiele 2000). Readers may notice similarities between the Africentric perspective and the strengths, ecological, resiliency, and empowerment perspectives. For instance, empowerment as a process begins when a client recognizes the impact that the environment has on the individual and family, specifically when there are systematic injustices embedded within the environment. In essence, this exemplifies the impact that the community, whether strong or unjust, can have on the potential of the individual or group. This is consistent with the belief in the interconnectedness of person and the environment that exists in the Africentric perspective.

The strengths, ecological, resilience, and empowerment perspectives are valuable for working with individuals, groups, communities, and societies. Each perspective posits an alternative method of problem identification, emphasizes client involvement, and is consistent with the Africentric worldview. In addition, scholars have emphasized the complementary nature of the perspectives (Cowger 1997; Early & GlenMaye 2000; Graybeal 2000; Hill 1998; Laursen 2000; West Stevens 1998; Wright & Anderson 1998. For instance, West Stevens (1998) speaks of the importance of identifying client strengths while using the empowerment process to clarify oppressive states that clients, specifically African American girls, may endure. In addition, Wright and Anderson (1998) believe that clinical work with urban African American families should involve the empowerment of the client or client system, and an analysis of the client's situation from a strengths orientation.

This chapter provides a new framework for child welfare practice that combines the strengths, empowerment, resilience, and ecological perspectives with an Africentric worldview. This framework provides practical and culturally sensitive methods of addressing child welfare issues with African American families. Specific goals of the framework are to (1) assess African American families through a method that allows these families to articulate their reality to practitioners; (2) use information to illustrate strengths and possibilities for families; (3) help families analyze choices and make decisions that empower and improve family functioning, as well as the larger community functioning; and (4) execute actions that achieve goals. Unlike other models, this model operates from the assumptions that (1) the child and family are connected to the larger community's functioning; (2) the family may have participated in child welfare interventions that used a Eurocentric model of family functioning; (3) children and families in the child welfare system have developed strengths that can be cultivated; (4) the child, family, and community must be active participants in planning, implementing, and evaluating the interventions; and (5) change often needs to be made in the child welfare and other institutional systems to support and maintain client changes and strengths.

Assessment involves creating a diagrammatic representation of African American families from a strengths perspective. Child welfare practitioners work with African American families to determine where strengths, talents, possibilities, and challenges exist. Imagine a set of three concentric circles. Alone, each circle represents an important layer. However, when the practitioner combines the three, they have a synergistic relationship. Figure 4.1 is a diagrammatic representation of assessment using an ecological Africentric perspective.

The outermost layer is the "larger society." This layer signifies the cultural norms and values that dominant society reinforces, as well as other cultural views. The next layer is the "Africentric." This layer represents the traditional cultural values and norms that the African American community generally espouses (e.g., values such as community responsibility, collective action, spiritual groundedness, and support for children). All of these cultural values and norms are consistent with the Africentric sphere, if the family holds them. The boundary between the Africentric and larger society (Eurocentric) layers is fluid. This signifies the biculturality, multiculturality, or the ability of African American families to operate from the Africentric or Eurocentric, Native American, Jewish, or other frameworks. The first and second layers of this diagram allow practitioners to document how African American families negotiate their existence in a society that holds values and norms that may be different from their specific worldview. The next layer represents the family unit. This is where the client's relationships with family members are identified. Finally, the innermost layer represents the individual. This is where practitioners document information concerning the individual's biopsychosocial spiritual functioning.

Each of these layers contains three overlapping circles that represent three

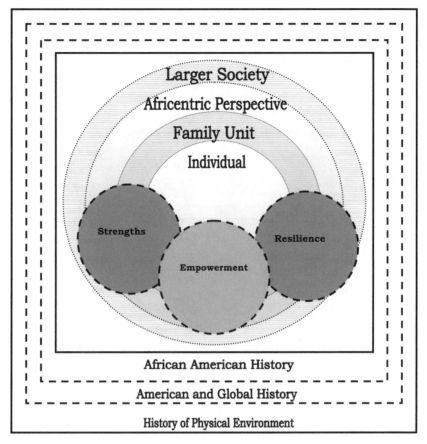

FIGURE 4.1   Diagram of Beckett & Lee Ecological Africentric Model

concepts: empowerment, resilience, and strengths. Strengths are descriptors of the positive coping skills that are available within a specific layer. For instance, a practitioner examining the Africentric layer may identify client strengths such as strong community relationships and a strong spiritual base. A practitioner examining the family layer of the diagram might identify client strengths such as loyalty to family members or extended family members who can provide services such as cooking, cleaning, or child care. In essence, strengths are the coping skills that can be cultivated and used for the client or client system's benefit, and to achieve the intervention goals.

Empowerment is the actual biopsychosocial spiritual or physical actions that the individual or family undertakes to gain personal, interpersonal, or community power. For example, some African American children, particularly girls, may appear boisterous and overanimated in their speech when judged by Eurocentric standards. However, a practitioner familiar with the history of African

Americans may notice that these behaviors are a way for oppressed and marginalized youth to gain a sense of respect and power. Viewing the behaviors in
this manner reframes the children's behavior from deviant and provides evidence of their "humanity."

Resilience refers to the "skills, abilities, knowledge, and insights that accu-
mulate over time as people struggle to surmount adversity and meet challenges" (Saleebey 1996, 298). These characteristics develop during hardships
and crises and may remain to help a family or individual endure future hardships and crises. Sometimes it is difficult for children or families to identify
their own resiliency. For instance, a child who has experienced physical abuse
may not realize the coping skills that he or she has developed. A thoughtful and
culturally competent practitioner should be able to reframe the child's situation and use language that identifies the child's resilient behaviors. For example, the practitioner can reframe a child's shy and withdrawn behavior as
appropriate protection in an abusive environment.

Following the child's move to a new situation, the practitioner might help
the child to verbally identify behaviors used to constantly watch for abuse and
congratulate her on developing such important and appropriate protective
skills. The practitioner should not ask the child to give up these skills, especially
since neither can predict what will happen in the future. The practitioner, nevertheless, can tell the child that she or he will help to protect the child from
abuse. Furthermore, the practitioner can support the child and foster family in
learning behavior appropriate for a new situation. They can support the child in
exploring the larger world and learning to appropriately protect her- or himself
in social relationships with peers and others.

Figure 4.1 represents the resiliency, empowerment, and strengths characteristics as overlapping circles because they are interrelated. (For discussion
of relatedness of strengths and resilience, see Fraser 1997.) Strengths are
important if families are to demonstrate resilience, and recognizing strengths
can be an important mechanism in the empowerment process. Each of the layers includes information about the culture, attitudes, values, and physical
environment.

Finally, history and the impact of historical events on African American
families are important to consider when working with these families. The series
of three borders around the concentric circles represent three specific histories;
each is essential when intervening with African Americans. They are American
and global history, African American history, and history of the physical environment and their influences on the client system in the past, present, and
future. American and global history includes events in American history and
the world that have influenced or currently influence the client. The 1930s stock
market crash and various changes in child welfare policies are examples. African American history includes the events of African Americans—such as slav-

ery, the Civil Rights movement, and segregation—and a timeline of the family's experiences as African Americans. The history of the physical environment includes events in the physical surroundings in which the family lives or has lived. For example, this border would document the influence of events such as natural disasters and the climate on the family's physical environment.

How can figure 4.1 assist in work with African American families? First, it provides at-a-glance information on family functioning. Specifically, the figure illustrates and provides information on family strengths, resiliency, and the actions that the family has engaged in to maintain and empower itself. Next, the figure provides information concerning how the family negotiates the boundary between the Africentric African American society and the larger society. Finally, it demonstrates the importance of the community and external environment on the lives of individuals. With this assessment tool, the individual is not the primary unit of analysis. Rather, the analysis is multileveled and allows the practitioner to understand how the individual functions in relation to the family unit and the larger society. The assessment tool underscores the importance of language and encourages a change from labeling persons "at-risk" to identifying how they have survived. In addition, the model reevaluates commonly defined concepts such as "risk factor" and "family structure," and reframes these to incorporate the values and unique experiences of African American families.

Practice with African American families should provide a mutually supportive environment where clients can evaluate their situations and make decisions concerning their functioning. It should not involve judging the family based on Eurocentric and other culturally inappropriate assumptions. Rather, practice with African American families should involve providing tools for these families to empower themselves.

The child welfare practitioner and family should engage in activities such as mutual goal setting and evaluation of choices through a risk-benefit analysis. Mutual goal setting may help the child welfare practitioner and family identify resources and choices that they had not acknowledged before. For example, an African American child who enters a new foster home may experience acclimation difficulties. A practitioner working from a traditional perspective may identify only two choices: either the child leaves and is placed in a new foster home, or the child stays and the family works to maintain the placement. However, the foster family may not be the only ones involved in the child's life. Are there connections that the child has to his or her biological family (e.g., mother, father, grandparents, or other relatives), to significant family friends, the church, or to other systems in the community? Does the child have connections to the foster family's relatives, such as the foster grandmother or grandfather? Understanding these relationships may introduce new choices for the child.

Reframing is important in work with African American families and children. Reframing is a way in which activities originally designated as negative are shown to contain important wisdom. For instance, a drug-addicted father may not have contact with his children. A practitioner operating from a traditional Eurocentric framework may concentrate on father absence as detrimental to the child and the child's mother. However, a practitioner operating from an ecological Africentric perspective of practice acknowledges the absence of the child's father, but also points out how the mother may use creative solutions to provide interactions with surrogate "otherfathers." The father's absence may force the family unit to develop coping mechanisms or resilience. The practitioner's ability to reframe circumstances may help the client see possibilities instead of negative circumstances.

Developing creative interventions based on an individual client's strengths, experiences, and comfort level are essential. For example, many African American families frequently read African American magazines, such as *Jet*, *Ebony*, *Ebony Jr.*, and *Essence*, or books from the Oprah Book Club. Materials from these sources (bibliotherapy) can be consciously included in intervention. For example, the practitioner might develop a therapeutic reading club. The participants can volunteer to select the book and lead the discussion on it for a particular session. The discussion of the books might relate to each participant and his or her family and provide a more intimate view of African Americans for the practitioners.

Storytelling, which feminist-oriented interventions often use (Saulnier 1996), is an important part of practice with African American families. Storytelling may include information about family rituals, beliefs, or family history. It is important to provide opportunities for the client to tell her, his, or their stories. For example, clients who use physical discipline when other forms of discipline are available may be identified as overly punitive and possibly unfit. However, the client's motivations and reasons can only be discovered if the client is allowed to articulate his or her story from a personal point of view. Perhaps physical discipline is a historical response to misbehavior that has been passed down from parent to child, or maybe the parent is unaware of the other forms of discipline that are available[1] or the possible effects of corporal punishment. In any instance, the client's stories are germane to understanding the client's reality. It may also be important to ask the parents what outcomes they want from the physical discipline. If they do not get that outcome, they may be more willing to try an alternative.

Another example occurs when there is confirmed child abuse and the child continues to deny it. Perhaps this child believes that if he or she speaks about abuse, the guilty parent will be arrested and become part of a system that has traditionally oppressed African Americans. Perhaps he or she has strong community roots and is afraid to disclose for fear that the practitioner may remove him or her from the community. However, the reasons will not be understood unless the practitioner asks the child to tell his or her story; that is, to talk about what he or she thinks would happen if the parents were identified as parents who hit too hard or in other ways inflict harm. Both of these examples illustrate that practitioners can only make accurate assessments and work with clients when the clients' reality is understood.

This model involves reevaluating commonly held beliefs that govern family structure, family role expectations, and family functioning. This entails de-pathologizing nontraditional family structures and understanding the reasons for, and strengths within, these structures. For example, child welfare practitioners who identify female-headed households in their caseload as dysfunctional and less stable than nuclear families stigmatize the African American community, devalue the work of women, and overlook the informal support structures that female-headed households may provide. Sudarkasa (1996) states, "Female headed households are not just the consequence of teenage pregnancies. Many are alternative forms of family organization that mature Black women have adopted in the face of the demographic, economic, political, and social realities of Black life in America" (29). The demographic reality is that the sex ratio is such that if all African American men (including those in prison, out of the country, and/or gay) were married to African American women, there would still be single African American women (Davis 1979).

Rethinking the traditional family structure involves understanding the validity and importance of kinship care and fictive kin within the African American community. Fictive kin, such as "othermothers" are persons who are not related by blood, but share a bond that creates positive benefits for both persons as well as the community (Hill-Collins 2000; James 1993). Othermothers such as grandmothers, aunts, sisters, and even neighbors may be important stakeholders in a child's situation. Child welfare practitioners who ignore the importance of kinship care–based family structures may undervalue an important strength of the African American community, and make mistakes during the intervention that isolate or negate important components of a child or adult's support system.

Finally, this model involves moving African American knowledge from the periphery of theoretical interventions and discourses into mainstream discussions. hooks (1981) describes this process as centering; it prevents one from expecting any one theory to explain behaviors of all people. This process recognizes African American knowledge as legitimate, central, and powerful.

The Future of Child Welfare from an Ecological Africentric Perspective

Using the ecological Africentric perspective when working with African American children and families in the child welfare system is only the first step in assisting African Americans. To truly make an impact, child welfare practitioners need to pay attention to large system-level issues, such as how child welfare agencies develop programs and policies. For example, current child welfare policies concerning adoption prioritize young (i.e., less than forty-five years of age), heterosexual, married couples (Hill 1998). This emphasizes the importance of the nuclear family and assumes that a one-size-fits-all approach to child welfare is appropriate. However, this priority ignores the strengths, resilience, and validity of alternative valid family structures (Sudarkasa 1996); thus, the number of acceptable choices for African American children in the child welfare system is decreased. Practitioners operating from a traditional Eurocentric framework may consider the young nuclear family the best family structure, without examining current research on alternative family structures. As the American population ages, child welfare and other practice areas will likely consider the use of alternative family structures for Euro-Americans as well.

Using the model in the program development context involves reevaluating the way in which child welfare needs are identified and addressed. Operating from a traditional Eurocentric framework may contribute to a practitioner incorrectly identifying needs. For example, some African American families may have extended family units residing under one roof. A practitioner operating from the assumption that nuclear family homes are best for children may develop a program that links persons to single-family affordable housing units. However, this action may not take into consideration the existing strengths of the extended family unit. If the practitioner moves family members, valuable services such as child care or transportation may be lost. Instead, a more appropriate model might begin with examining the roles and responsibilities of family members to each other and to the children, and determining the family's feelings about what supports its optimal level of functioning. Through analysis, a practitioner may acquire an understanding of the complexity of the family unit; the children may be residing in a very crowded yet well-organized and supportive household.

This chapter presents a model that helps practitioners of all racial and ethnic groups better understand and more effectively intervene with African Americans. Beckett (1994) originally developed the Multicultural Communication Process Model (MCCPM) to address any intervention in which the practitioner and client differed on some sociocultural characteristic (e.g., age, ethnicity, gender, race, social class). The model incorporates human service values, practice theories, research findings, and principles of communication theory. The purpose of this model is to enhance practice by promoting and increasing multicultural understanding, self-awareness, and competence. Figure 4.2 summarizes the premises of the MCCPM.

The Beckett MCCPM has eight strategic and interdependent practical components that include acquiring knowledge about African Americans. Other parts of the model incorporate skills demonstrating self-awareness and professional use of self. Note that this is a process model and includes neither sequen-

❖ Communication is the basic medium for interaction and achieving intervention goals

❖ Multicultural communication is between individuals and groups who differ in some way.

❖ The differences may be along any dimension including age, gender, ethnicity, disability, nationality, place of residence, race, religion, sexual orientation, social class, and social, educational and economic statuses.

❖ Culture largely determines broad group patterns of communication and it attaches meanings to verbal and nonverbal symbols.

❖ Demographics, status, affiliation, and ethnographic characteristics such as nationality, ethnicity, language, and religion all define culture.

❖ Individual cultures each have values, etiquette, and rules of behavior while cultural differences also occur between individuals of the same ethnicity or nationality.

❖ Multicultural communication is generic to all relationships, and essential to all therapeutic relationships.

❖ Both verbal and nonverbal, effective and problematic communication patterns are learned.

❖ Ineffective communication can be unlearned and/or improved with practice, openness, and by substituting other more effective approaches.

FIGURE 4.2   Premises of the Multicultural Communication Practice Model

tial components nor a linear conceptualization. Instead, a practitioner may begin at any component in the model, simultaneously concentrate on multiple components, or attend to each component several times as the practitioner becomes more knowledgeable and skillful in multicultural practice. One may use the MCCPM to guide knowledge building and multicultural competency for one group, then another, and another, and so on (Beckett & Dungee-Anderson 1996; Beckett & Dungee-Anderson 1998; Beckett et al. 1998) The eight components are as follows:

1. *Know yourself.* A deliberate, ongoing self-discovery process that requires the practitioner to continually assess his or her cultural values and beliefs, and their influence on interpersonal interactions. This process enhances sensitivity to other cultures, prepares for learning about other cultures, and increases effective multicultural interventions.

2. *Acknowledge cultural differences.* The ability to acknowledge individual, group, organizational, and societal differences. Acknowledging differences ensures learning from other cultures and decreases miscommunication. Straightforward and open discussion of differences does not suggest a racist or other oppressive orientation; nor does it prevent persons from seeing multicultural commonalties, nor perpetuate stereotypes.

3. *Know other cultures.* The understanding of how other cultural values and patterns motivate behaviors of individuals, couples, families, groups, organizations, and/or societies. Learning about other cultures is another weapon against miscommunication, and it enhances multicultural practice. This knowledge prevents the practitioner from projecting her or his culture into interactions with the client and helps her or him to plan culturally appropriate intervention strategies.

4. *Identify and value differences.* The use of direct verbal and nonverbal communications throughout the helping process that define and underscore the practitioner's positive regard for differences. Practitioners must look for, identify, and discuss cultural differences between him- or herself and the client. Discomfort about discussing subjects of gender, age, race, sexual orientation, and other characteristics that are crucial to a person's identity and behavior inhibit effective communication, constructive interactions, and appropriate interventions.

5. *Identify and avoid stereotypes.* A process of open dialogue that identifies relevant and specific cultural stereotypes that the practitioner and others apply to the client's diverse group memberships. This component includes the practitioner's commitment to recognize and avoid the use of stereotypes. To eliminate stereotypes, one must first become aware of those that are accepted and used and must also increase knowledge of groups. The most effective method is to have multiple experiences with culturally different groups.

6. *Empathize with persons from other cultures.* The use of an implicit and explicit practice focus of communicating genuine understanding of the client's experience in a society with values, beliefs, and operational rules that differ from those of the practitioner. To achieve empathy, the practitioner must temporarily give up his or her own worldview in order to experience another's.

7. *Adapt rather than adopt.* The practitioner's conscious attentiveness to his or her own expectations that clients adopt Euro-American (mainstream) values, beliefs, and behaviors. This stance increases awareness that encourages the practitioner's positive adaptations to clients' cultural variables. The practitioner can appropriately adapt his or her behavior to the multicultural interaction or take on the client's reality without changing his or her *basic* values and realities. Practitioners must consider the client's val-

ues and behaviors in order to communicate effectively with the client and must adapt to them in order to provide culturally acceptable, relevant, and effective interventions.

8. *Acquire recovery skills.* A continual focus on the practitioner's recognition, responsibility, and sensitive handling of practice errors occurring during the helping process. Practitioners skilled in multicultural practice differ from the novice, not for mistakes they make but by their ability to recover from the errors. If a practitioner makes no mistakes in multicultural interventions, she or he may not be taking enough personal and professional risks. The practitioner who is confident that she or he can recover from mistakes is likely to be less anxious about making mistakes.

The practitioner uses the MCCPM to actively intervene or supervise intervention. It is appropriate for intervention with various client systems including individuals, couples, families, groups, communities, organizations, social policies, and societies. It is appropriate for direct intervention, as well as for management and administration. In addition, the MCCPM also addresses the two types of intervention errors Dungee-Anderson (Dungee-Anderson & Beckett 1995) conceptualized that practitioners commonly make. Type 1 errors are *relationship errors* caused by problems in the practitioner's *self-awareness.* They include the behaviors of the practitioner that intentionally or unintentionally sabotage the intervention process: (1) engaging in power struggles with the client; (2) actively deciding "shoulds" and "should nots" for the client; and (3) lacking awareness of one's own issues and feelings, and thereby attributing them to the client. Type 1 errors prevent establishing an effective helping process with clients and contribute to Type 2 practice errors. Type 2 errors are *faulty interventions* caused predominantly by inadequate *knowledge* of multicultural content and/or arising from problems in *self-awareness* that promote misguided and faulty application of multicultural content in practice. Type 2 errors frequently occur when practitioners lack knowledge about differences between and within cultural groups. Type 1 and Type 2 practice errors result in ineffective multicultural practice. Table 4.1 shows how the practitioner can replace inappropriate Eurocentric interventions with interventions based on the models herein presented.

Research that provides information and meaning concerning the African American community without judging it based on Eurocentric guidelines is crucial to understanding the African American community. Further, research that investigates the African American community's involvement in the child welfare system is especially needed. Both qualitative and quantitative research is valid and necessary for understanding and working with the African American community. Traditional positivist research is important because it produces

TABLE 4.1

Comparison of Eurocentric and Ecological Africentric Assessments

Practice Situation	Traditional Eurocentric Assessment	Ecological Africentric Assessment
Child arrives for services without a biological parent. Instead, the child is accompanied by her grandmother, aunt, or older friend.	A practitioner's initial response may be to assume that the parent is not concerned about the child. Further, the practitioner may fear violating the child's confidentiality and resist disclosing to the grandmother, aunt, or friend. An effort is made to contact the child's parents and stress the importance of the child being accompanied by a biological parent.	The practitioner wonders about the relationship between the child and the adult. Perhaps the adult is an "othermother" or provides support for the mother. The practitioner gathers information about the family relationships before deciding that the biological parents are not concerned about the child's well-being.
Child lives in a crowded dwelling	Child's living arrangement is substandard and does not provide privacy for family members. Effort is made to find appropriate housing for all involved.	The practitioner examines the relationship between the persons in the dwelling. Perhaps the living arrangement provides support for extended family members who have "fallen on hard times." Perhaps services such as child care, transportation, financial, and/or emotional support are provided by this arrangement. The practitioner assesses the roles of the persons in

(continued)

Practice Situation	Traditional Eurocentric Assessment	Ecological Africentric Assessment
		the dwelling and determines what they contribute or have the potential to contribute. Practitioner may ask clients if they want to advocate for larger housing units in their neighborhood.
A male child has frequent angry outbursts in school. Many of these outbursts are directed toward girls or women. Upon reviewing the client files, the practitioner determines that the child's biological father does not have regular contact with the child.	The child lacks a male role model. He may have anger that exists due to his father's lack of involvement in the client's life. An effort should be made to enroll the youngster in a mentoring program as well as anger management classes.	The practitioner does not assume that the absence of a biological father causes negative behaviors. Rather, the practitioner determines who the important influences are in the child's life. Perhaps there is an uncle, cousin, or even a neighbor that is an informal mentor for the child. Instead of assuming that the child's system "lacks mentors," the practitioner seeks to cultivate existing relationships within the child's system.
An African American family brings an African American child welfare practitioner a small gift.	This is a violation of the client/practitioner relationship and agency policies. The practitioner should refuse the	The practitioner views the gift as a small token of the family's appreciation and trust. Trust is important

(continued)

Practice Situation	Traditional Eurocentric Assessment	Ecological Africentric Assessment
	gift and educate the family about the importance of maintaining an objective therapeutic relationship.	to many African Americans and may sometimes be as important as or more important than professional credentials. The practitioner should express that he or she does not require gifts, but should not refuse the small gift without understanding the motivations behind it. This is an opportunity to review agency policies with the clients. Further, this provides the impetus for the agency to review the cultural sensitivity of its policies.
Child refuses to go to school or has difficulty remaining attentive at school. However, the child is able to sit for extended periods of time while his or her hair is braided or twisted.	Child may have attention deficit hyperactivity disorder (ADHD). Effort should be made to determine if behaviors qualify for a diagnosis of ADHD. In addition, a behavior program should be initiated by the parent(s). Perhaps the child has to earn the right to have hair braided or twisted.	Hair is seen as an important part of the child's identity. The child may have ADHD; an evaluation should be conducted. However, perhaps the hair braiding or hair twisting time could be used in the therapeutic process. For instance, perhaps the human service provider could encourage the primary caregiver to engage

(continued)

TABLE 4.1 Comparison of Eurocentric and Ecological Africentric Assessments
(continued)

Practice Situation	Traditional Eurocentric Assessment	Ecological Africentric Assessment
		the child in a non-threatening way while the child's hair is being done. Perhaps the practitioner may develop a girls group in which clients learn to braid hair, take photographs, and coordinate a fashion show.

large amounts of data that researchers analyze using various statistical techniques. Researchers may use statistical techniques to quantify the impact of multiple variables (e.g., race, class, gender, occupation) on the lives of African American children and families. Qualitative data are important because they provide meaning to the experiences of African American children and families. No matter what research methods or statistics are used, a greater effort must be made to (1) utilize a wellness rather than an illness model; (2) integrate research that focuses on African Americans into the mainstream literature; and (3) develop research models informed by an ecological Africentric perspective. This requires a level of analysis that includes both person-centered and system-centered research (Cowen & Work 1988). Research on successful achievement of individuals and systems, in spite of the odds, should be the central agenda; this emphasizes the empowerment potentials for all systems.

Conclusions

Throughout history, African American children and families have created a community that has withstood discrimination and oppression. African American families have developed mechanisms that promote the nurturing of all members. Sometimes statistics that emphasize the "challenging and unfortunate plight of African Americans" overshadow accomplishments. For instance, statistics that detail the number of African American children who are born into poverty, die from firearms, or commit suicide omit the fact that fewer

African Americans experience these circumstances than the general child population. They also omit the fact that most African American children are not committing suicide or dying from firearms. In essence, these statistics fail to recognize the strengths, resilience, and talents that the majority of African American children and families display on a daily basis.

NOTE

1. The authors are not condoning physical maltreatment. In this instance, the authors mean physical punishment that does not leave marks such as bruises and is not done out of anger or to humiliate.

REFERENCES

Ackerson, B., & W. D. Harrison. 2000. "Practitioners' Perceptions of Empowerment." *Families in Society: The Journal of Contemporary Human Services* 81:238–245.

Adams, V., & J. Nelson. 2001. "Hope, Happiness, and African American Fathers: Changes between 1980 and 1992." *African American Research Perspectives* 7:148–156.

Akbar, N. 1991. "Paradigms of African American Research." In *Black Psychology*, edited by R. Jones, 709–726. Berkeley, CA: Cobb & Henry.

Anderson, M. 1986. In *Famous Black Quotations and Some Not So Famous*, compiled by J. Bell, 56. Chicago: Sabayt Publications.

Anderson, R., I. Carter & G. Lowe. 1999. *Human Behavior in the Social Environment: A Social Systems Approach*. 5th ed. New York: Aldine DeGruyter.

Beckett, J. 1976. "Working Wives: A Racial Comparison." *Social Work* 21:463–471. Reprinted in *Science, Sex, and Society*, edited 1980 by A. E. Kammer, C. S. Granrose, & J. B. Sloan. Newton, MA: Women's Education Equity Act Program, Education Development Center.

———. 1985. "Effective Intervention with Black Clients." *Fortifying African-American Networks: Fifteenth Annual National Conference Proceedings*, 16–26. National Association of Black Social Workers, Ann Arbor, MI.

———. 1988. "Plant Closings: How Older Workers Are Affected." *Social Work* 33:29–33.

———. 1994. *Cross-Cultural Communication: A Video/Workbook Self-Instructional Training Package*. Richmond, VA: Virginia Geriatric Education Center, Virginia Commonwealth University, Medical College of Virginia.

Beckett, J., & S. Coley. 1987. "Ecological Intervention with the Elderly: A Case Example." *Journal of Gerontological Social Work* 11:137–157.

Beckett, J., & D. Dungee-Anderson. 1996. "A Framework for Agency-Based Multicultural Training and Supervision." *Journal of Multicultural Social Work* 4:27–48.

———. 1998. "Multicultural Communication in Human Service Organizations." In *Diversity in the Workplace: Issues and Perspectives*, edited by A. Daly, 191–214. Washington, DC: National Association of Social Workers.

———. 2000. "Older Persons of Color: Asian/Pacific Islander Americans, African Americans, Hispanic Americans, and America Indians." In *Gerontological Social Work: Fundamentals, Service Settings, and Special Populations*. 2nd ed. Edited by R. Schneider & N. Kropf, 257–301. Pacific Grove, CA: Brooks/Cole/Wadsworth.

Beckett, J., D. Dungee-Anderson, L. Cox & A. Daly. 1998. "African Americans and Multicultural Interventions." *Smith College Studies in Social Work* 67:540–563 (special issue on social work intervention with African Americans).

Beckett, J., & H. Johnson. 1995. "Human Development: Biological, Psychological, and Sociocultural Perspectives." In *Encyclopedia of Social Work*, editor in chief, R. Edwards, 1385–1405. Washington, DC: National Association of Social Workers.

Billingsley, A. 1968. *Black Families in White America*. New Jersey: Prentice-Hall.

———. 1973. Black Families and White Social Science. In *The Death of White Sociology*, edited by J. Ladner, 431–450. New York: Vintage Books.

Billingsley, A., & J. Giovannoni. 1972. *Children of the Storm: Black Children and American Child Welfare*. New York: Harcourt Brace Jovanovich.

Bloom, M. 1984. *Configurations of Human Behavior*. New York: Macmillan.

Blundo, R. 2001. "Learning Strengths-Based Practice: Challenging Our Personal and Professional Frames." *Families in Society: The Journal of Contemporary Human Services* 82: 296–304.

Boardman, J., B. Finch, C. Ellison, D. Williams & J. Jackson. 2001. "Neighborhood Disadvantage, Stress, and Drug Abuse among Adults." *Journal of Health and Social Behavior* 42:151–165.

Bowman, P. 1991. "Organizational Psychology: African American Perspectives." In *Black Psychology*, edited by R. Jones, 509–532. Berkeley, CA: Cobb & Henry.

Bronfenbrenner, U. 1979. *The Ecology of Human Development: Experiments by Nature and Design*. Cambridge: Harvard University Press.

Brown, A., & B. Bailey-Etta. 1997. "An Out-of-Home Care System in Crisis: Implications for African American Children in Child Welfare System." *Child Welfare* 76:65–84.

Brown, A., & R. Gourdine. 1998. "Teenage Black Girls and Violence: Coming of Age in an Urban Environment." *Journal of Human Behavior in the Social Environment* 1:105–124.

Brown, T. 2001. "Exposure to All Black Context and Psychological Well-Being: The Benefits of Racial Concentration." *African American Research Perspectives* 7:157–172.

Carter, C. 1999. "Church Burning in African American Communities: Implications for Empowerment Practice." *Social Work* 44:62–69.

Chestang, L. 1976. "Environmental Influences on Social Functioning: The Black Experience." In *The Diverse Society*, edited by P. Cafferty & L. Chestang, 59–74. Washington, DC: National Association of Social Workers.

Child Welfare League of America. January 1998. "Family Foster Care Fact Sheet." Retrieved from www.cwla.org/cwla/fostercr/familyfcfacts98.html.

Children's Defense Fund. August 2001. "Every Day in America." Retrieved from www.childrensdefense.org/everyday.htm.

Courtney, M., R. Barth, J. Berrick, D. Brooks, B. Needell & L. Park. 1996. "Race and Child Welfare: Past Research and Future Directions." *Child Welfare* 75:99–137.

Cousins, L., & T. Mabrey. 1998. "Re-Gendering Social Work Practice and Education: The Case for African American Girls." *Journal of Human Behavior in the Social Environment* 1:91–104.

Cowen, E., & W. Work. 1988. "Resilient Children, Psychological Wellness, and Primary Prevention." *American Journal of Community Psychology* 16:591–607.

Cowger, C. 1997. "Assessing Client Strengths: Assessment for Client Empowerment." In *The Strengths Perspective in Social Work Practice*. 2nd ed. Edited by D. Saleebey, 59–73. New York: Longman Publishers.

Daly, A., J. Jennings, J. Beckett & B. Leashore. 1995. "Effective Coping Skills of African Americans." *Social Work* 40:240–248. Reprinted 1996 in *Multicultural Issues in Social Work*, edited by P. Ewalt, E. Freeman, K. Stuart Kirk & D. Poole. Washington, DC: National Association of Social Workers.

Danzy, J., & S. Jackson. 1997. "Family Preservation and Support Services: A Missed Opportunity for Kinship Care." *Child Welfare* 76:31–45.

Davidson, B. 1997. "Service Needs of Relative Caregivers: A Qualitative Analysis." *Families in Society: The Journal of Contemporary Human Services* 78:502–510.

Davis, L. 1979. "Racial Composition of Groups." *Social Work* 24:208–213.

———. 1993. *Black and Single*. Chicago: Noble Press.

Denby, R., C. Curtis & K. Alford. 1998. "Family Preservation Services and Special Populations: The Invisible Target." *Families in Society: The Journal of Contemporary Human Services* 79/1:3–14.

Department of Health and Human Services. 1998. "Current Estimates as of January 1999: DHHS, Administration for Children and Families." Retrieved from www.acf.dhhs.gov/programs/cb/publications/afcars.

———. 2002. "Retaining Foster Parents." (DHHS Publication No. 0EI-07-00-00601). Washington, DC: U.S. Government Printing Office.

DeVito, J. 2001. *The Interpersonal Communication Book*. 9th ed. New York: Addison Wesley Longman.

Dodson, J., & S. Ross. 1977. *Afro-American Culture: Expressive Behaviors*. Atlanta, GA: Atlanta University of Social Work.

DuBois, B., & K. Miley. 2002. *Social Work: An Empowering Profession*. Boston: Allyn & Bacon.

Dungee-Anderson, D., & J. Beckett. 1995. "A Process Model for Multicultural Social Work Practice." *Families in Society: The Journal of Contemporary Human Services* 76:459–466.

Early, T. 2001. "Measures for Practice with Families from a Strengths Perspective." *Families in Society: The Journal of Contemporary Human Services* 82:225–232.

Early, T., & L. GlenMaye. 2000. "Valuing Families: Social Work Practice with Families from a Strengths Perspective." *Social Work* 45:118–130.

Fawcett, S., A. Paine-Andrews, V. Francisco, J. Schultz, K. Richer, R. Lewis, E. Williams, K. Harris, J. Berkely, J. Fischer & C. Lopez. 1995. "Using Empowerment Theory in Collaborative Partnerships for Community Health and Development." *American Journal of Community Psychology* 23:5–698.

Fields, J., & L. Casper. 2001. *America's Families and Living Arrangements: March 2000*. Current Population Reports, series P20-537. U.S. Census Bureau. Washington, DC.

Ford-Gilboe, M. 2000. "Dispelling Myths and Creating Opportunity: A Comparison of the Strengths of Single-Parent and Two-Parent Families." *Advances in Nursing Science* 23:41–58.

Fraser, M. 1997. *Risk and Resilience in Childhood: An Ecological Perspective*. Washington, DC: National Association of Social Workers.

Fraser, M., J. Richman & M. Galinsky. 1999. "Risk, Protection, and Resilience: Toward a Conceptual Framework for Social Work Practice." *Social Work Research* 23:131–144.

Gary, L., & G. Weaver. 1991. "Mental Health of African Americans: Research Trends and Directions." In *Black Psychology*, edited by R. Jones, 727–768. Berkeley, CA: Cobb & Henry.

Germain, C. 1979. *Social Work Practice: People and Environments*. New York: Columbia University Press.

Germain, C., & A. Gitterman. 1980. *The Life Model of Social Work Practice*. New York: Columbia University Press.

———. 1996. *The Life Model of Social Work Practice*. 2nd ed. New York: Columbia University Press.

Gibbs, J., & D. Fuery. 1994. "Mental Health and Well-Being of Black Women: Toward Strategies of Empowerment." *American Journal of Community Psychology* 22:559–578.

Gleeson, J., J. O'Donnell & F. Bonecutter. 1997. "Understanding the Complexity of Practice in Kinship Foster Care." *Child Welfare* 76:801–826.

Goldstein, H. 1973. *Social Work Practice: A Unitary Approach.* Columbia: University of South Carolina Press.

———. 1997. "Victors or Victims?" In *The Strengths Perspective in Social Work Practice.* 2nd ed. Edited by D. Saleebey, 21–35. New York: Longman Publishers.

Graybeal, C. 2001. "Strengths-Based Social Work Assessment: Transforming the Dominant Paradigm." *Families in Society: The Journal of Contemporary Human Service* 82:233–242.

Green, R., & P. Ephross. 1991. *Human Behavior Theory and Social Work Practice.* Hawthorne, NY: Aldine de Gruyter.

Greif, G. 1986. "The Ecosystems Perspective 'Meets the Press.'" *Social Work* 31:225–226.

Guba, E. 1990. *The Paradigm Dialog.* Beverly Hills, CA: Sage.

Gutierrez, L. 1990. "Working with Women of Color: An Empowerment Perspective." *Social Work* 35:149–154.

Gutierrez, L., L. GlenMaye & K. DeLois. 1995. "The Organizational Context of Empowerment Practice: Implications for Social Work Administration." *Social Work* 40:249–258.

Gutierrez, L., H. Oh & R. Gillmore. 2000. "Toward an Understanding of Empowerment for HIV/AIDS Prevention with Adolescent Women." *Sex Roles: A Journal of Research* 2:581–612.

Hartman, A. 1978. "Diagrammatic Assessment of Family Relationships." *Social Casework* 59:465–476.

———. 1993. The Professional Is Political. *Social Work* 38:365–366.

Hartman, A., & J. Laird. 1983. *Family-Centered Social Work Practice.* New York: Free Press.

Hayes, V. 1991. "African American Strengths: A Survey of Empirical Findings." In *Black Psychology*, edited by R. Jones, 379–408. Berkeley, CA: Cobb & Henry.

Hearn, G. 1958. *Theory Building in Social Work.* Toronto: University of Toronto Press.

Hecht, M., M. Collier & S. Ribeau. 1993. *African American Communication: Ethnic Identity and Cultural Interpretation.* Newbury Park, CA: Sage Publications.

Helms, J. 1990. *Black and White Racial Identity: Theory, Research, and Practice.* New York: Greenwood Press.

Hill, R. 1972. *The Strengths of Black Families.* New York: Emerson Hall.

———. 1998. "Enhancing the Resiliency of African American Families." *Journal of Human Behavior in the Social Environment* 1:49–61.

Hill-Collins, P. 2000. *Black Feminist Thought: Knowledge, Consciousness, and the Politics of Empowerment.* New York: Routledge.

hooks, b. 1981. *Ain't I a Woman: Black Women and Feminism.* Boston: South End Press.

Jackson, J., ed. 2000. *New Directions: African American in a Diversifying Nation.* Washington, DC: National Policy Association.

James, S. 1993. "Mothering a Possible Black Feminist Link to Social Transformation." In *Theorizing Black Feminisms: The Visionary Pragmatism of Black Women*, edited by S. James & A. Busia, 44–54. New York: Routledge.

Kagan, J. 1984. *The Nature of the Child.* New York: Basic Books.

Kendall, J. 1996. "Creating a Culturally Responsive Psychotherapeutic Environment for African American Youths: A Critical Analysis." *Advances in Nursing Science* 18:11–28.

Kohn, L., & K. Hudson. 2002. "Gender, Ethnicity, and Depression: Intersectionality and Context in Mental Health Research with African American Women." *African American Research Perspectives* 8:174–184.

Kortenkamp, K., & J. Ehrle. 2002. *The Well Being of Children Involved with the Child Welfare System: A National Overview* (Series B, no. 43). Washington, DC: Urban Institute.

Laursen, E. 2000. "Strength Based Practice with Children in Trouble." *Reclaiming Children and Youth* 9:70–75.

Lee, J. 1996. "The Empowerment Approach to Social Work Practice." In *Social Work Treatment: Interlocking Theoretical Approaches*. 4th ed. Edited by F. Turner, 218–249. New York: Free Press.

Lindahl, K. 2002. *The Sacred Art of Listening: Forty Reflections for Cultivating a Spiritual Practice*. Woodstock, VT: Skylight Paths Publishing.

Lum, D. 1992. *Social Work Practice and People of Color: A Process-Stage Approach*. Pacific Grove, CA: Brooks/Cole/Wadsworth.

Lutz, J. 1956. *Concepts and Principles Underlying Social Casework Practice*. New York: National Association of Social Workers.

Maluccio, A. 1981. *Promoting Competence in Clients: A New/Old Approach to Social Work Practice*. New York: Free Press.

McKinnon, J., & K. Humes. 2000. *The Black Population in the United States: March 1999*. Current Population Reports, series P20-530. U.S. Census Bureau. Washington, DC.

McLoyd, V. 1991. "What Is the Study of African American Children the Study Of?" In *Black Psychology*, edited by R. Jones, 419–440. Berkeley, CA: Cobb & Henry.

McRae, M., & D. Noumair. 1997. "Race and Gender in Group Research." *African American Research Perspectives* 3:68–74.

Meyer, C. 1983. *Social Work Practice: A Response to the Urban Crisis*. New York: Free Press.

Miley, K., M. O'Melia & B. DuBois. 2001. *Generalist Social Work Practice: An Empowering Approach*. 3rd ed. Boston: Allyn & Bacon.

Miller, J. 1978. *Living Systems*. New York: McGraw-Hill.

Morton, M. 2000. "Institutionalizing Inequalities: Black Children and Child Welfare in Cleveland, 1859–1998." *Journal of Social History* 34:141–162.

Myers, L. 1991. "Expanding the Psychology of Knowledge Optimally: The Importance of Worldview Revisited." In *Black Psychology*, edited by R. Jones, 5–14. Berkeley, CA: Cobb & Henry.

National Child Welfare Training Center. 1982. *A Sourcebook in Child Welfare: Serving Children and Black Families*. Ann Arbor: School of Social Work, University of Michigan.

———. 1983. *Serving Black Families and Children: A Sourcebook in Child Welfare*. Ann Arbor, MI: School of Social Work, the University of Michigan.

Neighbors, H. 1997. "The (Mis)Diagnosis of Mental Disorders in African Americans." *African American Perspectives* 3:1–11.

Nobles, W. 1976. *A Formative and Empirical Study of Black Families*. Final report submitted to the Office of Child Development under contract number 90-C-255. San Francisco, CA: Westside Community Mental Health Center, Inc.

Norton, D. 1976. "Residential Environment and Black Self-Image." In *The Diverse Society*, edited by P. Cafferty & L. Chestang, 75–92. Washington, DC: National Association of Social Workers.

O'Donnell, J. 1999. "Involvement of African American Fathers in Kinship Foster Care Services." *Social Work* 44:428–441.

Palmer, N. 1997. "Resilience in Adult Children of Alcoholics." *Health & Social Work* 22:201–209.

Perkins, D. 1995. "Speaking Truth to Power: Empowerment Ideology as Social Intervention and Policy." *American Journal of Community Psychology* 23:765–795.

Pincus, A., & A. Minahan. 1973. *Social Work Practice: Model and Method*. Itasca, IL: Peacock.

Polk, L. 1997. "Toward a Middle-Range Theory of Resilience." *Advances in Nursing Science* 19:1–13.

Raider, M., & M. Pauline-Morand. 1998. *Social Work Practice with Low-Income, Urban, African-American Families*. New York: Edwin Mellen Press.

Rapp, R. 1997. "The Strengths Perspective and Persons with Substance Abuse Problems." In *The Strengths Perspective in Social Work Practice.* 2nd ed. Edited by D. Saleebey, 77–94. New York: Longman Publishers.

Richmond, M. 1917. *Social Diagnosis.* Philadelphia: Russell Sage Foundation.

Rothenberg, P. 1999. *Race, Class, and Gender in the United States.* 4th ed. New York: Worth Publishers.

Saleebey, D. 1996. "The Strengths Perspective in Social Work Practice: Extensions and Cautions." *Social Work* 41:296–304.

———. 1997. "Introduction: Power in the People." In *The Strengths Perspective in Social Work Practice.* 2nd ed. Edited by D. Saleebey, 3–18. New York: Longman Publishers.

Saulnier, C. 1996. *Feminist Theories and Social Work: Approaches and Applications.* New York: Hawthorn Press.

Schiele, J. 2000. *Human Services and the Afrocentric Paradigm.* New York: Haworth Press.

Shaw, M., & P. Costanzo. 1982. *Theories of Social Psychology.* 2nd ed. New York: McGraw-Hill.

Siporin, M. 1975. *Introduction to Social Work Practice.* New York: Macmillan.

Solomon, B. 1976. *Black Empowerment: Social Work in Oppressed Communities.* New York: Columbia University Press.

Staples, L. 1990. "Powerful Ideas about Empowerment." *Administration in Social Work* 14: 29–42.

Sudarkasa, N. 1996. *The Strength of Our Mothers: African and African American Women and Families: Essays and Speeches.* Lawrenceville, NJ: Africa World Press.

Trierweiler, S., & G. Stricker. 1998. *The Scientific Practice of Professional Psychology.* New York: Plenum Press.

Truth, S. 1851. "If the First Woman." [Hallmark greeting card, 2002.] Kansas City, MO: Hallmark Cards.

von Bertalanffy, L. 1968. *General Systems Theory: Foundations, Development, Applications.* New York: George Braziller. Original work published 1937.

Washington Post, March 21, 2001. "Report Says Minorities Get Lower-Quality Health Care; Moral Implications of Widespread Pattern Noted," A2.

West Stevens, J. 1998. "A Question of Values in Social Work Practice: Working with the Strengths of Black Adolescent Females." *Families in Society: The Journal of Contemporary Human Services* 79:288–297.

White, J. 1991. "Toward a Black Psychology." In *Black Psychology*, edited by R. Jones, 5–14. Berkeley, CA: Cobb & Henry.

Wright, O., & J. Anderson. 1998. "Clinical Social Work Practice with Urban African American Families." *Families in Society* 79:197–205.

Yancy, A. 1998. "Building Positive Self-Image in Adolescents in Foster Care: The Use of Role Models in an Interactive Group Approach." *Adolescence* 33:130–253.

Zastrow, C., & K. Kirst-Ashman. 1990. *Understanding Human Behavior and the Social Environment.* Chicago: Nelson-Hall.

5

African American Families in Context

Internal and External Phenomena

MELVIN N. WILSON

LAKEESHA N. WOODS

GINA R. HIJJAWI

The family is a network of persons who share resources, residences, emotional bonds, and obligations and support each other in childrearing tasks (Brown, Cohon & Wheeler 2002). The African American family is a natural supportive network that provides its members with opportunities for at least economic and instrumental cooperation, informal communications, and reciprocated social and emotional obligations (Wilson & Tolson 1990). Through patterns of kin contact that are proximal, available, frequent, and functional, a family provides its members with a sense of group and personal identities, behavioral rules, roles and responsibilities, enduring solidarity, and emotional affiliations and attachments. The African American familial support system aptly has been described as a kin insurance policy because of the support provided during emergencies (McAdoo 1982).

The societal context of African Americans has changed dramatically since 1990, greatly challenging the African American family. A dramatic increase has occurred in the number of internal issues such as divorce, nonmarital births, and single-parenting rates; and external issues such as economic hardship, unemployment, incarceration, and health challenges. An especially significant concern is the prevalence of health and social problems like AIDS and substance abuse, which have taken their toll on African American family life. This chapter investigates the current context of the African American family and identifies existing familial specific processes and outcomes through examination of two areas. First, the chapter examines the internal structure of the African American family through consideration of the effect of social phenomena on family roles and processes. Second, the chapter explores external phenomena and systems, such as the economy, incarceration, health challenges, and the child welfare system, which confront the traditional structure or current circumstances of African American family life.

Internal Challenges to Family Functioning

Family Roles

An important aspect of African American family life is the roles that various members of the family play. The two most critical roles in families involve giving care to family members and providing the family with financial resources. In traditional families, mothers are caregivers and fathers are family providers. As evidenced by extended kin involvement, mothers and fathers are not the only persons to take on the role of caregivers and providers in the family. Alternate family members may assume the roles whether living inside or outside of the home. Older children may care for younger siblings, especially when parents are at work. Grandmothers and other extended family members also take on the caregiving role. African American families include a diverse set of income earners. Single-mother families, extended family households, and two-parent families in which the mother also works are situations in which someone other than the father assumes the familial role of provider.

African American grandmothers' role as surrogate parents is not a new phenomenon, and grandmothers are involved consistently in parenting (Burton & DeVries 1992; Wilson, Tolson, Hinton & Kiernan 1990). Pearson, Hunter, Ensminger, and Kellam (1990) reported a significant level of involvement in child rearing for grandmothers, second only to mothers. Grandparents, particularly grandmothers, contribute to child socialization directly (through participating in child care) and indirectly (through contributing to the values and atmosphere of the household). Wilson (1984) found that African American grandmothers are more involved with their grandchildren when they live in the child's home and when the mother is single than in other living arrangements.

The 1990s brought new reasons for the formation of grandmother-only families. Even within the narrower category of adolescent single parenting, there can be diversity in family functioning. Apfel and Seitz (1991) suggest that four models of grandmother involvement in families with adolescent mothers exist, including replacing, sharing, supporting, and mentoring the adolescent mother. Grandmothers perform such tasks as buffering the grandchild from negative interactions with the mother, teaching the mother child-rearing skills, or assuming a pseudo-parenting role that allows the mother to return to school or get a job (Apfel & Seitz 1991; Flaherty 1988).

Extended family members can serve as support systems as well as assistants in child rearing. Kinship care has foundations in African culture, where kinship networks often provided mediation services in the resolution of disputes (Wilhelmus 1998). The extended family also emerged as a response to the history of adversity African Americans have faced in the United States (Brown, Cohon & Wheeler 2002). Extended family households may be protective for children whose families struggle with economic and social adversity (Brown, Cohon &

Wheeler 2002). McAdoo (1982) found that kin support systems greatly facilitated maternal stress management. Stevens (1988) indicated that mothers who sought support from extended family members were more skillful in parenting. Similarly, Thompson and Ensminger (1989) found that single mothers have higher parental competence when another adult is present in the home. The presence of another adult family member was related to more positive and less punitive parenting (Brassard 1979; Colletta 1979). To address the high number of children in foster care, particularly African Americans, the foster care system has increasingly turned to placements with relatives or kinship care arrangements (Wilhelmus 1998). Generally, it appears that extended family members can help alleviate stress in African American families and thereby increase the quality of child socialization. The extended family structure reflects a resilience of African American families that enables them to utilize their resources to overcome difficulties.

Given the myriad of roles African American family members assume, role boundaries are important to consider when studying African American family life. In families in which more than one generation of adults lives in the same household, conflicts may arise regarding the delegation of roles. When both a mother and a grandmother are acting as caregivers for the children, for example, it is quite likely that occasional disagreements regarding the appropriate punishments for children's misbehaviors will arise. Ambiguities may exist concerning the limits of each adult's authority in child rearing. Staples and Johnson (1993) suggested that traditional gender roles of fathers as providers and mothers as nurturers have inhibited the exploration of parenting for each gender. More research is needed to explore the many aspects of parenting for diverse African American groups. In addition, research that incorporates the children's as well as parents' views of parenting and those of the parents is critical to understanding the interactive nature of child rearing.

African American Parenting and Child Outcomes

It is important to account for the possible influence that any household members may have on the parent-child relationship. Wilson, Kohn, Curry-El, and Hinton (1995) examined the influence of family structure on four child-rearing behaviors of African American mothers. Parental support, control, demand, and punishment were considered. Results indicated that mothers with higher income, higher levels of education, and more children reported more nurturance and punishment behaviors and less demand behaviors. A higher number of adults in the household was related to less punishment. Specific household composition did not appear to be as predictive of parenting behaviors as were number of adults and number of children.

Creighton (1995) examined parenting among sixty diverse African American families. Three distinct parenting dimensions emerged from the mothers' reports: control, which is consistent with the results of Wilson and associates (1995); support, which includes positive, warm, and nurturing attitudes toward the child; and discipline, which refers to the belief that a parent should maintain authority. Three dimensions emerged from the children's reports: support, which is similar to that found with the mothers; discipline/guidance, which refers to the belief that their mothers will follow through with discipline; and flexibility/encouragement, which concerns the extent to which children feel their mothers view them as mature, competent individuals. Children in extended family households reported their mothers to be more flexible and encouraging than did children in other households. In addition, children perceived their mothers to be less supportive when there was another adult present in the home (Creighton 1995). It is apparent that some constructs, such as support, control, and discipline, are legitimate for describing African American parenting. More research is needed that addresses the children's views of family functioning.

African American mothers have been found to be more parent-oriented than their white counterparts. African American mothers have been described negatively as expecting unyielding obedience to parental authority and as not considering their children's needs or desires (Kamii & Radin 1967; Radin & Kamii 1965). Baumrind (1972) described African American mothers as rejecting their daughters and stated that, in comparison to white Americans, African American parents did not enrich their daughters' environment or encourage individuality or independence. Portes, Dunham, and Williams (1986) found that African American mothers were less permissive than were white American mothers. None of these findings, however, describe the nature of African American families or within-group variations in processes and outcomes.

Baumrind (1971) developed four parenting styles—authoritarian, authoritative, permissive, and neglectful—based on a large, mostly white sample of parents and children. Authoritarian parents were those who placed a high value on obedience for its own sake and exerted a high level of control and low level of warmth toward children. Authoritative parents valued obedience, not for its own sake, but in order to assure that their children behaved properly. Authoritative parents exercised high levels of control and warmth. Permissive parents were least likely to exert control over their children, displaying a low level of control and high level of warmth. Indifferent parents exhibited low levels of both control and warmth.

Taking a cultural specific approach, family researchers and practitioners have begun to develop broader, more ecologically valid conceptualizations of their African American family functioning, rather than viewing African American families as a variation of mainstream families. African American families, which once were viewed as dysfunctional, emerge as strong, functional, and flexible (Peters 1988). Discipline, which once was believed to be too harsh in comparison to mainstream practices, has been shown to be functional and appropriate for many African American children and parents.

Baumrind (1971) found that authoritative parenting styles correlated with the most positive child outcomes. Although this relationship appears to be true for mainstream populations, a follow-up study indicated that alternative patterns might be more common for ethnic minorities (Baumrind 1972). Although the sample of African Americans was too small to draw any conclusions, some surprising results occurred for African American girls whose parents fell into the authoritarian category. In contrast to the less favorable child outcomes found for authoritative parenting in the larger sample, African American daughters of authoritarian parents were more mature and independent.

Peters (1976, 1981) reported that the more "authoritarian" style of discipline is functional for African American children and that their parents do not view discipline negatively, but rather as a means of preparing their children for the world and protecting them in dangerous environments. It is plausible that the attitudes of parents (and perhaps children) regarding the structure and reasoning behind child-rearing practices are diverse and may relate to child outcomes and family functioning. Kelley, Power, and Wimbush (1992) examined the disciplinary practices of low-income, urban African American mothers and found a wide range of styles, from parent-oriented to child-oriented. The results suggested that physical punishment in African American families might not be indicative of an authoritarian parenting style, but rather a result of other factors, such as maternal marital status, religiosity, age, and education.

Brody and Flor (1998) coined the term "no nonsense parenting" to describe the more authoritarian and parent-focused parenting style many African American parents employ and to identify a parenting style that more accurately explains their parenting. High levels of parental control, including physical punishment, combined with warmth and affection, characterize no nonsense parenting. It is intended to shield children from becoming victims or perpetrators of antisocial activities and to communicate parents' vigilance and concern for their children's welfare. No nonsense parenting is positively related to child self-regulation and social competence in children of rural, single-parent families, and the children construe the parenting practice as a sign of parental involvement and concern (Brody & Flor 1998).

Researchers also have examined the role of parental involvement and expectations in predicting academic outcomes. Parental involvement in the schooling process has been associated with higher grades and test scores (Dye 1989; Reynolds 1989). Similarly, Thompson, Alexander, and Entwisle (1988) found that higher parental expectations were associated with higher first-grade reading achievement, particularly for children who live with more than one adult. McAdoo (1986) found that African American fathers socialize their daughters to be more competent and independent at an early age. His later work suggested a need for a theory that describes father-child relationships over the life span and within the family, taking into account racial, ethnic, and social class differences (McAdoo 1988). Other work has shown fathers to be more active in spousal support than in child rearing (Slaughter & Dilworth-Anderson 1988).

Despite the limitations of generalizability, earlier work on African American parenting has helped shape the current trends in research. Future research is needed that addresses the relationship of child outcomes and parenting style, involvement, and expectations for African American children. Another avenue of research on African American families concerns the participants in child rearing (such as fathers and extended family members) and their roles within the family. Much of the research on parenting has focused on mothers rather than on fathers. The exclusion of fathers from research probably is due to the fact that mothers are more likely to be the primary caregivers for children. When possible, studies of parenting should include fathers who are involved in their children's upbringing, regardless of whether they live with their children.

External Challenges to Family Functioning

Although it is critical to investigate African American family functioning across a variety of living situations, it also is important to understand the changing face of the political, social, and economic contexts in which they develop. Various external forces seriously can alter family structure by removing a family member, introducing a new member to the household, or changing the role of a member within the family. External challenges influence everyday family life, as well as the roles that members of the family assume.

Parental Absence

It is tempting to blame the high rate of father absence on the moral characteristics of certain father/husbands; however, it must be understood that the economic, social, and health contexts in which African American men live also play a part in their ability to function within their families. Like other men, African American fathers want to participate in and support their families (Bowman 1990). Factors such as widespread economic marginality and incarceration, however, have impaired their ability to do so. Health impairments and incarceration increasingly are affecting maternal involvement as well.

Poverty and Unemployment

Economic marginality has serious implications for family structure and functioning in the African American community. The persistent and concentrated poverty of high portions of African American families (Gephart & Pearson 1988), especially single-parent African American families, is probably the most important factor correlated with extended family formation. Although most African American families are not poor, 23.6 percent of them live in poverty (U.S. Bureau of the Census 1999). Among one-parent families, poverty is particularly evident, as 39.3 percent of African American female-headed families were classified as poor as recently as 1999 (U.S. Bureau of the Census 1999). More importantly, African American single mothers often blamed their depressive conditions on low income and chronic money problems than on any other stressful life event (Belle, Longfellow & Makosky 1982). The chronic effects of low income present the most difficulties for African American families.

Postindustrial technological changes during the last two decades have rendered obsolete many of the jobs that African American men once had. With the increase in white-collar service jobs, African American men who primarily held unskilled or semiskilled labor positions have become either unemployed or underemployed at jobs that do not pay enough to cover basic sustenance. In 1995, 9.9 percent of black males were unemployed as compared to 5.4 percent nationally and 4.2 percent of white males, illustrating that even when black men are employed, it is at significantly lower rates than their white counterparts. Discrimination affects group earnings, and the unemployment rate of African Americans negatively affects their earnings to a greater degree than for any other racial group (Boushey 1998). African American men also receive lower pay than do white men, as evidenced by the fact that, in 1998, African American men earned 75 percent as much as did white men (Center for Policy Alternatives 2000). Median household incomes for African Americans also are approximately only 62 percent of the incomes of white households.

Fathers/husbands suffering from chronic unemployment or underemployment may adopt poor coping strategies for dealing with their inability to provide financially and may be more likely to leave the family. Chronic unemployment, thus, may be related to divorce. Unemployed and underemployed fathers also may fail challenges to starting a new family and may choose not to marry the mother of their children. In a nationally representative sample, Bowman (1993) found married men more likely than single men to be employed. This finding indicates that economically marginal men possibly are more likely to divorce or never marry. Rates of teen parent marriages also have decreased as the rate of joblessness has increased (Bowman 1993). Bowman (1990) found that 41 percent of young adults between the ages of nineteen and twenty-eight were unemployed. As both unemployment and teen births rise, the fact that teen fathers are most likely to be involved in the family if they have been employed within the preceding year (Danziger & Radin 1990) implies a decrease in many young fathers' involvement in their families.

Incarceration

Incarceration has proven to be a serious threat to African American family life and functioning, impacting the entire family network including the mother, father, child, and extended family. Families not only suffer loss of income, but they lose a child care provider, role model, and emotional supporter. Incarceration also influences men in ways that render them less capable to return to their family roles after released from prison. The United States' prison and jail population has escalated continually since 1973. The national rate of incarceration represents a level of incarceration six to ten times that of most industrialized nations (The Sentencing Project 2001). African American men are incarcerated at much higher rates than are any other group in the United States. Although they represent about 6 percent of the population, African American men comprise 32 percent of America's prison population (Jackson 1997; King 1993). African American men are imprisoned at a rate of 4,617 per 100,000 compared with the white rate of 630 per 100,000 for white men (The Sentencing Project 2001). In some inner-city African American communities, 50 percent of all men have been incarcerated (Jackson 1997; King 1993).

Incarcerated men often become dependent on their families for money, clothing, or other personal items while they are imprisoned. One of the biggest problems associated with the imprisonment of a family member is loss of that member's income (King 1993). External stressors hamper family members' abilities to cope with other day-to-day problems as well (King 1993). Particularly, the wives or partners of inmates often face dire circumstances and feel overwhelmed. Many wives and partners are left alone to deal with the emotional strain on their families. Partners of inmates may experience depression, loneliness, or anger. Most wives express concern regarding raising their children alone, their husband's release, community isolation, and their husband's treatment while in prison (Adalist-Estrin 1994). The wives and partners also must make the decision of how much information to tell their children regarding their father's imprisonment. In deciding what information to disclose, mothers take into account the nature of their husbands' or partners' crimes and the children's ages. Many mothers conceal the father's actual whereabouts from their preschool-age children. Mothers of older children may wish to tell the truth about the father's whereabouts, lest their children hear the information elsewhere (Fishman 1990).

The female inmate population also is increasing. Women, particularly poor women of color, represent the fastest growing prison population (National Women's Law Center 1995). Female inmates are disproportionately women of color, with African American women comprising 46 percent of the population nationwide (National Women's Law Center 1995). The incarceration rate of African American women is 375 per 100,000 compared with the white female incarceration rate of 53 per 100,000 (The Sentencing Project 2001). The rise in the prison population is remarkable given declining crime rates since 1992. The decline, however, has been overridden by the increasing impact of lengthy mandatory sentencing policies, which include mandatory minimums; "three strikes" policies; and "truth in sentencing," which mandates that offenders serve 85 percent of their sentences.

The shift in family structure caused by a family member's incarceration has implications for family functioning. Extended family members may fill the roles of child care provider and emotional supporter. Younger children may have to increase their responsibility within the family, and mothers may have to seek other employment. Parental incarceration interferes with children's ability to successfully master developmental tasks and to overcome the effects of trauma, parent-child separation, and substandard care (Fishman 1990). Fishman found children often have problems dealing with separation and loss. Some of the problems include insomnia, nightmares, bed-wetting, loss of appetite, overeating, a drop in school grades, delinquent behavior, and less frequently, suicide ideation. Behavior problems of children include aggressive reactions, tension, withdrawal, hostility, and acting out. King (1993) found that children may suffer from depression, are prone to feeling abandoned, and often feel lonely and angry. Additionally, children can become the target of wives' frustration and anger resulting in part from quality of life changes. Such psychosocial factors can lead to negative long-term effects including intergenerational incarceration. For instance, children of incarcerated parents are at high risk for delinquency (29.6 percent), gang involvement (22.2 percent), and incarceration (10 percent) (Gabel & Johnston 1995). Also, children of prisoners are five to six times more likely than are their peers to become incarcerated.

The experiences and attitudes that fathers develop while imprisoned also profoundly affect the family. Incarceration separates African American men from their source of identity and well-being in the community. The stigma of serving a jail sentence may raise men's doubts regarding their abilities to fulfill parental and spousal roles. They also may fear being replaced and that their children will forget them or lose respect for them. Such role strain can lead to withdrawal from family relationships, engagement in risky behaviors, and discouragement of children from identifying fathers as role models (Bowman 1989; King 1993).

Health Challenges

Health challenges pose a serious threat to the African American nuclear family. High mortality rates are the largest contributor to the steady decline in the ratio of African American men to women (Gibbs 1990). Not only are African American men dying faster and younger than are men of other ethnicities, but the cause of death among African American men is different. The "new morbidity" refers to life-threatening diseases that are primarily the result of social phenomena, including homicide, suicide, drug problems, and AIDS (Gibbs 1990).

Homicide is the largest cause of mortality in African American males under age forty-five (Gibbs 1990). The death rate for black males ages fifteen to nineteen is 202.4 deaths per 100,000 and 300.8 deaths per 100,000 for black males ages twenty to twenty-four (National Center for Health Statistics 1997). In 1997 alone, 49 percent of homicide victims were black males, and 94 percent of black murder victims were slain by black offenders. African American men are also dying as a result of suicide. Since 1960, the suicide rate for African American men between the ages of fifteen and thirty-five had tripled (Allen-Meares & Burman 1995). Among black males aged fifteen to nineteen years, the suicide rate increased 146 percent between 1980 and 1995 (Centers for Disease Control 1998).

Serious issues with alcohol and drug abuse have rendered parents unfit and unable to care for their children. Alcohol and drug abuse, particularly the use of crack cocaine, has produced grandmother-only households where children of addicted parents live with grandparents (Burton 1992; Minkler, Roe & Price 1992). Studies by Burton (1992) and Minkler, Roe, and Price (1992) suggest that grandmother-only parenting has serious implications for the nature of family life and child rearing because of the added stress of having an addicted adult child as well as the stress of "off-time" parenting.

Acquired immune deficiency syndrome (AIDS), contracted primarily by intravenous drug use and unprotected sexual intercourse, is a major contributor to the new morbidity of African Americans. Representing only 12 percent of the U.S. population, African Americans make up 37 percent of all reported AIDS cases and 57 percent of HIV diagnoses, according to the Centers for Disease Control (CDC 1999). Fifty-eight out of every one hundred thousand African Americans contract AIDS, which is twice the contraction rate for Latinos and eight times the rate for whites (CDC 1999). African American men comprise over 35 percent of all adult AIDS cases yet constitute only 4 percent of the U.S. population (U.S. Bureau of the Census 2000). AIDS is growing fastest among African American women; 63 percent of women with AIDS are African American (CDC 1999). Mortality from AIDS in African Americans is concentrated in people between the ages of twenty-five and forty-four, a statistic that has serious implications for family life and parental involvement (Kain 1993).

Although the social, economic, and personal statuses of African American women serve as a catalyst for many of the challenges that African American families experience, the socioeconomic and health status of African American men appears to be a central source of the problems their families experience. Men, husbands, and fathers experience economic strife, incarceration, illness, and increased mortality more than do women, wives, and mothers. It is important that researchers and practitioners heed to the changing demographics of African Americans and understand the causes and implications of these changes. Specifically, attention must be paid to differences in the structure of single parenthood and to the roles of fathers and grandmothers in family functioning and child rearing.

Child Welfare

History and Composition

In the United States, systems have been designed to ensure that the family environment is healthy for its members. The child welfare system specifically is interested in the well-being of family members who are unable to fully care for and defend themselves—children. Beginning in the nineteenth century, childhood began to be viewed as a particularly innocent and vulnerable time that required special consideration and protection (Barnett, Manly & Cicchetti 1993). Orphanages were established to house children whose parents were deceased or whose families could not provide for them. Finally, the free foster home, stimulated by the abolition of slavery, was established. It began as a form of indenture, as parents were not paid for their care and the children had to work for shelter and care (Chipungu 1997).

The child welfare system has been most concerned with child maltreatment. Child maltreatment is defined as "the physical or mental injury, sexual abuse or exploitation, negligent treatment, or maltreatment of a child by a person who is responsible for the child's welfare, under circumstances which indicate that the child's health or welfare is harmed or threatened thereby, as determined in accordance with regulations prescribed by the Secretary of the U.S. Dept of Health and Human Services" (Tatara 1997). Violence is considered an act carried out with the intention of causing physical pain or injury to another, and abuse is an act of violence with high probability of causing injury (Straus, Gelles & Steinmetz 1980). The categories of child maltreatment are physical (major, minor, or unspecified physical injury); neglect (deprivation of necessities; failure by caretakers to provide shelter, nourishment, health care, education, supervision, and clothing); sexual abuse, which is the fastest growing category; emotional maltreatment (failure to provide emotional and psychological support); and emotional abuse (commission of abusive acts that are emotionally detrimental).

Child maltreatment is not only a symptom of individual or family trouble, but of neighborhood and community trouble as well. High-risk neighborhoods and families are a context for child maltreatment. Areas with a high absolute rate of child maltreatment and areas with a higher rate of child maltreatment than would be predicted knowing its socioeconomic character are considered high-risk (Garbarino, Kostelny & Grady 1993). Family instability increases the risk of child maltreatment, and African American families experience more changes and disruptions than do other ethnic minorities or whites (Hampton 1997;Wilson & Saft 1993). Single parenthood, divorce, poverty, substance abuse, living in a shelter, and institutionalization have been implicated as conditions that increase a child's vulnerability to negative developmental outcomes (Sternberg 1993).

African American children are separated disproportionately from their families by the child welfare system and placed in foster care (Kapp, McDonald & Diamond 2001). The total number of children in foster care has increased due in part to parental substance abuse and the deterioration of the economy. Children also are staying longer in foster care, and a significant number reenter foster care (Wells & Guo 1999). Children of color constitute 40 to 50 percent of the foster care population, although they comprise only 20 percent of the national population (Garland et al. 1998; McRoy, Oglesby & Grape 1997). Youth of color, especially African American youth, are more likely to remain in care longer, receive fewer services and contacts with caseworkers, and have a faster rate of reentry into the child welfare system than are white youth (Avery 2000; Garland et al. 1998; McRoy, Oglesby & Grape 1997; Wells & Guo 1999).

In addition to minority youth, the following categories of children have slower rates of reunification: infants, children in poor health, children who are from a single parent or relative home, eligible for AFDC, or entered foster care because of dependency or neglect; children who did not receive preplacement services; and children placed in kinship care (Courtney 1994; Davis, Landsverk & Newton 1997; Wells & Guo 1999). Children experiencing long delays in placement are more likely to have substantial disabilities, enter because of neglect, and be male, older when they enter care, part of a sibling group, and involuntarily removed from the birth parent's home (Avery 2000). Children with health problems, from families receiving government aid, and who entered foster care because of dependency had the fastest rates of reentry into the child welfare system (Courtney 1995; Wells & Guo 1999). Children who were older at exit, spent three months or less in care, were placed in nonrelative care, and had a higher number of placements during their first period of care also had high rates of reentry. The rising numbers of children entering the system are met with declining numbers of available foster homes (Wilhelmus 1998).

Challenges for African American Families

Child welfare programs never were conceived to serve African American children (Billingsley & Giovannoni 1972). Programs often fail to acknowledge the cultural experiences and expectations of African Americans, as suggested by the fact that child abuse rates between 1975 and 1985 decreased for whites but not for blacks (Hampton 1997). Current child welfare policies reflect the dominant values of society as they relate to families and children in general and to historical oppression of African Americans in particular. The current concept of child abuse in the United States is more political than scientific, and it implies behavior that is improper or immoral without providing a specific definition. Definitions are based on value judgments (Hampton 1997). The dominant American values of individualism, work ethic, sanctity of family, children as parents' property, and children as the responsibility of society influenced the development and provision of child welfare services for African American children (Chipungu 1997). Child welfare services, thus, are a result of a complex blend of racism, professionalism, sectarianism, and bureaucracy (Billingsley & Giovannoni 1972).

African American families may be the victims of a decision-making system for removing children from their birth families based on personal characteristics rather than on actual behavior (Hampton 1986). Unnecessary removal can occur when child welfare practitioners and policy makers fail to recognize cultural differences and variations in parenting and caregiving (Leashore, McMurray & Bailey 1997). For example, misperceptions of authoritarian parenting, which is adaptive for some children in dangerous environments, may cause professionals to misinterpret the environment in which some African American children are reared. When the cultural background of those labeling behaviors is vastly different from those who are being labeled, the potential for misinterpretations of behavior is exacerbated (Sternberg 1993). Socioeconomic differences between clinicians and African American parents create social distance and misunderstanding. Given popular biases that members of ethnic minorities, particularly those with low socioeconomic status (SES), are more tolerant of abusive behavior, professionals are mandated to err on the side of invading family privacy under the guise of protecting the children. Ethnic background, professional training, education, and social class influence the way behaviors are labeled abusive or normative (Sternberg 1993). Decisions often are based on deficits of available resources, personal values and biases, notions of ideal family, and accepted agency practice. Ethnic identity and SES influence the probability of being considered abusive. Without economic means to provide basic care, poor African American families are more likely to be reported for child abuse and neglect. In order to break the cycle, economic support and opportunities for poor and working-class families are needed (Leashore, McMurray & Bailey 1997).

More recent research also has identified several challenges African Americans face within the child welfare system in maintaining their parenting rights and abilities. Garland and associates (1998) tested the visibility hypothesis, which suggests that minority children have a higher probability of being placed in foster care when living in geographic locations where they are in small proportion, therefore more visible. In addition to high visibility, locally underrepresented minority groups may lack supports that could be protective against foster placement. Garland and associates found that minority youth were overrepresented in foster care and found support for the visibility hypothesis in that the more visible a child was in the community, the more likely that the child would be placed in foster care. The visibility phenomenon was specific to African American children, suggesting that race and racial distribution were determining factors in foster care placement rather than simply were confounds of SES.

Policy changes also may pose challenges for families. Avery (2000) asserted that many children grow up in foster care rather than in adoptive homes as a result of agency administrative and policy problems. Welfare reform potentially can increase reports of child maltreatment, increase the number of children entering the public child welfare system, slow rates of reunification, and hasten rates of reentry (Wells & Guo 1999). Stein (2000) found that child welfare policy changes have increased the number of children in foster care as well, in part due to professionals who misinterpret the reasonable efforts requirement in federal law.

The Adoption Assistance and Child Welfare Act (AACWA) of 1980 was designed to make reasonable efforts to prevent removal of children from their own home, limiting the number of children in foster care and promoting family reunification (Wells & Guo 1999). The Adoption and Safe Families Act (ASFA) of 1997 reflects a shift in philosophy from the family preservation and reunification theme prevalent since 1980 to a focus on achieving permanency through adoption. It attempts to balance efforts to reunite families, limit time spent in foster care, and provide a safe and stable permanent home (Wells & Guo 1999). The ASFA arose from concerns that efforts to reunite families favored parental rights over a child's safety and need for stability (Stein 2000). Stein concluded that the ASFA creates a false dichotomy that places parents' rights against children's rights. Although the ASFA sanction of termination of parental rights without reasonable efforts to reunite children with parents who committed severe abuse protects children, media-sensationalized cases have caused some parents to be punished with little evidence of social benefit for children. Stein concluded that the ASFA might have the opposite of its intended consequence, increasing the number of children who are available for adoption, but not necessarily the number of children actually adopted.

Professionals in the legal and child welfare systems also may present challenges for families in general and African Americans in particular. In some jurisdictions, general courts preside over child welfare cases. Family courts may suffer from inexperienced judges, different judges in the course of a single case, prolonged delays, overcrowded dockets, and inattention to permanency issues as well (Stein 2000). The child welfare system suffers from similar problems. Stein found that a minority of child welfare staff has formal social work education. Professionals may have insufficient service training and knowledge about specific disabilities and a subsequent lack of skills needed to engage clients (Avery 2000; Stein 2000). The child welfare system also suffers from inadequate resources, high turnover of child welfare workers, and unmanageable caseloads. The high caseloads and limited intervention skills might cause workers to attend to the least difficult client, who may be a foster parent, as opposed to biological parents with significant problems.

Negative attitudes and insufficient knowledge can create agency policies, practices, structures, and a climate that impede rapid placement of hard-to-place children. Private and public agencies have been reluctant either to establish or to use specialized minority adoption recruitment programs (McKenzie 1993). Caseworkers not convinced of the adoptability of a child appear to take reduced recruitment efforts on behalf of the child (Avery 2000). Some agency practices and attitudes continue to present obstacles for potential adoptive minority parents, with many African American families interested in adoption being screened out for various reasons (McRoy, Oglesby & Grape 1997).

Finally, the concept of the nuclear family negatively impacts African Americans involved in the child welfare system. Foster care draws on the nuclear family model, which is idealized and considered the most common or healthy family structure. According to Brown, Cohon, and Wheeler (2002), the foster care model cannot adequately capture the lives of kinship care families, which can serve as a solution to increasing child welfare rates, declining availability of foster parents, and continued concern for culturally competent placements for children (Wilhelmus 1998). The foster care model fails to capture the variety of family situations in kinship care families and the adaptive and flexible nature of the families (Brown, Cohon & Wheeler 2002).

Relative placement may ease the disruption that abused and neglected children experience upon removal from their homes. Whereas foster care places children with new, more stable families, kinship care moves children to a more stable part of their own families. Kinship care, unlike traditional foster care, draws on family support resources and inherent strengths (Brown, Cohon & Wheeler 2002). Despite the benefits and utility of kinship care, little evidence exists that caseworkers involve others, such as extended family, in the permanence planning process (Gleeson, O'Donnell & Bonecutter 1997). The nuclear family is not the typical family in America, due to growing marital instability that has caused contemporary families to become more malleable, fluid, and diverse (Brown, Cohon & Wheeler 2002). The idealization of the nuclear family, however, is significantly responsible for overlooking the extended family as a placement resource. Gleeson, O'Donnell, and Bonecutter (1997) concluded that the low rate of accomplishing permanent plans within a two-year period is due to the slow termination of parental rights, and the failure to discuss adoption early, and the failure to involve the extended family.

As ethnic differences in conceptualization (Rose & Meezan 1995) and management of child maltreatment exist, consideration of cultural context and an ecological framework are necessary to reform the child welfare system to make it more efficacious and equitable for African Americans. An ecological framework includes a progressive, mutual adaptation of organism and environment; the importance of quality of life for families and of socially rich environments in creating that life; and important aspects of human behavior that take place as a result of interactions that are shaped or controlled by indirect forces (Hampton 1997). A minority perspective on child welfare issues is needed for critiquing societal and professional ideologies and for understanding the stratification system from the viewpoint of the underprivileged. A minority worldview would combat the notion of poverty being attributed to laziness, depravity, and weakness, thus facilitating treatment rather than punishment of the underprivileged (Gould 1997).

Without culturally relevant services and prevention efforts, an orientation toward strengthening family and reducing violence is unlikely. The child welfare system must increase its capacity to provide family preservation services to families for whom placement is imminent. A quest for permanence for African American children is more than a demand for additional adoption services; it requires improving policy provisions available to vulnerable families, restructuring service delivery, and expanding permanency options to reflect social and cultural realities of African American family life. It is vital and potentially cost effective to mobilize and utilize available family resources and community-based support services to facilitate family and community preservation. Evaluation of the effectiveness of reform approaches also will be necessary to ensure proper service provision.

Conclusions

In the face of literature that often uses white families as the standard by which to evaluate all families, it is imperative to consider the context of African American life and examine African American families from a culture-specific perspective. Although part of the dominant culture, African American families function in distinctive ways as a result of external factors and African cultural values. External challenges such as economic marginality, incarceration, and health impediments have contributed to the mother-only composition of some African American homes. The involvement of extended family members in African American families is consistent with the communal and familial African cultural values. Assistance from extended family and fictive kin also is a response to the challenges some African American families face, and in part explains greater recovery from divorce and adequate functioning of many African American children in comparison to their white counterparts. More authoritarian parenting styles are responses to societal dangers African American children may face. Research (e.g., Baumrind 1972; Brody & Flor 1998) has found a parenting style consisting of both authoritarian and nurturing components adaptive for African American youth. Unlike Baumrind's authoritarian parenting style that is considered negative, many parents, children, and researchers deem the more parent-centered style as positive. It is thus vital to alter assumptions about family practices and what constitutes a family, recognizing that concepts such as the nuclear family are ideologically and culturally extolled rather than inherently advantageous arrangements (Brown, Cohon & Wheeler 2002), and that family structures and parenting styles that contrast the established norms are not inherently maladaptive.

While much of the research now being conducted on African American families is very valuable, there are still many areas to be explored. As indicated in the chapter, a multitude of factors influence African American structure, functioning, and outcomes and should be considered in both research and social intervention endeavors. A dearth of research exists examining the child welfare system's efficacy for African Americans and the effects of maltreatment on African American children, due in part to the lack of attention to the racial composition of targeted populations. Research on ethnic differences is contradictory, and more research is needed to understand the cultural differences and variables of maltreatment that have an impact on child maltreatment in the African American community (Wilson & Saft 1993). Culturally sensitive research will elucidate the cultural considerations (e.g., a professional's awareness of the client's and his or her own cultural background) that can help promote adaptive, effective child welfare system functioning and service delivery. A culturally sensitive and ecological perspective of child maltreatment is necessary for an effective prevention strategy. Cultural competence at the service delivery level of the child welfare system can be achieved only with recognition of the significance of culture in children's development, and would be reflected in an effort to maintain children in their own cultures.

The changing demographics of society require that the ever-increasing diversity be considered while recognizing complex interactions between the individual and the environment. Closer attention to both internal and external variables affecting African American families will facilitate an understanding of the complex nature of the family and the context in which it exists. In order to help families, a greater understanding of their cultural and societal context is necessary. A theoretical perspective that incorporates considerations of context and culture will aid in a comprehensive understanding of African American family life and elucidate the accomplishments as well as the needs of the African American family.

REFERENCES

Adalist-Estrin, A. 1994. "Family Support and Criminal Justice." In *Putting Families First: America's Family Support Movement and the Challenge of Change*, edited by S. L. Kagan & B. Weissbourd, 161–185. San Francisco: Jossey-Bass.

Allen-Meares, P., & S. Burman. 1995. "The Endangerment of African American Men: An Appeal for Social Work Action." *Social Work* 40/2:268–274.

Apfel, N. H., & V. Seitz. 1991. "Four Models of Adolescent Mother-Grandmother Relationships in Black Inner City Families." *Family Relations* 40/4:421–429.

Avery, R. J. 2000. "Perceptions and Practice: Agency Efforts for the Hardest-to-Place Children." *Children and Youth Services Review* 22/6:399–420.

Barnett, D., J. T. Manly & D. Cicchetti. 1993. "Defining Child Maltreatment: The Interface between Policy and Research." In *Child Abuse, Child Development, and Social Policy*, edited by D. Cicchetti & S. L. Toth, 7–73. Norwood, NJ: Ablex Publishing.

Baumrind, D. 1971. "Current Patterns of Parental Authority." *Developmental Psychology Monographs* 4/1 (pt. 2).

——. 1972. "An Exploratory Study of Socialization Effects on Black Children: Some Black-White Comparisons." *Child Development* 43:261–267.

Belle, D., C. Longfellow & V. P. Makosky. 1982. "Stress, Depression and the Mother-Child Relationship: Report of a Field Study." *International Journal of Sociology of the Family* 12/2:251–263.

Billingsley, A., & J. M. Giovannoni. 1972. *Children of the Storm: Black Children and American Child Welfare.* New York: Harcourt Brace Jovanovich.

Boushey, H. 1998. "Two Alternative Tests of the Wage Curve: Does Discrimination Matter?" Retrieved May 27, 2002 from www.panix.com/~dhenwood/Race_curve.html.

Bowman, P. J. 1989. "Research Perspectives on Black Men: Role Strain and Adaptation across the Adult Life Cycle." In *Black Adult Development and Aging,* edited by R. L. Jones, 117–150. Berkeley, CA: Cobb & Henry.

———. 1990. "Coping with Provider Role Strain: Adaptive Cultural Resources among Black Husband-Fathers." *Journal of Black Psychology* 16/2:1–21.

———. 1993. "The Impact of Economic Marginality among African American Husbands and Fathers." In *Family Ethnicity: Strength in Diversity,* edited by H. P. McAdoo, 120–137. Thousand Oaks, CA: Sage Publications.

Brassard, J. 1979. "The Ecology of Divorce: A Case Study Analysis of Personal Social Networks and Mother-Child Interaction in a Divorced and Married Family." Paper presented at the annual meeting of the National Council on Family Relations, Boston, MA.

Brody, G. H., & D. L. Flor. 1998. "Maternal Resources, Parenting Practices, and Child Competence in Rural, Single-Parent African American Families." *Child Development* 69/3: 803–816.

Brown, S., D. Cohon & R. Wheeler. 2002. "African American Extended Families and Kinship Care: How Relevant Is the Foster Care Model for Kinship Care?" *Children and Youth Services Review* 24/1–2:53–77.

Burton, L. J. 1992. "Black Grandparents Rearing Children of Drug-Addicted Parents: Stressors, Outcomes, and Social Service Needs." *Gerontologist* 32/6:744–751.

Burton, L. M., & C. DeVries. 1992. "Challenges and Rewards: African American Grandparents as Surrogate Parents." *Generations* 16/3:51–54.

Center for Policy Alternatives. 2000. "Drive for Equal Pay Builds Greater Economic Security across the States." *Alternatives: Newsletter of the Center for Policy Alternatives* 8/3. Retrieved May 26, 2002 from www.stateaction.org/alternatives/altbody.cfm?volume =8.3.

Centers for Disease Control. 1998. "Suicide among Black Youths, United States 1980–1995." Retrieved June 2000 from www.cdc.gov/mmwr/preview/mmwrhtml/00051591.htm.

———. 1999. "HIV/AIDS among African Americans." Retrieved June 2, 2002, from www .cdc.gov/hiv/pubs/facts/afam.htm.

Chipungu, S. P. 1997. "A Value-Based Policy Framework." In *Child Welfare: An Africentric Perspective,* edited by J. E. Everett, S. P. Chipungu & B. R. Leashore, 290–305. New Brunswick, NJ: Rutgers University Press.

Colletta, N. 1979. "Support Systems after Divorce: Incidence and Impact." *Journal of Marriage and the Family* 41:837–846.

Courtney, M. 1994. "Factors Associated with the Reunification of Foster Children with Their Families." *Social Services Review* 68:81–108.

———. 1995. "Reentry to Foster Care of Children Returned to Their Families." *Social Services Review* 69:228–241.

Creighton, C. L. 1995. "Parenting in African American Families: Mothers' and Children's Perceptions." Pre-dissertation manuscript, University of Virginia.

Danziger, S. K., & N. Radin. 1990. "Absent Does Not Equal Uninvolved: Predictors of Fathering in Teen Mother Families." *Journal of Marriage and the Family* 52/3:636–642.

Davis, I., J. Landsverk & R. Newton. 1997. "Duration of Foster Care for Children Reunified within the First Year of Care." In *Child Welfare Research Review*. Vol. 2. Edited by J. Berrick, R. Barth & N. Gilbert, 272–293. New York: Columbia University Press.

Dye, J. 1989. "Parental Involvement in Curriculum Matters: Parents, Teachers, and Children Working Together." *Educational Research* 31:20–35.

Fishman, L. T. 1990. *Women at the Wall: A Study of Prisoners' Wives Doing Time on the Outside.* New York: State University of New York Press.

Flaherty, M. J. 1988. "Seven Caring Functions of Black Grandmothers in Adolescent Mothering." *Maternal-Child Nursing Journal* 17/3:191–207.

Gabel, K., & D. Johnston. 1995. *Children of Incarcerated Parents.* New York: Lexington Books.

Garbarino, J., K. Kostelny & J. Grady. 1993. "Children in Dangerous Environments: Child Maltreatment in the Context of Community Violence." In *Child Abuse, Child Development, and Social Policy*, edited by D. Cicchetti & S. L. Toth, 167–189. Norwood, NJ: Ablex Publishing.

Garland, A. F., E. Ellis-MacLeod, J. A. Landsverk, W. Ganger & I. Johnson. 1998. "Minority Populations in the Child Welfare System: The Visibility Hypothesis Reexamined." *American Journal of Orthopsychiatry* 68/1:142–146.

Gephart, M. P., & R. W. Pearson. 1988. "Contemporary Research in the Urban Underclass." *Items: Newsletter of Social Science Research Council* 42:1–10.

Gibbs, J. T. 1990. *Young, Black, and Male in America: An Endangered Species.* Dover, MA: Auburn House.

Gleeson, J. P., J. O'Donnell & F. J. Bonecutter. 1997. "Understanding the Complexity of Practice in Kinship Foster Care." *Child Welfare* 76/6:801–826.

Gould, K. H. 1997. "Limiting Damage Is Not Enough: A Minority Perspective on Child Welfare Issues." In *Child Welfare: An Africentric Perspective*, edited by J. E. Everett, S. P. Chipungu & B. R. Leashore, 58–78. New Brunswick, NJ: Rutgers University Press.

Hampton, R. L. 1986. "Race, Ethnicity, and Child Maltreatment: An Analysis of Cases Recommended and Reported by Hospitals." In *The Black family: Essays and Studies.* 3rd ed. Edited by R. Staples, 172–185. Belmont, CA: Wadsworth.

———. 1997. "Child Abuse in the African American Community." In *Child Welfare: An Africentric Perspective*, edited by J. E. Everett, S. P. Chipungu & B. R. Leashore, 220–246. New Brunswick, NJ: Rutgers University Press.

Jackson, K. L. 1997. "Differences in the Background and Criminal Justice Characteristics of Young Black, White, and Hispanic Male Federal Prison Inmates." *Journal of Black Studies* 27/4:494–509.

Kain, E. 1993. "Race, Mortality, and Families." In *Family Ethnicity: Strength in Diversity*, edited by H. P. McAdoo, 60–78. Thousand Oaks, CA: Sage Publications.

Kamii, C., & N. Radin. 1967. "Class Differences in Socialization Practices of Negro Mothers." *Journal of Marriage and the Family* 29:302–310.

Kapp, S. A., T. P. McDonald & K. L. Diamond. 2001. "The Path to Adoption for Children of Color." *Child Abuse and Neglect* 25:215–229.

Kelley, M. L., T. G. Power & D. D. Wimbush. 1992. "Determinants of Disciplinary Practices in Low-Income Black Mothers." *Child Development* 63:573–582.

King, A. O. 1993. "The Impact of Incarceration on African American Families: Implications for Practice." *Families in Society* 74:145–153.

Leashore, B. R., H. L. McMurray & B. C. Bailey. 1997. "Reuniting and Preserving African American Families." In *Child Welfare: An Africentric Perspective*, edited by J. E. Everett, S. P. Chipungu & B. R. Leashore, 247–265. New Brunswick, NJ: Rutgers University Press.

Lindsey, D. 1991. "Factors Affecting the Foster Care Placement Decision: An Analysis of the National Survey Data." *American Journal of Orthopsychiatry* 61:272–281.

McAdoo, H. P. 1982. "Stress Absorbing Systems in Black Families." *Journal of Applied Family and Child Studies* 31/4:479–488.

———. 1986. "A Black Perspective on the Father's Role in Child Development." *Marriage and Family Review* 9:77–133.

———. 1988. "The Roles of Black Fathers in the Socialization of Black Children." In *Black Families*, edited by H. P. McAdoo, 257–269. Beverly Hills, CA: Sage.

———. 1995. "Stress Levels, Family Help Patterns, and Religiosity in Middle and Working-Class African American Single Mothers." *Journal of Black Psychology* 21/4:424–449.

McKenzie, J. 1993. "Adoption of Children with Special Needs." In *The Future of Children*, edited by I. Schulman, 3/1:62–76.

McRoy, R. G., Z. Oglesby & H. Grape. 1997. "Achieving Same-Race Adoptive Placements for African American Children: Culturally Sensitive Practice Approaches." *Child Welfare* 76/1:85–104.

Minkler, M., K. M. Roe & M. Price. 1992. "The Physical and Emotional Health of Grandmothers Raising Grandchildren in the Crack Cocaine Epidemic." *Gerontologist* 32/6: 752–761.

National Center for Health Statistics. 1997. "Report on Final Mortality Statistics, 1995." Retrieved June 2002 from www.cdc.gov/nchs/data/statnt/statnt23.pdf.

National Women's Law Center. 1995. "Chicago Legal Aid to Incarcerated Mothers." Retrieved May 27, 2002 from www.unix.oit.umass.edu/~kastor/walking-steel-95/ws-women in prison.html.

Pearson, J. L., A. G. Hunter, M. E. Ensminger & S. G. Kellam. 1990. "Black Grandparents in Multigenerational Households: Diversity in Family Structure and Parenting Involvement in the Woodlawn Community. *Child Development* 61:434–442.

Peters, M. F. 1976. "Nine Black Families: A Study of Household Management and Childrearing in Black Families with Working Mothers." PhD diss., Harvard University.

———. 1981. "Childrearing Patterns in a Sample of Black Parents of Children Age One to Three." Paper presented at annual meeting of the Society for Research in Child Development.

———. 1988. "Parenting in Black Families with Young Children: A Historical Perspective." In *Black Families*, edited by H. P. McAdoo, 228–241. Beverly Hills, CA: Sage.

Pinderhughes, E. E. 1991. "The Delivery of Child Welfare Services to African American Clients." *American Journal of Orthopsychiatry* 61/4:599–605.

Portes, P. R., R. M. Dunham & S. Williams. 1986. "Assessing Child-Rearing Style in Ecological Settings: Its Relation to Culture, Social Class, Early Age Intervention, and Scholastic Achievement." *Adolescence* 21/83:723–735.

Radin, N., & C. Kamii. 1965. "The Childrearing Attitudes of Disadvantaged Negro Mothers and Some Educational Implications." *Journal of Negro Education* 34:138–146.

Reynolds, A. 1989. "A Structural Model of First-Grade Outcomes for an Urban, Low Socioeconomic Status, Minority Population." *Journal of Educational Psychology* 81:594–603.

Rose, S. J., & W. Meezan. 1995. "Child Neglect: A Study of the Perception of Mothers and Child Welfare Workers." *Children and Youth Services Review* 17/4:471–486.

The Sentencing Project. 2001. "National Inmate Population of Two Million Projected for 2001." Retrieved May 27, 2002 from www.sentencingproject.org.

Slaughter, D. T., & P. Dilworth-Anderson. 1988. "Care of Black Children with Sickle Cell Disease: Fathers, Maternal Support, and Esteem." *Family Relations* 37:281–287.

Staples, R., & L. B. Johnson. 1993. *Black Families at the Crossroads*. San Francisco: Jossey-Bass.

Stein, T. J. 2000. "The Adoption and Safe Families Act: Creating a False Dichotomy Between Parents' and Families' Rights." *Families in Society* 81/6:586–592.

Sternberg, K. J. 1993. "Child Maltreatment: Implications for Policy from Cross-Cultural Research." In *Child Abuse, Child Development, and Social Policy*, edited by D. Cicchetti & S. L. Toth, 191–211. Norwood, NJ: Ablex Publishing.

Stevens, J. H. 1988. "Social Support, Locus of Control, and Parenting in Three Low-Income Groups of Mothers: Black Teenagers, Black Adults, and White Adults." *Child Development* 59:635–642.

Straus, M. A., R. J. Gelles & S. Steinmetz. 1980. *Behind Closed Doors: Violence in the American Family*. New York: Doubleday.

Tatara, T. 1997. "Overview of Child Abuse and Neglect." In *Child Welfare: An Africentric Perspective*, edited by J. E. Everett, S. P. Chipungu & B. R. Leashore, 187–219. New Brunswick, NJ: Rutgers University Press.

Thompson, M., K. Alexander & D. Entwisle. 1988. "Household Composition, Parental Expectations, and School Achievement." *Social Forces* 67:424–451.

Thompson, M. S., & M. E. Ensminger. 1989. "Psychological Well-Being Among Mothers with School-Age Children: Evolving Family Structures." *Social Forces* 67/3:715–730.

U.S. Bureau of the Census. 1999. "Poverty 1999." Retrieved June 2, 2002 from www.census .gov/hhes/poverty/poverty99/pv99est1.html.

———. 2000. "Black Population in the United States: March 2000." Retrieved June 2, 2002 from www.census.gov/population/socdemo/race/black/ppl-142/tab01.txt.

Wells, K., & S. Guo. 1999. "Reunification and Reentry of Foster Care." *Children and Youth Services Review* 21/4:273–294.

Wilhelmus, M. 1998. "Mediation in Kinship Care: Another Step in the Provision of Culturally Relevant Child Welfare Services." *Social Work* 43/2:117–126.

Wilson, M. N. 1984. "Mothers' and Grandmothers' Perceptions of Parental Behavior in Three-Generational Black Families." *Child Development* 55:1333–1339.

Wilson, M. N., L. P. Kohn, J. Curry-El & I. D. Hinton. 1995. "The Influence of Family Structure Characteristics on the Child-Rearing Behaviors of African American Mothers." *Journal of Black Psychology* 21/4:450–462.

Wilson, M. N., & E. W. Saft. 1993. "Child Maltreatment in the African American Community." In *Child Abuse, Child Development, and Social Policy*, edited by D. Cicchetti & S. L. Toth, 213–247. Norwood, NJ: Ablex Publishing.

Wilson, M. N., T.F.J. Tolson, I. D. Hinton & M. Kiernan. 1990. "Flexibility and Sharing of Childcare Duties in Black Families." *Sex Roles* 22/7–8:409–425.

Wilson, M. N., & T. F. Tolson. 1990. "Familial Support in the Black Community." *Journal of Clinical Child Psychology* 19/4:347–355.

6

Child-Rearing Practices in African American Families

CARMEN P. MOTEN

Socialization is the process by which a child acquires functional skills for social interaction to become a self-sufficient, competent adult (Wilson et al. 1995). The cultural styles and child-rearing practices unique to African American families provide supportive and nurturing environments for the development of their children (Richardson 1981). The objective of this chapter is to provide a selective literature review related to the parenting styles of African American families in the socialization of their children, and thereby inform child welfare policy, practice, and research. The chapter examines parental expectations, child-rearing practices, and parent training intervention programs.

Parental Expectations

Various scholars have sought to delineate values that have been paramount in African American families, irrespective of socioeconomic status. These values include commitment to education, self-help, service to others, and a strong religious and spiritual orientation. Several authors have noted that these values are not exclusive to African Americans. To some degree they are embraced by cultures in most, if not all, parts of the world (Billingsley 1992; Sudarkasa 1997).

Studies of African American and other ethnic families have shown that the attitudes, economic stressors, expectations, and behaviors of their parents affect children's academic performance abilities. Parents' expectations of their children's academic abilities are one of the best predictors of children's perceptions of their abilities (Vasta et al. 1995). Studies have shown that children who view themselves as academically skilled are more motivated to succeed, more persistent in their work, and more willing to seek out challenging tasks or problems (Boggiano, Main & Katz 1988; Harter 1988; Harter & Connell 1984; Schunk 1984; Vasta et al. 1995). As significant, children with low expectations of their academic abilities are less motivated to succeed. One study found that even among children whose academic skills were high, those who held a low opinion of their competence approached new tasks with less effort and optimism than did their classmates. Thus, for some children, academic success may hinge as much on academic self-concept as it does on academic ability (Phillips 1984, 1987).

The value of academic success to the child may seem obvious, but its effects can reach beyond the classroom. For example, a three-city study on welfare, children, and families suggests that preschoolers and adolescents in families of lower socioeconomic status are often more developmentally placed at risk compared with middle-class American children in either the cognitive or behavioral realms. Of greatest concern are the preschoolers of families who have experienced sanctions (a reduction or elimination of benefits) and/or left welfare; these preschoolers show rates of behavior problems three times higher than the national norms. To leave public assistance, particularly after being sanctioned, may be especially stressful for families with young children who must balance child care, employment, and parenting responsibilities. Also of concern are adolescents of recipients of welfare and sanctioned former recipients who show evidence of being placed at risk for academic failure and poor mental health (Chase-Lansdale et al. 2002).

Beyond the overriding goal of preparing children to succeed in academia, self-help is an active value in many African American families. This communal helping value focuses on outreach efforts aimed toward building a community-based support network of existing organizations for the purpose of providing public education and awareness, and physical and mental health services. The presence of formal and informal social and interpersonal community networks can promote increased social connection with others and provide social support for positive parenting (Sampson 1992). Communities in which residents seldom interact may promote social isolation, which can lead to non-optimal parenting (Furstenberg et al. 1993). Noteworthy, despite gains from housing subsidies, families receiving housing assistance are more likely to reside in undesirable communities where concerns about children, crime, and social isolation are greater (Quane, Rankin & Joshi 2002).

Religion and spirituality are values that have been vital in African American families, irrespective of socioeconomic status. It is important that children understand, respect, and obey the spiritual being that makes them a living human soul. Religion and spirituality provide a foundation of meaning through which life events can be understood (Blaine & Crocker 1995; Ellison 1993; Peterson & Roz 1985), and linking spiritual meaning, faith, and belief to life events may foster coping capabilities and increase levels of social support (Sherkat & Reed 1992). Attending church (or other places of worship), praying, evangelizing to non-Christians, fellowshipping with other Christians, and reading the Bible daily (or other forms of worship) have been linked to stronger mental and physical well-being in African American families (Blaine & Crocker 1995). Church attendance may provide social interactions that result in families under stress and strain receiving positive reflective appraisals, parental assistance, and spiritual guidance from individuals with similar values and experiences (Demo & Hughes 1990; Ellison 1993). The church also provides opportunities for individuals to attain positions of leadership in accordance with the laws of God (or one's spiritual being), which may be unavailable in mainstream/secular society (Demo & Hughes 1990). Such roles may enhance coping abilities that can be applied not only in the church but also in the wider environment. Finally, the church provides role models for younger African American members and is a mechanism for community action (Murry 2000; Taylor, Thornton & Chatters 1987).

Child-Rearing Practices

Baumrind (1989), in a series of research studies, has described three general styles of parenting that have been found to produce direct outcomes in children across all ethnic groups and socioeconomic status: authoritarian, authoritative, and permissive (McAdoo 1997; MacDonald 1992; Vasta et al. 1995). Parents who are low in warmth but high in control are termed authoritarian parents. Authoritarian parents are very demanding, lacking nurturance and clarity in communication, exercising strong control over their children's behavior, and enforcing their demands with threats and punishment. Children of authoritarian parents often lack empathy and self-confidence; are easily upset, displaying moodiness, aggression, or disobedience; and demonstrate apathy, dependence, and conduct problems (Baumrind 1989; Vasta et al. 1995).

Parents who are high in both warmth and control are referred to as authoritative parents. These parents tend to have high expectations for their children,

TABLE 6.1
Patterns of Parental Child-Rearing Practices

Pattern	Control High	Low	Clarity of Communication High	Low	Maturity Demands High	Low	Warmth/ Nurturance High	Low
Authoritarian	X			X	X			X
Authoritative	X		X		X		X	
Permissive		X	X			X	X	

Source: Based on D. Baumrind, "Childcare Practices Anteceding Three Patterns of Preschool Behavior," *Genetic Psychology Monographs* 75 (1967):43–88.

but make demands on them as well as set clear limits on behavior and maintain a supportive and nurturing environment. This parenting style has the most positive effects on early social development. Children of authoritative parents generally are competent, nonaggressive, self-reliant, high on self-esteem, sociable, altruistic, considerate, curious, self-confident, independent, academically successful, cooperative, and obedient with their parents (Baumrind 1989; Vasta et al. 1995).

Parents who are high in warmth but low in control are called permissive parents. These parents are loving and emotionally sensitive but set few clear limits on behavior. Surprisingly, children of permissive parents in some ways resemble those of authoritarian parents; they often lack self-reliance, maturity, and self-control (Baumrind 1989; Vasta et al. 1995).

In the ensuing studies, child-rearing practices in African American families will be presented through complex realms of cultural beliefs, expectations, interactions, and traditions, when compared with authoritarian, authoritative, and permissive parenting styles. There is surprisingly scarce empirical research on family relationships and child-rearing practices of families receiving public assistance. A challenge for researchers, policy makers, child welfare administrators, and clinicians will be not only to determine the child-rearing practices of families in mainstream society, but also to examine the parenting styles of parents of children in the welfare system, particularly those involved in child welfare services. These efforts will provide a richer empirical understanding of how risk factors impact the physical and behavioral development of children across all racial and ethnic groups and socioeconomic status.

In a study of child-rearing (disciplinary) practices, Bradley (1998) examined the types of disciplinary methods used in African American families. One hundred twenty-one African American parents (age eighteen to seventy-nine years) completed a self-report questionnaire. African American parents preferred to use nonphysical forms of discipline and seemed to refute the opinions of those social scientists who asserted that African American parents engage in very little give-and-take dialogue with their children. However, the findings also seem to be consistent with the notion that African American parents embrace a more authoritative approach to discipline. In each case, when the parents used physical/punitive punishment, the situation involved a child who directly challenged the authority of the parent.

Likewise, in a preliminary study, Hill (1995) examined the relationship of African American family environment and parenting style of 174 ninth and eleventh graders and college freshmen (96 percent African American). They completed the J. R. Buri's Parent Authority Questionnaire (PAQ) and the R. H. Moos Family Environment Scale (FES). Authoritarianism was positively correlated with control and negatively correlated with expressiveness and independence. Authoritativeness was positively correlated with cohesion, organization, achievement, and intellectual orientation. Authoritativeness was negatively associated with expressiveness. Permissiveness was negatively correlated with conflict and positively correlated with expressiveness. The responses on the FES were compared between parents and adolescents. On seven of the ten PAQ and FES subscales, there were significant correlations between mothers and adolescents, whereas on only one subscale were fathers and adolescents significantly correlated.

As important, Taylor, Casten, and Elickinger (1993) assessed the association of kinship support with psychosocial adjustment and child-rearing practices for 125 African American adolescents (52 boys and 73 girls) in grades nine through twelve from single- and two-parent households. Findings revealed that kinship support was positively associated with adolescent adjustment and with authoritative child-rearing practices in single- but not two-parent households. Results also indicate that child-rearing practices mediated the effects of kinship support. When the effects of authoritative child-rearing practices were controlled, significant relations found between kinship support and adolescent adjustment were no longer apparent. The importance of kinship support among African American families is key to the social, emotional, and cognitive development of children.

In a series of studies involving African American mothers, Bluestone and Tamis-LeMonda (1999) examined sociodemographic and psychological determinants of child-rearing and disciplinary practices among 114 working- and middle-class African American mothers (mean age 37.4 years) of children ages five to twelve using the Parenting Dimensions Inventory (PDI). Results revealed significant variation among parents in their disciplinary strategies. Reasoning, which is characteristic of authoritative parenting, was the most frequently reported strategy. It is suggested that maternal education, socioeconomic status, child-rearing history, and maternal depression differentially predicted child-centered parenting, reasoning, and mothers' tendencies to let a situation go. The study emphasized the importance of extending evidence-based models of child-rearing determinants to underrepresented areas of African American families in order to gain a fuller understanding of the factors that contribute to diverse styles of parenting.

Reis (1993), in a study on African American and Caucasian adolescent mothers' child-rearing beliefs and behaviors, assessed whether African American mothers were more likely than Causasian mothers to advocate some authoritarian child-rearing practices. African American and white mothers with desirable attitudes toward parenting and positive parenting behaviors exceeded the number expected on the basis of chance alone. In contrast, African American mothers were not as punitively oriented in either words or deeds as depicted in sociological analyses. The results point to the importance of recognizing diversity in parental attitudes and behavior both between and within racial and ethnic groups in the broader context of the changing role of adolescent mothers in our society.

In a series of studies involving the impact of child-rearing practices on academic performance, Taylor, Hinton, and Wilson (1995) investigated the effects of parenting style, parental involvement, and parental expectations of ability on academic outcomes for African American students. African American families with at least one child in the five- to eighteen-year-old age group from the National Survey of Families and Households Data were used. Results revealed that parental expectations of ability did not significantly predict academic outcomes of students. Students with parents who use an authoritarian parenting style received lower grades in school than did students whose parents practiced an authoritative style. The grades of students with permissive parents were also found to be lower than that of students with authoritative parents. It was concluded that child-rearing practices (warmth/nurture and control) and parental involvement significantly predicted academic outcomes. Steinberg, Brown, and Bradford (1993) addressed the issues of parenting and ethnic differences in adolescent academic achievement. Using data collected from a large sample of high school students, Steinberg and colleagues challenged three widely held explanations for the "high" school performance of Asian American adolescents and the "low" school performance of African American and Hispanic American adolescent group differences in (1) child-rearing practices, (2) familial values about education, and (3) students' belief about the career rewards of academic success. They found that Caucasian students benefit from the combination of authoritative parenting and peer support for achievement, whereas Hispanic youngsters experience a combination of parental authoritarianism and low peer support. Among Asian American students, peer support for academic excellence offsets the negative consequences of authoritarian parenting. Among African American students, the absence of peer support for achievement undermines the positive influence of authoritative parenting.

Noteworthy, Radziszewska et al. (1996) examined whether the relationship between child-rearing practices and adolescent depressive symptoms, smoking, and academic grades varies according to ethnicity, gender, and socioeconomic status. The study included 3,993 fifteen-year-old African American, Caucasian, Hispanic, and Asian adolescents. The results are generally consistent with the literature: adolescents with authoritative parents had the best outcomes and those with authoritarian parents were least well adjusted, while the permissive style produced intermediate results. For the most part, this pattern held across ethnic and sociodemographic subgroups. There was one exception, suggesting that the relationship between child-rearing practices, especially the authoritarian style, and depressive symptoms may vary according to gender and ethnicity. In sum, intensive research is needed to replicate and explain this pattern in terms of ecological factors, socioeconomic status, cultural norms, and socialization goals and practices.

As important, Jackson, Clark, and Hermons (1993) used standardized scores to illustrate the relationship between socioeconomic status and academic performance among urban African American children. California Achievement Test scores in mathematics were collected for 79 Caucasian and 212 African American third graders (146 boys and 145 girls). The influence of social class was apparent in the fact that middle-class African Americans had higher test scores than did Caucasian children from working-class backgrounds. The results support the thesis of Blau (1981) that regardless of race, middle-class children receive more praise and are treated with less authoritarianism, resulting in greater individual self-confidence and self-esteem.

Parent Training Intervention Programs

Given that children in the welfare system are growing in number and are placed at risk for behavior problems (Fisher and Chamberlin 2000), there is surprisingly limited empirical research on parental training programs that meet the needs of parents of children in the system, specifically ethnic and culturally diverse programs.

In mainstream society, however, parental discipline styles (e.g., parental strategies for managing and controlling child behavior) and conflict management (e.g., behaviors that aid in exploring a given problem and that generate potential solutions) have been primary targets for many parental training programs. These programs have consistently documented that positive and nurturing parental discipline and conflict management styles of parenting lead to improvements in child and adolescent conduct (Webster-Stratton 1998, 2001), consistent with the authoritative approach. More specifically, therapeutic foster home placements that embrace a more authoritative approach to discipline have shown significant reductions in delinquency among adjudicated youth (Chamberlin and Reid 1998; Fisher and Chamberlin 2000).

Evidence indicates that negative parental control and harsh parental discipline (as shown among authoritarian parents) during toddlerhood, as early as age two, predict increased risk for child aggression and behavior problems one, two, and five years later (Campbell 1994; Hann & Borek 2001). Some of this work has examined the role of early child negative emotionality and finds that both child negativity and parental coercion/permissiveness predict child behavior problems (Hann and Borek 2001; Vasta et al. 1995).

In middle childhood, and in early and later adolescence, consistent relationships between highly conflictual, inconsistent, harsh, and restrictive (authoritarian) parenting and child delinquent and antisocial behavior have been found in research using concurrent correlational designs (Hann & Borek 2001; Knight, Virdin & Roosa 1994). Predictive longitudinal studies also indicate that harsh and inconsistent parenting predicts later youth conduct problems (Hann & Borek 2001; Patterson et al. 1998; Wasserman et al. 1996). However, the direction of this influence may change over time, with a reciprocal relationship between disciplinary style and antisocial behavior in early and middle child-hood, but fading reciprocity as the child moves into adolescence (with parental behavior predicting child behavior) (Cohen & Brook 1995; Hann & Borek 2001). Also, there is some evidence that the experience of parental physical/punitive discipline may more strongly predict early childhood behavior problems than it does adolescent conduct problems (Feehan et al. 1991; Hann & Borek 2001). It is important to note, however, that modest to moderate effects of parental disci-pline and parent-child conflict with behavior problems still are detected in ado-lescence (Hann & Borek 2001; Neighbors, Forehand & Bau 1997; Steinberg et al. 1994).

Given these findings, it is essential for future research on parent training interventions relevant to child behavior problems include diverse ethnic ran-dom samples and methodologies sensitive to potential cultural distinctions. These efforts will provide not only a richer empirical understanding of how risk factors are similar or different across ethnic groups but also a much stronger base on which to develop evidence-based interventions relevant to our nation's diverse population and real-world settings (i.e., child welfare system) (Hann & Borek 2001). In many cases, this process will involve building collaborative rela-tionships with child welfare administrators, researchers, community leaders, and policy makers, as well as providers of mental health services.

Conclusions

Socialization is a life process built upon a paradox. The paradox is that at the same time we are both social and individual beings, connected with family and ancestors in a multitude of ways, as well as ultimately alone in the world (Damon 1983).

The selected literature presented in this chapter examines the parenting styles of African American families and the complex ways in which African American parental expectations, child-rearing practices, and parent training intervention programs impact the socialization of African American children. These family characteristics will enhance the growth and development of Afri-can American children to become self-sufficient, competent adults.

Unless we also explore the social, political, and economic realities of Afri-can American families receiving public assistance and those involved in child welfare services, we may overlook the possibility of producing changes in social, political, and economic policies by local, state, or federal governing agencies that determine and support culturally sensitive programs and evidence-based interventions for African American families and their children.

NOTE

The views expressed in this chapter are those of the author and should not be construed as the official position of the National Institute of Mental Health (NIMH).

REFERENCES

Baumrind, D. 1989. "Rearing Competent Children." In *Child Development Today and Tomorrow*, edited by W. Damom. San Francisco: Jossey-Bass.

Billingsley, A. 1992. *Climbing Jacob's Ladder*. New York: Simon & Schuster.

Blaine, R., & J. Crocker. 1995. "Religiousness, Race, and Psychological Well-Being: Exploring Social Psychological Mediators." *Personality and Social Psychology Bulletin* 21:1031–1041.

Blau, Z. 1981. *Black Children/White Children: Competence, Socialization, and Social Structure*. New York: Free Press.

Bluestone, C., & C. S. Tamis-LeMonda. 1999. "Correlations of Parenting Styles in Predominantly Working and Middle-Class African American Mothers." *Journal of Marriage and the Family* 61/4:881–893.

Boggiano, A. K., D. S. Main & P. A. Katz. 1988. "Children's Preference for Challenge: The Role of Perceived Competence and Control." *Journal of Personality and Social Psychology* 54:134–141.

Bradley, C. 1998. "Child Rearing in African American Families: A Study of the Disciplinary Practices of African American Parents." *Journal of Multicultural Counseling and Development* 26/4: 273–281.

Campbell, S. B. 1994. "Hard-to-Manage Preschool Boys: Externalizing Behavior, Social Competence, and Family Context at Two-Year Follow-Up." *Journal of Abnormal Child Psychology* 22/2:147–166.

Chamberlin, P., & J. B. Reid. 1998. "Comparison of Two Communities' Alternatives to Incarceration for Chronic Juvenile Offenders." *Journal of Consulting and Clinical Psychology* 66/4:624–633.

Chase-Lansdale, L., R. L. Coley, B. J. Lohman & L. D. Pittman. 2002. "Welfare Reform: What About the Children?" In *Welfare, Children, and Families: A Three City Study* (Policy Brief 02-1). Baltimore, MD: Johns Hopkins University.

Cohen, P., & J. S. Brook. 1995. "The Reciprocal Influence of Punishment and Child Behavior Disorder." In *Coercion and Punishment in Long-Term Perspectives*, edited by J. McCord, 154–164. New York: Cambridge University Press.

Damon, W. 1983. *Social and Personality Development: Infancy through Adolescence*. New York: W. W. Norton.

Demo, D., & M. Hughes. 1990. "Socialization and Racial Identity among Black Americans." *Social Psychology Quarterly* 53:364–374.

Ellison, C. G. 1993. "Religious Involvement and Self-Perception of Black Americans." *Social Forces* 71/4:1027–1055.

Feehan, M., R. McGee, W. R. Stanton & P. A. Silva. 1991. "Strict and Inconsistent Discipline in Childhood: Consequences for Adolescent Mental Health." *British Journal of Clinical Psychology* 30:325–331.

Fisher, P. A., & P. Chamberlain. 2000. "Multidimensional Treatment Foster Care: A Program for Intensive Parenting, Family Support, and Skill Building." *Journal of Emotional & Behavioral Disorders* 8/3:155–164.

Furstenberg, F. F., A. Belzer, C. Davis, J. A. Levine, K. Morrow & M. Washington. 1993. "How Families Manage Risk and Opportunity in Dangerous Neighborhoods." In *Sociology and the Public Agenda*, edited by W. J. Wilson, 231–238. Newbury Park: Sage.

Hann, D. M., & N. Borek. 2001. *Taking Stock of Risk Factors for Child/Youth Externalizing Behavior Problems*. Department of Health and Human Services. National Institutes of Health Publication number 02-4938.

Harter, S. 1988. "Development Processes in the Construction of the Self." In *Integrative Processes and Socialization: Early to Middle Childhood*, edited by T. D. Yawkey & J. E. Johnson. Hillsdale, NJ: Erlbaum.

Harter, S., & J. P. Connell. 1984. "A Model of the Relationship among Children's Academic Achievement and Their Self-Perceptions of Competence, Control, and Motivational Orientation." In *The Development of Achievement Motivation*, edited by J. Nichols. Greenwich, CT: JAI Press.

Hill, N. E. 1995. "The Relationship between Family Environment and Parenting Style: A Preliminary Study of African American Families." *Journal of Black Psychology* 21/4: 408–423.

Jackson, M., S. B. Clark & W. Hemons. 1991. "Class, Caste, and the Classroom: Effective Public Policy vs. Effective Public Education." *Western Journal of Black Studies* 15/4:242–247.

Knight, G. P., L. Virdin & M. Roosa. 1994. "Socialization and Family Correlates of Mental Health Outcomes among Hispanic and Anglo American Children: Consideration of Cross-Ethnic Scalar Equivalence." *Child Development* 65:212–224.

MacDonald, K. B. 1992. "Warmth as a Developmental Construct: An Evolutionary Analysis." *Child Development* 63:753–773.

McAdoo, H. P. 1997. *Black Families*. Thousand Oaks, CA: Sage Publications.

Murry, V. M. 2000. "Extraordinary Challenges and Ordinary Life Experiences of Black American Families." In *Family Stress and Change*. 2nd ed. Edited by P. C. McKenry & S. H. Price, 333–358. Thousand Oaks, CA: Sage Publications.

Neighbors, B. D., R. Forehand & J. J. Bau. 1997. "Interparental Conflict and Relations with Parents as Predictors of Young Adult Functioning." *Development and Psychopathology* 9:169–187.

Patterson, G. R., M. S. Forgatch, K.L. Yoerger & M. Stoolmiller. 1998. "Variables That Initiate and Maintain an Early-Onset Trajectory for Juvenile Offending." *Development and Psychopathology* 10:531–547.

Peterson, L. R., & A. Roz. 1985. "Religiosity, Anxiety, and Meaning and Purpose: Religion's Consequences for Psychological Well-Being." *Review of Religious Research* 27:49–62.

Phillips, D. A. 1984. "The Illusion of Incompetence among Academically Competent Children." *Child Development* 55:2000–2016.

———. 1987. "Socialization of Perceived Academic Competence among Highly Competent Children." *Child Development* 58:1308–1320.

Quane, J. M., B. H. Rankin & P. Joshi. 2002. "Housing Assistance, Housing Costs, and Welfare Reform." *Welfare, Children and Families: A Three-City Study* (Policy Brief 02-4). Baltimore, MD: Johns Hopkins University.

Radziszewska, B., J. L. Richardson, C. W. Dent & B. R. Hay. 1996. "Parenting Style and Adolescent Depressive Symptoms, Smoking, and Academic Achievement: Ethnic, Gender, and Socioeconomic Status Differences." *Journal of Behavioral Medicine* 19/3:289–305.

Reis, J. 1993. "Black and White Adolescent Mothers' Child-Rearing Beliefs and Behaviors." *Infant Mental Health Journal* 14/3:221–233.

Richardson, B. B. 1981. *Racism and Child-Rearing: A Study of Black Mothers*. Ph.D. diss., Claremont Graduate School.

Sampson, R. J. 1992. "Family Management and Child Development: Insights from Social Dis-organization Theory." In *Facts, Frameworks, and Forecasts: Advances in Criminological Theory*, edited by J. McCord, 63–93. New Brunswick, NJ: Transaction Books.

Schunk, D. H. 1984. "Self-Efficacy Perspective on Achievement Behavior." *Educational Psychologist* 19:48–58.

Sherkat, D. E., & M. D. Reed. 1992. "The Effects of Religion and Social Support on Self-Esteem and Depression among the Suddenly Bereaved." *Social Indications Research* 26:259–275.

Steinberg, L. D., S. M. Brown & B. Bradford. 1993. "Ethnic Differences in Adolescent Achievement: An Ecological Perspective." *Annual Progress in Child Psychiatry and Child Development* (528–543).

Steinberg, L., S. D. Lamborn, N. Darling, N. S. Mounts & S. M. Dornbusch. 1994. "Over-Time Changes in Adjustment and Competence among Adolescents from Authoritative, Authoritarian, Indulgent, and Neglectful Families." *Child Development* 65:754–770.

Sudarkasa, N. 1997. "African American Families and Family Values." In *Black Families*, edited by H. P. McAdoo, 9–40. Thousand Oaks, CA: Sage Publications.

Taylor, L., I. D. Hinton & M. N. Wilson. 1995. "Parental Influences on Academic Performance in African American Students." *Journal of Child and Family Studies* 4/3:293–302.

Taylor, R. D., R. Casten & S. M. Elickinger. 1993. "Influence of Kinship Social Support on the Parenting Experiences and Psychological Adjustment of African-American Adolescents." *Developmental Psychology* 29/2:382–388.

Taylor, R. J., M. C. Thornton & L. M. Chatters. 1987. "Black Americans' Perceptions of the Sociohistorical Role of the Church." *Journal of Black Studies* 18:123–138.

Vasta, R., M. M. Haith & S. A. Miller. 1998. *Child Psychology: The Modern Science.* 3rd Ed. New York: John Wiley.

Wasserman, G. A., L. S. Miller, E. Pinner & B. Jaramillo. 1996. "Parenting Predictors of Early Conduct Problems in Urban, High-Risk Boys." *Journal of the American Academy of Child and Adolescent Psychiatry* 35/9:1227–1236.

Webster-Stratton, C. 1998. "Preventing Conduct Problems in Head Start Children: Strengthening Parenting Competencies." *Journal of Consulting and Clinical Psychology* 66/5: 715–730.

———. 2001. "Nipping Early Risk Factors in the Bud: Preventing Substance Abuse, Delinquency, and Violence in Adolescence through Interventions Targeted at Young Children (Zero to Eight Years)." *Prevention Science* 2/3:165–192.

Wilson, M. N., L. P. Kohn, J. Curry-El & I. D. Hinton. 1995. "The Influence of Family Structure Characteristics on the Child-Rearing Behaviors of African American Mothers." *Journal of Black Psychology* 21/4:450–462.

7

Best Practices in Kinship Care for African American Mothers and Their Children

MARIAN S. HARRIS

Large numbers of African American children continue to be removed from the care of their birth mothers by the child welfare system and placed in kinship care. According to Petit, Curtis, Woodruff, Arnold, Feagans, and Ang (1999), African American children are overrepresented in kinship care. Yet, despite the ease with which they enter the child welfare system, limited research has been conducted to develop relevant knowledge regarding best practices for these children and their birth mothers. Although kinship care has been a noted topic of investigation in social work during the past several years, few studies have utilized African American mothers as research participants (Harris 1999). There has not been an emphasis on services that are contextually designed and implemented from an Africentric worldview. It is imperative to have knowledge and understanding of all members of the African American family and the significance of birth mothers in the lives of their children, when these children are placed in kinship care. This chapter will focus on collective identity versus individual identity and its relationship to best practices for African American birth mothers and their children placed in kinship care. The chapter is delineated into four sections. The first provides an overview of the history of African American mothers and their children. The second section examines collective identity and motherhood. The third discusses collective identity and intergenerational parenting, and the fourth section describes guidelines for assessment and intervention in child welfare practice.

History of African American Mothers and Their Children

Mothers have always had a very important role in African American culture and in the lives of their children. The role of the birth mother in a child's life encompasses helping in the development of a strong sense of self and ethnic identity,

nurturing, caregiving, modeling, educating, providing experiences for socialization and recreation, economic support, and assisting in the maintenance of intergenerational family connections. Despite the dehumanizing experiences of
slavery, African American mothers were vigilant in their efforts to develop and
maintain strong bonds with their children. According to Patterson (1967), "slave
mothers did everything to keep their children within their household and to dis-
courage any attempt at forming permanent unions outside" (cited in Mintz & Price
1976, 74). Many mothers ran away from their slave masters to keep their children
from being taken away from them and sold at slave auctions. It was even more
heartbreaking to learn of children running away to try and find their birth mothers and/or fathers. Mothers who departed with their children confronted special
difficulties. It was not easy to feed, clothe, care for, and protect children while on
the run. The physical burden of carrying babies or youngsters four or five years of
age was extreme, while the seven- or eight-year-olds had trouble keeping up and
often tired quickly. One runaway mother took her child despite his being "sick
with a sore mouth and cannot speak." Mothers themselves often suffered mal-
adies. Pregnant women also ran away. Twenty-one-year-old Lucille, a Louisiana
woman who set out in 1833, was "in an advanced stage of pregnancy." Nancy was
seven or eight months pregnant and was limping because of a sore toe when she
ran away in 1834, shortly before Christmas (Franklin & Schweninger 1999, 63–64).

   Although some mothers were able to obtain their freedom, many had children who were born prior to their emancipation. Many of these mothers risked
their lives to help their children who were in bondage. For example, the mother
of Kitty, a slave, had more influence than the typical slave and was able to conceal her when she ran away from her master (Franklin & Schweninger 1999).
Some children ran away and were assisted by free relatives in their quest to be
reunited with their mothers.

   From 1865 until 1871, many African American children and their families
were able to get land, work, and other direct services from the Freedmen's
Bureau (DuBois 1901). This government funded and regulated agency provided
in-home services to children and their families. Many African American mothers made tremendous sacrifices in order to keep their children when they
became emancipated.

   During the late 1800s, many civic and religious organizations (e.g.,
churches, lodges, women's clubs, men's clubs) in the African American community provided services to children and their families (Hill 1972). Mothers and
their children were able to live in their own homes and familiar neighborhoods
because of the support received from many of these organizations. Such informal support systems were highly significant in facilitating the maintenance of
the relationships between mothers and their children.

   The strong bond between African American mothers and their children has
existed from slavery to the present time. African Americans place a high value

on the relationship between mothers and their children. Best practices for them encompass knowledge and skills regarding the history of African American mothers and their children, as well as those factors inherent in African American culture that support rather than negate this bond.

The relationship between African American children and their mothers should be assessed within a cultural context. Although the institution of slavery had a profound impact on the lives of mothers and children, African American culture always placed a high value on mothers and their relationship with their children. Although the family was defined from a legal perspective as mother and child during slavery (Zipf 2000), children have always been significant in the African and African American culture because they represented continuation of life. It is imperative to understand this history in order to effectively plan and implement services that will enhance their lives, family relationships, and especially the well-being of children.

Mothers and Other Interconnections

The sharing of a collective identity becomes apparent when one examines the relationship of African American mothers with their children, extended family, and other interconnections in their lives. In African culture, as well as African American culture, it has been the norm for birth mothers to be assisted by other women in the community in caring for their children. These caregivers can be kin or "fictive kin" (Stack 1974). "Fictive kin relations are maintained by consensus between individuals, and in some contexts can last a lifetime" (Stack 1974, 59). This collective network of fictive kin is important in the lives of African American children and their mothers. It is imperative to understand that these female caregivers have been a central part of African American motherhood for a very long time.

Historically, not only were African American children cared for by their kin or fictive kin, but it was also common for neighbors to provide child care for children in their community. Neighbors cared for and were concerned about children collectively in the community rather than simply caring for the children in their individual families. African American mothers were cooperative and supportive of each other as a collective rather than an individual entity in child rearing. Othermothers and grandmothers play the following roles in the upbringing of the African American child: formal and informal caregiving (fostering and adopting); nurturing; providing emotional and financial support, goods, and services; child care; modeling; and maintaining intergenerational and community connections.

Othermothers are key not only in supporting children but also in helping blood mothers who, for whatever reason, lack the preparation or desire for motherhood. In confronting racial oppression, maintaining community-based child care and respecting othermothers who assume child care responsibilities serve a critical function in African American communities. Children orphaned by sale or death of their parents under slavery, children conceived by rape, children of young mothers, children born into extreme poverty or to alcoholic or drug-addicted mothers, or children who for other reasons cannot remain with their blood mothers have all been supported by othermothers, who, like Ella Baker's aunt, take in additional children even when they have enough of their own (Collins 1991, 120–121).

It is important for practitioners to accurately assess all aspects of the parent-child relationship and understand the dynamics of African American mothers' child-rearing behavior and history. Many children have been cared for by kin because of conflicting feelings regarding parenting expressed by birth mothers (e.g., some mothers have experienced feelings of ambivalence about parenting) (Hess & Folaron 1991). Many of these feelings can be traced to the oppression experienced by African American mothers (e.g., some African American women view motherhood as a form of exploitation and oppression). However, others view motherhood as a status symbol, a basis for development of self, as well as a "catalyst for social activism" (Collins 1991, 118). The African American community, as well as other interconnections, are crucial in assisting mothers who have conflictual feelings regarding parenting when their children are placed in kinship care. These interconnections include kin and fictive kin who provide support and care for African American children whenever necessary. The interconnection of kin, as well as fictive kin, is a viable part of the African American family network. Interconnections are an important source of support for African American mothers and their children, since many of these mothers do not have the physical, social, emotional, and financial resources needed for them to function in their parenting roles.

Collective Identity and Kinship Care

The extended family is inherent in the definition of family in African American culture. Extended family members have been caring for each other throughout the history of African Americans in an informal way. Prior work has highlighted the significance of extended family for African Americans (Hill 1972, 1997; McAdoo 1978, 1980; Stack 1974). Extended family members are quite important in the support networks of most individuals, and many African Americans live with extended family members. In fact, the weight of the evidence has shown that African Americans are more likely than European Americans to live with extended family (Angel & Tienda 1982; Beck & Beck 1989; Pickney 2000; Taylor et al. 1991;). According to the U.S. Bureau of the Census (1990), 13 percent of all

African American children lived with their grandparents, as compared with only 3 percent of European American children; in 56 percent of the African American families, the mother of the children also lived in the home.

Stack (1974) studied the extended family patterns of poor African American families living in a midwestern inner city and found that "kin and friends exchange and give and obligate one another. They trade food stamps, rent money, a TV, hats, dice, a car, a nickel here, a cigarette there, food, milk, grits, and children" (32). Inherent in this system are the blood and nonblood relatives who are bound together through reciprocal support, as well as a strong sense of caring and responsibility. This extended family structure is indicative of the collective identity that characterizes individuals in African American culture.

Although extended family support has been prevalent in African American as well as African culture throughout history, it is a family structure that promotes family survival through formalized kinship care. African American children whose birth mothers are unable to care for them can continue to be connected to their extended family and culture when placed in kinship care. Kinship care placements tend to last longer than nonrelated foster care placements (Berrick, Barth & Needell 1994; Crosson-Tower 1998). Many child advocates have stated that kinship care should be the placement of choice when children cannot remain in the care and custody of their birth mothers and/or fathers. Several factors should be considered when assessing the home of any extended family member prior to kinship care placement:

1. The nature and quality of the relationship between the child and the relative
2. The ability and the desire of the kinship parent to protect the child from further abuse and maltreatment
3. The safety of the kinship home and the ability of the kin to provide a nurturing environment for the child
4. The willingness of the kinship family to accept the child into the home
5. The ability of the kinship parent to meet the developmental needs of the child
6. The nature and quality of the relationship between the birth parent and the relative, including the birth parent's preference about the placement of the child with kin
7. Any family dynamics in the kinship home related to the abuse or neglect of the child
8. The presence of alcohol or other drug involvement in the kinship home (Child Welfare League of America 1994, 44–45)

The inclusion of these factors in the assessment, as well as culturally sensitive work with extended family members, can facilitate a high quality of care for children placed in kinship care.

Many children in kinship care also tend to maintain closer connections and/or contacts with their birth parents (Lewis & Fraser 1978; Needell 1994). For example, Needell studied six hundred kin and foster care providers (African American, Caucasian, and other). Findings revealed the following:

1. Regular contact with birth parents was maintained to a much greater degree with kin.
2. Eighty-one percent of kinship foster parents compared with 58 percent of foster parents had some contact with the birth parents.
3. Regarding visitation between children and their birth parents, more than half (56 percent) of children in kinship homes saw their birth parents at least once a month, which was true for less than one-third (32 percent) of foster children.
4. Nearly one-fifth (19 percent) of kin children saw their birth parents more than four times a month; virtually no (3 percent) foster children did.
5. More than three-fourths (79 percent) of kinship foster parents arranged visits directly with the birth parent.
6. Visitation with birth parents, when it did occur, was more likely to be arranged directly by African American kinship caretakers and foster parents than Caucasian, Hispanics, or others.
7. Although many providers saw a warm relationship between the child and the birth parent, more kinship than foster parents felt that the child had a "close" relationship with their birth parent (61 percent vs. 40 percent).
8. Many providers also asserted that birth parents viewed the placement positively. Slightly more kinship providers than foster parents reported that the birth parents were at least somewhat pleased with the placement (84 percent vs. 78 percent), however, this difference was not statistically significant.

These findings point to the continuity of the relationship between children, extended family, and birth parents when children are placed with kin. Harris (1999) examined the quality of extended family support for African American birth mothers whose children had been placed in kinship care and returned to their care versus mothers whose children remained in kinship care. Both groups of mothers were deeply rooted in their extended family systems. Child care and emotional support were the types of assistance received most often from these two groups of mothers. Mothers in both groups expressed warm and positive feelings about their extended family members helping them in a time of crisis. Nineteen of the mothers reported that extended family members played a significant role in their lives. This and other studies show some of the positive aspects of kinship care placements, as well as the sense of collective identity evidenced through the actions of extended family in their relationships with mothers and their children placed in kinship care. This collective identity is maintained in the context of the extended family system.

Although extended family readily accept relatives in their homes and want to maintain a sense of collective identity, many of these placements are problematic for all members of the family. Many birth mothers have long-standing conflictual relationships with extended family members. Sometimes these relationships become exacerbated when children are placed in kinship care. The result is ongoing interaction filled with hostility, resentment, anger, and rage. According to Crumbley and Little (1997), kinship caregivers may experience anger toward the parent for the following reasons: (1) attempts to be reunited with the child (i.e., in the relative's opinion, the parent is irresponsible); (2) freedom from the responsibilities of parenthood; (3) failure as a parent; (4) embarrassment and hurt to the child or family; (5) sabotage of or competition with the caregiver's authority and efforts; or (6) efforts to force the relative to "choose" (loyalty) between the child or the parent (13–14). Birth parents may attribute anger with the kinship caregiver to: (1) the kinship caregiver's acceptance of the child in his or her home (i.e., "If you hadn't accepted my child, the court would have left the child with me; you gave them an alternative to me"); (2) the kinship caregiver having reporting the parent to an agency (i.e., for abuse or neglect); (3) the kinship caregiver's attempts to not have the child returned to the parent; (4) the kinship caregiver's success with the child (i.e., health, school performance, behavior); (5) jealousy of the kinship caregiver's relationship with and attachment to the child; or (6) feelings that the kinship caregiver is undermining the parent's role and relationship with the child (i.e., verbally demeaning the parent, buying the child's loyalty and affection with toys, "spoiling" the child) (Crumbley & Little 1997, 22). These relationships are traumatic for the children as well as other family members. Children are often caught in the middle of these conflictual relationships between parents and kinship caregivers and sometimes are forced to take sides with one or the other. No child should ever be put in this position because of the potential for emotional damage to the child. "A real concern is that the child might be caught up in existing family dynamics, such as mother-daughter conflict between grandmother caretaker and the child's parent, or sibling rivalry between father and his sister, the caregiver aunt" (Downs et al. 2000, 348).

Another disadvantage hypothesized in another study was that birth parents can continue to do whatever they want and still have easy access to their children; therefore, they have less incentive to do the things essential to facilitate family reunification (Meyer & Link 1990). However, findings from a study by Harris (1997) contradicted this hypothesis. Specifically, birth mothers who had been reunified with their children reported that they had been encouraged by extended family members to do whatever the child welfare system required to have their children returned to them. Another disadvantage is the limited services and supports received by children and kin caregivers (Dubowitz 1990; Mason & Gleeson 1999; Needell 1994; Walker, Zangrillo & Smith 1994). Finally, many birth mothers pose a risk to their children because they continue to abuse alcohol, drugs, and/or other addictive substances and cannot get the necessary treatment for their substance abuse problems. These mothers continue to maintain contact with their children who are placed in kinship care. While there are advantages as well as disadvantages of kinship care, these placements reaffirm a sense of interdependence (collective identity) in the African American extended family, as these family members repeatedly provide care for children and encourage their continued relationships with their birth mothers.

Guidelines for Assessment and Intervention

It is imperative for those practitioners who work with African American birth mothers and their children placed in kinship care to provide culturally sensitive services. The initial phase of this work includes the development of a keen sense of self-awareness. Practitioners must have an understanding of self that entails identifying, acknowledging, and addressing their own biases, prejudices, racist thoughts, and feelings. Practitioners must also acknowledge and discuss worker and client differences and how these differences can hamper the development and maintenance of a positive working relationship; differences in child-rearing practices is an essential part of this awareness. "Most important is the capacity to integrate the personal experience of self and ethnicity in the disciplined process of understanding how these impact on other people, especially the clients social workers serve" (Devore & Schlesinger 1996, 191).

Practitioners must communicate respect for and understanding of the history of African Americans including their continued experiences with racism, discrimination, and oppression; these experiences have an enormous impact on the lives of African American birth mothers, their children, and other family members. It is imperative to be aware of the effects of ongoing racism, discrimination, and oppression on children, birth mothers, kin caregivers, and other family members. Practitioners cannot assess, understand, and address the many complexities inherent in kinship care without a strong knowledge base about the history of African Americans. This history documents the significance of family and kinship ties during slavery and the ways African Americans have been able to develop and sustain a rich ethnic, cultural, and family heritage in spite of slavery, racism, discrimination, and oppression. Understanding this history also includes the meaning of family in African American culture. Family includes one's own family, as well as other African Americans. It is important for practitioners to acquire a thorough understanding of the support network of birth mothers and children. This support network can be used as a positive resource for birth mothers and their children. It is highly significant for practitioners to demonstrate verbal and nonverbal respect for caregivers, especially elderly caregivers. This respect includes the utilization of titles such as Mrs.,

Ms., and Mr. Failure to do so may suggest that one does not respect the wisdom and life experiences of older African Americans. The communication of respect is key to successful work with African American caregivers, birth mothers, and children in kinship care.

African Americans place a high value on responsibility and loyalty to family. Their survival is predicated on a strong degree of interdependence (i.e., collective identity). Practitioners should utilize the knowledge and strengths of the extended family, rooted in collective identity, to facilitate a nonadversarial working relationship. Birth mothers, kin caregivers, and other extended family members must be included in all facets of planning and decision making for children placed in kinship care. A culturally competent practitioner will seek information regarding the child, mother, kin caregivers, other extended family members, and/or culture to get clarity or understanding. Practitioners should understand and utilize the Africentric worldview in their work with African American birth mothers and their children. The principles inherent in this worldview include (1) the interconnectedness of all things; (2) oneness of mind, body, and spirit; (3) collective identity; (4) consanguineal family structure; (5) consequential morality; (6) analogue thinking; (7) phenomenological time; and (8) spirituality (Schiele 2000, 17–35). Practitioners should also acquire an understanding of African American vernacular in order to communicate with African American birth mothers, children, and family members in a culturally competent manner. Most important, practitioners should avoid labeling and stereotyping children, birth mothers, and others members of African American families.

Many birth mothers and caregivers have conflicting relationships. According to Crumbley and Little (1997), some parents experience feelings of anger, abandonment, jealousy, and competition when their children are placed in kinship care. Practitioners should encourage birth mothers and caregivers to discuss conflicting issues, and birth mothers and caregivers should be assisted in gaining awareness of the continued negative impact on the family system when family members fail to openly and honestly discuss long-standing conflicting issues. The short- and long-term consequences of conflicting relationships on children with their birth mothers and kin caregivers should be assessed and addressed by practitioners. Relationship issues need to be addressed in order for birth mothers and kin caregivers to be able to work together in teaching children the skills needed to survive in the African American culture, as well as in the larger racist and oppressive society. Practitioners should maintain a neutral and objective frame of reference and should not engage in collusion with children, birth mothers, or kin caregivers. They should encourage birth mothers and caregivers to be consistent in child rearing and their adherence to boundaries; consistency is very important in child rearing.

One way for practitioners to understand African American children in kinship care is to have knowledge about child development. "Development unfolds in individual, family and community contexts that influence its course. To understand a particular child's development we must attend to the transactions between that individual child and the layers of ecological context that surround him" (Davies 1999, 44). This knowledge should include an understanding of African American children from a familial, societal/environmental, and cultural/ethnic context. Practitioners need awareness and insight regarding the development of the ethnic sense of self for African American children. The ethnic self is usually formed between the ages of three and five years and firmly established between the ages of six and twelve, although this formation continues throughout the life span. "Social and cultural attitudes about race are screened through the beginning ethnic sense of self matrix and require buttressing by parents, family, community, and other external forces" (Bowles 1988, 108–109).

African American birth mothers experience feelings of separation and loss when their children are placed in kinship care, and children experience maternal deprivation when they are separated from their mothers. According to Jenkins and Norman (1972), the feelings of birth parents can range from bitterness to thankfulness. "The separation trauma, guilt, sense of loss, devaluation of self, and identity conflicts experienced by children and their biological families are real, as are the emotional bonds and attachments between them" (Leashore, McMurray & Bailey 1991, 252). Caregivers may also experience several losses including interruption in their life cycles, interference with space and privacy, and changes in their roles and relationships with their children and grandchildren (Crumbley & Little 1997). There is a need for practitioners to understand the impact of these losses on African American children, birth mothers, and caregivers in order for them to work effectively with the entire family system.

Conclusions

Large numbers of African American children continue to be removed from the care of their birth mothers and placed in kinship care. Extended family members serve as kin caregivers for these children and have been important in the African and African American cultures. Many policies and practices of government funded and regulated programs are contrary to the beliefs and characteristics of the African American family system that have prevailed throughout history. For example, African American extended family members have served as caregivers for children in their families from slavery through contemporary times without government intervention. However, when extended family members serve as caregivers for children under the auspices of a government funded and regulated kinship care program, their homes must be licensed and they must adhere to the policies and procedures of the formalized child welfare system. These policies include rules against the use of corporal punishment when disciplining children. Many African American caregivers do not feel that corporal punishment is harmful to children, and many of them adhere to the adage "Spare the rod, and spoil the child." There has always been informal adoption of children in many African American families; however, in contemporary times kinship caregivers are strongly encouraged by child welfare practitioners to formally adopt children in their care or to become the subsidized guardian of these children. It is essential to have knowledge and understanding of the history of African Americans including the risks and sacrifices of African American mothers during and after slavery. An understanding of the past of African Americans will enhance our understanding of the present.

Family forms the core of African American culture. A strong mother/child bond as well as familial and kinship ties have always been important to African American mothers. These familial relationships include kin and fictive kin. Kin and fictive kin relationships continue to be an integral part of the African American family system. These relationships help birth mothers and their children to develop and maintain a sense of collective identity with other family members.

African American children have been cared for by kin, fictive kin, othermothers and neighbors. The sharing of a collective identity is most evident in the relationship of African American mothers with their children, extended family, and interconnections in their lives. These interconnections are an important part of the support system for African American mothers and their children in kinship care. Best practices for these mothers and their children must be designed and implemented in the context of African American culture.

REFERENCES

Angel, R., & M. Tienda, 1982. "Headship and Household Composition among Blacks, Hispanics and Other Whites." *Social Forces* 61:508–531.

Beck, R.W., & S. H. Beck. 1989. "The Incidence of Extended Households among Middle-Aged Black and White Women: Estimates from a Five-Year Panel Study." *Journal of Family Issues* 10:147–168.

Berrick, J., R. Barth & B. Needell. 1994. "A Comparison of Kinship Foster Homes and Family Foster Homes: Implications for Kinship Care as Family Preservation." *Children and Youth Services Review* 161/2:33–63.

Bowles, D. D. 1988. "Development of an Ethnic Self-Concept among Blacks." In *Ethnicity and Race: Critical Concepts in Social Work*, edited by C. Jacobs & D. D. Bowles, 103–113. Silver Spring, MD: National Association of Social Workers.

Child Welfare League of America. 1994. *Kinship Care: A Natural Bridge*, 44–45. Washington, DC: Child Welfare League of America.

Collins, P. E. 1991. Black Women and Motherhood. In *Black Feminist Thought: Knowledge, Consciousness, and the Politics of Empowerment*, 115–137. New York: Routledge, Chapman, and Hall.

Crosson-Tower, C. 1998. "Children in Family Foster Care." In *Exploring Child Welfare: A Practice Perspective*, 316–354. Needham Heights, MA: Allyn & Bacon.

Crumbley, J., & R. J. Little. 1997. "Clinical Concepts." In *Relatives Raising Children: An Overview of Kinship Care*, 9–35. Washington, DC: Child Welfare League.

Davies, D. 1999. "Risk and Protective Factors: The Child, Family, and Community Contexts." In *Child Development: A Practitioner's Guide*, 44–83. New York: Guilford Press.

Devore, W., & E. G. Schlesinger. 1996. "Adapting Strategies and Procedures for Ethnic-Sensitive Practice: Direct Practice." In *Ethnic-Sensitive Social Work Practice.* 4th ed., 187–225. Needham Heights, MA: Allyn & Bacon.

Downs, S. W., E. Moore, E. J. McFadden & L. B. Costin. 2000. "Foster Care: A Service for Children and Their Families. In *Child Welfare and Family Services: Policies and Practice*, 307–380. Needham Heights, MA: Allyn & Bacon.

DuBois, W.E.B. 1901. "The Freedmen's Bureau." *Atlantic Monthly*, 87:354–365.

Dubowitz, H. 1990. *The Physical and Mental Health and Educational Status of Children Placed with Relatives: Final Report.* Baltimore, MD: University of Maryland.

Franklin, J. H., & L. Schweninger. 1999. "Whither Thou Goest." In *Runaway Slaves: Rebels on the Plantation*, 49–74. New York: Oxford University Press.

Harris, M. S. 1997. *Factors That Affect Family Reunification of African American Birth Mothers and Their Children Placed in Kinship Care.* Ph.D. diss., Smith College School for Social Work, Northampton, MA.

———. 1999. "Comparing Mothers of Children in Kinship Foster Care: Reunification vs. Remaining in Care." In *Kinship Care: Improving Practice through Research*, edited by J. P. Gleeson & C. F. Hairston, 145–166. Washington, DC: Child Welfare League of America.

Hess, P. M., & G. Folaron. 1991. Ambivalence: A Challenge to Permanency for Children. *Child Welfare* 70/4:403–424.

Hill, R. P. 1972. *The Strengths of Black Families.* New York: Emerson Hall.

———. 1997. *The Strengths of African American Families: Twenty-Five Years Later.* Washington, DC: R & B Publishers.

Jenkins, S., & E. Norman. 1972. *Filial Deprivation and Foster Care.* New York: Columbia University Press.

Leashore, B. B., H. L. McMurray & B. C. Bailey. 1991. "Reuniting and Preserving African American Families." In *Child Welfare: An Africentric Perspective*, edited by J. E. Everett, S. P. Chipungu & B. R. Leashore, 247–265. New Brunswick, NJ: Rutgers University Press.

Lewis, R. E., & M. Fraser. 1978. "Blending Informal and Formal Helping Networks in Foster Care." *Children and Youth Services Review* 9/3:153–169.

Martin, E., & J. E. Martin. 1978. "The Extended Family: How Is It Formed and What Does It Do?" In *The Black Extended Family*, 5–16. Chicago: University of Chicago Press.

Mason, S. J., & J. P. Gleeson. 1999. "Adoption and Subsidized Guardianship as Permanency Options in Kinship Foster Care: Barriers and Facilitating Conditions." In *Kinship Care: Improving Practice through Research*, edited by J. P. Gleeson & C. F. Hairston, 85–114. Washington, DC: Child Welfare League of America.

McAdoo, H. P. 1978. "Factors Related to Stability in Upwardly Mobile Black Families." *Journal of Marriage and the Family*, 40:761–776.

———. 1980. "Black Mothers and the Extended Family Support Networks." In *The Black Woman*, edited by L. F. Rodgers-Rose, 125–144. Berkeley, CA: Sage Publications.

Meyer, B. S., & M. K. Link. 1990. *Kinship Care: The Double-Edged Dilemma.* Rochester, NY: Task Force on Permanency Planning for Foster Children.

Needell, B. 1994. "Kinship Care: Rights and Responsibilities, Services and Standards." In

From Child Abuse to Permanency Planning, edited by R. P. Barth, M. Courtney, J. D. Berrick & V. Albert, 195–219. New York: Aldine DeGruyter.

Mintz, S. W., & R. Price. 1976. "Kinship and Sex Roles." In *The Birth of African-American Culture: An Anthropological Perspective*, 61–80. Boston: Beacon Press.

Petit, M. R., P. A. Curtis, K. Woodruff, L. Arnold, L. Feagans & J. Ang. 1999. "Out-of-Home Care." In *Child Abuse and Neglect: A Look at the States*, 67–128. Washington, DC: Child Welfare League of America.

Pickney, A. 2000. "Social Institutions." In *Black Americans*, 105–130. Upper Saddle River, NJ: Prentice-Hall.

Schiele, J. H. 2000. "The Afrocentric Worldview." In *Human Services and the Afrocentric Paradigm*, 17–35. New York: Haworth Press.

Stack, C. D. 1974. "Personal Kindreds." In *All Our Kin: Strategies for Survival in a Black Community*, 45–61. New York: Harper & Row.

Taylor, R. J., L. M. Chatters, M. B. Tucker & E. Lewis. 1991. "Developments in Research on Black Families." In *Contemporary Families, Looking Forward, Looking Back*, edited by A. Booth, 275–296. Minneapolis, MN: National Council on Family Relations.

U.S. Bureau of the Census. 1990. *Marital Status and Living Arrangements.* Current Population Reports, series P-20. Washington, DC: U.S. Government Printing Office.

Walker, C. D., P. Zangrillo & J. M. Smith. 1994. "Parental Drug Abuse and African-American Children in Foster Care." In *Child Welfare Research Review*. Vol. 1. Edited by R. Barth, J. D. Berrick & N. Gilbert, 109–122. New York: Columbia University Press.

Zipf, K. L. 2000. "Reconstructing 'Free Woman': African-American Women, Apprenticeship, and Custody Rights During Reconstruction." *Journal of Women's History* 12/1:8–31.

8

Unwed African American Fathers' Participation in Child Welfare Permanency Planning

Caseworkers' Perspectives

WALDO E. JOHNSON JR.

VAUGHN D. BRYANT

Introduction

This chapter addresses caseworkers' perceptions of unwed fathers' involvement in permanency planning in child welfare services for their children. It examines how paternal statuses, namely noncustodial and nonresidential, affect caseworkers' capacity and inclinations to engage unwed fathers in child welfare permanency planning. It also explores how gender, socioeconomic status, child welfare, and family policies and practices collectively shape institutional opportunities and responses to paternal participation among unwed fathers in child welfare services.

In the United States today, nearly one-third of all births occur outside of marriage (McLanahan & Garfinkel 2001). While these households include a diversity of family structures, including never-married, divorced, separated, and widowed (Boyd-Franklin 1989; Osborne 2002), those headed by single women are more likely to experience chronic poverty and remain the focus of public policy discourse and initiatives regarding family formation (Franklin & Smith 1991; Johnson 1998; Nichols-Casebolt 1988; Roschelle 1997). Today, fathers, as a group, are less likely to reside with their children (Blankenhorn 1995; Hamer 2001; Seltzer 1996). As such, when caseworkers are faced with the prospect of having to engage unwed, nonresident fathers in child welfare permanency planning, the prospect of doing so raises far more anxiety than relief.

Societal Expectations Regarding Parental Behavior and Child Responsibility

The principal attribution regarding nonresident fathers (of which African American fathers are disproportionately represented) is that they are peripheral to the lives of their children and families (Hamer 2001; Johnson 1998; Mead 1986; Murray 1984). In fact, these fathers are often described as "absent fathers" or, more recently, "deadbeat dads." While a number of nonresident fathers are indeed uninvolved and absent from their children's lives, many are not (Johnson 2001a). In fact, these two terms, absent fathers and nonresident fathers, are not interchangeable, although they are often expressed. By definition, men who do not reside with their children are nonresident fathers, but they are not necessarily absent from the lives of their children. In contrast, many nonresident fathers are indeed involved in their children's lives, but their involvement is often obscured and, therefore, is often undocumented (Hamer 2001; Johnson 1998). Unwed fathers are especially at risk of being portrayed as uninvolved if they do not have legal custodial status or reside with their children. Paternal involvement is defined in terms of father engagement (direct interaction with child in the form of caretaking, play, or leisure); accessibility or availability to the child; and responsibility for the child, as distinct from performance of care (Lamb et al. 1987). A growing body of research literature examines the presence and involvement of fathers in children's lives and makes clear distinctions about these differences and their impact on child well-being (Johnson 1996; Lamb 1997; Pleck 1997). In contrast, absence does not necessarily mean uninvolved (Danziger & Radin 1990).

Demographic Profile of Unwed Fathers

What are the causes of declining paternal noninvolvement? The couple relationship status among unwed parents may be central to understanding why paternal involvement potentially waxes and wanes (Johnson 2001a). Although marriage as an institution is currently hailed as the mechanism by which good health outcomes, happiness, and prosperity for both men and women is facilitated (Waite & Gallagher 2000), the social characteristics of parents (particularly the fathers) whose children are in or at risk of child welfare intervention do not resemble those who enjoy such marital benefits. Yet, paternal involvement among resident and nonresident unwed fathers is both similar and strikingly different. Unwed fathers are less likely to have established legal paternity that legitimizes them in gaining access to their children. Instead, they must negotiate with the mothers of their children regarding acceptable paternal expectations, roles, and activities that may be conditioned on factors within and beyond their control. Although sustaining paternal involvement is often presumed inclusive in cohabiting parent relationships, changes in the couple relationship status generally affect paternal involvement and can negate all previous paternal and parental arrangements (Johnson 2002b; Roschelle 1997).

The distinctions in paternal involvement among unwed fathers in committed, cohabiting relationships with the mothers of their children versus how noncustodial (and often) nonresident fathers sustain involvement cannot be overemphasized. Patterns of paternal involvement among unwed fathers in cohabiting relationships may more closely resemble paternal involvement among married fathers, at least in the ways in which it is assessed. Paternal involvement has been traditionally measured in the context of intact, nuclear families (Johnson 1998). Paternal presence, also traditionally assessed in terms of father's residential status (Hamer 2001; Johnson 1996), is based on conventional ideals that emphasize financial support, discipline, and to a lesser degree, emotional involvement with children. These characteristics are inextricably linked as desirable characteristics of how fathers should parent. Unwed fathers who cohabit with the mothers of their children, compared with nonresident unwed fathers, are more likely to have work experience and employment, although only part-time and low paying (Danziger & Radin 1990; Johnson 2002a). Paternal provision of financial and other material support is a strong predictor of paternal involvement among unwed fathers; only the couple relationship status is stronger (Johnson 2001a) and serves as an interface phenomenon that sustains involvement.

Robertson (1997) reported that unwed noncustodial fathers are less likely to hold jobs than other men. This difference in work effort is attributed to the poor health of these men, as well as their involvement in high-risk behaviors (e.g., drug use and criminal activity) (Stone 2002). African American men are disproportionately represented among nonresident and noncustodial unwed fathers compared with Latino and white fathers (Lerman & Ooms 1992). Roy (1999) reported that the "new degrees of economic marginalization brought on by the postindustrial economy threaten the regular involvement of African American men with their children." As noncustodial fathers, they exercise limited legal access to their children. Their nonresident status further limits their parental involvement. These disadvantaged statuses, combined with unemployment, severely truncate paternal involvement, family development, and child well-being.

As fathers, their absence from their children's residence and inability to provide financial support have been traditionally viewed as their lack of commitment to their children's lives (Johnson 2001a). While it is true that these fathers' demographic characteristics (e.g., socioeconomic statuses, resident status, human and social capital, problem behavior) exacerbate the fragility of their relationships with their children's mothers, many unwed fathers remain committed parents (Hamer 2001; Roy 1999; Stone 2002). For example, the findings of a recent examination of paternal involvement among unwed fathers in the Fragile Families and Child Well-Being Study (Johnson 2001a) suggest that the parenting couple's relationship status is the best predictor of paternal involvement. Fathers cohabiting with the mothers reported the highest degree of involvement with their children. Their partners, the mothers of their children, confirmed the fathers' reports. Eighty-eight percent of the mothers and 91 percent of the fathers reported that the father contributed money and other material things during the pregnancy, and 88 percent of both the mothers and the fathers reported that fathers made nonfinancial contributions such as assisting with household chores and other responsibilities.

Even among nonresident fathers, paternal involvement was fairly high. When both nonresident fathers and the mothers of their children were queried about the father's involvement, 82 percent of the mothers and 88 percent of the fathers reported that the fathers contributed money and other things during pregnancy. When queried about nonfinancial contributions made by the unwed father, 78 percent of the mothers and 80 percent of the fathers reported that the fathers assisted with household chores and other responsibilities. These findings, although not as high and consistent as those among cohabiting unwed parents, suggest that unwed parenting and specifically nonresident fathers demand further study to better understand the relationships and circumstances of unwed parenthood and their impact on child well-being (Johnson 2001a). Paternal intentions among cohabiting and nonresident fathers were identical (i.e., all fathers expressed a desire to be involved in raising their children). In addition, 91 percent of mothers and 85 percent of nonresident fathers reported that the father promised to provide financial support for the child in the coming year.

Among unwed parents, dissolution of the parents' romantic relationship is a chief cause of declining paternal involvement (Johnson 2001a). Earlier research suggests that the couple relationships among unwed parents are highly fragile and susceptible to breakup because of financial strains (Johnson, Levine & Doolittle 1999; Roy 1999) and maternal and paternal families of origin involvement in the couple relationship dynamics (Johnson 2001b; Stone 2002). Relationships with other partners after the dissolution of the parents' couple relationship may also threaten a father's ability to sustain involvement with his child if legal paternity has not been established.

Collectively, these research findings form a demographic profile of unwed fathers. Often the statuses of nonresident and noncustodial fathers are largely determined by their human capital (education, work preparation and training, labor force participation) and social capital characteristics (physical and mental health statuses, relationships with children's mothers as maternal and paternal families of origin), which often results in their inability to assume traditional, socially sanctioned parental roles. Caseworkers, as agents of the state, often misinterpret their absence and lack of sustaining financial support as uninvolvement, and fail to value their current or future involvement with their children.

Study Sample and Research Methods

Source of Data

Five focus group discussions about fathers in the child welfare system in Illinois are the sources for the data analyzed in this study. Participant selection was guided by the goal of obtaining expert opinion on child welfare practice with parents at the field level. To ensure expert opinion, participation was limited to caseworkers and direct service supervisors who had at least one year of experience in working with families involved in the child welfare system and were currently providing services. The study sought participants both from in-home and out-of-home service programs in order to obtain a more general overview of practice with fathers. To further the latter objective, the study also recruited volunteer participants both in Chicago and in downstate Illinois. Not-for-profit child welfare agencies and interagency work groups were recruited whose work was known through previous or ongoing collaboration in consultation on best practice issues or program evaluation (O'Donnell et al. in press).

Thirty-four caseworkers and supervisors participated in the five focus group discussions in 1999. The number of participants per group ranged from five to eleven. Participants in two of the focus groups worked in downstate Illinois child welfare agencies that have a long history of providing foster care and family preservation services. Two of the three focus groups in Chicago were drawn from participants in interagency work groups that explore current child welfare practice in a variety of services, including foster care and family preservation. The third Chicago group comprised staff from a network of agencies serving teen parents (O'Donnell et al. in press).

Table 8.1 provides an overview of the sex and racial characteristics of the participants as well as the kinds of services they provided. Overall, and in four of the five focus groups, female participants outnumbered male. To ensure an atmosphere of confidentiality, the focus group facilitators did not ask each participant to identify professional characteristics such as length and types of professional experiences. However, individual remarks in the discussions revealed that experience ranged from one year to more than twenty years. In two of the groups, participants provided only foster care services; the other three groups reflected a broader mix of services that included foster care, family preservation, and/or teen parenting services.

Implementation of Focus Groups

Administrators in the participating agencies and work group facilitators advised staff in advance of the purpose of the focus groups, when and where they were to be held, and the requirement of one year experience. To encourage participation, the focus groups were held during the noon break and a box lunch was available to all participants. Participation was strictly voluntary. Prior to the beginning of each focus group, the two facilitators described focus group procedures, informed participants of the confidentiality of the discussion, and reviewed the contents of a written consent for voluntary participation that each potential participant was asked to sign. All of the discussions were audiotaped. The length of the focus groups ranged from sixty-seven to eighty-one minutes.

TABLE 8.1

Demographic Characteristics and Services Provided by Focus Group Participants

	Gender	Race	Area(s) of Service	Location of Services
Group 1 (N = 6)	Females 2 Males 4	African American 5 White 0 Latino 1	Teen parenting Family preservation Foster care	Chicago
Group 2 (N = 5)	Females 4 Males 1	African American 5 White 0 Latino 1	Family preservation	Chicago
Group 3 (N = 5)	Females 2 Males 3	African American 4 White 0 Latino 1	Foster care Family preservation	Chicago
Group 4 (N = 11)	Females 11 Males 0	African American 2 White 9 Latino	Foster care	Downstate Illinois
Group 5 (N = 7)	Females 6 Males 1	African American 0 White 7 Latino 0	Foster care	Downstate Illinois

Note: N = 34 participants.

To ensure confidentiality, each participant was assigned a letter of the alphabet, starting with "A," which was then used by the facilitators and other group members to refer to that participant during the discussion. As a precaution against any possible inhibiting of discussion, the researchers for this study were affiliated with universities and conducted each of the groups rather than the researcher who was associated with the public child welfare agency (O'Donnell et al. in press).

All focus group participants contributed to the discussions. The facilitators did not discern either censuring or conforming among participants during the discussions, nor did the recorder who conducted a review of the audiotape after each session. In each focus group, discussion was marked by disagreement among participants with the views expressed as well as descriptions of practice experiences that differed from those of other participants. Although discussions were often lively, the tone was always conversational and professional.

The major question posed in each of the focus groups was whether participants' practice experiences corroborated research findings that fathers, especially noncustodial fathers, are rarely involved in child welfare services. Follow-up questions directed participants to identify and explore factors that influence paternal involvement.

Data Analysis

Transcripts were made of all the audiotapes of the focus groups. Transcripts were analyzed in several stages using the constant comparative analysis procedures described by Padgett (1998). The process was iterative. In the first stage, the transcripts were reviewed and each participant statement was coded in accordance with individual content such as "fathers are afraid of getting in trouble" or "fathers expect caseworkers to have answers." This process was repeated until the researchers were satisfied that the raw data were accurately and exhaustively reflected by codes. The researchers then organized the codes into larger categories (e.g., "fathers are afraid of caseworkers") and analyzed the list of categories for latent themes. In the final stage of analysis, the transcripts were reread and a comparison of the final themes with the texts were made to ensure comprehensiveness and fit. In each stage of the process, a process referred to as analytic triangulation was used (Padgett 1998) (i.e., each researcher worked with the data independently and then came together to compare findings, identify differences in findings, and reach consensus through discussion and re-review of the data). It should be noted that although all of the researchers have expertise in child welfare, they have different professional orientations. One is an attorney specializing in child welfare law, one had previously worked in child welfare services for eighteen years, and the third has conducted extensive research on fragile families, including teen parenting. This diversity fostered a richer analysis of the focus group discussions and contributed significantly to extracting the essence of these discussions.

Findings

"All He's Done Is Neglect His Kids": Unwed Fathers as Indifferent Parents

Disclosures provided by focus group participants largely depicted unwed fathers as indifferent parents. These depictions were based on the caseworkers' perceptions of paternal functioning and were shaped, in part, by the fathers' noncustodial and nonresidential statuses. Their visible absence from the households in which their children reside and their obvious failure to undertake and sustain expected parenting roles provided "substantiated" evidence, from the caseworkers' perspectives, that unwed fathers are less than responsible parents. Implicitly, unwed fathers share responsibility for the child's current at-risk status, even if they did not perpetrate in the offense that brought the children into protective services or reside in the home in which it occurred.

The unwed fathers' noncustodial and nonresident statuses are proxies for assessing parental involvement, commitment, and the status of the couple relationship. The perceived noninterest and inadequacy of unwed African American fathers to provide for their children was strongly articulated in the perspectives drawn from the five focus group discussions. At least one informant in each of the focus groups reported that the child welfare system values mothers as more crucial to children's developmental well-being than fathers. This perception potentially shapes caseworkers' view of unwed fathers as indifferent parents, in spite of the fathers' best efforts to sustain involvement. The perception that mothers are more important to children's development influences direct child welfare practice with regard to the range of services offered by the child welfare system to assist parents, differentiation in parenting standards for men and women, and the distinction in burden of proof levels required of men and women in their roles as parents. When unwed fathers do not reside with their children, the caseworkers tended to view their absence as further confirmation of their lack of commitment to the children. When asked about the commitment of noncustodial fathers to their children, one informant remarked:

> I think there is a gender stereotype when it comes to fathers because society looks at [unwed] mothers [as] being the sole parent and kids as needing mothers more than fathers to raise [them]. But I have found that [noncustodial] fathers are capable of raising their sons and their daughters but they have to go through so many hoops and go through so many changes to even get there, even though they don't have a criminal record. If they step forward, society says "no," there are things that you have to prove to us that you are able to be a parent. That is more discouraging to [these] fathers than anything. It makes them say, "Hey, it's not worth it. Why should I have to prove that I am a parent to anyone?" This is what I've found with most [noncustodial] fathers. They don't feel they have to prove anything. "Give me a chance like you give mothers a chance."

The caseworker contends that child welfare practice treats unwed fathers unfairly. Citing that society views mothers as the sole parent (especially in child welfare service determinations), according to this informant, unwed fathers who step up and show interest in being involved (or assuming custody) appear to be fighting a losing battle. Because the fathers are perceived as indifferent to date, their motives for "resurfacing" and showing interest in their children are often questioned. The perceived failure to provide financial assistance heretofore suggests that they are incapable of providing the mother and child with what they most urgently need—material support—and invalidates them as custodial parents. It also raises concerns about their ability to undertake nonfinancial parental responsibilities for which they are presumed even less prepared.

Children who come into the child welfare system are often viewed as "fatherless" because a disproportionate number are born out of wedlock and, even if the father resides or has contact with the child, it is often undetected or undocumented by their mothers' caseworkers. Although father involvement in affective parenting roles is increasingly recognized in the child development literature (Lamb 1997), mothers perform most of the direct care and child-rearing roles even in intact, married families (Rosier 2000). If the children of unwed fathers are poor and require state intervention, it is presumed that their fathers are not successfully executing their expected parental role. This societal attribution is accepted with little or no empirical support and widely regarded as fact in each case, without a clear understanding of the ways in which father involvement is undertaken among unwed fathers, especially if the fathers do not reside with their children.

Child welfare intervention is presumed appropriate when parental and familial supervision and support are inadequate and children are at risk of physical and/or emotional harm. Caseworkers as agents of the state are charged and empowered to intervene and, if necessary, remove children if they are so exposed. A child's impoverished status may be cause for intervention, but generally does not warrant removal from parental custody. Caseworkers are expected to provide custodial parents with supportive services aimed at preventing homelessness, hunger, and malnutrition (O'Donnell 1999). Child neglect and abuse resulting from the rise in substance abuse among custodial parents has become the chief cause for child welfare intervention and removal of children, along with other health-related problems (O'Donnell 2001). The informants in this study acknowledge that African American unwed fathers are unlikely to have custody or reside with their children when child welfare intervention occurs: "Even when we try to contact the father, 90 percent of the time, father is uninterested in gaining custody. Most of the fathers were not around when the children came into care."

Noting that participants in this and other focus groups reported that they had interacted with less than 10 percent of the fathers of children in their caseloads, the contention that 90 percent of all noncustodial fathers are uninterested in their children is based largely on information provided by the mothers of their children and subject to bias. It raises skepticism about the veracity of these reports and questions whether the 10 percent of noncustodial fathers who are interested is a nontrivial number of cases. As one caseworker acknowledged, "When we try to connect with the fathers," efforts to connect unwed fathers with their children who entered the child welfare system are not routinely or systematically undertaken.

In the 10 percent of cases where the noncustodial fathers express interest in gaining parental custody of their children in foster care, the findings suggest that the child welfare system is unlikely to welcome the fathers' initiative to step forward. The fathers are routinely subjected to a child welfare system, comprising caseworkers and judges, who are unlikely to be sympathetic to their overtures. The fathers often are held to similar parenting goals and expectations in treatment and reunification plans for gaining custody as the former custodial parent. This is reflected in the following disclosure: "If I get a report [from mom] that 'I don't know who he is or I know who he is but we're not talking, he's in another relationship,' I'd be skeptical and I would want to do a home study and the background checks."

While conducting individual and environmental assessments are appropriate to ensure that the parent and environment are child-safe and supportive, many noncustodial African American fathers are subjected to criminal background checks in which their rights to custody are often mitigated by traffic violations and dated criminal arrests. This consequence is reflected in the following statement by one of the caseworkers: "I find amongst African American fathers, even if they have a criminal record that is even fifteen years old, judges will shut that down. Whereas if the man [father] is white, the court is more likely to overlook the criminal record, look at his family as well, and think about the resource that the father could be."

A criminal record typically does not disqualify a custodial parent from sustaining custody. In contrast, noncustodial parents, especially unwed fathers, are held to different standards, and criminal records can invalidate a noncustodial father's access to custody. A criminal background check conducted by a caseworker that yields a criminal record can preempt any further individual assessment of fitness as a custodial parent. The informant perceived that there is a racial bias against African American fathers. This perception is widely held by African American males (Johnson, Levine & Doolittle 1999).

The informant's perception that parenting roles are gender biased is a salient one. This gender bias may be unduly applied in families where flexibility in parenting roles is limited by socioeconomic status (Johnson 2002a). Unwed African American fathers may have limited opportunities and support to develop nurturing and other nonmaterial skills in child care because they are often under intense pressure to undertake instrumental roles for which they are often unprepared to engage. When caseworkers assess noncustodial fathers for fitness as custodial parents, they are rarely assessed in terms of their preparedness to assume socially sanctioned parental roles (providing financial support) or provided assistance or services to undertake these roles.

Assessing unwed fathers from a strengths perspective, the informant contended that the fathers were capable of being custodial parents when their desire to care for their children is supported by their families and the child welfare system. The caseworker sympathized with those unwed fathers who show interest in caring for their children but are met with resistance, especially from the courts and the child welfare system. Further elaboration is offered.

The informant implied that judges' racial bias against African American fathers affects their ability to gain custody of their children. Recognizing the uneasy tension that results from African American males' distrust of the justice system, the informant suggests that court personnel, including judges and lawyers, view nonresident fathers as dispensable and unworthy of consideration as custodial parents, especially if they have prior involvement in the criminal justice system. The fathers must prove themselves worthy. This perception is reflected in remarks made by another caseworker that questioned noncustodial fathers' commitment to their children:

> Was the father there once mom left the hospital? Was he trying to inter-act? With an infant, I think there's greater responsibility due to the fact that they [the infant] can't communicate. The immune system isn't there; there may be special dietary requirements. We know there are special feeding and diaper changing requirements and I would want to know that a dad can step up and perform those functions. For me, this is one case where I would suggest step forward and perform those functions. There's a lot of things that go on like diaper changing, bottle feeding that he needs to know that I can't take for granted that he know."

This caseworker's skepticism about the noncustodial father's commitment to his child was based on the father's commitment to the child's mother. While it is important that couples support one another in order to strengthen the parenting relationship, the caseworker narrowly frames paternal commitment as attitudes and behaviors that more accurately assess the status of the couple's relationship. Fathers' visits to the hospital following delivery are increasingly an unreliable measure of their commitment to their children given the declining length of hospital stays. In light of the fact that these fathers and mothers are not only unwedded but in most cases, not residing together, a number of factors might mitigate a father's visit to the hospital including the mother's early discharge, work and/or other family commitments, and lack of transportation and/or funds to travel to the hospital. Johnson, Levine, and Doolittle (1999) suggest that a father's visit to the hospital following birth is culturally bound in the contexts of marriage and social class. This suggestion will be examined later in the context of couple relationship dynamics. Finally, the determination of the father's commitment is based solely on the mother's report. Mothers in estranged couple relationships who experience a great deal of acrimony during pregnancy or breakup before delivery are highly unlikely to report to caseworkers favorable sentiments about their estranged partners' paternal commitments.

Two points raised in this response merit further examination. First, the latter perception that mothers are more responsible for home things like raising children, however widely shared within American society, contributes to the feminization of parenting, especially with regard to gender-appropriate

parenting roles and their value in the marketplace and society. It implicitly rel-
egates the role of child care to one of lesser importance (within the home where
the market value of those skills and products has traditionally been under-
assessed and uncompensated). It also suggests that socializing male children to
develop proficiency and skills for domestic concerns like child rearing is not
normative. This point is further elaborated in subsequent responses: "I'm not
proud to admit it but I feel relieved when I hear that dad is not interested
because it means less work. Now I can focus on the one person here, the mom."

Because these fathers do not reside with their partners and children, they
are presumed to be uninvolved in the care of their children, as reflected in the
former respondent's statement, "Now, I can focus on the one person here, the
mom." This presumption does not allow for the fact that a father may provide
financial support (thus maintain expected paternal obligation) but not reside
or have legal custody. Paternal involvement examined solely from an instrumental or affective perspective limits our understanding not only of its effects
on child well-being but also the multiple, interactive roles in which fathers and
mothers may partake in parental role development.

Second, when caseworkers assess noncustodial fathers' current or previous
involvement with the children based, in part, on the status of the father's relationship with the child's mother, the potential to minimize or totally miss nonresident fathers' commitment to their children is also exacerbated. Although
closely associated, fathers' romantic commitment to and involvement with
their children's mothers and paternal involvement with and commitment to
their children are distinctive. Clearly, caseworker's observations of paternal
involvement and dynamics are critical data for making assessments and recommendations about nonresident fathers' future involvement when permanency
plans are under way for their children. However, these respondents are reflective of most caseworkers who have limited to no opportunities for such observations. Is it possible that child welfare casework practice's heavy focus on
maternal involvement and performance obstructs its ability to recognize the
ways in which paternal involvement among nonresident fathers naturally
occurs?

In an earlier response to inquiry about nonresident fathers' interest in
their children, the caseworker proposed to determine the nonresident father's
worthiness as a custodial parent based on factors that are largely affected by the
father's relationship with the mother. Given fathers' lower levels of child care
involvement notwithstanding, the veracity of mothers' reports regarding the
whereabouts and involvement of nonresident fathers is affected by a number of
factors, namely couples' relationship status, and is indeed open to suspicion.
Caution should be exercised in assessing paternal involvement based solely on
mothers' reports (Johnson 2001a). Since the relationships between nonresident
parents are often nonromantic and uninvolved, these findings suggest that the

parents' relationship status is somewhat predictive of the nonresident father's paternal involvement but not entirely (Johnson 2001a). Although the differences in mother and father reports among nonresident fathers are statistically significant, paternal involvement among nonresident fathers was far higher than previously documented.

For example, the father's visit to the hospital following the baby's birth may be more accurately an indication of status of the couple relationship than a gauge of his commitment to his child. This may have particular importance in estranged couple relationships. The father's visit to the hospital immediately following the baby's birth may be normative among intact couples but among noncohabiting couples, the father's visit to the hospital may be a stronger measure of the couple's intimate relationship than the father's commitment to the baby (Johnson 2001b). Clearly, the range of relationship statuses among unwed nonresident parents immediately following birth is broad and dynamic. In addition, increasingly shortened length of hospital stays, the physical and geographical distance fathers must potentially travel to see the baby, and limited financial resources, as well as other commitments such as work and providing care for other children, in addition to the acrimony that often exists between nonresident parents as couples, might prevent nonresident fathers from visiting the hospital (Johnson 2001b).

Among the caseworkers participating in the focus groups, there was broad agreement that having to work with nonresident fathers potentially increased workers' caseloads. In defense of their reluctance to try to engage nonresident fathers, the following observations were made: "Bottom line, it's much easier for men to have kids and not do anything about it. I'm not putting down men but that's the way it is; moms are stuck with it, dads don't have to be there."

This response suggests that many caseworkers see nonresident fathers as men uninterested in the welfare of their children. These respondents contend that when efforts to reach out to nonresident fathers via service plans and supports are extended, they do not follow through on tasks or simply do not show up. This routinely results in the caseworkers' decisions to dismiss or ignore them as parents. This perception is based on two assumptions: first, mothers are usually the parents who assume responsibility for child care. This perception is not restricted to nonresident fathers of out-of-wedlock children but all fathers, irrespective of their marital statuses (Rosier 2000). Families with children displaced in the public child welfare system are disproportionately poor, families of color, and single heads of households, thus increasing the likelihood that the families of children in substitute care are headed by mothers. Similar to responses in an earlier section of this chapter, these caseworkers contend that mothers, not fathers, were the parents they engaged as they worked toward developing parental service plans, family reunification, and ultimately permanency planning. In their view, fathers simply were not there. Caseworkers suggested that in cases where there was some father involvement, the fathers conveniently were not around when the caseworker came to the home.

Mothers Make Better Parents

Despite the variety of responses to questions raised during the focus groups, participants in all of the groups identified two factors that informed their over-all views of fathers as child welfare clients. Parenthetically, both of these factors support the position taken by Jaffe (1983) and others that social services are female dominated and have tended to focus on mothers' needs and maternal issues. One factor is that on the whole, mothers make better child welfare clients than fathers.

The informant identifies several of the countless obligations of parents in their roles as responsible custodial parents of infant children. Indeed, bottle preparation and feeding, changing diapers, and even properly holding the baby are necessary parenting skills that all custodial parents should master. Another informant made the following case: "Women are raised to be more responsible for home things. They are the ones who are in the home and observe their mothers or relatives raising children while men are out doing masculine things."

This stereotypic perspective is widely shared in American society. Some noncustodial fathers are unlikely to have mastered these parental caregiving skills because of their potentially less frequent visitation and direct care provision for their children (as well as their placing more value on mastering "masculine things" like earning wages, which is also broadly shared as a core paternal role). In addition, many noncustodial fathers express discomfort and anxiety about providing care for infants (Johnson 2002b). It is unclear to what extent their discomfort and anxiety are shared by fathers of infant children in general. As such, providing child care education, training, and assistance to fathers so that they gain confidence and proficiency in care provision to infant children is appropriate. This may be even more critical for first-time and young, nonresident fathers.

Informants noted that in most of their cases, the mothers had been primary caregivers before child welfare involvement. Their lives were therefore usually more disrupted by the child welfare intervention than the fathers', and they usually appeared more motivated than fathers to work with the child welfare system to restabilize themselves and their families. Mothers were also much more available than fathers in part because their whereabouts were usually known and caseworkers had gathered personal information about them at the time of case opening. Several caseworkers also noted that mothers were usually better able to tolerate the child welfare environment. In contrast to fathers, most of the mothers had experience with service bureaucracies such as public assistance. Caseworkers noted that the inevitable paperwork, procedural requirements, and delays the mothers encountered in the child welfare system did not confuse and alienate them to the degree that they did fathers. "Child welfare and society as a whole believe that children should be with their mothers. That holds up in service, why do we need to look at them [dads]; they [children] have a mother."

Caseworkers described mothers as being more patient with and accepting of the "system" than fathers, who wanted greater clarity and predictability with respect to time frames and outcomes than caseworkers could provide. Interestingly, they did not raise the possibility that fathers may simply have been less hesitant than mothers to voice complaints that both felt. Also, as noted earlier, participants believed that many fathers feared involvement with child welfare services for a variety of reasons that would not have affected most of the mothers.

Several of the young female caseworkers reported that gender conflicts often hampered their work with fathers. "I do counseling but it never fails that when I get to the home, dad would never be there. He had a game, etc. It was a man-woman thing that women [even as caseworkers] can't tell me [dad] anything."

Caseworkers interpreted these fathers' unavailability as resentment toward women in positions of authority and reported that the fathers often reacted in a "macho" manner, which the female caseworkers interpreted as trying to control them as they did other women in their lives. These caseworkers appeared very annoyed at what they perceived as power struggles initiated by the fathers, and they were unable to find successful strategies for resolving the conflicts.

Fathers Are Neither Trained Nor Expected to Be Primary Child Caregivers

A second factor raised by participants in all of the focus groups is that working with fathers on child welfare issues is difficult because men in our society are neither expected nor trained to be primary caregivers of children. Caseworkers noted that the fathers had rarely been primary or even secondary caregivers of their children. This fact complicated casework with fathers in several ways. For example, many of the fathers with whom the caseworkers came in contact remained aloof because they considered child welfare involvement as a matter primarily for mother involvement. One informant articulated this perception by saying, "We try to engage the fathers, but very seldom is it followed through with by father."

This response was characteristic of the sentiment that largely permeated the five focus groups. Recognizing that some fathers may indeed be irresponsible in terms of their commitments, this generalization is endogenous in that caseworkers view fathers as irresponsible because they are nonresident and often not providing care in traditional, clearly visible ways. Does being a non-resident father (who has out-of-wedlock children for whom he may not have established legal paternity) limit the ways in which paternal interest, or more important, paternal involvement can be undertaken and assessed? When case-workers assert that they try to engage nonresident fathers, what does this mean? Clearly, among those participating in the five focus groups, their engagement of nonresident fathers varied significantly. However, the generalization that non-resident fathers are more interested in "playing ball" than addressing child welfare issues regarding their children is a gross overexaggeration. Many non-resident fathers may have other obligations including work and care for other children and/or family members.

Several informants reported that fathers often blamed the mothers for whatever circumstances brought the family to the attention of child welfare authorities and often did not perceive that they also bore responsibility for any maltreatment that their child had suffered. Many informants expressed exas-peration that these same fathers often felt little obligation to participate in ser-vices and neither saw themselves as part of the problem nor as significant contributors to a desired outcome for the child. In addition, even those fathers who were concerned about their children's welfare and wanted to assume cus-tody on their own children faced serious handicaps because of their lack of child care skills and experience. Caseworkers noted that some of these fathers did not understand that they needed to parent a particular child and were frustrated or angry when asked to participate in services such as parenting classes that they felt were unnecessary. Other fathers attempted to accomplish all that was asked of them but were daunted by the time required and, as noted in the findings, by the suspicion and mistrust with which their intentions to obtain custody were received by the court and, sometimes, by service providers.

Implications for Child Welfare Policy and Practice in Permanency Planning

The custodial and residential statuses of unwed fathers shape, in part, the con-text and the range of involvement they undertake. Current research suggests that unwed fathers who reside with their children are more involved than pre-viously documented. This increased involvement appears to be more closely linked to the status of their relationship with the custodial parent than his presence in the household. In fact, many of these fathers may also maintain res-idence with other family members and friends simultaneously. Therefore, a bet-ter understanding of the residential patterns among low-income, unwed fathers is warranted as a means of strengthening family bonds and keeping children within their families of origin.

Similarly, current research suggests that paternal involvement among unwed fathers who do not reside with their children is also greater than previously documented, although significantly less than residential unwed fathers. Child welfare policy and practice would be well served by better understanding the pathways paternal involvement among these fathers has undertaken. The fact that paternal involvement among all unwed fathers declines over time heightens the urgency to understand these parenting relationships. Successful interventions aimed at engaging unwed fathers in permanency planning can evolve from empirical and practice-base examinations.

Paternal commitment among unwed fathers, broadly assessed by providing financial support and presence, may be shaped by the range of financial and nonfinancial options allowed by the custodial parent and opportunity to undertake these forms of involvement. The lower socioeconomic status that broadly defines these fathers suggests that traditional measures for assessing paternal commitment in permanency planning place them at a disadvantage in determining their fitness as custodial parents. Child welfare policy and practice must be sensitive to the nuanced ways in which parenting expectations and obligations are negotiated among unwed parents.

Child welfare policy and practice would also be well served by distinguishing the status of the couple relationship from the possibility for positive coparenting relationships among unwed parents, especially in determining paternal fitness for custodianship. The impracticality is reflected in the dissolution of marital relationships in which a father's fitness for sustaining custody of his child is independent of the status of his relationship with the child's mother. Better assessment tools and processes for determining unwed fathers' capacity to undertake custody of their children in foster care, independent of their relationships with the custodial parent, will level the playing field aimed at treating unwed parents fairly.

Current child welfare initiatives aimed at shortening the timelines for achieving permanency outcomes raise three interrelated issues concerning the role of the child welfare system in addressing the needs and interests of fathers described by informants in the study: the type of goal or goals that should guide child welfare interventions with fathers; whether the child welfare system should focus resources on certain groups of fathers; and what constitutes a "reasonable" effort to assist interested fathers in assuming a parental role (O'Donnell et al. in press).

Few of the informants discussed their practice with fathers in which the father might assume a supportive rather than primary role as an intervention goal. The failure to exhaust the range of ways in which unwed fathers might be involved or sustain involvement is crucial to conceptualizing the status of fathers in child welfare services. Caseworkers typically view fathers as primary custodians, and given the high threshold in terms of paternal expectations and obligations, few, if any, fathers passed their test. It is interesting to note that caseworkers also failed to provide supportive services for fathers to engage and sustain paternal roles by which they routinely assessed their fitness as custodial parents (e.g., financial support). Neither did they offer or provide services that would enable fathers to provide nonfinancial support as engaged parents such as providing direct care as a component of their intervention with the family. Even caseworkers serving intact families approached nonresident fathers as possible alternative caregivers rather than a potential resource to help the mother provide a stable, nurturing environment for their children (O'Donnell et al. in press). The views of the informants are consistent with findings of research previously cited with respect to the limitations of paternal involvement in child welfare work both with nonresident fathers and fathers in intact-parent families (O'Donnell 1999, 2001a). Consideration for the multiple roles that fathers might play in sustaining involvement with their children has important implications for the Adoption and Safe Families Act of 1997. This act requires termination of parental rights when children have been in foster care for fifteen of the last twenty-two months except when the best interest of the child clearly excludes termination. The legislation does not encourage caseworkers to exceed routine "diligent search" procedures in looking for presumed absent or unknown fathers.

Research on the variety of direct and indirect support that fathers can provide their offspring suggests that these limitations may not serve children's needs well. The findings of this focus group study signal the need to reexamine the goals of child welfare practice with respect to the range of objectives that may be achieved through paternal involvement within the mandated time frames for achieving permanency for children. For example, the families of origin of nonresident fathers are key resources in enhancing unwed fathers' capacities to become sole or partial custodians of their children (Johnson 2001b). When caseworkers assess the resources of nonresident fathers for gaining custody, their assessments should include genealogy that maps out family members who could provide financial and nonfinancial support to the fathers and their children. The addition of such an ecological assessment would not only improve the unwed father's profile but also potentially enhance the caseworker's recognition of family support available to the child.

The findings of this study also raise the question regarding the amount of caseworker time and effort that should be expended on nonresident fathers, whose behavior or circumstances indicate that they are not likely to provide any resources for their children or assume any parenting role in the near future. Caseworkers should be required to conduct searches for nonresident fathers and to offer services to fathers who want them. As previously stated, current child welfare practice does not routinely initiate the due diligent search to identify nonresident fathers to offer supportive services that enhance their fitness to become custodial parents. Changes in child welfare policy aimed at removing inequities would improve child welfare practice with unwed fathers. However, the informants in this study raised serious questions about how much of the limited time given to achieve permanency for children should be spent on attempts to engage fathers whom mothers describe as "one-night stands" or who otherwise have demonstrated no interest in their child. These are indeed legitimate questions that must be addressed. Yet, the dynamics of unwed couples and parenting relationships suggest that caseworkers must exert more effort in making these determinations before summarily dismissing unwed fathers as "absent" or "uninvolved." Relying solely on information provided by the custodial parent about the nonresident father's involvement should be open to suspicion and at least substantiated by other sources including the unwed father and his as well as the custodial parent's family of origin. Improved assessment tools and processes for determining paternal involvement throughout the service cycle, from case opening through closing, are warranted.

Similar questions arise with respect to the level of casework efforts on behalf of fathers who display ongoing ambivalence toward parenting a child, who lack very basic parenting skills, or who have a history of not providing care or resources for their children. This is a clear case where early contact with the noncustodial father and assessment of his family resources would be appropriate and useful given the shortened time frames for reunification or termination of parental rights. Child welfare staff should assess carefully the parenting potential of nonresident fathers and focus their time and resources on those fathers whose motivation and circumstances are predictive of ongoing paternal involvement and support. For fathers who are available but display little potential to help parent their children, the current practice of offering services but not making extra efforts to motivate or involve fathers may be the most practical means of satisfying fathers' legal rights to services while not impeding children's rights to permanency on a timely basis. A key factor to implementing such an approach is the development of assessment methods that accurately gauge fathers' motivation and parenting potential. To date, such methods of assessments have not been routinely applied when decisions regarding permanency planning are made. Some critical components of this kind of assessment may already be known and used by practitioners. For example, focus group participants identified paternal family support and the quality of the father's relationship with the child's mother as predictors of paternal involvement (Johnson 2001b). There is no evidence to date, however, that practitioners have a set of procedures or tools that specifically help them to assess paternal strengths and weaknesses.

The focus group discussions also generated questions about the types of services that should be offered to fathers who demonstrate good parenting potential. Informants tended to deny that fathers may have service needs that are different from those provided to mothers, or at least upheld the importance of providing "equal" services for mothers and fathers so that neither had a unfair advantage in the competition to gain custody of their children. Such responses appear to reflect institutional justifications and limitations for supporting the needs of parents in distress than a conceptual understanding of the gender distinctions in societal expectations of parenting that caseworkers themselves employ in assessing paternal commitment and involvement. In addition to perpetuating a "race to the finish" approach to service, this viewpoint overlooks much of what the research literature tells us about how fathers perceive their responsibilities and what unique kinds of assistance they may need to enhance their parenting capacity. For example, despite the increase in the number of fathers who have added to their repertoire of parenting roles, many fathers, particularly among minorities, continue to see the role of breadwinner as the primary contribution a father makes to his children (Johnson 2002a; Leashore 1981). For such men, the motivation to become involved with their children may be strongly affected by their ability to fulfill this role. In order to effectively serve this clientele, child welfare policy and practice must broaden the range of services offered.

Few of the informants appeared sensitive to this paternal need and consequently did not inquire about role conflicts or explore the kind of help a father might need to undertake job searches or vocational training. They routinely ignored these issues because as child welfare workers, they were not required to provide such services. Similarly, participants assumed that all services, such as parenting classes, were gender neutral without asking fathers whether such services helped them to better understand parenting or addressed any of their specific concerns about being a good parent. Recognition of the difficulty in addressing these issues notwithstanding, child welfare policy must confront them head-on if child welfare practice with unwed fathers is to be improved.

One of the major challenges facing the child welfare system is the development of practice-based knowledge of what fathers can be helped and how. The focus group discussions suggest that this development may be impeded by current time constraints on service provision, particularly in substitute care services (O'Donnell et al. in press). Family preservation services may be a promising area in which to develop and test paternal involvement. Because these services are not subject to the legal time restrictions imposed on foster care, family preservation staff have a greater opportunity to assist interested fathers to acquire the motivation, skills, and abilities to provide care for their children in either a primary or secondary capacity. Also, these services are often provided without court involvement, which may facilitate engagement of those fathers who are reluctant to participate in child welfare services due to fear of the judicial system. From a practice perspective, family preservation services may be a more suitable service area than foster care for the development of skills and knowledge about working with both resident and nonresident fathers. Absent the intensive time pressures, child welfare practitioners would have greater opportunity to learn more about how to engage fathers; how to make accurate assessments of fathers' motivation, abilities, and service needs; as well as what kinds of services and service approaches work best for fathers in various circumstances. Focusing on paternal involvement in family preservation may also promote timely permanency for those children who subsequently need to go into foster care, as caseworkers will have a clearer idea of whether the father can play a role in achieving permanency (O'Donnell et al. in press).

The challenge of child welfare policy and practice to provide family supportive services in a dynamic environment in which changes in societal expectations and obligations of parents have not kept pace with changes in family formation patterns can no longer be delayed. The findings of this study, however, suggest that increasing paternal involvement in child welfare service can be difficult, particularly among minority fathers, given the strong distrust that many of these fathers feel toward the child welfare system. This dilemma should not impede progress. The combined contribution of longitudinal child welfare research, policy, and practice focused on unwed fathers in parenting relationships represents the best chance for understanding and strengthening paternal involvement and minimizing out-of-family foster placement and paternal involvement in permanency planning. Their children deserve no less.

REFERENCES

Blankenhorn, D. 1995. *Fatherless America: Confronting Our Most Urgent Social Problem.* New York: Basic Books.

Boyd-Franklin, N. 1989. *Black Families in Therapy: A Multisystems Approach.* New York: Guilford Press.

Danziger, S., & N. Radin. 1990. "Absent Does Not Equal Uninvolved: Predictors of Fathering in Teen Mother Families." *Journal of Marriage and the Family* 52:636–642.

Franklin, D., & S. Smith. 1991. "Adolescent Mothers and Persistent Poverty: Does Delaying Parenthood Still Make a Difference?" Paper presented at the Chicago Urban Poverty and Family Life Conference, Irving B. Harris School of Public Policy Studies, University of Chicago.

Gadsden, V., & M. Hall. 1996. "Intergenerational Learning: A Review of the Literature." Commissioned paper for the National Center on Fathers and Families. Philadelphia: University of Pennsylvania.

Hamer, J. 2001. *What It Means to Be Daddy: Fatherhood for Black Men Living Away from Their Children.* New York: Columbia University Press.

Jaffe, E. 1983. "Fathers and Child Welfare Services: The Forgotten Clients?" In *Fatherhood and Family Policy,* edited by M. Lamb & A. Sagi, 129–137. Hillsdale, NJ: L. Erlbaum.

Johnson, D. 1996. "Father Presence Matters: A Review of the Literature." Commissioned paper for the National Center on Fathers and Families. Philadelphia: University of Pennsylvania.

Johnson, E., A. Levine & F. Doolittle. 1999. *Fathers' Fair Share: Helping Poor Men Manage Child Support and Fatherhood.* New York: Russell Sage Foundation.

Johnson, W. 1998. "Paternal Involvement in Fragile, African American Families: Implications for Clinical Social Work Practice." *Smith College Studies in Social Work* 68/2:215–232.

———. 2001a. "Paternal Involvement among Unwed Fathers." *Children and Youth Services Review* 23/6–7:513–536.

———. 2001b. "Young, Unwed African American Fathers: Social and Developmental Indicators of Their Paternal Involvement." In *Forging Links: African American Children—Clinical and Developmental Perspectives*, edited by A. Neal-Barnett, J. Contreras & K. Kerns, 147–174. Westport, CT: Praeger.

———. 2002a. "Time Out of Bound: High School Completion and Work Preparation among Urban, Poor, Unwed African American Fathers." In *African American Education: Race, Community, Inequality, and Achievement: A Tribute to Edgar G. Epps*, edited by W. Allen, M. Spencer & C. O'Connor, 229–256. Oxford, UK: JAI/Elsevier Science.

———. 2002b. "Social Work Strategies for Sustaining Paternal Involvement among Unwed Fathers: Insights from Field Research." *Professional Development: The International Journal of Continuing Social Work Education* 4/5(3/1):70–83.

Lamb, M. 1997. "Fathers and Child Development." In *The Role of the Father in Child Development*, edited by M. Lamb, 1–18. New York: John Wiley & Sons.

Lamb, M., J. Pleck, E. Charnov & J. Levine. 1987. "A Biosocial Perspective on Paternal Behavior and Involvement." In *Parenting across the Lifespan: Biosocial Perspectives*, edited by J. Lancaster, J. Altman, A. Rossi & L. Sherrod, 11–42. New York: Academic.

Leashore, B. 1981. "Human Services and the Unwed Father: The Forgotten Half." *The Family Coordinator* 23/4:487–534.

Lerman, R., & T. Ooms. 1992. *Young Unwed Fathers: Changing Roles, Emerging Policies*. Philadelphia: Temple University Press.

McLanahan, S., & I. Garfinkel. 2001. "Unwed Parents: Myths, Realities and Policymaking." National report, Fragile Families and Child Well-being Study. Retrieved from http://crcw.princeton.edu.

Mead, L. 1986. *Beyond Entitlement: The Social Obligations of Citizenship*. New York: Free Press.

Murray, C. 1984. *Losing Ground: American Social Policy, 1950–1980*. New York: Basic Books.

Nichols-Casebolt, A. 1988. "Black Families Headed by Single Mothers: Growing Numbers and Increasing Poverty." *Social Work*, 306–313.

O'Donnell, J. 1999. "Involvement of African American Fathers in Kinship Foster Care Services." *Social Work* 44/5:428–441.

———. 2001. "Paternal Involvement in Kinship Foster Care Services in One Father and Multiple-Father Families." *Child Welfare* 80/4:453–479.

O'Donnell, J., W. Johnson, L. D'Aunno & H. Thornton. In press. "Fathers in Child Welfare: Caseworkers' Perspectives." In *Child Welfare*.

Osborne, C. 2002. "Diversity among Unmarried Parents: Human Capital, Attitudes, and Relationship Quality." Working paper, Center for Research on Child Well-Being, Princeton University.

Padgett, D. 1998. *Qualitative Methods in Social Work Research: Challenges and Rewards*. Thousand Oaks, CA: Sage Publications.

Pleck, J. 1997. "Paternal Involvement: Levels, Sources, and Consequences." In *The Role of the Father in Child Development*, edited by M. Lamb, 66–103. New York: John Wiley & Sons.

Robertson, J. 1997. "Young Residential Fathers Have Lower Earnings: Implications for Child Support Enforcement." *Social Work Research* 21/4:211–223.

Roschelle, A. 1997. *No More Kin: Exploring Race, Class, and Gender in Family Networks*. Thousand Oaks, CA: Sage Publications.

Rosier, K. 2000. *Mothering Inner City Children: The Early School Years.* New Brunswick, NJ: Rutgers University Press.

Roy, K. 1999. "Low Income Single Fathers in an African American Community and the Requirements of Welfare Reform." *Journal of Family Issues* 20:432–457.

Seltzer, J. 1996. "Fathers by Law: Effects of Joint Legal Custody on Nonresident Fathers' Involvement with Children." Paper presented at the Conference on Father Involvement. Family and Child Well-Being Network of the National Institute of Child Health and Human Development, Bethesda, MD.

Stone, G. 2002. "Nonresidential, Never-Married Fathers: Policy Advocacy Opportunities." *Professional Development: The International Journal of Continuing Social Work Education* 4/5(3/1):57–60.

Waite, L., & M. Gallagher. 2000. *The Case for Marriage: Why Married People Are Happier, Healthier, and Better Off Financially.* New York: Doubleday.

PART THREE

Using an Africentric
Perspective for Practice
and Service Delivery

In part 3 of our 1991 book, we asserted that child neglect was the primary reason for the disproportionate number of African American children in child welfare and that, as such, it escaped the public's attention. Twelve years later, child neglect continues to be the major reason for the disproportionate involvement of African American children in our nation's child welfare system.

Similarly, in 1991 we asserted that a significant reduction in child welfare cases is more likely to occur with improvements in housing, health care, employment, and education. Unfortunately, twelve years later, substantive improvements in these and related areas have been few. Thus, the primary reason for the disproportionate number of African American children in child welfare, and the needed improvements to reduce this number, remain as they were twelve years later.

With our first book, we hoped to elevate the importance of race in child welfare and argued that race must be considered if more effective services were to be achieved. Today, we assert that it is imperative that race be considered in order to reduce the disproportionate number of African American children in child welfare. For example, it is imperative that federal policy and local practices support kinship, subsidized legal guardianship, and effective neighborhood-based services. In addition, housing assistance, accessible and quality health care, training and employment services, and an improved and enhanced system of education in public schools are needed.

Culturally sensitive policies and practices are needed to effectively address the critical social and economic factors that are related to child maltreatment. For example, substance abuse prevention and intervention services, domestic violence and parenting programs, and policies and programs to reduce poverty and unemployment are critically necessary to abate the abuse and neglect of children. The social and economic costs of failing to provide these and other important policies and services are great including: the death of children, an increase in the likelihood of juvenile and violent crimes and the financial costs associated with them, and the long-term emotional and psychological consequences of abuse and neglect. Estimates of the financial costs alone suggests that child abuse and neglect costs $258 million each day and about $94 billion each year. It should be noted that these estimates, while alarming, probably understate the annual costs (U.S. Department of Health and Human Services 2003). For some, these costs suggest that child welfare in the United States has become an industry with African American children as the chief commodities.

The chapters included in the next part of this book use the Africentric perspective as a common thread for pursuing effective child welfare practice and service delivery. Part 3 does not address all of the practice and service delivery challenges confronting child welfare, nor all of the opportunities available for prevention and intervention. Rather, they highlight some prominent and important areas for effective practice with African American families and children (i.e., substance abuse, homelessness, and HIV/AIDS; kinship care; family preservation and neighborhood-based services; and adoptions). Excluded areas include legal guardianship with subsidy, long-term foster care, residential care, group homes, and so on. While many of these excluded areas are more traditional approaches and practices, we are excited about and encourage the development of innovative, emerging, and responsive practices such as legal guardianship with subsidy.

This part begins with Okundaye, Lawrence-Webb, and Smith's consideration of the interrelated problems of substance abuse, homelessness, and HIV/AIDS. Drawing on the Africentric and ecological perspectives, they emphasize the need for a culturally relevant perspective, provide an overview of these problems, and address the implications for practice with African American families and children. In the following chapter, Mills and Usher highlight the kinship care approach as an effective model of care. They make clear linkages between kinship care and the Africentric perspective, which are exemplified by the adage "It takes a *community* to raise a child." A call to action for family and community care models of practice is made, building on the strengths of African American extended families and a tradition and history of community care (e.g., informal child care and adoptions). Kinship care, family group decision making, and strengths-based empowerment are practice approaches that can provide family continuity for children in need of care.

Viewed as a universal and enduring theme among African Americans, Carten and Dumpson highlight family preservation and the emerging interest in neighborhood-based services. Family-centered practice as central to permanency planning is emphasized. Preserving families through self-help and improving neighborhood conditions is supported, and accessible, continuous, integrated, and culturally competent systems of care located in neighborhoods where African American families and children live with prevention as an important goal are encouraged. Developing models of neighborhood-based services are presented, and linkages with an Africentric perspective are made (e.g., communalism, mutual aid, collectivism, shared parenting, consanguineal family structure).

The problem of mental health disparities in the child welfare system is addressed in Manning's chapter. The lack of integration between mental health and child welfare systems poses a particularly disturbing problem for African American foster children who are more at risk for mental health disorders, and have limited access and low utilization of mental health services. Manning recommends a culturally competent system of care model. In an effective "system of care," schools, community mental health centers, psychiatric treatment programs, substance abuse services, recreational services, vocational services, primary health care organizations, and child welfare agencies coordinate services to most effectively address the needs of these children while allowing them to remain in their community.

In the final chapter of part 3, McRoy provides a comprehensive and critical analysis of the challenges faced by public adoption agencies in placing African American children. Inequities and barriers in the delivery of child welfare services for African American families and children are considered, particularly in the context of adoption services. Racial discrimination in hiring child welfare personnel and a poorly trained child welfare workforce are addressed. In addition, this chapter highlights the long-standing cultural tradition of informal adoptions among African Americans, as well as the impact of current adoption policies and legislation. The call for culturally competent staff and locating services in African American communities is clear in this chapter, as is the call for creating specialized recruitment and retention services of African American adoptive families, and financial and other supportive services for these families.

REFERENCE

U.S. Department of Health and Human Services, Children's Bureau. 2003. "Emerging Practices in the Prevention of Child Abuse and Neglect." Retrieved from www.calib.com/nccanch/prevention/emerging.

9

Substance Abuse, Homelessness, HIV/AIDS, and African American Children

JOSHUA N. OKUNDAYE

CLAUDIA LAWRENCE-WEBB

PAMELA L. THORNTON

> When spider webs unite, they can tie up a lion.
>
> —Ethiopian proverb (Smith 1992)

Introduction

Substance abuse, homelessness, HIV/AIDS, and the overrepresentation of African American children in the American child welfare system present a combination of problems that continue to be overwhelming, resulting in a pressing need for developing alternative systems of service provision. In so doing, more attention needs to be given to the theoretical frameworks and paradigms that guide service delivery. Given the complexity of the challenges that substance abuse, homelessness, and HIV/AIDS create, any approach not grounded within a culturally relevant perspective is likely to have limited utility and compromised outcomes for African American children.

Current statistics on the pervasiveness of substance abuse, homelessness, and HIV/AIDS reveal that nine million to ten million children under the age of eighteen are directly affected by substance-abusing parents (Woodside 1988). For example, in 1994, eleven states had an average of 35 percent of their substantiated cases involve substance abuse, with the percentage ranging from 4 percent to 65 percent (Wiese & Daro 1995). Curtis and McCullough (1993) as cited in Resnik, Gardner, and Rogers (1998) "report that the Child Welfare League found that 83 percent of child protective services providers interviewed believed that problems associated with substance abuse increased the time they spent investigating a case. In addition, 93 percent of the respondents reported that substance abuse was increasingly a factor in initial investigations. However, only 65.9 percent reported that their agency provided training associated with family substance abuse" (102). Sixty percent of homeless women have children ages zero to seventeen, while 41 percent of homeless men have children ages zero to seventeen. Most of these children are young: 20 percent are ages zero to two, 22 percent are ages three to five, 20 percent are ages six to eight, and 33 percent are between the ages of nine and seventeen. Age was not given for 5 percent. Homeless families have, on average, two children. Members of these families comprise 34 percent of all homeless people using services (www.urban.org/housing/homeless/homeless.html).

Case studies conducted by housing service provider organizations found that the foster care system often fails to provide children with appropriate services to address the problems (child abuse, neglect, parental substance abuse, etc.) that brought them to the system (Roman & Wolfe 1997). "Frequent movements of children within foster care have impacted the system's ability to provide treatment relevant to the problems presented" (10). Case studies also indicated that alcohol and substance abuse illnesses frequently interact with foster care placement and homelessness. Homeless people with a foster care history are more likely than other homeless people to have their own children in foster care (Nelson 1995; Roman & Wolfe 1997). Adult and adolescent AIDS cases total 765,559 with 635,451 cases in males and 130,104 cases in females. Through the same time period, 8,908 AIDS cases were reported in children under age thirteen. Total deaths of persons reported with AIDS are 448,060, including 442,882 adults and adolescents, and 5,178 children under age fifteen, and 412 persons whose age at death is unknown (www.cdc.gov/hiv/stats .htm#cumrace). Resnik, Gardner, and Rogers (1998) believe that "increased parental substance abuse and associated HIV infection also contribute to the problem of so-called border babies" (103). Children experiencing HIV/AIDS and other problems associated with substance abuse have contributed to the increased number of kinship care placements within the child welfare system (Lawrence-Webb, Okundaye & Hafner 2001).

The singularity or combination of substance abuse, homelessness, and HIV/AIDS creates special problems for children and their families within the child welfare system. Many of the social conditions and problems experienced by children such as poverty, child abuse/ neglect, mental illness, and medical ailments often have their roots in the sometimes-difficult underlying problems of substance abuse, homelessness, and HIV/AIDS within family systems. These are the problems that child welfare workers find the most difficult to address because many behaviors that may be associated with such conditions may also be attributed to other social problems. Documentation of cause and effect to explain how children end up in the child welfare system becomes complex. Families often deny all three conditions as existing and needing intervention. Many children and their families find these situations to be embarrassing, shameful, and the most frowned upon by society. This makes the ability to identify the problem and intervene even more difficult (Child Welfare League of America 1992; Feig 1998; McCullough 1991). These problems have serious consequences for providing child welfare services because they require an array of interdisciplinary services to allow for the protection of children while seeking to establish or maintain them in permanent living situations within or outside of their families. Addressing the difficult challenges created by these conditions requires a complex integration of skillful social workers who can interface with other disciplines and a service delivery system that recognizes how their different philosophies, missions, and interventions are sometimes counterproductive to a helping process that requires collaboration and respect.

Service delivery has several barriers. For example, in the course of service provision, issues of substance abuse are addressed with parents but may not be systematically addressed with children, or the problem of homelessness is addressed with the family but may not incorporate services for substance abuse and HIV/AIDS although these problems may be a catalyst for the homelessness of families and children. The fragmentation of the delivery of services across a variety of problems that affect families and children is a long-standing problem (Ambrosino et al. 2001). When some integrated services are available to African American families within existing service frameworks, they may not necessarily be culturally sensitive or integrate the expertise necessary to promote the well-being of the family.

Another barrier is that many programs tend to focus on concrete services (e.g., housing, drug treatment, medication) as opposed to inclusion of mind and body needs or "soft" services of the spirit and soul. The oneness of mind and body (spirituality) is embedded in the lives of many African Americans and as such, it should be integrated in interventions. Thus, while concrete services such as housing are extremely important, these "houses" would not automatically transform into "homes" without the healing of mind and body (Lawrence-Webb, Okundaye & Hafner 2001).

The purpose of this chapter is to provide an overview of the problems of substance abuse, homelessness, and HIV/AIDS among African Americans involved in the child welfare system. An integrated approach to these problems from two theoretical perspectives, Africentric and ecological, are utilized to guide discussion of these problems. Finally, this chapter proposes a model service delivery system that is congruent with the Africentric perspective in order to guide practitioners to a more practice-oriented understanding of the problem and a web approach to service delivery.

Nature of the Problems

Situations that African American children experience today did not exist to the same degree and intensity that they did forty years ago. It was only in the mid-1960s and their introduction into the modern child welfare system that the government began to track levels of poverty among African Americans and to monitor the number of African American children receiving services. Eligibility workers and early social workers did not keep track of the race and/or ethnicity of children in the adoption and foster care processes until the passage of the Flemming Rule in the 1960s brought to the full attention of the federal government the racist and discriminatory practices of denying large numbers of African American children access to Aid to Families with Dependent Children (AFDC) welfare benefits (Lawrence-Webb 1995).

The Flemming Rule was a 1960s federal administrative ruling that would not allow states to arbitrarily deny welfare benefits to African American children without ensuring that they were living in safe and protected environments (Lawrence-Webb 1995). The Flemming Rule ushered in the changes to the 1960s legislation regarding foster care payments, child abuse/neglect investigations, and the 1962 public welfare amendments. Service emphasis was on removing children from their homes and placing them in foster care. This led to an influx of a disproportionate number of African American children entering the child welfare system that continues today. As a result of children's needs for home placements and decreases in traditional foster care homes, initiatives were proposed to promote a reliance on relative placements—a historical cultural resource for African American children. Legislation included the Child Abuse Prevention and Treatment Act of 1974 (PL 93-247), Indian Child Welfare Act of 1978 (PL 95-608), Adoption Assistance and Child Welfare Act of 1980 (PL 96-272), and the Adoption and Safe Families Act of 1997 (PL 105-189). At the same time, however, services to assist these families did not incorporate an Africentric perspective that supports and enhances family strengths.

The current situation warrants the modification of theoretical paradigms for understanding African American children and their families, as well as for creating new techniques and interventions. This chapter proposes linking the Africentric perspective with an ecological systems perspective to assist African American children and their families with the interrelated problems of substance abuse, HIV/AIDS, and homelessness.

Parental substance abuse is associated with a large percentage of child welfare cases. In fact, the major reason for the increase in children entering foster care since the 1980s is attributed to the consequences of parental substance abuse (Azzi-Lessing & Olsen 1996; Dore & Doris 1998). Parental substance abuse is reported by child welfare workers in the range of 20 percent to 90 percent of cases (Jaudes, Ekwo & Van Voorhis 1995). A 1999 report by Advocates for Children and Youth states that in Maryland, "parental substance abuse is associated with at least two-thirds of maltreatment cases."[1] Parental substance abuse is also associated with two-thirds of all foster care cases as a reason for removal and a key barrier to reunification for many of the children in foster care for extended periods.[2]

Since the late 1980s, attention has focused on the growing numbers of infants born addicted or negatively affected during pregnancy due to mothers' alcohol and other drug use (Rathus, Nevid & Fichner-Rathus 1998). According to Ambrosino et al. (2001), "five thousand infants are born with fetal alcohol syndrome, the third leading cause of birth defects leading to mental retardation" (240). These conditions have evolved as some of the primary concerns in child welfare. Further, substance abuse is frequently accompanied by a host of other difficult problems that make working with these families challenging. Among the most common are HIV/AIDS, economic and housing insecurity, mental illness, domestic violence, and dangerous neighborhood environments (Oakley & Dennis 1996). Research has shown that child welfare clients with an identified substance abuse problem have more problems overall than other clients (USDHHS 1999a). Caseworkers report that these are among the most difficult and frustrating cases to manage (Semidei, Radel & Nolan 2001).

Current trends in the incidents of HIV/AIDS disproportionately affect racial minority populations, especially women, youth, and children. The U.S. Department of Health and Human Services (USDHHS 2000) reports that African Americans have the highest incidence of HIV than any other ethnic groups. For example, from July 1998 through June 1999, African Americans accounted for 46 percent of adult AIDS cases, while representing only 12 percent of the total U.S. population (USDHHS 2000). The greatest increase has been among racial and ethnic minority women through heterosexual transmission. Substance abuse is one of the primary mechanisms by which these vulnerable groups become HIV-infected. When considered jointly, heterosexual contact and intravenous drug users comprised 36 percent of the reported cases of AIDS (USDHHS 2001).

The Centers for Disease Control and Prevention (CDC) estimates that 1 in 50 black men and 1 in 160 black women are infected with HIV, making them ten times more likely than whites to be diagnosed with AIDS and ten times more likely to die from it. As of December 2000, the number of persons living with AIDS was at an all-time high (322,685), 61 percent of which were black or Hispanic (USDHHS 2001). Thus, it is painfully evident that the epidemic is a significant threat to the lives of African Americans (Shinn & Weitzman 1996).

Finally, this epidemic has already affected African American children. For example, in 2000, more than 125,000 American children lost one or both parents to AIDS, 80 percent of whom were African American or Hispanic (United Press International 2001). The disproportionate representation of African Americans experiencing chronic disease in the United States is linked to poverty and a lack of access to health care facilities. HIV/AIDS and substance abuse are examples of such chronic illnesses (Ambrosino et al. 2001).

The Mayors' Survey on Hunger and Homelessness in America's cities found that families with children comprised 36 percent of the homeless population (U.S. Conference of Mayors 1998). On average, homeless families have two children (USDHHS 1999b). Of the homeless population, 50 percent are estimated to be African American. This number is based on data collected in urban environments and does not necessarily account for homelessness in rural areas. In addition, it is estimated that 37 percent of homeless individuals in urban areas are substance abusers. Having an addiction cannot be solely viewed as the cause of homelessness; however, it does make it difficult for those experiencing such chronic conditions as substance abuse and HIV/AIDS to compete for the limited housing options available (Daskal 1998). For instance, landlords and shelters may be reluctant to provide shelter to them and their children as a result of these disabilities (National Coalition for the Homeless 1997). In a profile of women enrolled in a methadone maintenance program, up to 50 percent were homeless (Kaltenback 1994).

Substance abuse, HIV/AIDS, along with poverty, declining employment opportunities and restrictions, and welfare, as well as a lack of affordable rental housing contribute to the problem of homelessness experienced by children (Koegel, Burnam, & Baumohl 1996; Roman & Wolfe 1997; U.S. Bureau of the Census 1998). Homelessness often occurs in conjunction with parental substance abuse, chronic mental illness, and unsafe behavior (Oakley & Dennis 1996). All of these factors increase homeless people's risk for contracting HIV. A survey of sixteen U.S. cities found that 3 percent of homeless people were HIV positive, compared with less than 1 percent of the general adult population (Allen et al. 1994).

Unfortunately, people with HIV/AIDS may die before they receive the housing assistance that they need. Stigma and fear of the illness continue to thwart efforts to build HIV/AIDS housing for people with HIV/AIDS. According to a Los Angeles study, approximately two-thirds of people with AIDS experienced homelessness (Shelter Partnership 1999). Robbins and Nelson (1995) found that 36 percent of people with HIV/AIDS were homeless since learning that they had contracted the disease. Since HIV/AIDS drains one physically as well as financially, it is often difficult for families in this situation to adequately provide the basic essentials for living, shelter being one of these essentials. The impact of homelessness on children has been known to make them three times more likely to have emotional or behavioral problems, repeat a grade, or be suspended or expelled from school. In comparison with housed children, they experience more poor health, depression, anxiety, developmental delays, behavioral problems, and low self-esteem (Shinn & Weitzman 1996). HIV/AIDS, coupled with homelessness/substance abuse and the possible loss of a parent, has a serious impact on the child physically, psychologically, socially, and spiritually.

As a result of the complex nature of the interrelated conditions of substance abuse, HIV/AIDS, and homelessness, interventions with and on behalf of children have taken on a greater urgency. Culturally effective paradigms are needed to ensure the safety and protection of children. Thus, a relevant paradigm shift is especially important due to the magnitude of these problems and their direct impact on the rise in kinship care living arrangements for children and greater use of extended family systems in the African American community. To meet this demand, there have been major changes in family preservation and permanency planning for children, mandating the exploration of family resources and promoting family preservation initiatives in order to cut costs and bridge cultural differences. Significant changes in the roles and expectations for placements and length of stay in foster care have been made to improve the system. The impetus for these changes has been the Child and Family Services Review Initiative that requires documentation of service intervention outcomes (Morgan 2002). The Child and Family Services Review mandate is part of current child welfare legislation in foster care, child protection, and adoption that requires caseworkers to document not just the services they provide but the effectiveness or outcome of those services. Unfortunately, these changes have placed greater demands on a child welfare system that is already overwhelmed—hence, the rise in privatization of managed care organizations for child welfare services. What is proposed here is an alternative for how to work with such complex issues in both public and private agencies.

Conceptual Framework

Turner (1997) provides some guidelines for linking mainstream theories with the Africentric perspective. According to Turner, metaparadigms—for example, Dorman's 1988 ecosystems perspective and cybernetic epistemology, or the social systems models—are more congruent with the Africentric perspective than models that look for linear causality. Turner further contends that "metaparadigms view phenomena as interconnected and interrelated in a causal network and view individual behavior as something that can be understood only in context. These metatheories, or metaparadigms, are like transparencies that are content free and therefore not subject to ethnocentric bias" (55).

With this in mind, this chapter uses some key concepts from the Africentric and ecological perspectives to create a framework that is culturally relevant and useful for addressing the problems previously identified. The Africentric perspective implicitly contends that differences in culture, worldview, and historical experiences exist between African Americans and European Americans. The Africentric perspective delineates and explicates some of these differences, many of which have implications for the construction of paradigms of human behavior. The principles of the Africentric perspective include the interconnectedness of all things; oneness of mind, body, and spirit; collective identity;

consanguineal family structure; consequential morality; analogue thinking; phenomenological time; and spirituality (Turner 1997). While all of these principles are relevant to this discussion, the chapter highlights the first four principles because of their relative similarities and connection to the ecosystems principles.

The Africentric perspective is a theoretical paradigm whose central core is based on African philosophy and religion. The foundation of that core is that all living things are one with nature, interdependent with each other. No matter how small, life is significant in the larger context of the universe. The life and existence of humans does not take preference over the fragile existence of plants and other living things. Turner (1997) states that in African cosmology or philosophy, people are perceived as being interconnected to everything in their environment. People are embedded in nature as a part of it and interconnected to all of it, not separate from it. All people are considered interconnected to each other, to those who have died, and to those who are not yet born. The link between people of the past and present is maintained through oral traditions that help to solidify interdependent relationships and social networks across time and space.

The concept of understanding sees human nature as holistic, encompassing the mind, body, and spirit (Turner 1997). Unlike the Eurocentric perspective that attempts to understand humans by examining them through the separation of the mind from the body, Africentrism suggests that this arbitrary separation is counterproductive to understanding the full and true nature of humans. In African philosophy and religion, life is circular in nature and there is no division between these entities. There is no beginning and end to life. Every living thing has a physical, mental, and spiritual component down to the smallest blade of grass. The living and the dead are connected in spirit and ancestry (Mbiti 1970). It is through the living that the spirit of the dead continues to live due to ancestral lines; hence the saying, "I am the spirit of my ancestors." This view of being one with the universe is not an uncommon phenomenon in Eastern religions and Native American culture. For example, there is a Native American song that speaks of "the spirit of the wind carrying one home to one's self" (Eighteenth Annual World Celebration Gathering of Nations PowWow, April 26–28, 2001, Albuquerque, NM).

African psychological identity differs from the Eurocentric ideal of individualism in that it is collective (Nobles 1972). In many African cultures, the tribe, as the basic human unit, seeks to ensure its collective survival. To share a collective identity is to know that one is not alone and that others share the joys and sorrows of life (White 1984).

According to Nobles (1972), the ethos, in a very real sense, is not something for the betterment of the individual, but rather something for the community of which the individual was an integral part. "For the traditional African, to be human was to belong to the whole community" (Mbiti 1970, 5). The concept of collective identity is juxtaposed to the Western ideal of rugged individualism and fierce insistence on individuals being independent as opposed to interdependent (Nobles 1972; Turner 1997).

The belief of being one with the world and cognizant of one's significance and insignificance when evaluating one's self in the larger context of the universe supports the concept of collectivism. All living things are interdependent and therefore responsible to and for each other. This concept is applied to the utilization of resources within the larger world and within smaller systems such as communities and families. One should never take more than is required and is never asked to contribute more than one is capable of providing. This sense of communal responsibility is applied in all aspects of life (Turner 1997).

The interconnectedness and interdependence of living things expressed in collective identity are seen throughout Africa in the consanguineal family. The family as an institution includes all related through the bloodline and by marriage. The term "extended family" is also used to describe this type of structure (Sudarkasa 1996). "Nuclear ethnocentric" families, in contrast, include only the conjugal unit and its children. From an Africentric perspective, the nuclear unit is not the central or basic unit. The genetic or bloodline is the basic unit. Thus, even if the conjugal unit dissolves, the family remains intact (Turner 1997). For African Americans, this collectivism is highly emphasized in community responsibility and family life. The bonds and relationships in family are supported by the consanguineal or bloodlines within family systems.

Sudarkasa (1996) discusses the significance of consanguineal family relationships within the African American community, while Stack (1974) highlights the nature of kinship relationships and arrangements representative of the collectivist nature that continues to be a part of how African American families and communities function. It is quite common to hear the saying that "blood is thicker than water." This saying symbolically represents the importance of blood relatives being there for each other, in good and bad times.

The Africentric perspective provides a unique opportunity to work with African Americans utilizing a theoretical paradigm that is culturally sensitive and captures the nature of this population group. The concepts of being one with the universe or interconnectedness of all things; the integration of mind, body and spirit; collectivism or collective identity; and consanguineal family structure are all a part of Africentrism.

The ecological systems perspective, a unifying theoretical frame of reference (Allen-Meares, Washington & Welsh 1986; Fine 1992; Garbarino et al. 1992), directs us to focus on the social ecology of a community to enhance our understanding of various challenges that families, communities, and nations face. The perspective, which is drawn from ecological ideas and general systems theory, is specifically concerned with providing a broad context for social work practice. The following are the four central ideas or principles of the perspective.

First is the principle that all systems are made up of separate but interrelated members (parts) that constitute an ordered whole (Hutchinson 1999). For example, a family by definition first exists separately from other families and the community. Second, it has boundaries that are more or less permeable, but which clearly delineate the family as both a unit and as subgroups of individuals within it (Meyer 1988).

Next is the principle that all systems are interconnected, with each part impacting all other parts and the system as a whole (Hutchinson 1999). The reciprocity or mutuality in these relationships is like a thread pulled through fabric; it shapes the garment all the way through; even the distortions that it creates are organic to the material of which it is a part (Meyer 1988). Third is the principle that all systems are subsystems of other larger systems (Hutchinson 1999). There is commonality in having a shared history, culture, and daily life experience (Meyer 1988). The fourth principle is that all systems maintain boundaries that give them their identities; and systems tend toward homeostasis, or equilibrium (Hutchinson 1999).

Thus, like Africentrism and its principles of the interconnectedness of all things and being one with the universe; the integration of mind, body, and spirit; collectivism or collective identity; and consanguineal family structure, the underlying philosophical position of the ecological systems perspective is that the person is connected to others, as well as to the social institutions, cultural forces, and the physical space that make up his or her environment. Both perspectives share the same basic views of the world. Like Africentrism, ecological systems principles allow us to view individuals, families, and groups holistically—that is, to recognize the interrelatedness of each person to his or her environment (Meyer 1988). Indeed, it makes sense at this juncture to see the interconnectedness of substance abuse, HIV/AIDS, homelessness, and child welfare problems identified in this chapter.

Interrelatedness: Substance Abuse, HIV/AIDS, Homelessness, and Child Welfare

When parents are suffering from chronic substance abuse, HIV/AIDS, or homelessness, there are impacts on the children. Children within a family are merely a subsystem of the larger family and, regardless of the type of care they receive from their parents, there is commonality in having a shared history, culture, and daily life experience (Meyer 1988). They maintain boundaries that give them their identities. Even within what one may consider a dysfunctional situation of drugs, alcohol, and homelessness, there may be a sense of equilibrium to children because they know what to expect and knowing is better than not knowing.

Using these integrated principles presents an opportunity to draw upon the connectedness between persons and to utilize these in an innovative way to assist children and families in developing alternatives to detrimental situations. Within this paradigm shift, the traditional view of providing services is integrated into a culturally competent approach that takes into account the social and psychological forces impacting parents that have rendered them and their children in precarious conditions. The focus of interventions should no longer be limited to the psychosocial deficits of individuals, families, and communities, but extended to the body-soul-family-neighborhood-society nexus.

Finally, grounding interventions with African American families in Africentric and ecological systems perspectives fosters interventions that are complementary and capable of emphasizing the importance of the African philosophy of collective consciousness. Exploring as well as enhancing, supporting, developing, and using resources that families may already possess such as community connections, agencies and organizations, churches, and mutual support systems are part of cultivating the collectiveness of being responsible for each other during difficult and profitable times. Here, family preservation and kinship care become critical interventions for ensuring the safety, permanency, and well-being of all children. The goal is to use the resources of the family as a means of providing the least restrictive environment for the child while maintaining his/her connection to the family system.

This approach supports the belief that children are better off in their own family systems with support and services than in any other living arrangement because it provides them with a sense of continuity, permanence, identity, and nurturance (Scannapieco & Jackson 1996). It is when children are removed from their homes that they lose a part of who they are and where they belong. When a child is placed in care, he or she experiences the loss of the previous caregiver, the familiar environment, and established relationships. Even though the child's previous family environment and relationships may have been less than perfect and sometimes even abusive and traumatic, the child grieves the loss of loved ones just the same (Edelstein, Burge & Waterman 2001).

The larger context of services should incorporate helping individual children and their families to understand this loss, deal with the grief associated with it, and move on to protective ways of coping. Services should emphasize what should be done in their own best interest and that of their larger community. This requires a reeducation process that alters the child and family's worldview of their importance and significance to the larger community. The sense of belonging and being valued as an individual is paramount to a collective identity. Utilizing this collective identity helps the child and the family to place themselves in the larger world and to develop self-esteem and viable skills for surviving hostile environments—hence, for example, the rise in rites of passage programs. These programs have their origin in African culture in which adolescents are guided in their transition from youth to adulthood (Harvey & Warfield-Coppock 1989). Children are assisted in understanding their history, their connection to it, and their responsibility to themselves and their community.

Using ecological and Africentric perspectives to guide interventions necessitates a shift in the perception of a model of linear causality. Practitioners depart from previous models of causality that imply direct cause and effect from one element to another, including the impact of a practice method upon a case problem. Also, because systems theory emphasizes holism and focuses on the interaction between and among systems, a wider view of the situation becomes necessary so as to account for everything that impinges upon the unit of attention. This view requires concentration on the person, the environment, and their differential interaction as an ecological whole rather than as separate entities (Bloom 1998; Feig 1998; Harden 1998; Resnik, Gardner & Rogers 1998). Therefore, it becomes clear that sometimes parents end up in difficult situations, not totally attributable to themselves but sometimes wholly attributable to their environment and sometimes attributable to both. For instance, sometimes parents abuse substances as a maladaptive coping strategy of painful or difficult circumstances in which they find themselves. It is quite conceivable that if a parent loses a job, he or she may use drugs or alcohol to cope with that loss. The situation becomes more stressful due to the debilitating behaviors in which the parent is engaging, which could in turn lead to homelessness and child abuse/neglect. Thus, a child welfare issue emanates from a structural or social condition (i.e., job loss).

It is recommended that the ecological system assessment be linked to holistic intervention strategies that are intended to treat interrelated problems at multiple levels. This recommendation should be extended to the Africentric perspective. Practitioners must have at their disposal proven interventions that are both person and environment changing. For example, a practitioner may teach a parent social skills that facilitate adjustment in society while simultaneously working with the children in the school and with community agencies to develop a natural support network for the family. "Ideally, the choice of intervention should be based on strategies that have been validated (by reports from practitioners or empirically or both) for a particular situation" (Allen-Meares & Lane 1987, 520).

Implications for Social Work Education, Policy, Practice, and Research

Substance abuse, HIV/AIDS, and homelessness cross every field of human services, especially social work. As this chapter has argued, the maltreated child population cannot be served without considering the role of these interacting elements. The educational system that trains social workers and other human service providers needs to recognize this. Social workers and other human service providers need to have taken at least one to three credit hours of substance abuse course work, human sexuality, and related health courses, as well as courses emphasizing poverty issues. Those already in the field should be required to include such vital training in their continuing education agenda.

Effective policies and programs for African American children and their families experiencing substance abuse, HIV/AIDS, and homelessness should have some common elements (USDHHS 1999b). First and foremost, they should incorporate Africentric elements as a means of addressing issues of cultural sensitivity. The assessment and treatment philosophy should be holistic in nature, and the goal of treatment should be guided by the best interest of the child in the context of the family and community, and in conjunction with permanency and a safe protective environment in which the child can develop. Programs should have a multidisciplinary approach to addressing these issues and view them as interrelated and part of the larger picture.

Policies, research, and programs on homelessness, substance abuse, HIV/AIDS, and child welfare should be interfaced with each other. For example, substance abuse treatment, homelessness, and HIV/AIDS programs may be located in a multidisciplinary center with the child welfare agency in the community. This could enhance and improve the coordination of services for children, families, and treatment providers. In addition, it would allow for centralized services in the community where children live, promote and make outreach efforts easier, promote cross-training of staff, and coordinate housing efforts for the hard-to-place populations of HIV/AIDS and substance abusers with children. This can be achieved by consolidating a resource where parents can explore admission to abstinence-based residential or risk-reduction residential programs, as well as independent transitional housing managed by social service programs, providing home-based services like chore services, meal delivery, health care especially for those with HIV/AIDS, and adult day health.

Conclusions and Recommendations

This chapter has argued that one of the greatest challenges child welfare and other human services providers and advocates face is creating clinically sound and culturally competent interventions that will lead to greater effective and efficient delivery of services to families experiencing integrated problems of substance abuse, HIV/AIDS, and homelessness. It has also attempted to provide a different vision for viewing the impact of these problems for African American children in the child welfare system and to promote a model of intervention that incorporates the Africentric and ecological systems perspectives. The ideas offered here should serve as part of an ongoing process and effort to understand the complex nature of problems that the child welfare system faces today and thus tailor appropriate responses. Child welfare practitioners, researchers, policy makers, students, teachers, community developers, and others are encouraged to consider the paradigm shift proposed.

In social work, there is both room and need for evaluation, for the construction of practice models, and for discovery of knowledge about the system into which the practitioner intervenes. Social work needs discovery-oriented research in order to develop new knowledge about the systems that practitioners attempt to change and evaluate (Gilgun 1992). The ecological systems theory has been a part of social work curriculum for many decades and as such, the integration suggested in this chapter should be quite a natural paradigm shift for the profession. Interventions grounded in the Africentric and ecological perspectives allow for policy and practice innovations across fields of practice including child welfare.

The interconnectedness of problems, ideas, and concepts outlined in this chapter can be adapted and incorporated into proven methods of intervention across theoretical boundaries. Efforts should be made to use traditional models to highlight the importance of a search or journey that would ultimately create safe and more fulfilling lives for children. However, at the same time, studies should be made to integrate new visions of evaluating conditions from more culturally sensitive perspectives that address the whole person and system. Understanding the child welfare system and its past history of the treatment of African American children and families encourages the promotion of new ways of intervening and working with them from an Africentric perspective that respects the dignity of the child and promotes not only their wholeness but that of the family.

NOTES

1. "Protecting Our Children: 1999 Report on Maryland's Child Welfare System," Advocates for Children and Youth, Baltimore, MD. December 9, 1999, 5.
2. U.S. General Accounting Office referenced in HHS, 1999, 46.

REFERENCES

Adoption and Safe Families Act of 1997. Public Law 105-189.
Adoption Assistance and Child Welfare Act of 1980. Public Law 96-272.
Allen, D. M., J. S. Lehman, T. A. Green, M. L. Lindegren, I. M. Onorato & W. Forrester. 1994. "HIV Infection among Homeless Adults and Runaway Youth, United States, 1989–1992." *AIDS* 8/11:1593–1598.
Allen-Meares, P., & B. Lane. 1987. "Grounding Social Work Practice in Theory: Ecosystems." *Social Casework: The Journal of Contemporary Social Work* 68/9:515–521.
Allen-Meares, P., R. Washington & B. Welsh. 1986. *Social Work Services in the Schools.* Englewood Cliffs, NJ: Prentice-Hall.

Ambrosino, R., J. Heffernan, G. Shuttlesworth & R. Ambrosino. 2001. *Social Work and Social Welfare: An Introduction.* 4th ed. Belmont, CA: Wadsworth-Thomson Learning.

Azzi-Lessing, L., & L. J. Olsen. 1996. "Substance Abuse–Affected Families in the Child Welfare System: New Challenges, New Alliances." *Social Work* 41/1:15–23.

Bloom, M. 1998. "The Bridges of Child Welfare/Substance Abuse County." In *Substance Abuse, Family Violence, and Child Welfare: Bridging Perspectives,* edited by R. L. Hampton, V. Senator & T. P. Gullotta, 124–142. Thousand Oaks, CA: Sage.

Centers for Disease Control and Prevention. December 2000. Semi-Annual HIV/AIDS Surveillance Report 12/2. Retrieved from www.cdc.gov/hiv/stats.htm#cumrace.

———. 2001. *HIV and AIDS—United States, 1981–2001: Morbidity and Mortality Weekly Report (MMWR) 2001* 50/21:430–434. Atlanta: Centers for Disease Control and Prevention.

Child Abuse Prevention Act of 1974. Public Law 93-247.

Child Welfare League of America. 1992. *Children at the Front: A Different View of the War on Alcohol And Drugs.* Washington, DC: Child Welfare League of America.

Daskal, J. 1998. *In Search of Shelter: The Growing Shortage of Affordable Rental Housing.* Washington, DC: Center on Budget and Policy Priorities.

Dore, M. M., & J. M. Doris. 1998. "Preventing Child Placement in Substance-Abusing Families: Research-Informed Practice." *Child Welfare* 77/4:407–426.

Edelstein, S. B., D. Burg & J. Waterman. 2001. "Helping Foster Parents Cope with Separation, Loss, and Grief." *Child Welfare* 80/1:5–25.

Feig, L. 1998. "Understanding the Problem: The Gap between Substance Abuse Programs and Child Welfare Services." In *Substance Abuse, Family Violence, and Child Welfare: Bridging Perspectives,* edited by R. L. Hampton, V. Senatore & T. P. Gullotta, 62–95. Thousand Oaks, CA: Sage.

Fine, M. 1992. "A Systems-Ecological Perspective on Home-School Intervention." In *The Handbook of Family-School Intervention: A Systems Perspective,* edited by M. Fine & C. Carlson, 1–17. Englewood Cliffs, NJ: Prentice-Hall.

Garbarino, J., N. Dubrow, K. M. Kostelny & C. Pardo. 1992. *Children in Danger: Coping with the Consequences of Community Violence.* San Francisco: Jossey-Bass.

Gilgun, J. F. 1992. "Hypothesis Generation in Social Work Research." *Journal of Social Service Research* 15/3–4:113–135.

Harden, B. J. 1998. "Building Bridges for Children: Addressing the Consequences of Exposure to Drugs and to the Child Welfare System." In *Substance Abuse, Family Violence, and Child Welfare: Bridging Perspectives,* edited by R. L. Hampton, V. Senatore & T. P. Gullotta, 18–61. Thousand Oaks, CA: Sage.

Harvey, A. R., & N. Warfield-Coppock. 1989. *A Rites of Passage Resource Manual: Ten Age Pregnancy and Prevention.* Washington, DC: United Church of Christ, Commission for Racial Justice.

HUD. 1999. "Homelessness Programs and the People They Serve." Retrieved from www.huduser.org/publications/homeless/homelessness.

Hutchinson, E. D. 1999. *Dimensions of Human Behavior: Person and Environment.* Thousand Oaks, CA: Pine Forge Press.

Indian Child Welfare Act of 1978. Public Law 95-608.

Jaudes, P. K., E. Ekwo & J. Van Voorhis. 1995. "Association of Drug Abuse and Child Abuse." *Child Abuse and Neglect* 19/9:1065–1075.

Kaltenback, K. 1994. "Effects of In-Utero Opiate Exposure: New Paradigms for Old Questions." *Drug and Alcohol Dependence* 36:83–87.

Koegel, P., M. A. Burnam & J. Baumohl. 1996. "The Causes of Homelessness." In *Homelessness in America,* edited by J. Baumohl, 24–33. Phoenix, AZ: Oryx Press.

Lawrence-Webb, C. 1995. "African American Children in the Modern Child Welfare System: A Legacy of the Flemming Rule." *Child Welfare* 76/1:9–31.

Lawrence-Webb, C., J. N. Okundaye & G. Hafner. 2001. "Education and Kinship Caregivers: A New Vision." *Families in Society: The Journal of Contemporary Social Services* 84/1: 135–142.

Mbiti, J. S. 1970. *African Religions and Philosophies.* Garden City, NY: Anchor Books, Doubleday.

McCullough, C. 1991. "The Child Welfare Response." *The Future of Children* 1/1:61–70.

Meyer, C. H. 1988. "The Eco-Systems Perspective." In *Paradigms of Clinical Social Work*, edited by R. A. Dorfman, 275–294. New York: Brunner/Mazel.

Morgan, J. 2002. "Overview of National Adoptions Initiative." In *Children's Bureau Title IV-E Waiver Demonstration Project.* Washington, DC: Children's Bureau.

National Coalition for the Homeless. 1997. "America's Homeless Children: Will Their Future Be Different?" Retrieved from www.nch.ari.net/edsurvey97.

Nelson, K. 1995. "The Child Welfare Response to Youth Violence and Homelessness in the Nineteenth Century." *Child Welfare* 74/1:56–70.

Nobles, W. W. 1972. "African Philosophy: Foundations for Black Psychology." In *Black Psychology.* 3rd ed. Edited by R. L. Jones, 18–32. New York: Harper & Row.

Oakley, D., & D. L. Dennis. 1996. "Responding to the Needs of Homeless People with Alcohol, Drug, and/or Mental Disorders." In *Homelessness in America*, edited by J. Baumohl, 179–186. Phoenix, AZ: Oryx Press.

Rathus, S. A., J. S. Nevid & L. Fichner-Rathus. 1998. *Essentials of Human Sexuality.* Boston: Allyn & Bacon.

Resnik, H., S. Gardner & C. M. Rogers. 1998. "Child Welfare and Substance Abuse: Premises, Programs, and Policies." In *Substance Abuse, Family Violence, and Child Welfare: Bridging Perspectives*, edited by R. L. Hampton, V. Senatore & T. P. Gullotta, 96–123. Thousand Oaks, CA: Sage.

Robbins, G., & F. Nelson. 1995. *Looking for a Place To Be: A Report on AIDS Housing in America.* Washington, DC: AIDS Housing of Washington.

Roman, N. P., & P. B. Wolfe. 1997. "The Relationship between Foster Care and Homelessness." *Public Welfare* 55/1:4–9.

Scannapieco, M., & S. Jackson. 1996. "Kinship Care: The African American Response to Family Preservation." *Social Work* 41/2:190–196.

Semidei, J., L. F. Radel & C. Nolan. 2001. "Substance Abuse and Child Welfare: Clear Linkages and Promising Responses." *Child Welfare* 80/2:109–128.

Shelter Partnership. 1999. *A Report on Housing for Persons Living with HIV/AIDS in the City and County of Los Angeles.* Los Angeles: Los Angeles City Housing Department.

Shinn, M., & B. C. Weitzman. 1996. "Homeless Families Are Different." In *Homelessness in America*, edited by J. Baumohl, 109–122. Phoenix, AZ: Oryx Press.

Smith, D. D. 1992. *HIV/AIDS African Proverb Posters.* Washington, DC: American Red Cross.

Stack, C. B. 1974. *All Our Kin: Strategies for Survival in a Black Community.* New York: Harper & Row.

Sudarkasa, N. 1996. *The Strength of Our Mothers: African and African American Women and Families: Essays and Speeches.* Trenton, NJ: Africa World Press.

Turner, R. J. 1997. "Affirming Consciousness: The Africentric Perspective." In *Child Welfare: An Africentric Perspective*, edited by J. E. Everett, S. P. Chipungu & B. R. Leashore. New Brunswick, NJ: Rutgers University Press.

United Press International. 2001. *HIV/AIDS Epidemic in Minority Community.* Bethesda, MD: U.S. National Library of Medicine.

U.S. Bureau of the Census. 1998. *Poverty in the United States: 1997.* Current Population Reports, series P60-201. Retrieved from www.cenus.gov/hhes/www/poverty.html.

U.S. Conference of Mayors. 1998. *A Status Report on Hunger and Homelessness in America's Cities: 1998.* Washington, DC: U.S. Conference of Mayors.

USDHHS, Administration for Children and Families. 1999a. *Blending Perspectives and Building Common Ground.* Washington, DC: U.S. Government Printing Press.

USDHHS, Administration on Children, Youth and Families, Head Start Bureau. 1999b. *Serving Homeless Families: Descriptions, Effective Practices, and Lessons Learned.* Fairfax, VA: Head Start Publications Management Center.

USDHHS. 2000. *Substance Abuse Treatment for Persons with HIV/AIDS.* Washington, DC: U.S. Government Printing Press.

USDHHS, Public Health Service, Center for Disease Control and Prevention. 2001. *Semi-Annual HIV/AIDS Surveillance Report.* Washington, DC: USDHHS.

White, J. L. 1984. *The Psychology of Blacks: An Afro-American Perspective.* Englewod Cliffs, NJ: Prentice-Hall.

Wiese, D., & D. Daro. 1995. *Current Trends in Child Abuse Reporting and Fatalities: The Results of the 1994 Annual Fifty State Survey.* Chicago: NCPCA.

Woodside, M. 1988. "Research on Children of Alcoholics: Past and Future." *British Journal of Addiction* 83:785–792.

10

An Africentric Paradigm for Child Welfare Practice

CRYSTAL S. MILLS

DEBRA PORCHIA USHER

Introduction

Family group decision making as an approach to child protection in the United States is modeled, to some extent, after Family Group Conferences that were implemented in New Zealand as a result of the 1989 Child Welfare Act.[1] Family Group Conferences are rooted in the tribal traditions of the indigenous Mouries of New Zealand who, like African Americans, are a visible minority group that has been victimized by child welfare policies and practices. The practice of child welfare in New Zealand often resulted in the separation of Mourie children from their parents and their culture. Researchers have noted that it was typical to find three and four generations of Mourie families who were state wards and ultimately disenfranchised from their cultural and familial base (Walker et al. 2000). At one point during the mid-1980s there were six thousand children in the foster care system in New Zealand, and 72 percent of those children were Mourie children. Embracing Mourie tribal traditions in which family and clan connections are acknowledged and emotional attachments are respected, implementation of Family Group Conferences in New Zealand effectively reduced the number of children in government care from the implementation of the act in November 1989 to September 1992. One indicator of the effectiveness was the reduction in the number of agencies providing child welfare services from twenty-nine to five.

The child welfare experience for Mourie children in New Zealand parallels that of African American children in the United States. Prior to the implementation of Family Group Conferences in New Zealand, there were large numbers of Mourie children in foster care. There were not enough Mourie foster parents to provide appropriate services, and allegations of institutional racism were rampant. There was a vocal group of child advocates seeking reform, and much like the experience of the United States, there was a conservative push to make government child welfare services less expensive in New Zealand.

The convergence of forces in the field of child welfare caused the leaders in New Zealand to undertake extensive review of their child welfare policies and practices. Subsequent to the review, New Zealand implemented far-reaching national legislation with a focus on family and a minority perspective. Lore and law converged, and the 1989 Child Welfare Act, which reflects the values and traditions of the Mourie culture, developed.

In the United States, the convergence of forces led the federal government to institute incentives to encourage the development of innovative programming designed to support families and reduce the number of children in the foster care system. The success of New Zealand's child welfare reform was not lost to this process. Following New Zealand's lead, many states sought solutions to the problems in the child welfare system by turning to the history and traditions of African American culture, the result of which has been the increasing popularity and use of kinship care and family group decision making (Gleeson 1999). This chapter suggests that kinship care and family group decision making provide an Africentric paradigm for child welfare practice. In view of the history and traditions in the African American community, the use of kinship care and family group decision making provides a culturally and historically consistent approach to child welfare practice.

The Africentric Perspective

The Africentric perspective asserts that African Americans have a distinct history and worldview that challenge the universal application of Euro-American paradigms (Turner 1997). In the field of child welfare in the United States, kinship care and family group decision making emerge as an Africentric paradigm. Kinship care and family group decision making are the legacy of the African Diaspora and offer promise for culturally competent child welfare practice in the United States.

The use of kinship care and family group decision making in child welfare practice is reflective of values and constructs that are rooted in Africa and shaped in America. Africentric constructs such as collective identity and consanguine family provide a beginning point for understanding African American family values and characteristics that have historically supported informal kinship care and intrafamilial exchanges. Specifically, the collective identity is a traditional African value that was fostered during slavery when individual survival was vested in the group of like others. It was through the group that slaves received affection, companionship, love, and empathy with their suffering. Within the group, they learned how to avoid punishment, how to cooperate with their fellow slaves, and simultaneously how to retain self-esteem (Johnson & Roark 1984). Additionally, slave narratives and other accounts suggest that the numerous African American children who were orphaned by the sale, death, desertion, and dislocation of their parents during slavery were absorbed into extended and augmented kin groups (Staples & Johnson 1993). Adaptive "kin" obligations were transformed into larger communal obligations and became the basis for survival of a people (Gutman 1976).

Another Africentric construct, the consanguine family system, supports kinship as a major organizing theme for African American families. African American families are not solely organized around the nuclear family as a central or basic unit, but rather, kinship is the prominent organizing force. Similar to African tribal systems, African American kinship systems are typically organized around a base family household and several subunit family households that live in close proximity and engage in the exchange of resources and support (Martin & Martin 1978). The base family unit was distinguished as the home base with emotional ties with members of the various subunit households. Base family units were headed by a strong parental figure that provided direction and commanded respect from everyone within the kinship system. This parental figure was often in the personage of a grandmother, grandfather, great-grandparent, or other family member who provided authoritative direction on all matters of well-being for all family members. Though patterns of mobility in the 1980s and 1990s have reduced the proximity of living arrangements for many African American extended family systems, the emotional ties have not diminished. Even when great distances separate the subunits, cross-household cooperation and exchange are facilitated by the identified parental figure within the family system (Mills, Usher & McFadden 1999).

The African American Community

African Americans represent the largest ethnic minority group in the United States, and though America is an affluent society, many African American children grow up in conditions not unlike those in third world nations. Increasing numbers of African American children are growing up in poverty (Taylor et al. 1997) and vulnerable to exploitation, abuse, and multiple deprivations. The incidence of African American children separated from their parents is significant and in many ways comparable to that noted in countries ravaged by armed conflict.

The war that often separates African American children from their parents is waged through the drugs and crime that grip most large urban areas where the majority of African Americans reside (Henderson 1994; Hill 1993). Crack cocaine has taken its toll on African American families (Seamon 1992), as has the increasing incarceration of African American mothers (Dressel & Barnhill 1994). These two factors alone have effectively separated numerous African American children from their parents; and when the impact of the AIDS epidemic is added to the equation, the effect is quite devastating.

Reports of child victims in the African American community have prompted urgency in response from the child welfare community. However, child welfare policy has, in many instances, further victimized African American children. Increasingly, the literature points to the overrepresentation of African American children in the foster care system (Testa 1997; Wulczyn 1994)—a system that is overburdened, underfunded, and associated with negative child outcomes (Woodley-Brown & Bailey-Etta 1997).

An Africentric Paradigm for Child Welfare

There is general agreement that the well-being of African American children is best assured within the context of the African American community. Leaders have called for the implementation of family and community care models to address the needs of the large numbers of African American children who are separated from their parents. The old adage "It takes a community to raise a child" has been raised as a banner around which to rally, and the African American community has responded. Attempts have been made to build on the traditional strengths of the African American extended family system, and the history of community care, to develop an approach to child welfare that is grounded in family support, self-help, and self-determination. Such an approach must embrace the strengths/empowerment perspective and acknowledge the importance of culture and the positive influence of family in the development of the child's sense of self.

It is clear that both kinship care and family group decision making build on the history and traditions of African American people by emphasizing the use of family and community resources to support dependent children. Leaders in the field have noted that kinship networks in the African American community have the potential to support culturally competent, ecologically sound, family-supportive child welfare services (Danzy & Jackson 1997). As a formal approach for child welfare practice, kinship care, in conjunction with family group decision making, has increased in popularity and use by formal systems (Gleeson 1999).

Popularity notwithstanding, the many cross-cultural situations and the heterogeneity of kinship networks in the African American community call for sensitivity and understanding on the part of practitioners to the family's cultural context. The practitioner must be able to help the family identify and mobilize family strengths while working within the context of frequent negative concentric cultural, social, and economic forces. African American family systems continuously address the many challenges and threats of the twenty-first century, including racism, conflicting values, and policies that reflect concern more in "rhetoric" than "substantive" initiatives for families (Weick & Saleebey 1995).

Use of the kinship group to facilitate child welfare goals helps to ground practice and the worker in the family's cultural context and sensitizes the worker to the unique strengths of African American families. A focus on strengths and the translation of the strengths/empowerment perspective to work with the extended family system have been discussed relative to effective case management with kinship families (Mills & Usher 1996). Effective case management with kinship families is defined by a set of principles that include attention to cultural diversity, family self-definition, and the use of unique and varied family decision-making structures. The extended kinship network is viewed as viable and is engaged in deliberation and decisions for child protection, and is mobilized to support child welfare goals. The primacy of concentric culture is recognized, and the values of mutuality and intrafamilial exchange are supported (Mills & Usher 1996).

The kinship case management approach embraces the depiction of the extended kinship system as an adaptive, flexible system that has contributed to survival of African Americans against overwhelming odds (Billingsley 1968; Hill 1972). Child welfare workers trained in this approach acknowledge and are open to a diversity of living arrangements and support patterns within African American families. They respect the norm of the fluidity among the numerous branches of family within a complex extended kinship system and understand the importance and necessity of relying on the family for definitions and interpretations of family structures and systems (Mills & Usher 1996).

Integral to the kinship approach to case management is that exclusive focus on problems undermines the quest for solutions. Incorporating facets of the strengths perspective, the kinship approach views the African American community and its members as possessing a wide range of strengths, capacities, and potentials to support child protection and family preservation goals while providing a powerful vehicle for successful problem solving. Appreciation is shown for the family's cultural norms, and workers seek to expand knowledge and understanding of family structures through family communicators and family-controlled decision-making processes.

In today's practice of child welfare, the use of kinship care and family group decision making is congruent with the idea of Africentric child welfare practice and synonymous with empowerment practice where

- The family is the unit of focus.
- The family provides leadership in the identification of current roles and responsibilities within the extended family system.
- Emphasis is placed on assessing and building on family strengths and on the capacity of families to function effectively.
- Families are engaged in designing all aspects of the policies, treatment, and evaluation.
- Families are linked with a more comprehensive, diverse, and community-based network of supports and services.

This approach means working with families: identifying and talking with a family communicator, talking with the biological parents, working with the church and community leaders, and talking with the children. The key is being able to gather information from knowledgeable family members and persons in the community and helping the family use the information to plan for the safety of the child or children.

Systematic Assessment Using Family Information and Decisions

Systematic assessment helps the worker identify and delineate the family's definition of family, intrafamilial exchange patterns, strengths, resources, and naturally occurring helping systems within both the family and the community. Key family members obtain information on needs, strengths, resources, and supports through both objective assessment and subjective evaluation.

The professional provides information regarding the significance of legal requirements and timelines. This information guides the family around key decision points. Informed decisions and outcomes provide a framework for reflection and family self-assessment and the identification of intrafamilial and community-based supports necessary to ensure protection, continuity, and permanency for child members. Though daunting, the alignment of the legal requirements and family dynamics can be the most rewarding aspect of the family decision-making process for the professional helper and the kinship family system.

Family Leadership in the Decision-Making Process

The process of supporting family leadership in child welfare decisions is best accomplished by engaging the family in an extended family assessment. The extended family assessment is the cornerstone of effective family engagement, empowerment, and participation. The clarity provided by the social work professional throughout the assessment process is critical, as is the importance of working in concert with a family member in a leadership position. Moreover, family members need to be informed and knowledgeable of child welfare policies and legal mandates and must be encouraged to assume leadership in the decision-making process.

Identify and Mobilize Intrafamilial Resources

Sorting through the options for supports and exchanges begins with the family. By identifying the family communicator and uncovering the power base within the family system, the worker is better able to unravel the complexities of family organizational patterns. The use of standard instruments such as the genogram and the eco-map may facilitate the gathering of information and provide an opportunity to interactively identify how the family might come together to support child welfare goals.

Family Group Conferencing

The family group conference is a powerful tool through which the caseworker might be able to identify and mobilize intrafamilial resources. In the family group conference, family members come together and discuss the issues and resolutions. Family decision making assumes that families know better than any external professional about family issues and processes. It recognizes that families have strengths and the ability to access resources and use them to address family issues and concerns (Walker et al. 2000). Borrowing from the New Zealand model, family group decision making encourages family members to provide information on and make decisions about the use of family and community-based resources.

The extended family unit should be provided a neutral environment that is conducive to discussion, argument, and decision making. Decisions include family support, child placement options, and strategies to maintain connections between the children and the extended family. Oftentimes, simply providing a structured forum for family discussion helps facilitate the mobilization of resources internal to the family.

Using Natural Helping and Community Systems

The service delivery, or support mobilization plan, is developed with the family. Whenever possible, this plan should draw heavily on natural helping systems and intrafamilial resources and exchange patterns. The family with familial oversight of implementation should endorse this plan. When more formal supports are needed, the family should be connected to existing community-based resources. Helping families identify and mobilize community resources is critical to this approach. Strong communities foster strong families and strong families expand the community's resource base.

Benefits of the Approach

Kinship care and family group decision making in child welfare respect the family's cultural norms and expand cultural knowledge through information gathering with the family. The concept of family self-determination and self-assessment, and the belief that family systems are highly organized, self-governed systems are emphasized (Berg 1994). The focus on decision making and intervention recognizes and values family observations, input, and participation. The family is empowered to participate in and take control of child welfare decisions. Throughout the process, family definitions, family decisions, and natural helping systems are used and are integral to best practice.

Involving families in decisions about the care of dependent children effectively identifies intrafamily strengths and resources that may be used to promote child protection goals. This approach not only draws from extended family strengths, but also helps the worker adapt services in response to the unique resources and needs of families. The use of family group decision making within a kinship care environment builds upon core values in the African American community and incorporates informal exchanges in a formal plan to support child protection goals.

Family group decision making as an integral part of child welfare practice with kinship cases has been shown to enhance practice outcomes (Mills & Usher 1996). In a federal demonstration project designed to implement and demonstrate the effectiveness of a model of permanence practice with kinship cases, Mills and Usher (1996) used an intensive contact wraparound service delivery approach. Emphasis was placed on family empowerment and decision making using case management elements and themes that were successfully implemented under the New Zealand 1989 Child Welfare Act, such as the utilization of family definitions, family decisions, and natural helping systems to support permanence in kinship placements. Interns were used to link families with existing supports, create supports through the provision of direct services, advocate for the family, and coach the family in the development of resource acquisition skills. The results of this demonstration showed that the family decision-making approach utilized by the project was effective in maintaining family continuity for dependent children (Mills & Usher 1996).

Effective use of family group decision making for foster family continuity is discussed in the evaluation of the Family and Community Compact program (FCC) (Crampton & Jackson 2001). New Zealand's Family Group Conferences as implemented in the FCC program also inspired family group decision making. Similar to the Kinship Project, the FCC program was designed to provide a culturally appropriate intervention to promote safety and strengthen family and community connections for the child. A major difference between the two programs is the point of referral. The Kinship Project provided ancillary services to ongoing kinship cases, and the FCC program received referrals of substantiated child protection cases at the point of entry into the system. Of the ninety-six cases that participated in a family compact meeting (a family decision-making meeting) over a three-year period, fifty-eight (60 percent) developed a plan that kept the children out of foster care (Crampton & Jackson 2001).

In the child welfare community, there has been a commonly held misconception that family ties in the African American community were breaking, due to changes in social mobility patterns and the diminishing role of the senior generation in the rearing of youth. However, recent literature suggests that although the helping tradition within the extended family system has been threatened by racism and social ills since the sixties, many social workers and agencies have been able to build on traditions and cultural strengths to support children and families (Gray & Nybell 1990; Jackson-White et al. 1996; Taylor 1996). For example, informal adoption among African Americans rose sharply between 1970 and 1990 (Hill 1992), and the recent explosion in and resilience of kinship care in the African American community suggests that old and new concepts of kinship are well despite a myriad of stressors (Ruiz 2000).

As Sudarkasa (1993) notes, many researchers and policy makers studying African American families miss the "web of kinship" and patterns of cooperation because they focus narrowly on individual households. Often multiple households are involved in cooperative exchange within the larger extended kinship system (Sudarkasa 1993), and exchange patterns reflect extensive diversity in the organization of African American family systems. The kinship network includes both relatives and nonrelatives, who can be called upon to serve as supports, models, and advocates for the family within the larger social system, and this pattern of self-help activities has been extended to institutions in the wider African American community.

Early identification and mobilization of African American kinship networks to support at-risk children and families have the potential to prevent the need for child placement, provide temporary placements, and maintain family continuity and permanency for children who are permanently separated from their parents (Crampton & Jackson 2001; Mills & Usher 1996). If practitioners can help families build viable support networks, they can also increase the likelihood for successful family reunification, continuity, and permanency for African American children (Mills & Usher 1996).

NOTE

1. In September of 1992, Dr. Mills was among a group of child welfare advocates from the United States who visited New Zealand and gathered information on implementation of the 1989 Child Welfare Act.

REFERENCES

Berg, I. 1994. *Family Based Services: A Solution-Focused Approach.* New York: W. W. Norton.
Billingsley, A. 1968. *Black Families in White America.* Englewood Cliffs, NJ: Prentice-Hall.
Brown, K. 2000. "Political Freedom and the Widening of Group Consciousness among Middle and Lower Class Black Americans." *African American Research Perspectives* 6/2:18–24.
Chestang, L. 1976. "Environmental Influences on Social Functioning: The Black Experience." In *The Diverse Society: Implications for Social Policy,* edited by P. Cafferty & L. Chestang, 59–74. Washington, DC: NASW Press.
Crampton, D., & W. Jackson. 2001. In *Family Group Conferences: Perspectives on Policy, Practice, and Research,* edited by G. Burford & J. Hudson. Hawthorn, NY: Aldine de Gruyter.
Danzy, J., & S. Jackson. 1997. "Family Preservation and Support Services: A Missed Opportunity for Kinship Care." *Child Welfare* 76:31–44.
Dressel, P., & S. Barnhill. 1994. "Reframing Gerontological Thought and Practice: The Case of Grandmothers with Daughters in Prison." *The Gerontologist* 34:685–690.
Gleeson, J. 1999. "Kinship Care as a Child Welfare Service: What Do We Really Know?" In *Kinship Care: Improving Practice through Research,* edited by J. Gleeson & C. Hariston, 3–34. Washington, DC: CWLA Press.

Gray, S., & L. Nybell. 1990. "Issues in African American Family Preservation." *Child Welfare* 69/6:513–523.

Gutman, H. 1976. *The Black Family in Slavery and Freedom, 1760–1925.* New York: Random House.

Henderson, L. 1994. "African Americans in the Urban Milieu: Conditions, Trends, and Development Needs." In *The State of Black America*, edited by B. Tidwell. New York: National Urban League.

Hill, R. 1972. *The Strengths of Black families.* New York: Emerson Hall.

———. 1992. "The Strengths of Families of Color: Implications for Family-Based Practice." In *Empowering Families: Papers from the Sixth Annual Conference of Family Based Services.* Cedar Rapids, IA: National Association for Family-Based Services.

Hill, R. B. 1993. *Research on the African-American Family: A Holistic Perspective.* London: Auburn House.

Hungerford, G. 1996. "Caregivers of Children Whose Mothers Are Incarcerated: A Study of the Kinship Placement System." *Children Today* 24/1:23–28.

Jackson-White, G., C. D. Dozier, J. T. Oliver & L. B. Gardner. 1996. "Why African American Adoption Agencies Succeed: A New Perspective on Self-Help." *Child Welfare* 76: 239–253.

Johnson, M., & J. Roark. 1984. *Black Masters: A Free Family of Color in the Old South.* New York: W. W. Norton.

Maluccio, A., L. Ambramczyk & B. Thomlison. 1996. "Family Reunification of Children in Out-of-Home Care: Research Perspectives." *Children and Youth Services Review* 18: 287–305.

Martin, E., & J. Martin. 1978. *The Black Extended Family.* Chicago: University of Chicago Press.

Martin, J., & E. Martin. 1985. *The Helping Tradition in the Black Family and Community.* Washington DC: NASW Press.

Mills, C., & D. Usher. 1996. "A Kinship Care Case-Management Approach." *Child Welfare* 75:600–618.

Mills, C., D. Usher & E. McFadden. 1999. "Kinship in the African American Community." *Michigan Sociological Review* 13:28–45.

Rittner, B., & C. Doxier. 2000. "Effects of Court-Ordered Substance Abuse Treatment in Child Protective Services Cases." *Social Work* 45/2:131–140.

Ruiz, D. 2000. "Guardians and Caretakers: African American Grandmothers as Primary Caregivers in Intergenerational Families." *African American Research Perspectives* 6/1:1–14.

Scannapieco, M., & S. Jackson. 1996. "Kinship Care: The African American Response to Family Preservation." *Social Work* 41:190–196.

Seamon, F. 1992. "Intergenerational Issues Related to the Crack-Cocaine Problem." *Family and Community Health* 15/3:11–19.

Staples, R., & L. Johnson. 1993. *Black Families at the Crossroads: Challenges and Prospects.* San Francisco: Jossey-Bass.

Sudarkasa, N. 1988. "Interpreting the African Heritage in Afro-American Family Organization." In *Black Families*. 2nd ed. Edited by H. McAdoo, 27–43. Newbury Park, CA: Sage.

———. 1993. "Female-Headed African American Households: Some Neglected Dimensions." In *Family Ethnicity: Strength in Diversity*, edited by H. McAdoo. Newbury Park, CA: Sage.

Taylor, R. 1996. "Adolescents' Perceptions of Kinship Support and Family Management Practices: Association with Adolescent Adjustment in African American Families." *Developmental Psychology* 32:687–695.

Taylor, R., M. Tucker, L. Chatters & R. Jayakody. 1997. "Recent Demographic Trends in African American Family Structure." In *Family Life in Black America*, edited by R. J. Taylor, J. S. Jackson & L. M. Chatters, 14–62. London: Sage Publications.

Testa, M. 1997. "Kinship Foster Care in Illinois." In *Child Welfare Research Review*. Vol. 2. Edited by J. D. Berrick, R. P. Barth & N. Gilbert, 101–129. New York: Columbia University Press.

Turner, R. 1997. "Affirming Consciousness: The Africentric Perspective." In *Child Welfare: An Africentric Perspective*, edited by J. Everett, S. Chipungu & B. Leashore, 36–57. New Brunswick, NJ: Rutgers University Press.

Tutu, D. 1999. Introduction to *Kinship: A Family's Journey in Africa and America* by P. Wamba Dutton. New York: Penguin Publishing.

Van Sertima, I. 1976. *The African Presence in Ancient America: They Came Before Columbus*. New York: Random House.

Walker, H., G. Allan, T. Featherstone, A. Hewitt, G. Keith & D. Smith. 2000. *Family Decision Making: A Conferencing Philosophy*. New Zealand: Kinpower Associates.

Weick, A., & D. Saleebey. March 1995. "Supporting Family Strengths: Orienting Policy and Practice Toward the Twenty-first Century." *Journal of Contemporary Human Services*: 141–149.

Woodley Brown, A., & B. Bailey-Etta. 1997. "An Out-of-Home Care System in Crisis: Implications for African American Children in the Child Welfare System." *Child Welfare* 76:65–80.

Wulczyn, F. 1994. "Status at Birth and Infant Placements in New York City." In *Child Welfare Research Review*. Vol. 1. Edited by R. P. Barth, J. D. Berrick & N. Gilbert, 146–184. New York: Columbia University Press.

11

Family Preservation and
Neighborhood-Based Services

An Africentric Perspective

ALMA J. CARTEN

JAMES R. DUMPSON

> In African culture, the sons and daughters of one's aunts and uncles are considered brothers and sisters, not cousins. We do not make the same distinctions among relatives practiced by whites. We have no half brothers, or half sisters. My mother's sister is my mother, my uncle's son is my brother; my brother's child is my son, my daughter (Mandella 1994).

Introduction

When four young children are left alone in a housing development in Jacksonville, Florida, two neighborhood women convince police officers that they can provide the necessary care for their safety until the mother could be located. With the support of Children's Services, the plan succeeds, protecting the children from the secondary trauma of placement in an emergency shelter and inevitable placement in foster care during the mother's incarceration. In New York City, a Beacon School operates virtually around the clock in a neighborhood with heavy drug trafficking, providing on-site and referral services to other community-based agencies for families largely headed by single women who for many, means the difference between keeping their children at home or losing them to foster care. In a community outreach program operating from a storefront on the west side of Cleveland, Ohio, a neighborhood resident, who is now employed as a parent advocate after completing a leadership training program, encourages a mother in recovery from crack addiction to state what services she feels she needs to get her children returned from foster care.

These are examples of neighborhood-based services emerging in urban cities across the country that aim to keep children safely in their own homes and neighborhoods and out of foster care. The families using these services are typically poor families of color who are isolated from the mainstream and endeavoring to cope with neighborhood conditions that compound rather than buffer them against the disadvantages of poverty. These services are usually undertaken as collaborative partnerships between local government and many community stakeholders including nonprofit service providers, faith-based organizations, schools, informal neighborhood associations, and community residents. Although there is considerable variation among programs dependent upon geographic location, community resources, and family needs, all are anchored in the principle that children do best when supported by strong families, and families do best when supported by strong communities.

This chapter has four purposes: (1) to describe family preservation as a universal and enduring theme of the African American experience, (2) to review the policy framework for family preservation and neighborhood-based services, (3) to discuss concepts that form the conceptual framework and philosophical underpinnings of the two approaches, and (4) to identify related themes from the Africentric perspective.

Family Preservation: A Universal and Enduring Theme of the African American Experience

An Africentric perspective that forms the conceptual framework for the approach to child welfare services ascribed to in this book is premised on the assumption that contemporary problems impacting African Americans cannot be adequately understood or addressed without understanding the broader historical, social, and cultural context of the African American experience (Turner 1997). Child welfare services as they have evolved in the United States have been shaped by an opposing Eurocentric view that gave scant attention to the influence of larger systems on family functioning and child well-being, promoted myths and misconceptions about the worthiness or fitness of poor families to bring up their own children, and contributed to the overuse of foster care services as a practice intervention. For African American families these myths and misconceptions were compounded by racial stereotyping and a preference in the child welfare research for formulating study questions that examined indicators of family dysfunction and gave little attention to understanding why large numbers of families were doing well despite adverse social conditions (Morrison 1997).

Contrary to stereotypical thinking, poorly conceptualized research, and residual assumptions of a Eurocentric view, preserving the family has been a universal and enduring theme of the African American experience. Further, since arriving in the New World as slaves, African Americans have endeavored to preserve their families in the face of considerable barriers imposed by the dominant culture. There is extensive historical literature (Franklin 1969; Frazier 1957; Gutman 1976) about the central role of family in African civilization. In

African culture the nuclear family was part of an extended family network that branched into clans and tribes. These complex kinship groups formed a community bound together by a feeling of unity, affectional ties, and mutual aid and in which children were highly valued.

This tradition was brought to the New World by enslaved Africans and persisted despite inhumane practices of the slave system designed to destroy any semblance of family life. For example, under the slave codes, marriage among slaves was illegal, and slave owners could sell slaves with indifference to kinship ties for economic profit. Nonetheless, ceremonial marriages considered binding by the partners were common in the slave community, and the fidelity of former slaves to these unions and strength of kinship bonds are attested to by the large number of freed slaves searching for lost family members and legalizing marriages during Reconstruction (Billingsley 1968; Blassingame 1979).

Two-parent families were dominant in the African American community until well into the twentieth century, surviving cataclysmic changes that transitioned the country from an agrarian to urban society, mass migration from the rural South to northern cities, extreme economic hardships of the depression, and ghettoization. Because these changes occurred against a backdrop of Jim Crowism later institutionalized in law and public policy, African American families did not fully benefit from the social progress that propelled the country forward, or the federalization of safety net programs that resulted in a rising standard of living and new levels of security for other American families.

Nonetheless, the nuclear family, the dominant American family type during these years, demonstrated great staying power in the African American community. In 1940 the largest share of African American children under the age of eighteen years were living in families headed by two parents. This remained the case until the 1960s when two-parent families cared for 75 percent of children. It was not until the decade of the 1980s that a new picture began to emerge and the number of two-parent families began to decline. By 1986 the number had fallen to 49 percent (Billingsley 1992). According to current census data, an estimated 55 percent of black children are living in single-parent, mother-only homes.

Eurocentric biased research studies attributed changes in the structure of African American families, and the accompanying growth in child poverty rates, to moral shortcomings and weak identification with the work ethic of adult caretakers. Billingsley (1968) and Hill (1971) were the first scholars to challenge findings of methodologically flawed studies exemplified by the Moynihan report (1965) and established a new research agenda for examining the circumstances of African American families that acknowledges the persistent striving to preserve the family as central to an understanding of the African American community. The seminal work of these authors (Billingsley 1968; Hill 1971) gave a more realistic appraisal, and introduced general systems and strength-based approaches that took into account the political, economic, and social forces driving changes in the structure of the African American family, and identified strengths characteristic of African American families across socioeconomic strata. These contributions led to an expanded knowledge base for understanding African American families, and the development of resiliency theories now widely accepted as providing a more accurate framework for understanding the behaviors of many vulnerable and oppressed groups (Longres 2000; Martin & Martin 1986; McAdoo 1978).

Today, there is broad consensus that increases in the number of African American children growing up in single parent homes are the result of complex interactive trends in the last decades that have contributed to the increasing diversity of family types among all American families. Some of these changes have been more profound for African Americans than other ethnic groups and merit special attention. However, social, economic, and political context will no doubt continue to redefine and reshape the role and structure of the American family and provide a rationale for policy development responsive to the diversity of needs of many family types that have come to characterize American culture in the twenty-first century.

Current Trends

The life circumstances of the largest percentage of African Americans have improved significantly over the last decades on most well-being indicators including income, health, education, occupation, and life expectancy. At the same time, statistical trends show continuing racial disparities that are especially disturbing when examining child welfare trends.

For example, the National Survey of America's Families compared changes in family well-being on indicators of employment, family income, food hardship, family structure, and health insurance and health status by racial and ethnic categories of white, black, and Hispanic. Findings from the 1997–1999 surveys indicate that African American children are not faring better as a result of public policy changes. For example, child poverty rates for all children declined from 21 percent in 1996 to 18 percent in 1998, but remained essentially unchanged for African American children. And although African American parents experienced the greatest increase in employment in comparison with other ethnic groups, there was a worsening in their housing and food hardship (Staveteig & Wigton 1999).

Child welfare trend data paints a picture of a system that is increasingly used by children of color. For example, between 1986 and 1995 the number of children receiving foster care services increased significantly, rising from 280,000 to 486,000. In 1980, 47 percent of the children in foster care were children of color, and by 1995 that number had grown to 61 percent. And while African American children comprise 14 percent of the country's child population under the age of eighteen years, they comprise 44 percent of the foster care population and account for the largest share of children entering care and experiencing foster care reentry, and the longest stays in care (Child Welfare League of America 2000; USDHHS 2000).

Poverty remains a central element in the lives of children involved in child welfare services, and current data indicate that their circumstances are increasing in severity. For example, parental alcohol and substance abuse are contributing factors for 75 percent of the children entering care, an increasing number of children have not only lost their parents to AIDS but are HIV positive themselves, and a growing number are considered medically fragile or experience some form of physical disability. Some studies suggest that children in foster care are six times more likely than children not in foster care to have behavioral, emotional, or developmental concerns, and an estimated 30 percent are severely emotionally disturbed (Kortenkamp & Ehrle 2002). These data, combined with community conditions in neighborhoods with high foster care placement rates, underscore the daunting task that state child welfare systems face in moving toward a neighborhood-based model, which requires a continuum of easily accessible, high-quality services of sufficient scope and availability.

The Policy Framework for Family Preservation Neighborhood-Based Services

All states currently provide some form of family preservation services. These programs vary but share common features: they are offered to families who are at imminent risk of having children placed, interventions endeavor to solve crisis situations that place children at risk, and services are designed to keep children out of foster care. Research findings of the effectiveness of family preservation services in keeping children out of foster care and improving family functioning have been mixed (Littel & Shuerman 1995). Early studies of program effectiveness were quite promising but have been criticized because of flaws in methodological design. Studies employing more rigorous experimental research designs found no significant difference in outcomes for families using these programs and those using traditional child welfare services on key variables such as reducing foster care placement rates, maintaining child safety, and improving family functioning (USDHHS 2001). Although the reviews are mixed, family preservation services should be offered as one component of a broad array of a continuum of services for families and children.

In this chapter, family preservation is viewed as a conceptual approach and practice principle that should inform all aspects of public policy development as it directly or indirectly impacts the family. The First White House Conference on Children convened in 1909 and established the principle that children should not be removed from their own homes for the reason of poverty alone. The conference affirmed the importance of the biological family in the life of children and paved the way for the federalization of income assistance and family support services that were codified and expanded under the Social Security Act. This principle, however, has been ambiguously applied to child welfare policy and practice, and all but ignored in child welfare service developments for African American children (Billingsley & Giovannoni 1972; Grey & Nybell 1990).

The Eurocentric philosophical underpinning of American child welfare services is rooted in a tradition of "rescue and punishment" that extends back to the Elizabethan Poor Laws of 1601. This tradition reflected both humanitarian concerns for what was perceived to be in the best interest of dependent children and the social control interests of the state, which saw the family as a means for controlling deviance and reinforcing dominant social norms. The Orphan Trains Project undertaken in the mid-1800s illustrates the tradition of rescue and punishment. This social experiment began with the transporting of hundreds of children of poor, white, immigrant families living in the slums of New York City to the Midwest where they were placed in fostering arrangements with families believed capable of instilling within them the values of virtue, hard work, and self-reliance (Brace 1872; Cook 1995). By the time the trains had stopped running in 1939, thousands of children had been deported and the practice of removing children from the influence of communities and parents believed to be inadequate was firmly established. The tradition of rescue and punishment was reinforced by the increasing professionalization of social work, long the anchor profession in the field of child welfare that drew heavily on Freudian theories that are now known to have limited generalizability to culturally different groups. For African American families, this approach was strengthened by a Eurocentric perspective that labeled culturally different behavior as deviant and supported victim blaming stances (Billingsley & Giovannoni 1972; Morisey 1990). The literature is replete in its descriptions of the magnitude of the failures of this approach. Children were too quickly removed from their homes without sufficient cause, only to be placed in a system that mirrored discriminatory practices of the larger society and in which they experienced foster care drift—extended stays in placement with little hope of achieving permanent living arrangements, or forever in the process of being returned to their own homes (Bernstein 2001; Billingsley & Giovannoni 1972; Fanshel 1976; Maas & Engler 1964).

The Adoption Assistance and Child Welfare Reform Act of 1980 (PL 96-272) is considered landmark legislation in the field of child welfare. It was designed to correct extensive failures of the system and required states to make "reasonable efforts" to prevent children from entering into care in the first instance, to achieve early reunification with their families after being placed in care, and when this was not possible, placement in a permanent adoptive home. New financial incentives encouraged the use of preventive services and more stringent accountability requirements to prevent the overuse of foster care and to more carefully monitor early permanency planning efforts of agencies. The legislation affirmed in child welfare policy the primacy of the biological family in the life of the child and his or her right and developmental needs for consistent stable emotional attachments as a basic prerequisite for reaching the most optimum level of development. The act had three primary goals: to prevent the unnecessary separation of children from their families; to improve the quality of care provided; and to ensure permanency by reuniting children with their families, or the adoption of other permanent arrangements when this was not possible.

Despite considerable optimism following the passage of Public Law 96-272, the numbers of children entering the foster care system continued to rise and the numbers of those being discharged from care remained unchanged. Congress reacted to this situation by passing the Family Preservation and Support Services Program in 1993 as part of the Omnibus Budget Reconciliation Act, which established a five-year capped entitlement program to encourage states to develop family preservation and family support programs. The program supports the development of a broad range of services provided to children in their communities that target the family as a whole, are linked to a host of community services, focus on strengths, and require providers to include families as partners in identifying and meeting needs. States were provided $930 million over a five-year period for restructuring their child welfare systems through broad system reform (National Resource Center for Respite and Crisis Care Services 1994).

The Adoption and Safe Families Act of 1997 (PL 105-89) codifies under one statute two decades of child welfare reform efforts. The act reauthorized and expanded family preservation and family support services and endeavors to strengthen the permanency planning goals of Public Law 96-272. The new law does not require states to make reasonable efforts to reunify families in certain extreme situations; authorizes states to shorten the time frame for initiating termination of parental rights proceedings; makes concurrent planning mandatory and requires agencies to provide high-quality reunification services to birth parents while simultaneously seeking an alternative plan of permanency for the child; and standardizes outcome measures of safety, permanency, and child and family well-being as national standards for evaluating agency performance and timelines for state compliance (USDHHS 2000).

The intent of these reforms has been to achieve the dual and often competing goals of ensuring the safety of children while preserving families. Family-centered practice mediates these concerns and encourages the use of broad-based assessments and interventions that identify the family as the focus of attention within the context of the surrounding communities (Laird & Hartman 1985; Pecora, Whittaker & Maluccio 2000). Central to permanency planning is a family-centered focus that supports a more rational, systematic, family-oriented approach to the planning and delivery of child welfare services. For example, Maluccio, Fein, and Olmsted (1986) identify the following as key elements for permanency planning: (1) a philosophical orientation that underscores the importance of the biological family; (2) a theoretical perspective emphasizing the importance of attachments, stability, and continuity in relationships for children and promoting their most optimum development; (3) a case management method encouraging the use of case decision making that involves parents in the decision-making process; and (4) active collaboration among many community agencies and the professional disciplines involved with a family.

Conceptual Framework

Although guidelines for the development of neighborhood-based child welfare services began to appear in the child welfare literature in the early 1980s (Brown et al. 1982), a comprehensive systematic conceptual framework for a neighborhood-based model for child welfare is only beginning to become clearly articulated in the professional literature. Moreover, the approach is not necessarily new, but more accurately described as a synthesis and integration of constructs from many theoretical frameworks that have informed micro- and macro-level social work practice since the turn of the nineteenth century. As well, preserving the integrity of the family through self-help and improving neighborhood conditions are long-standing helping strategies in the African American community. Although understated in the literature (LaNey-Carlton 2001), the neighborhood approach was evident in the work of African American pioneers working at the turn of the century to mitigate the combined effects of urbanization and discrimination in the neighborhoods and families that had been popular resettlement sites of African Americans migrating from the rural South to urban cities in the North.

These early efforts spawned organizations and social work education programs in historically black colleges and universities that emphasized the interdependent reciprocal nature of the relationship between families and their environments (Haynes 1912; Weiss 1974). Problem-solving approaches adopted by early pioneers such as George Edmond Haynes, founder of the National Urban League, contributed to what is now embraced as the ecological perspective and person-in-the-environment approach to practice, a distinguishing feature of the social work profession.

With the increased professionalization of social work, twentieth-century developments saw a shifting from broad-based macro-level interventions that defined problem causation from an environmental and social justice perspective, to micro-level interventions that attributed problem causation to personal behaviors and favored individualistic psychodynamic approaches. By mid-century, these perspectives began to merge, forming the ecological approach for understanding the problems and needs of individuals, families, and communities (Bronfenbrenner 1979; Germaine & Gitterman 1980; Pincus & Minahan 1973). New practice paradigms were subsequently introduced based on an expanded view of people as being interdependent with their social environment and as those who looked to their environment to obtain the material, emotional, and spiritual resources necessary for carrying out major life tasks. The ecological perspective provides the integrating framework for the strengths perspective, empowerment model, and community capacity building that contributed to the theoretical basis of federal initiatives targeting poor urban communities during the war on poverty and model cities programs of the 1960s and 1970s, and more recently, under the empowerment zones and enterprise initiatives instituted under the Clinton administration (Chaskin et al. 2001; Morris 1997).

The neighborhood-based model for child welfare services builds on these developments and integrates several interrelated concepts. It is an approach that recognizes that problems confronted by poor families are symptomatic of the complex interaction of the personal and the public. Accordingly, services are most effective when delivery strategies include micro- and macro-level interventions that aim to improve interpersonal functioning and address structural flaws that contribute to social conditions that place children at risk and influence the quality and availability of family support services at the community level. Neighborhood-based services attempt to bring fundamental changes in the underlying philosophy of state child welfare systems and to transform what has traditionally been a highly specialized set of services offered only when children are at imminent risk to continuous, integrated systems of care that are preventive in thrust and culturally competent, with round-the-clock accessibility in the neighborhoods where families live.

The Edna McConnell Clark and Annie Casey Foundations are strong supporters of the neighborhood-based model and are currently funding neighborhood-based initiatives in several states. A primary goal of these initiatives is to redesign and restructure child welfare systems from traditional centralized departments where child protective services are the exclusive responsibility of the public child welfare agency to networks of services located in communities where they are needed the most. The model also requires that birth families be involved in decision making and views child protection as a shared responsibility of many community stakeholders.

The Edna McConnell Clark initiative, Community Partnerships for Protecting Children, has made capacity-building grants to four cities, including Cedar

Rapids, Iowa; Jacksonville, Florida; Louisville, Kentucky; and St. Louis, Missouri. The conceptual model of the Community Partnerships for Protecting Children initiative is based on a theory for change that integrates four core elements: (1) developing an individualized course of action, families are engaged in decision making and participate in family team meetings; (2) creating neighborhood networks that include the development of linkages with formal care systems as well as informal systems to support parents in the parenting role before a crisis occurs; (3) changing policies, practice, and the culture of public child protective services by encouraging the assignment of workers to neighborhoods and locating CPS staff in community-based agencies; and (4) establishing local decision-making bodies that include agency representatives and community residents who develop program priorities and review the effectiveness of strategies. These initiatives have been in operation since 1995 and are now into the second stage of implementation. Findings from an evaluation study completed by Chapin Hall Center for Children indicated good progress on implementation of key components of the initiative in all sites (White 1997).

Alabama, New Mexico, Pennsylvania, Ohio, and Maryland were among the first states to begin implementing the Annie Casey Foundation's Family-to-Family initiative in 1992. Los Angeles County has recently begun implementing the program, as has New York City. Other states adopting the model are Illinois, Oregon, Kentucky, Michigan, North Carolina, Colorado, and California (Annie Casey Foundation 1992). The initiative is designed to encourage change in four planning and evaluation domains including the policy context; program management and structure; program operations; and program impact. The initiative incorporates four core strategies: (1) recruitment, training, and support of resource families in the communities and neighborhoods where families live; (2) building community partnerships with many community organizations in addition to the public child welfare agency and other private child welfare organizations; (3) family team decision making that involves birth parents and community members in all placement decisions; and (4) self-evaluation based on hard outcome data for decision making and service planning (Annie Casey Foundation 1992).

A 1998 evaluation of the Family-to-Family initiative used a quasi-experimental design to assess progress in achieving goals and objectives, and examined program performance and outcomes across and within program sites in Alabama, Maryland, New Mexico, Ohio, and Pennsylvania. The study did not yield information about the full impact of the program in these sites, finding that some of the objectives were accomplished in some sites and some were not achieved in any site. Summary observations of the study were as follows: (1) the program had enjoyed the most success in sites that focused on reconstructing family foster care in the most vulnerable neighborhoods in large urban areas; (2) achieving enduring reform in the child welfare system is difficult but can be accomplished; and (3) many sites reported that the enhanced capability to produce, analyze, and interpret data was a significant benefit of participating in the program (Annie Casey Foundation 1992).

New York City: A Case Example

New York City is currently in the early stages of changing from a traditional to a neighborhood-based model using the Casey Foundation Family-to-Family model. Several preexisting conditions contributed to creating a receptive climate for reforms supporting the neighborhood-based model in children's services in New York City. Among these conditions were sustained efforts of an advocacy policy group comprising leaders from the health and human services, government, business, and philanthropic communities concerned about the fragmentation of children's services. In a 1990 report to the mayor, the group advised: "Services are most effective when they are designed, operated, and delivered in the community where recipients live. Assisting, upgrading, and empowering local service deliverers, whether public or private, to strengthen their communities is the most direct way to a stronger healthier city" (Agenda for Children Tomorrow 1990, 3).

The city's long history of privatization and partnering with the voluntary sector in delivering child welfare services was also a significant condition. Voluntary agencies have traditionally carried the largest share of responsibility for delivering prevention, substitute care, and adoption services under contractual agreements, with the public child welfare agency carrying full responsibility for child protective services and a limited number of directly operated programs. A well-organized advocacy community that has kept children's issues high on the social agenda, as well, characterizes New York City. One of these organizations has been tracking policy, budgetary, and political shifts that affect child well-being since 1993. These data are published and serve as a strong base for advocacy efforts (Citizens Committee for Children 2001). Finally, a controversial class action lawsuit filed against the city in 1973 charging racial discrimination against African American children in the operation of foster care programs gave the court a strong and continuing oversight role.

The death of a child whose family had a long history of involvement with the public child welfare agency and was known to several community-based agencies served as the catalyst for setting into motion events that culminated in massive efforts to fundamentally transform the child welfare system in New York City. The centerpiece of reform is the neighborhood-based service model used in the Family-to-Family initiative designed by the Annie Casey Foundation. The Casey Foundation also played a central role in supporting the work of what was known as the Marisol Panel, established to oversee implementation of the negotiated settlement of the nearly thirty-year-old class action lawsuit alleging racial discrimination against African American children, and the progress of reforms.

"Protecting New York City's Children" (Administration for Children's Services 1996) outlined a five-year reform plan for transforming child welfare services and beginning implementation of the Family-to-Family program. One of the first steps was to create a new agency responsible for overseeing children's services, with a mission to ensure the safety, permanency, and well-being of all New York City children (Administration for Children's Services 1996). A significant redirection in policy was awarding agency contracts on the basis of geographically defined neighborhoods. Agencies are now required to negotiate working partnerships and alliances with other agencies and service providers in the community, and to recruit foster parents willing and capable of serving as resource parents in the communities where children live. In keeping with the Family-to-Family model, the new approach emphasizes key strategies of recruitment, training, and support of resource families in their neighborhoods; building community partnerships; family team decision making; and self-evaluation based on hard data to monitor progress and support decision making.

Practice innovations include early case management conferences that bring parents together with many members of the child's support network (which may include caseworker, teachers, extended family, and medical personnel) within seventy-two hours after the placement to plan services that will result in the child's quick return home. Collaborative partnerships have been established with many public and private agencies such as the board of education, police department, health department, Health and Hospitals Corporation, and voluntary social service agencies. In addition, the five New York City metropolitan schools of social work have formed a consortium to collaborate with the agency on a number of child welfare workforce development initiatives.

Recent statistical data published by the agency show positive beginning trends. The foster care caseload has fallen from 49,814 in 1991 to 31,008 in 2001, adoptions are up 63 percent over the previous five years, more families are receiving preventive services, and a small but growing number of children are being placed in their neighborhoods. Foster care entry rates have presented a more erratic picture. For example, between 1996 and 1998 the number of children admitted to foster care peaked at 12,000 in 1998 and began a slow decline to 9,583 in 2000 (Administration for Children's Services 2001). As is the case with national trends, African American children comprise the largest percentage of children entering the system.

Family-to-Family is in the earliest stage of implementation in New York City, and impact data have yet to become available. As required by the Family-to-Family model, extensive data are being generated that can be used to evaluate program impact once these programs are fully under way and operationalized throughout the system. A two-year study conducted by the Citizens

Committee for Children to track the city's progress toward implementation of the neighborhood-based child welfare plan made several findings of the experiences of the program in the early stages of implementation. Study findings indicated consistently strong support among many stakeholders for the neighborhood-based model. The approach was also found to be highly successful in encouraging the development of neighborhood networks, improving communication and coordination among community-based organizations, and encouraging a sense of common purpose and shared mission. Significant obstacles to supporting families in their neighborhoods included the lack of suitable housing, the lack of quality family support services, and notable difficulties in recruiting foster parents in neighborhoods where families live. Finding additional funds needed to support the transition from traditional to neighborhood-based care for a system that has been persistently underfunded was noted as a substantial and ongoing challenge (Citizens Committee for Children 2001).

The Africentric Perspective

The Africentric perspective establishes culture as the context for understanding and explaining human behavior and is grounded in a holistic conceptualization of the human condition that assumes an interrelatedness and interconnectedness of all things. The neighborhood model is anchored in similar assumptions in that general systems theory and the ecological perspective inform it. Both support the development of practice paradigms that shift attention away from the exclusive focus on the individual to an emphasis on exchanges between individuals and families in interaction with their social environments, recognizing the need for social supports and connections within the broader context of community.

This philosophical perspective represents a significant departure from the Eurocentric perspective that emphasizes self-reliance, individualism, and family privacy. The underlying ideology driving the development of neighborhood-based services is more closely aligned with an Africentric perspective that stresses communal ideals, especially the care of children who are viewed as the collective responsibility of the community. The compatibility of these perspectives are reflected in themes of mutual aid, collectivism, shared parenting, and consanguineal family structure embedded in the illustrations of neighborhood-based services given in the introduction of this chapter.

Communal themes of the neighborhood-based model are reflected in strategies that encourage the development of community leadership and shared decision making. Community residents are seen as equal partners in determining what is in their best interest and that of their neighborhoods. The strategy of community inclusiveness is closely aligned to the African concept of democracy, which unlike the majority rule of Western democracy, requires that every voice be heard. Furthermore, the obligation of leadership from an African view is to promote consensus building, ensure that the needs of all members of the community are provided for, and empower members to meet their own needs.

These democratic principles are embedded in community capacity-building concepts discussed earlier and integral to the neighborhood model. At the macro level this translates to the requirement for child welfare agencies to support the development of working partnerships with community stakeholders that help provider agencies build capacity and community resources that help children remain safely in their own homes and communities. The role of the public agency is to build community consensus and political support to reinvest dollars in neighborhoods for job creation and economic development that improve and mitigate community conditions that place children at risk. At the micro level, these concepts are reflected in shared decision making supporting the parents' rights to self-determination by having an equal voice in decisions about the types of services that will affect the lives of their children in very profound ways.

Conclusions

This chapter describes the legislative trends of the last decades that have supported the development of neighborhood-based services as the latest effort to bring about fundamental changes in the nation's child welfare system. The neighborhood-based model has received strong philanthropic support, and a growing number of states are adopting the model in hopes of solving long-standing problems of child welfare systems in urban cities where foster care placement rates are high.

On a cautionary note, neighborhood services must not be viewed as the solution for continuing social and economic inequalities that are the root cause of problems confronted by families in urban cities. Nor can these services be seen as a substitute for high-quality, culturally competent foster care services that must remain an option for children living in persistently unsafe environmental conditions or whose families are unable or unwilling to provide for their protection and care.

This chapter identifies similarities in the underlying ideology of the neighborhood-based approach and the Africentric perspective that can create new opportunities for the development of culturally competent services. To take full advantage of these new opportunities requires that issues of race and class be squarely faced. There must also be a willingness to make necessary fiscal investments to address the cumulative effects of long-term institutional neglect and discrimination on these communities.

Race and class segregation have resulted in the concentration of the poorest families in communities characterized by deteriorating infrastructures. The abandonment of housing has created hardship in an area that is vital for both family and community stability and poses substantial obstacles to the implementation of neighborhood-based child welfare services. Further, for social and political activists dedicated to obtaining a more equitable share of resources for poor communities, these conditions are representative of a legacy of racism and planned attempts designed to undermine family life in the African American community that have persisted throughout history. The Adoption and Safe Families Act, which makes it easier for states to terminate parental rights, has been met with some suspicion in African American communities for these same reasons. Therefore, sustaining community leadership and establishing a measure of trust is needed for negotiating partnerships and power sharing in the face of persistent unmet needs and systemic inequities. Using a neighborhood-based approach requires a great deal of sensitivity on the part of all stakeholders.

REFERENCES

Administration for Children's Services. 2001. *Five Years of Reform in Children's Services: 1996–2001: Reform Update.* New York: Administration for Children's Services.

Agenda for Children Tomorrow. January 1990. *Three Public Policy Issues in Perspective: A Report to the Mayor.* New York: Agenda for Children Tomorrow.

Annie Casey Foundation. 1992. *Family to Family: Reconstructuring Foster Care: A Framework for Planning.* Greenwich, CT: Annie Casey Foundation.

Bernstein, N. 2001. *The Lost Children of Wilder: The Epic Struggle to Change Foster Care.* New York: Pantheon Books.

Billingsley, A. 1968. *Black Families in White America.* Englewood Cliffs, NJ: Prentice-Hall.

———. 1992. *Climbing Jacob's Ladder: The Enduring Legacy of African American Families.* New York: Simon & Schuster.

Billingsley, A., & J. Giovannoni. 1972. *Children of the Storm: Black Children and American Child Welfare.* New York: Harcourt Brace Jovanovich.

Blassingame, J. W. 1979. *The Slave Community: Plantation Life in the Antebellum South.* New York: Oxford University Press.

Brace, C. 1872. *The Dangerous Classes of New York and Twenty Years Work among Them.* New York: Wynkoop & Hallenbeck.

Bronfenbrenner, U. 1979. *The Ecology of Human Development.* Cambridge: Harvard University Press.

Brown, J. H., W. A. Finch, H. Northen, S. H. Taylor & M. Weil. 1982. *Child, Family, Neighborhood: A Master Plan for Social Service Delivery.* Washington, DC: Child Welfare League of America.

Chaskin, R., P. Brown, S. Venkatesh & A. Vidal. 2001. *Building Community Capacity.* Hawthorne, NY: Aldine de Gruyter.

Child Welfare League of America. 2000. National Fact Sheet. Children Reported as Abused and Neglected and Referred for Investigation.

Citizens Committee for Children. April 2001. *Closer to Home: Serving Children and Families in Neighborhoods Where They Live. Interim Report.* New York: Citizens Committee for Children.

Cook, J. F. 1995. "A History of Placing Out." *Child Welfare* 84/1.

Everett, J. E., S. Chipungu & B. Leashore. 1991. *Child Welfare: An Africentric Perspective*. New Brunswick, NJ: Rutgers University Press.

Fanshel, D. 1976. *Children in Foster Care: A Longitudinal Study*. New York: Columbia University Press.

Franklin, J. H. 1969. *From Slavery to Freedom*. New York: Vantage Books.

Frazier, E. F. 1957. *The Negro in the United States*. Rev. ed. New York: Macmillan.

Germaine, C., & A. Gitterman. 1980. *The Life Model of Social Work Practice*. New York: Columbia University Press.

Grey, S., & L. Nybell. 1990. "Issues in African American Family Preservation." *Child Welfare* 66/6: 513–523.

Gutman, H. 1976. *The Black Family in Slavery and Freedom, 1750–1925*. New York: Pantheon.

Hartman, A., & J. Laird. 1985. *A Handbook of Child Welfare Practice: Context, Knowledge, and Practice*. New York: Free Press.

Haynes, G. E. 1912. *The Negro at Work in New York: A Study in Economic Progress*. New York: Vintage Books.

Hill, R. B. 1971. *The Strengths of Black Families*. New York: National Urban League.

———. 1977. *Informal Adoption among Black Families*. New York: National Urban League.

Kortenkamp, K., & J. Ehrle. 2002. *The Well Being of Children Involved with the Child Welfare System: A National Overview* (Series B, no. 43). Washington, DC: Urban Institute.

Laird, J., & A. Hartman. 1985. *A Handbook of Child Welfare: Context, Knowledge, and Practice*. New York: Free Press.

LaNey-Carlton, I. 2001. *African American Leadership: An Empowerment Tradition in Social Welfare History*. Washington, DC: NASW Press.

Littel, J., & J. Schuerman. 1995. *A Synthesis of Research on Family Preservation and Family Reunification Programs*. U.S. Department of Health and Human Services, Office of Assistant Secretary for Planning and Evaluation. Washington, DC. Retrieved from http://aspe.os.dhhs.gov/hsp/hspyoung.htm#fampres.

Longres, J. 2000. *Human Behavior in the Social Environment*. 3rd ed. Itasca, IL: F. E. Peacock.

Maas, H., & R. F. Engler. 1964. *Children in Need of Parents*. New York: Columbia University Press.

Maluccio, A. N., E. Fein & K. A. Olmsted. 1986. *Permanency Planning for Children: Concepts and Methods*. New York: Routledge, Chapman, and Hall.

Mandella, N. 1994. *Long Walk to Freedom: The Autobiography of Nelson Mandella*. New York: Little, Brown.

Martin, E., & J. Martin. 1986a. *The Helping Tradition in the Black Family and Community*. Silver Spring, MD: National Association of Social Workers.

———. 1986b. *The Black Extended Family*. Chicago: University of Chicago Press.

McAdoo, H. P. 1978. "Factors Related to Stability of Upward Mobile Black Families." *Journal of Marriage and the Family* 40/4:761–776.

Morisey, P. G. 1990. "Black Children in Foster Care." In *Social Work Practice with Black Families*, edited by S. Logan, E. Freeman & R. McRoy, 133–147. New York: Longman.

Morris, H. 1997. "Building Public Private Partnerships." In *Removing Risks from Children: Shifting the Paradigm*, edited by A. Carten & J. R. Dumpson, 19–40. Silver Spring, MD: Beckham House.

Morrison, B. J. 1997. "Reframing the Research Agenda." In *Removing Risk from Children: Shifting the Paradigm*, edited by A. Carten & J. R. Dumpson, 49–62. Silver Spring, MD: Beckham House.

Moynihan, D. P. 1965. *The Negro Family: The Case for National Action*. Washington, DC: U.S. Government Printing Office.

National Resource Center for Respite and Crisis Care Services. November 1994. *Family Preservation and Family Support Services*. ARCH Fact Sheet no. 37.

Pecora, P. J., J. K. Whittaker & A. N. Maluccio. 2000. *The Child Welfare Challenge: Policy, Practice, and Research*. New York: Aldine de Gruyter.

Pincus, A., & A. Minahan. 1973. *Social Work Practice: Model and Method*. Itasca, IL: F. E. Peacock.

Research Triangle Institute & Jordan Institute for Families. December 1998. *Evaluation of Family to Family*. Baltimore, MD: Annie E. Casey Foundation.

Staveteig, S. & A. Wigton. February 2000. *Racial and Ethnic Disparities: Key Findings from the National Survey of America's Families* (Series B, no. B-5). Washington, DC: Urban Institute.

Turner, R. 1997. "Affirming Consciousness: The Africentric Perspective." In *Child Welfare: An Africentric Perspective*, edited by J. Everett, S. Chipungu & B. Leashore, 36–57. New Brunswick, NJ: Rutgers University Press.

USDHHS, Administration for Children and Families, Children's Bureau. November 2000. *Rethinking Child Welfare Practice under the Adoption and Safe Families Act of 1997: A Resource Guide*. Washington, DC: U.S. Government Printing Office.

——. Administration for Children and Families, Administration on Children, Youth, and Families, Children's Bureau. 2000. *Child Maltreatment 1998: Reports from the States to the National Child Abuse and Neglect Data System*. Washington, DC: U.S. Government Printing Office.

——. Assistant Secretary for Planning and Evaluation, and the Administration for Children and Families. January 2001. *Evaluation of Family Preservation and Reunification Programs, Interim Report*. Washington, DC: U.S. Government Printing Office.

Weiss, N. J. 1974. *The National Urban League, 1910–1940*. New York: Oxford University Press.

White, A. 1997. *Community Partnerships for Protecting Children, Citizen Power for Strong Families*. New York: Edna McConnell Clark Foundation.

Whittaker, J. K., J. Kinney, E. M. Tracey & C. Booth, eds. 1990. *Reaching High Risk Families: Intensive Family Preservation in Human Services*. New York: Aldine de Gruyter.

12

A Culturally Competent System of
Care for Addressing Mental Health
Disparities in Child Welfare

MAXWELL C. MANNING

Scope of the Problem

Mental health disparity in the child welfare system is a critical problem because of the disproportionate number of African American children who find themselves in out-of-home placements, particularly foster care (Brown & Bailey-Etta 1997; USDHHS 2002). Of the total foster care population, African American children represent 40 percent while white children comprise 38 percent, Hispanics represent 15 percent, and the other/unknown category comprises 8 percent. Furthermore, 68 percent of the foster care population resides in out-of-home placements (USDHHS 2002).

The *Surgeon General's Supplemental Report on Mental Health: Culture, Race, and Ethnicity* reported foster care children as a high-need population with a specific need for mental health services (USDHHS 2001b). African American children in the foster care population are unequally impacted by externalizing (behavioral) disorders (i.e., conduct disorders and post-traumatic disorders) (Garland et al. 2000, 1996). For example, a growing number of children entering foster care between the ages of two and five have developmental delay rates between 49 percent and 61 percent in comparison with 3 percent to 18 percent in the general population (Klee, Kronstadt & Zlotnick 1997; Silver et al. 1999). Similarly, Dubner and Motta (1999) analyze the relationship between foster care, sexual and physical abuse, and post-traumatic stress disorder (PTSD). They found that 60 percent of the children who had been sexually abused and were in foster care had PTSD, while 42 percent of those physically abused had PTSD. Other mental health disorders that impact children in the foster care system and those who have experienced maltreatment are adjustment disorders and reactive attachment disorders (McLeer et al. 1998, 1992). Stein, Rae-Grant, Ackland, and Avison (1994) examined a sample of 248 children and reported a 41 percent to 60 percent mental health disorder rate among children in foster care.

Other factors that place African American children who enter the foster care system at risk for needing mental health services are chronic poverty, homelessness, AIDS, drug abuse, loss of parent(s), coping with traumatic events, and adjustment to new family situations (Barbell 1997; Franck 1996; Leslie et al. 2000). Children in foster care often experience multiple and temporary placements and are at risk because of their failure to function in other systems (Chrenoff et al. 1994; McIntyre & Keesler 1986). For example, Berrick, Needell, Barth, and Jonson-Reid (1998) and Palmer (1996) report that children in traditional foster care experience disruptions that range from 38 percent to 57 percent during the first twelve to eighteen months of placement.

Because African American children are disproportionately represented in the foster care system and out-of-home placements, they are considerably more at risk for mental health disorders than white children (Brown & Bailey-Etta 1997; Sheppard & Benjamin-Coleman 2001). As a result, African American children have a considerable need for mental health services and are less likely than white children to receive mental health or psychological services, preferred child welfare services (i.e., family services, counseling), and referrals to psychotherapy (Close 1983; Courtney et al. 1996; Garland & Besinger 1996; Pilowsky 1995). In a sample of 2,803 black and white children in Virginia who had emotional or behavioral problems associated with out-of-home placement, black children were overrepresented at 41 percent compared with a state distribution of 23 percent. Black children (53 percent) received more out-of-home placements than white children (48 percent). However, even with no racial differences in the presenting problems, black children were three times more likely to receive detention center placements than hospitalization in comparison with white children even though there were no racial differences in the presenting problems (Sheppard & Benjamin-Coleman 2001). Garland and Besinger (1996) reported on 142 court-ordered children referred for a variety of services: African American children (46 percent) were referred significantly ($X^2 = (N = 142)$ 6.38, $p < .05$) less times for counseling than Caucasian children (70.8 percent). African American children (0 percent, 18 percent, and 6 percent respectively) also were referred less for support groups, psychological evaluations, and educational services than whites (12.5 percent, 27.1 percent, and 8.3 percent respectively).

African Americans, Mental Health, and the Child Welfare System

The problems of access to and utilization of mental health services by African Americans are further compounded by the historical mistrust and racism experienced by the African American community when interacting with the mental health system (Morton 2000; Williams & Williams-Morris 2000). As a people, African Americans have historically utilized their families, spirituality, and natural healers in the community to cope with mental health problems. But when these systems and supports break down, African Americans must turn to the mental health system (USDHHS 2001b).

Even though African Americans have mental illness percentages that are similar to whites—i.e., major depression (12 percent to 18 percent), dysthymia (5 percent to 7 percent), panic disorder (4 percent to 35 percent), and phobic disorder (22 percent to 22 percent)—African American children in the foster care system have rates ranging from 41 percent to 60 percent (Klee, Kronstadt & Zlotnick 1997; McLeer et al. 1998, 1992; Silver et al. 1999; USDHHS 2001b). The mental illness prevalence rates of African American children in the foster care system represent a high-need population. However, African Americans with mental illness lack mental health services and receive half the number of services as non-Hispanic whites (USDHHS 2001b). Further, two-thirds of African Americans who have mental illness receive no mental health services (USDHHS 2001b).

Because African American children are overrepresented in the child welfare system and in out-of-home placements (i.e., foster care), they are at risk for experiencing a variety of emotional disturbances (Brown & Bailey-Etta 1997; Courtney et al. 1996; McCabe et al. 1999). Their at-risk status is corroborated by the high rates of emotional disturbance—rates that range between 60 percent and 80 percent (Garland et al. 1996; Landsverk & Garland 1999; Pilowsky 1995).

The rate of emotional disturbance among children in the child welfare system has been compared with the rates for children with both the special education and mental health systems. In child welfare, the rate is 41.8 percent, compared with 70.2 percent and 60.8 percent, respectively, for children in special education and the mental health systems (Garland et al. 2001). However, since the latter two systems are designed for treating emotionally disturbed individuals, the lower rate in child welfare supports the need for more mental health intervention in the child welfare system. Children are referred to these other systems primarily, if not solely, for their mental health problems. Garland et al. (2001) report that 41.3 percent of a child welfare sample ($N = 1,715$) demonstrated some type of emotional disturbance (e.g., ADHD, conduct disorder, oppositional disorder, and mood disorders) with ADHD/disruptive disorders accounting for 38.7 percent of the diagnosed cases.

Other researchers report that children in the foster care system have a six times greater occurrence of externalizing disorders (i.e., disruptive behavior, hyperactivity, delinquency, and aggression) than other children. The rates of emotional disturbance among those in foster care range from 35 percent to 85 percent. These behaviors are typically more chronic, disruptive, and difficult to treat. For example, Zima, Bussin, Freeman, Yang, and Berlin (2000) report that in a sample of 302 children between the ages of six to twelve in foster care in Los Angeles County, 18 percent had some mental health problem (e.g., bipolar disorder or major depression). An analysis of 15,507 cases conducted by DosReis, Zito, and Safer (2001) estimated a 57 percent mental health disorder rate among foster care children, with depression and attention deficit hyperactive disorder being the most pronounced disorders.

Zima, Bussing, Freeman, Yang, and Berlin (2000) report that 80 percent of a sample of 302 randomly selected foster care children received a psychiatric diagnosis, and 43 percent of their parents perceived a need for mental health services. Consistent with these findings, African American children in foster care have similar rates of mental disorders as white children in foster care but receive fewer mental health services (Garland & Besinger 1996; McCabe et al. 1999). As a result, African American children have longer stays, unmet goals in permanency plans, and a decreased likelihood of returning to their families (Brown & Bailey-Etta 1997; Courtney et al. 1996).

To address the concerns about longer foster care stays, unmet goals, and children remaining in the system, the child welfare system has expanded its traditional services. These traditional services consist of investigation, family/crisis counseling and/or protective supervision, foster care, shelter care, adoptive home supervision, and alternative care placement (i.e., group homes and residential care). Expanded services include services such as therapeutic foster care, home builder's services, and wraparound services. Although these services help to address high rates of mental disorders, out-of-home placements, and other factors burdening the child welfare system, they fall short of addressing the long-standing, more chronic mental health disorders experienced by many children in child welfare. Leslie, Landsverk, Ezzet-Lofstrom, Tschann, Slymen, and Garland (2000) reported that a sample of 1,078 Los Angeles children entering the foster care system had greater physical, developmental, and psychological needs than children in the general population. They also reported an increase in sexual and physical abuse, neglect, and out-of-home foster care placements. Negative factors (i.e., chronic mental health disorders, escalating abuse and neglect rates, and increasing out-of-home placements) are further exacerbated by a lack of access to appropriate, culturally competent mental health services. African American children and their families report that they are underserved by and lack access to the mental health services system (Cunningham & Freiman 1996; Costello et al. 1997; Chabra et al. 1999).

Barriers to Delivering Mental Health Services to African Americans in the Child Welfare System

The disproportionate delivery of mental health services to African American foster children in comparison with white foster children can be attributed to barriers such as a lack of access to mental health services, an insufficient number of culturally competent providers, and an unresponsive system (Smiles &

Roach 2002; USDHHS 2001b). The historical mistrust by African Americans of the mental health community has also created an atmosphere of tension and a provider/consumer disconnect (Morton 2000; William & William-Morris 2000). During certain historical periods, African Americans were either denied services or received services in segregated settings. They have also been stigmatized and stereotyped, while little attention has been given to their cultural strengths and resources (Williams & Williams-Morris 2000). Present barriers to mental health services for children fall into three categories: (1) structural barriers, (2) perceptual barriers related to consumers referred for mental health services, and (3) perceptual barriers related to recipients of mental health services (Fisher et al. 1997; Hoagwood et al. 2000; Pavuluris, Luk & McGee 1996; Stiffman et al. 2000). Frequently, African Americans are concerned about being stigmatized and whether they will receive the appropriate care (Stroul & Friedman 1986; USDHHS 2001b). African American children and their families also often lack the insurance necessary to receive appropriate services, and when available the system is too fragmented and complex for them to negotiate (Owen et al. 2002; Snowden & Thomas 2000; USDHHS 2001b).

Other barriers such as long waiting lists, lack of transportation, denial of a mental health problem, and negative perceptions of mental health providers limit access for African Americans to mental health services (Fisher et al. 1997; Hoagwood et al. 2000; Pavuluris, Luk & McGee 1996; Stiffman et al. 2000).

Funding for mental health services significantly affects access to treatment for African Americans in general and African American children in foster care in particular. For example, children in foster care show high utilization of mental health services funded through state Medicaid programs (Landsverk 2000). The proportional relationship between utilization and funding is notable because it demonstrates the impact that available funding can have on access to mental health services.

Since African Americans often fall in the costliest 5 percent of mental health users, they present a major problem to the mental health system (Snowden 1993). The overrepresentation of African Americans as high mental health users is reflected in their vulnerability to inpatient psychiatric care and the use of hospital emergency rooms (Snowden & Cheung 1990; Snowden & Holschuh 1992). The use of these services is costly. Other factors that impact the use of mental health services by African American children include the child welfare system's ability to assess the mental health needs of these children, to engage and support the extended family, and to provide in-home support (Albers, Reilly & Rittner 1993; Gould 1991; Logan, Freeman & McRoy 1990; Mech 1985; Stenho 1982). These factors can be characterized as system weaknesses that do not encourage the development of culturally competent service delivery (Morton 2000; William & William-Morris 2000).

Mental Health Services for African American Children in Foster Care: Culturally Competent Strategies

Access to mental health services for African American children in foster care has been exacerbated by the lack of training, referral guidelines, cultural knowledge, self-assessment, family and community involvement, and knowledge of the system of care model. Too often, African American children are treated without consideration for their culture, specific needs, and historical context (Albers, Reilly & Rittner 1993; Gould 1991; Logan, Freeman & McRoy 1990; Mech 1985; Stehno 1982). Any child welfare models for improving mental health service delivery to African Americans in the child welfare system must incorporate lessons learned from the *system of care* model.

The system of care model was introduced in 1986 and focuses on five key principles: (1) attention to individual needs and cultural preferences of the child and family; (2) a focus on strengths rather than deficits; (3) involvement of families in the care of children and the development of services and programs; (4) interagency collaboration and coordination in service management and delivery; and (5) use of the least restrictive service setting (Stroul & Friedman 1986). Integrating the concept of cultural competence can strengthen the system of care model, specifically as it applies to African Americans (Cross et al. 1989).

For African American children and their families, the concept of cultural competence is germane to addressing the issues of access to mental health services within the child welfare system. Many African American children and their families mistrust the child welfare system, and these feelings are further complicated by a weak referral nexus to the mental health system (Williams & Williams-Morris 2000). Both the child welfare and mental health systems can become more responsive to African Americans by collaborating to improve their understanding of cultural responses, particularly those related to mental health (Cross et al. 1989).

Culturally competent training increases the provider's understanding of the client's situation by emphasizing the diversity within the African American culture and among people of African descent (Manning 2000). Child welfare workers are often unaware of cultural differences and lack the training required to determine the efficacy of mental health treatment. These workers may be able to complete the referral, but lack the knowledge and ability to provide culturally competent services. Moreover, child welfare workers also may have difficulty identifying culturally competent mental health professionals (Benjamin & Manning 1999).

Similarly, when a referral is made, child welfare workers may not know how to encourage and nurture a successful referral (Benjamin & Manning 1999).

Since African Americans may be initially resistant to treatment, child welfare workers may have to actively prepare and support African American children and families in formalizing the mental health treatment referral plan. The providers' preparation for a mental health treatment referral plan might encompass educating clients about mental health issues, building trust, and framing the treatment process in the context of the client's strengths (Benjamin & Manning 1999). The concept of a strengths-based approach will be discussed in more detail later.

An African American cultural perspective on mental health becomes the central theme in preparing for assessment and treatment. Related to this central issue is the need for more providers to receive cultural competence training. To increase the effectiveness of preparation for mental health treatment, child welfare workers must be trained in culturally competent theories, techniques, and practices (Benjamin & Manning 1999). For example, the Cross, Bazron, Dennis, and Isaacs (1989) model has been recognized for its foundational principles and implementation in child-serving systems. The model identifies the essential elements of cultural competence as the following: to value diversity, perform cultural self-assessments, understand the dynamics of difference, institutionalize cultural knowledge, and adapt to diversity.

Foremost, child welfare workers must acknowledge and respect the importance of values held by the African American family. By examining diversity and the dynamics of difference, child welfare workers will be less likely to view African Americans as a monolithic or stereotyped community. Understanding and supporting the concept of diversity facilitates a stronger relationship between child welfare workers and African American clients. These and other culturally competent strategies greatly contribute to knowledge about the interrelationships within the African American community.

The process of self-assessment can also promote cultural competence among child welfare workers, if it leads them to examine their attitudes and beliefs about African Americans (Cross et al. 1989). Assessment requires self-reflection about racial identity, family background, and experiences with both African Americans and their cultural value system. Through self-assessment, child welfare workers can identify attitudes, beliefs, and perceptions that hinder their sensitivity to African Americans. They must consider the values that have historically maintained solidarity within the African American community—that is, the strengths of African Americans and an African-centered worldview (Graham 1999; Hill 1997). These two core values permeate an Africentric worldview, imbibing it with a survival mechanism and African heritage identity. Child welfare workers who exhibit positive attitudes about the historical strengths of the African American community are less likely to erect barriers to referring their clients for mental health treatment.

During the 1980s, the mental health system incorporated several changes for increasing access to mental health services by children in general and African American children in the child welfare system in particular. These changes primarily focused on the lack of access to mental health services, not only in the child welfare system but also in the juvenile justice and education systems, and is known as the *system of care* model (Vinson 2001), which at its core is child-centered, family-focused, and community-based. In theory, the theme of these three values is consistent and compatible with the cornerstone of African American values (Stroul & Friedman 1986). However, it is incumbent upon service providers to exert greater effort in ensuring that service delivery reflects these values. More important, culturally competent professionals and community stakeholders must infuse into the system of care a respect for the Africentric perspective that honors strengths and an African-centered worldview—two qualities required for increasing access to mental health services and changing the attitudes of African Americans, professional providers, and the community about mental health services (Manning 2000). With culturally competent implementation, many of these strategies have exceptional potential for positively impacting the African American family, particularly children in the child welfare system.

The community must also become more engaged in child welfare assessment and intervention. Specific strategies that facilitate community involvement include the participation of culturally diverse professionals, community affiliation and engagement, cooperation among groups, information dissemination and feedback, and community action. To involve African American children and families, child welfare workers should recruit a cadre of culturally diverse professionals who are respected in the African American community. Upon recruitment, these professionals can assist in developing and establishing relationships by focusing on strengths, values, and historical identification with African American children and their families (community affiliation). African American children and families can engaged in self-healing (community engagement), a process supported by community members (cooperative group effort) whose experiences include successful transition from the child welfare system. These successful African American community members can also help educate (community dissemination and feedback) and assist African American children and families to constructively interact with the mental health system. Finally, the African American community and the child welfare and mental health systems can act together to improve the mental health well-being of African American children and families in the child welfare system (community action).

When African American children and families become a part of the *change* team, they become more educated about how to successfully access and utilize the array of mental health services available to them. As part of the educational process, they become more familiar with the *system of care* model and its use in supporting a variety of service delivery levels (for example, outpatient, family-based, crisis intervention services, and respite services). The *system of care* model is very important because its core principles—(1) a focus on individual needs, preferences, and culture; (2) family strengths and involvement; (3) collaboration and coordination of service delivery and child placement in the least restrictive setting—encourage positive and healthy views of people, and it is particularly supportive of African American children and their families. The model also stresses a more integrated approach to service delivery, especially child welfare and mental health services. Consequently, the model can be a fundamental tool by which African American children and families in the child welfare system may receive more culturally competent mental health services, and thus, feel more empowered to provide the care that their children need (see fig. 12.1).

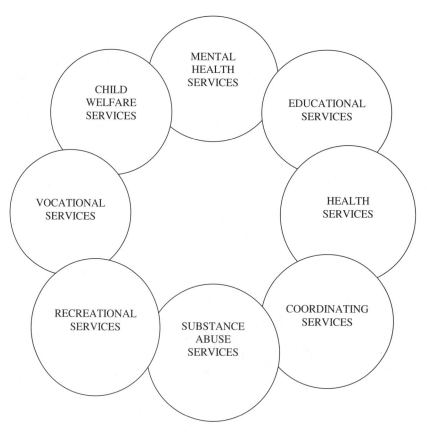

FIGURE 12.1   System of care framework.
Source: Data from Stroul and Friedman 1986

Conclusions

A culturally competent *system of care* model is the philosophical centerpiece inherent to understanding the major role that African American children and families play in resolving their own problems and moving beyond the child welfare system. African American children and families must become more engaged in the assessment and treatment plans for mental health services while simultaneously dismantling the barriers that hinder access to care.

In addition, child welfare workers can strengthen their cultural competence by examining, understanding, and practicing the elements of valuing diversity, conducting cultural self-assessments, acknowledging the dynamics of difference, institutionalizing cultural knowledge, and adapting to diversity. These elements facilitate a better rapport with African American children and families and allow for more supportive referrals for mental health services. Also, child welfare workers can advocate for more culturally appropriate, child-based, and family-centered treatment.

Child welfare workers can also become more culturally competent by becoming more knowledgeable about cultural similarities and differences among African American children and families. They should assess the dynamics of differences between their personal cultural beliefs and those shared or not shared by the clients. Worker self-assessment should include a critique of the extent to which they value diversity and cultural knowledge and adaptation.

If child welfare workers are culturally competent, they can express an appreciation for the Africentric perspective that values strengths and an African-centered worldview. This appreciation expresses a high regard for values such as the interconnectedness of all things, the spiritual nature of human beings, nurturing that encourages achievement, and strong kinship bonds. By valuing the culture of African American children and their families, service delivery is enhanced and children who need mental health services are more likely to receive them. Culturally competent approaches to service delivery are more integrated, comprehensive models of mental health treatment.

More interdisciplinary, culturally competent systems incorporate the values of strength, an African-centered worldview, and Africentric perspective into their *system of care* model. These values, worldview, and perspective offer an excellent foundation for developing a culturally competent child welfare system that has the capacity for rendering comprehensive services, starting with client referrals for mental health services, when appropriate. Additionally, child welfare workers who employ culturally competent practices can enhance the understanding of and intervention with these children and families by mental health providers.

Culturally competent child welfare workers can be significant players in facilitating access to mental health services for African American children and families in the child welfare system. These workers can influence service delivery by advocating the importance of culturally competent mental health services. Their investment in the delivery of culturally competent mental health services increases the likelihood that such services will be readily accessible to a population that has displayed a strong mistrust for the mental health system, decisively turning inward to their cultural foundation for self-treatment (e.g., family, friends, churches).

If increased access to effective mental health services is desired for African Americans in the child welfare system, these services must be broadened to promote an understanding of mental health and culturally competent practices. Moreover, from a culturally competent perspective, child welfare workers must embrace the values important in African American families. Embracing an Afri-centric perspective creates opportunities for culturally competent child welfare workers and mental health practitioners to collaborate during service delivery and thus facilitate healthy emotional, behavioral, and social changes in the lives of African American children and families in the child welfare system.

REFERENCES

Albers, E. C., T. Reilly & B. Rittner. 1993. "Children in Foster Care: Possible Factors Affecting Permanency Planning." *Child and Adolescent Social Work Journal* 10:329–333.

Barbell, K. 1997. *Foster Care Today: A Briefing Paper.* Washington, DC: Child Welfare League of America.

Benedict, M. I., R. B. White, R. Stallings & D. A. Courtney. 1989. "Racial Differences in Health Care Utilization among Children in Foster Care." *Children and Youth Services Review* 11:285–297.

Benjamin, M., & M. Manning. 1999. "How to Provide Culturally Competent Services to Children." In *Cultural Competency in Managed Behavioral Healthcare*, edited by V. H. Jackson & L. Lopez, 15–39. Providence, RI: Manisses Communication Group.

Berrick, J. D., B. Needell, R. P. Barth, & M. Jonson-Reid. 1998. *The Tender Years: Toward Developmentally Sensitive Child Welfare Services for Very Young Children.* New York: Oxford University Press.

Brown, A. W., & B. Bailey-Etta. 1997. "An Out-of-Home Care System in Crisis: Implications for African American Children in the Child Welfare System." *Child Welfare* 76/1:65–84.

Burns, B. J. 1991. "Mental Health Service Use by Adolescents in the 1970s and 1980s." *Journal of the American Academy of Child and Adolescent Psychiatry* 30/1:144–150.

Chabra, A., G. F. Chavez, E. S. Harris & R. Shah. 1999. "Hospitalization for Mental Illness in Adolescents: Risk Groups and Impact on the Health Care System." *Journal of Adolescent Health* 24:349–356.

Chrenoff, R., T. Combs-Orme, C. Reisley-Curtiss & A. Heisler. 1994. "Assessing the Health Status of Children Entering in Foster Care." *Pediatrics* 93:594–601.

Close, M.M. 1983. Child Welfare And People Of Color: Denial Of Equal Access. *Social Work Research and Abstract* 19:13–20.

Costello, E. J., E. M. Farmer, A. Angold, B. J. Barns & A. Erkanli. 1997. "Psychiatric Disorders among American Indians and White Youth in Appalachian Mountains Study." *American Journal of Public Health* 87:827–832.

Courtney, M. E., R. P. Barth, J. D. Berrick, D. Brooks, B. Needell & L. Park. 1996. "Race and Child Welfare Services: Past Research and Future Directions." *Child Welfare* 75:99–135.

Courtney, M. E., & Y.L.I. Wong. 1996. "Comparing the Timing of Exits from Substitute Care." *Children and Youth Services Review* 18:307–334.

Cross, T. L., B. J. Bazron, K. W. Dennis & M. R. Isaacs. 1989. *Towards a Culturally Competent System of Care: A Monograph on Effective Services for Minority Children Who Are Severely Emotionally Disturbed.* Washington, DC: National Institute of Mental Health, Child and Adolescent Service System Program.

Cunningham, P. J., & M. P. Freiman. 1996. "Determinants of Ambulatory Mental Health Service Use for School-Age Children and Adolescents." *Mental Health Research* 31: 409–427.

DosReis, S., J. M. Zito, D. J. Safer & K. L. Soeken. 2001. "Mental Health Services for Youths in Foster Care and Disabled Youths." *American Journal of Public Health* 91/7:1094–1100.

Dubner, A. E., & R. W. Motta. 1999. "Sexually and Physically Abused Foster Care Children and Posttraumatic Stress Disorder." *Journal of Consulting and Clinical Psychology* 67/3:367–373.

Fisher, A. J., R. A. Kramaer, R. C. Grosser, M. Alegia, H. R. Bird, K. H. Bourdon, S. H. Goodman, S. Greenwald, S. M. Horwitz, R. E. Moore, W. E. Narrow & C. W. Hoven. 1997. "Correlates of Unmet Need for Mental Health Services by Children and Adolescents." *Psychological Medicine* 27/5:1145–1154.

Frame, M. W., & C. B. Williams. 1996. "Counseling African Americans: Integrating Spirituality in Therapy." *Counseling and Values* 41/1:116–128.

Franck, E. J. 1996. "Prenatally Drug-Exposed Children in Out-of-Home Care: Are We Looking at the Whole Picture?" *Child Welfare* 75:19–34.

Garland, A. F. & B. A. Besinger. 1996. "Racial/Ethnic Differences in Court Referred Pathways to Mental Health Services for Children in Foster Care." *Children and Youth Services Review* 19/8:651–666.

Garland, A. F., R. L. Hough, J. A. Lansdverk, J. A. McCabe, M. Kristen, M. Yeh, W. C. Ganger & B. J. Reynolds. 2000. "Race and Ethnic Variations in Mental Health Care Utilization among Children in Foster Care." *Children's Service* 3/3:133–147.

Garland, A. F., R. L. Hough, K. M. McCabe, M. Yeh, P. A. Wood & G. A. Aarons. 2001. "Prevalence of Psychiatric Disorders in Youths across Five Sectors of Care." *Journal of the American Academy of Child and Adolescent Psychiatry* 40/4:409–418.

Garland, A. F., J. L. Landsverk, R. L. Hough & E. Ellis-MacLeod. 1996. "Type of Maltreatment as a Predictor of Mental Health Service Use for Children in Foster Care." *Child Abuse and Neglect* 20/8:675–688.

Gould, K. H. 1991. "Limiting Damage Is Not Enough: A Minority Perspective on Child Welfare." In *Child Welfare: An Africentric Perspective*, edited by J. E. Everett, S. P. Chipungu & B. R. Leashore, 58–78. New Brunswick, NJ: Rutgers University Press.

Graham, M. 1999. "The African-Centered Worldview." *Journal of Black Studies* 30/1:103–123.

Harvey, A. R. 2000. "Individual and Family Interventions Skills with African Americans: An Africentric Approach." In *Culturally Competent Practice: Skills, Interventions, and Evaluation*, edited by R. Fong & S. Furuto, 225–240. Needham, MA: Allyn & Bacon.

Hill, R. B. 1997. *The Strengths of African American Families: Twenty-Five Years Later.* Washington, DC: R & B Publishers.

Hoagwood, K., S. Horowitz, A. Stiffman, J. Weisz, D. Bean, D. Rae, W. Compton, L. Cottler, L. Bickman & P. Leaf. 2000. "Concordance between Parent Reports of Children's Mental Health Services and Service Records: The Services Assessment for Children and Adolescents (SACA)." *Journal of Child and Family Studies* 9:315–331.

Klee, L., D. Kronstadt & C. Zlotnick. 1997. "Foster Care's Youngest: Preliminary Report."
    American Journal of Orthopsychiatry 67:290–299.
Knitzer, J., & S. Yelton. 1990. "Collaborations between Child Welfare and Mental Health:
    Both Systems Must Exploit the Program Possibilities." *Public Welfare* 48:24–34.
Landsverk, J. 2000. "Child Welfare and the Identification of Mental Health Needs." *Proceed-
    ings in the Report of the Surgeon General's Conference on Children's Mental Health: A
    National Action Agenda.* Washington, DC: USDHHS.
Landsverk, J., I. Davis, W. Ganger, R. Newton & I. Johnson. 1996. "Impact of Child Psychoso-
    cial Functioning on Reunification from Out-of-Home Placement." *Children and Youth
    Services Review* 18:447–462.
Landsverk, J., & A. F. Garland. 1999. "Foster Care and Pathways to Mental Health Services."
    In *The Foster Care Crisis: Translating Research into Policy and Practice*, edited by P. A. Cur-
    tis, G. D. Dale & J. C. Kendall, 193–210. Lincoln: University of Nebraska Press.
Leslie, L. K., J. Landsverk, R. Ezzet-Lofstrom, J. M. Tschann, D. J. Slymen & A. F. Garland.
    2000. "Children in Foster Care: Factors Influencing Outpatient Mental Health Service
    Use." *Child Abuse and Neglect* 24:465–476.
Logan, S. M., E. M. Freeman & R. G. McRoy. 1990. *Social Work: A Culturally Specific Perspective.*
    New York: Longman.
Manning, M. 2000. "Culturally Competent Assessment of African American Communities
    and Organizations." In *Culturally Competent Practice: Skills, Interventions, and Evaluation*,
    edited by R. Fong & S. Furuto, 119–131. Needham, MA: Allyn & Bacon.
McCabe, K. M., M. Yeh, R. L. Hough, J. Landsverk, M. S. Hurlburt, S. W. Culver & B. Reynolds.
    1999. "Racial/Ethnic Representation across Five Public Sectors of Care for Youth." *Jour-
    nal of Emotional and Behavioral Disorders* 7:72–82.
McIntyre, A., & T. Y. Keesler. 1986. "Psychological Disorders among Foster Children." *Jour-
    nal of Clinical Child Psychology* 15:297–303.
McLeer, S. V., E. Deblinger, M. S. Atkins, E. B. Foa & D. L. Ralphe. 1988. "Post-Traumatic
    Stress Disorder in Sexually Abused Children." *Journal of the American Academy of Child
    and Adolescent Psychiatry* 27:650–654.
McLeer, S. V., E. Delinger, D. Henry & H. Orvashel. 1992. "Sexually Abused Children at High
    Risk for PTSD." *Journal of the American Academy of Child and Adolescent Psychiatry*
    31:875–879.
Mech, E. V. 1985. "Public Social Services to Minority Children and Their Families." In *Chil-
    dren in Need of Roots*, edited by R. O. Washington & J. Boros-Hull, 133–186. Davis, CA:
    International Dialogue Press.
Morton, M. J. 2000. "Institutionalizing Inequalities: Black Children and Child Welfare in
    Cleveland, 1859–1998." *Journal of Social History* 34/1:141–163.
Owen, P. L., K. Hoagwood, S. M. Horowitz, P. J. Leaf, J. M. Poduska, S. G. Kellam & N. S. Ia-
    longo. 2002. "Barriers to Children's Mental Health Services." *Journal of the American
    Academy of Child and Adolescent Psychiatry* 41/6:731–738.
Palmer, S. E. 1996. "Placement Stability and Inclusive Practice in Foster Care: An Empirical
    Study." *Children and Youth Services Review* 18:589–601.
Pavuluris, M. N., S. L. Luk & R. McGee. 1996. "Help-Seeking for Behavior Problems by Parents
    of Preschool Children: A Community Study." *Journal of the American Academy of Child
    and Adolescent Psychiatry* 35:215–222.
Pilowsky, D. 1995. "Psychopathology among Children Placed in Family Foster Care." *Psychi-
    atric Services* 46:906–910.
Realmuto, G. M., G. A. Bernstein, M. A. Maglothin & R. A. Pandey. 1992. "Patterns of Utiliza-
    tion of Outpatient Mental Health Services by Children and Adolescents." *Hospital and
    Community Psychiatry* 43:1218–1223.

Schiele, J. 1997. "The Contour and Meaning of Afrocentric Social Work." *Journal of Black Studies* 27:800–819.

Sheppard, V. B. & R. Benjamin-Coleman. 2001. "Determinants of Service Placement Patterns for Youth with Serious Emotional and Behavioral Disturbances." *Community Mental Health Journal* 37/1:53–65.

Silver, J., P. DiLorenzo, M. Zukoski, P. Ross, B. J. Amster & D. Schlegel. 1999. "Starting Young: Improving the Health and Developmental Outcome of Infants and Toddlers in the Child Welfare System." *Child Welfare* 78:148–165.

Smiles, R. V., & R. Roach. 2002. "Race Matters in Health Care." *Black Issues in Higher Education* 19/7:22–30.

Snowden, L. 1993. "Emerging Trends in Organizing and Financing Human Services: Unexamined Consequences for Ethnic Minority Populations." *American Journal of Community Psychology* 21/1:1–13.

Snowden, L. R., & F. K. Cheung. 1990. "Use of Inpatient Mental Health Services by Members of Ethnic Minority Groups." *American Psychologist* 45:347–355.

Snowden, L. R., & J. Holschuh. 1992. "Ethnic Differences in Emergency Psychiatric Care and Hospitalization in a Program for the Severely Mentally Ill." *Community Mental Health Journal* 28:281–291.

Snowden, L. R., & K. Thomas. 2000. "Medicaid and African American Outpatient Treatment." *Mental Health Services Research* 2:115–120.

Stehno, S. M. 1982. "Differential Treatment of Minority Children in Service Systems." *Social Work* 27:39–45.

Stein, E. N. Rae-Grant, S. Ackland & W. Avison. 1994. "Psychiatric Disorders of Children in Care: Methodology and Demographic Correlates." *Canadian Journal of Psychiatry* 39: 341–347.

Stiffman, A. R., E. Hadley-Ives, P. Dore, M. Polgar, V. E. Horvath, C. Striley & D. Elze. 2000. "Youths' Access to Mental Health Services: The Role of Providers' Training, Resource Connectivity, and Assessment of Need." *Mental Health Services Research* 2:141–154.

Stroul, B. A., & R. M. Friedman. 1986. *A System of Care for Severely Emotionally Disturbed Children and Youth*. Washington, DC: Georgetown University. CASSP Technical Assistance Center.

USDHHS, Administration on Children, Youth, and Families. 2001a. *Child Maltreatment 1999*. Washington, DC: U.S. Government Printing Office.

USDHHS. 2001b. *Mental Health: Culture, Race, Ethnicity: A Supplement to Mental Health: A Report of the Surgeon General*. Rockville, MD: USDHHS.

USDHHS. 2002. *The AFCARS Report: Interim Estimates as of August, 2002*. Retrieved from www.acf.dhhs.gov/programs/cb/publications/afcars/report7.

Vinson, N. B. 2001. "The System-of-Care Model: Implementation in Twenty-Seven Communities." *Journal of Emotional and Behavioral Disorders* 9/1:30–43.

Williams, D. R., & R. Williams-Morris. 2000. "Racism and Mental Health: African American Experience." *Ethnicity and Health* 5/3–4:243–268.

Zima, B. T., R. Bussing, S. Freeman, X. Yang & T. R. Berlin. 2000a. "Help-Seeking Steps and Service Use for Children in Foster Care." *Journal of Behavioral Health Services and Research* 27/3:271–286.

Zima, B. T., R. Bussing, S. Freeman, X. Yang, T. R. Berlin & S. R. Forness. 2000b. "Behavior Problems, Academic Skills Delays, and School Failure among School-Aged Children Foster Care: Their Relationship to Placement Characteristics." *Journal of Child and Family Studies* 9:87–103.

13

African American Adoptions

RUTH G. MCROY

Introduction

Much of the literature on African American adoptions describes the challenges faced by public adoption agencies seeking to find adoptive families for the growing number of African American children needing permanent placement. Children who are available for adoption are those who have had their parental rights terminated and/or have the permanency goal of adoption.

According to the April 2001 Adoption and Foster Care Analysis and Reporting System (AFCARS) data, there are 588,000 children in foster care and 134,000 have a plan of adoption. Of those needing adoptive placement, 32 percent are white, 45 percent African American, 12 percent Hispanic, 1 percent Native American, 1 percent Asian/Pacific Islander, and 9 percent unknown. Even though African American children encompass a greater proportion of legally free children needing adoptive placement, they are the group of children least likely to be adopted (Westat 1986 as cited in Lakin & Whitfield 1997). Barth (1997) reported that African American children in California were twice as likely to remain in out-of-home care as to be adopted (33 percent vs. 16 percent). White children were found to be twice as likely to be adopted as to remain in out-of-home care, and Latino children were equally as likely to remain in care as to be adopted.

In addition to race/ethnicity, age is another major influential factor on the likelihood of a child being adopted. Infants are adopted at higher rates than older children, and the likelihood of adoption decreases as a child ages (Barth 1997). Thus, based only on age, African American children should have higher rates of adoption than children of other racial groups because they tend to enter out-of-home care at younger ages than other children (Barth 1997). However, after controlling for age, Barth found that white children have a likelihood five times greater than African American children of being adopted versus remaining in care. In the same study he found that Latino children are 2.5 times as likely to be adopted as African American children. Barth's findings in California are consistent with those of Mont (1993) in New York and Kossoudji (1997) in Michigan.

Some suggest that transracial adoption, the placement of children of one racial background with families of a different racial background, is the answer to this growing problem, as there are insufficient numbers of African American families interested in adopting the African American children lingering in the nation's child welfare system (Simon, Altstein & Melli 1994). Others suggest that African American families are interested in adopting, and minority specializing agencies have been especially successful in making in-racial placements (McRoy, Oglesby & Grape 1997). This chapter examines important issues in African American adoption practice and offers suggestions, using an Africentric perspective, for improving service delivery outcomes.

Child Welfare Service Delivery Issues

African American children are overrepresented in the U.S. child welfare system. For example, in 2000, they comprised 14.7 percent of the population of children under eighteen in the United States but 38 percent of the children in foster care. Hispanic children represented 17.1 percent of the child population and 15 percent of children in foster care. Native American or Alaskan Native represented 0.9 percent of the U.S. child population and 2 percent of those in foster care. Asian or Pacific Islander children represented 3.5 percent of the U.S. child population and 1 percent of the foster care population (O'Hare 2001). The overrepresentation of African American children who need adoptive placement is partly related to inequities in the child welfare delivery system. These include both services to minority children in need of homes, as well as services to those seeking to adopt.

Racial discrimination within state child welfare systems has been identified as a cause of increasing numbers of children of color in out-of-home care. Despite the increase of people of color in higher-level work positions in recent decades, people of color are still marginally represented in child welfare positions (Lakin & Whitfield 1997). In 1992, the National Child Welfare Training Center reported that 78 percent of child welfare workers were white and 80 percent of child welfare supervisors were white. The majority have not received training in service provision to African Americans (Courtney et al. 1996; McRoy, Oglesby & Grape 1997). This may influence children of color entering the system at disproportionate rates and returning to their families at lower rates. African American and Native American children have the highest out-of-home placement rates (Lakin & Whitfield 1997; Mason & Williams 1985).

Moreover, according to the National Association of Black Social Workers (NABSW), the underlying cause for removal and subsequent out-of-home placements is neglect, as opposed to abuse or abandonment. Since neglect is associated with poverty, it is therefore correctable (Hill 1998). For example, the NABSW notes that some African American children are removed from their biological parents because siblings sleep in the same bed. Additionally, in 1986, "homelessness was a factor in over 40 percent of placements into foster care in New Jersey . . . and in 18 percent of those placements, it was the sole precipitating cause of placement" (1). Another factor, often related to neglect, that is becoming a growing reason for child removal is parental substance abuse. Alcohol and drug abuse are factors in the placement of more than 75 percent of the children entering care (USDHHS 1999).

Once removed from their homes and placed in foster care, African American children often remain in care for longer and may be less likely to be adopted. This is not a new concern. Historically, agency adoptions were not considered an available option for African American children or parents. Dependent African American children were informally adopted by the African American extended family (Hill 1997), since they were excluded from service provision by many private adoption agencies until the mid-1920s. Such agencies were segregated and designed to meet the needs of white couples seeking healthy white infants placed for adoption by unmarried mothers (Jackson-White et al. 1997; Morgernstern 1971; Rosenthal & Groze 1990). In the 1930s with the shift from private services to public social services, dependent African American children entered the child welfare system, but were primarily offered foster services rather than adoption. According to Billingsley and Giovannoni (1972), "In discussing the adoption of African American children, a leading child welfare text concludes that a number of characteristics of Black people make the extension of adoption services to Black children hopeless" (87). Thus, although "integrated" services were offered to African American children in the child welfare system, child welfare agencies did not adapt services to meet their needs. Instead, they tended to blame African American parents and their communities for agencies not offering adoption services to this population (Billingsley & Giovannoni 1972).

In 1955, the Child Welfare League of America (CWLA) reported that survey results indicated that African American children were remaining in care about twice as long as other children (CWLA 1955). Similarly, in 1959, Maas and Engler reported that many African American children in foster care were in need of adoption, but were less likely to be adopted. A few years later, Jeter (1963) also found that African American children were remaining in foster care for longer periods of time than white children and adoption was not being offered on an equitable basis. Jeter also identified ongoing discrimination in service provision, noting that African American children were primarily being served by public agencies and private voluntary agencies were primarily serving white children (Altstein & McRoy 2000).

Criteria used by adoption agencies had been generally exclusive of African American families, and very few have been approved as adoptive parents. Traditional mainstream agencies found it difficult to attract eligible African American families for African American children. This difficulty was largely due to perceptions by workers in the child welfare system that African American families were "beset with pathology" (Jackson-White et al. 1997, 246) and were not interested in adopting. Strengths in the African American community, such as reliance on extended family members, were seen as pathologies. Many adoption agencies screened out caregivers who were over the age of forty or who were single parents. African American children became labeled as "hard to place," and African American prospective parents were labeled "hard to reach" (Billingsley & Giovannoni 1972; Jackson-White et al. 1997, 246).

When children are not placed for adoption, they typically remain in foster care. The impact on these children (some of whom age out of the system) is devastating. They are three to six times more likely than children not in the child welfare system to have emotional, behavioral, and developmental problems. These difficulties include conduct disorders, depression, difficulties in school, and impaired social relationships. Experts estimate that approximately 30 percent of children in care have moderate to severe emotional problems. Fifty-eight percent of young children in foster care in 1995 had serious health problems. Additionally, 62 percent of children in foster care had been exposed to prenatal drug use, placing them at additional risk for health problems (CWLA 1998). Fifty percent of the children in care have entered because of abuse and neglect. Increasingly, parental drug and alcohol use is a factor in the placement of children in care.

Children in foster care frequently have substantial educational needs, including job training and educational skills. These children tend to perform at lower levels in school than children who are not in foster care, lag behind in their education by at least one year, and have lower educational attainment than the general population (CWLA 1998).

Informal Adoptions in African American Communities

Partly in response to the child welfare system's inability or unwillingness to serve African American children, and in part due to the value placed on children and kin in African American families, informal adoptions have evolved as a resource for dependent African American children. Informal adoption has a strong and enduring history in the African American community where families have traditionally relied on extended or kinship relatives for preservation and survival. Thus, when African American children were unable to live with their immediate families, blood relatives or other members of the surrounding community frequently absorbed the children into their homes (Jackson-White et al.

1997). According to Turner (1997), "Children were highly valued in African culture, where the concept of an illegitimate child was non-existent; all children were legitimate" (48).

During slavery, the community's response to the disruption of family bonds was to absorb children left without parents into existing family networks (Williams 1997). Following emancipation, as African American children were excluded from the evolving child welfare services and predominantly white charity organizations and settlement houses (Altstein & McRoy 2000), it was the African community, in concert with the self-help efforts of churches, women's clubs, benevolent societies, fraternal organizations, and extended families, that "came to the rescue of thousands of related and non-related African American children who had no means of support (Brown & Bailey-Etta 1997). During the twentieth century, poverty, racism, and socioeconomic and psychological stressors have necessitated the continuation of the pattern of extended family as a buffer against negative external forces (Danzy & Jackson 1997). Williams (1997) cites the example of a young mother who, recognizing she was ill equipped to raise her child alone, selected a responsible adult within her external family unit to share parenting. When she left the child with the family, the mother viewed it as a responsible decision and in the best interest of her child. It would surprise her to find that some child welfare workers view her decision to leave her child with a relative or friend as abandonment (Williams 1997, 268). Instead, the informal adoption of children is one example of a long-standing cultural tradition of self-help in the African American community.

Relatives without legal sanction, notably grandparents, aunts, and uncles, have adopted over one million African American children. The practice of informal adoption is closely tied to the traditions of kinship care. In light of this, informal adoption has been the traditional response to out-of-wedlock teen pregnancy (Sandven & Resnick 1990). Hill (1972) defines the practice as "the absorption of a daughter's illegitimate child into the immediate family, as well as the practice of 'giving' such a child to a member of the extended family to raise for an indeterminate period in order to ameliorate severe economic or emotional strain upon the immediate family" (210). The natural mother surrenders some, but not all, of her rights to the social mother (Stack 1974), often the grandmother. With the boundaries of the family being quite flexible, the grandmother acts as mother, the natural mother as older sister (Hill 1972; Yoest 1990), and children of a generation regard themselves as brothers and sisters, without divisions into siblings and cousins (Sandven & Resnick 1990).

Since informal adoption provides a relatively easy resolution to an unplanned pregnancy and does not address the underlying cause of the pregnancy, young women who have "gifted" their first child soon "replace" it with another (Sandven & Resnick 1990; Yoest 1990). Closely correlated is the notion of censure these young women may experience when considering formal adoption versus "gifting" the child within the kinship community (Sandven & Resnick 1990). This practice results in relatively few voluntary relinquishments of African American infants. Currently, less than 3 percent of white unmarried women and less than 2 percent of African American unmarried women place children for adoption (Mosher & Bachrach 1996).

However, 22 percent of Sandven and Resnick's (1990) sample of unwed teen mothers stated if they had some control in selecting the adoptive family, they may have considered placing a child for adoption. The authors suggested that if the African American adolescent mother perceives she has some control in the process of placing her infant, and if it is presented with sensitivity to cultural values, she may choose formal adoption more frequently in the future.

Yoest (1990), identifying concerns about informal adoptions, noted that such practices leave the child in legal limbo. For example, should the informal parent die, the child is ineligible for social security benefits. With no one having ultimate responsibility for them, informally adopted children are sometimes shifted from one home to another. Also, as the extended family network in the African American community has declined, the resources that previously enabled older African American women, and others, to care for needy children have diminished.

Barriers to Formal Adoptions

Many child welfare workers believe that although African American families informally adopt, they are not willing or able to adopt formally through agency channels. This belief may be based on agencies' long lists of white families waiting to adopt in comparison with the shorter lists of prospective African American parents. For example, in 1996 in Texas 636 white families adopted, while only 299 African American families adopted. Yet, according to Hill (1993), a National Urban League African American Pulse Survey found that one-third of African American–headed households were interested in formally adopting.

Sydney Duncan, founder of Homes for Black Children, and Zena Oglesby, founder of the Institute for Black Parenting, two African American–specializing adoption agencies, noted that "the dearth of African American formal adoptive homes is due to a social services system that is not sensitive to the African American community" (Yoest 1990). According to the North American Council on Adoptable Children (1993), minority agencies place 94 percent of their African American children in-racially, while nonminority specializing agencies place only 51 percent of their African American children in-racially. These types of specialized programs have demonstrated that it is possible to recruit and retain African American families as adoptive parents (McRoy, Oglesby & Grape 1997).

"Screening out" prospective adoptive families, not lack of interest, represents a major barrier to African American adoptions. In a National Urban

League study of eight hundred African American applicants for adoption, only two were approved for adoption (McRoy, Oglesby & Grape 1997). In fact, in a comparative study of minority adoptive parents working with thirteen traditional agencies and three agencies that specialized in minority adoptions, Rodriguez and Meyer (1990) found that agency policies, lack of culturally competent staff, and some community attitudes were obstacles to the successful recruitment and retention of adoptive families for older minority children (McRoy, Oglesby & Grape 1997; Rodriguez & Meyer 1990).

Historically, because agencies developed "screening out" criteria to very selectively choose from large pools of childless white couples seeking to adopt the relatively small number of white infants needing homes, they rarely have been involved in recruiting families for older children of color. Williams (1997) suggests that the criteria and procedures of traditional adoption are neither appropriate for African American families nor responsive to their economic status, thereby screening out potential families. When determining the suitability of a prospective family for adoption, many child welfare agencies require that the adoptive parents be a two-parent, middle-income family with no children and under forty-five years old (Hill 1993; Jackson-White et al. 1997; Rodriguez & Meyer 1990). However, it is the antithesis of this prototype that represents most minority families interested in adoption—one parent, low income, with children, and over forty-five years old (Hill 1993).

Cultural insensitivity and lack of knowledge on the part of the worker leads to the application of middle-class standards as the measuring rod of acceptability of African American parents. Hollingsworth (1998) reported that there may be a sufficient number of families of color who are willing to adopt healthy infants if agency recruitment and eligibility policies are responsive to the lifestyle and culture of such families. Some workers' inability to understand the families with whom they work, especially within the context of the external family and viewing the African American family through a pathological lens (Hill 1993), has led to an excess of African American children without homes.

The use of white, middle-class standards effectively screens out the majority of African Americans wishing to adopt, especially if their lifestyles do not match the lifestyles of Anglo families in their socioeconomic bracket. For example, some child welfare workers may perceive African American families with multiple children as being too crowded to adopt. If the worker is not culturally competent, he or she will not recognize that multiple children in the home is part of the African American community culture, not part of an overcrowded lifestyle (Grape 2000).

Other organizations have identified child welfare service delivery barriers to African American adoptions. For example, the 1994 National Association of Black Social Workers (NABSW) position statement on preserving African American families described the barriers of the traditional adoption process that prospective African American adoptive families face as follows: "The emphasis on high income, educational achievement, residential status, high fees, and other accoutrements of a White, middle-class lifestyle eliminate African American applicants by the score" (1). Similarly, according to the North American Council on Adoptable Children, the most frequent barriers to minority adoptions are "institutional/systemic racism, lack of people of color in managerial positions, fees, 'adoption as business mentality', communities of color historical tendencies toward informal adoption, negative perceptions of agencies and their practices, lack of minority staff, inflexible standards, general lack of recruitment activity and poor recruitment techniques" (NACAC 1991). Brown and Bailey-Etta (1997) also noted systemic issues within the child welfare system that perpetuate barriers to adoption. They identified the following: lack of adequate staff and resources; sporadic training of staff; and unclear and lack of preservation services to prevent initial out-of-home placements.

Friends of Black Children, a North Carolina adoption project, identified similar barriers to adoption within the African American community (Washington 1987). These barriers included inflexibility of working hours; complexity and length of application forms, financial reports, and legal documents; lack of timely response to initial inquiries and slowness in processing applicants; difficulty in using or accepting the services of community volunteers; undeveloped recruitment materials, strategies, and techniques; and inadequate systems for keeping track of children and families (Washington 1987).

Prospective adoptive families also may feel that fees often charged by private adoption agencies are inappropriate due to negative historical associations with the buying and selling of African slave children (Rodriguez & Meyer 1990). Some families feel they should not be paying for a child nor for the service to obtain the privilege to adopt an African American child, especially when there is a shortage of homes for African American children. Other families may also feel resentful of having to pay to "open their homes and hearts to children in need" (Jones 1992; McRoy, Oglesby & Grape 1997, 100). Moreover, some private agencies that rely on agency fees to sustain their operations are sometimes confronted with the dilemma of deciding "where would you place a minority kid . . . with a White family that can afford to pay, or with a Black family that can't?" (Hollingsworth 1998, 108).

The issue of money has a two-pronged effect as a barrier to adoption for African American families. Brown and Bailey-Etta (1997) reported that families in their study stated they were unable to afford another child or already had obligations to a child within their external family unit. Subsidies for adoption would be beneficial in defraying the cost of taking in another child (Hollingsworth 1998). Yet in a study by Rodriquez and Meyer (1990), 63 percent of families stated the federal and state subsidies, particularly for special needs children, were not explained to them.

In recent decades, adoption agencies have been prompted to reconsider how their practices and policies impact the number of African American children needing adoption. Factors such as growing numbers of African American children lingering in foster care, the passage of legislation such as the Adoption Assistance and Child Welfare Act of 1980 (PL 96-272) and the Adoption and Safe Families Act of 1997 (PL 105-89), and the development of private sector African American adoption programs have led agencies to develop active recruiting programs for prospective African American parents, and some have been successful in finding and retaining African American families.

Some agencies have responded to the presumed shortage of African American adoptive families being approved for adoption by placing African American children in white foster and adoptive families. The 1994 Multiethnic Placement Act (MEPA, PL 103-382) prohibits any foster care or adoption agency or entity that receives federal financial assistance from denying a placement solely on the basis of race. In 1996, the act was amended by the provisions for Removal of Barriers to Interethnic Adoption as part of the Small Business Job Protection Act (PL 104-188). Under this amendment, "agencies could no longer assume that children have needs related to their race, color, or national origin" (Hollinger 1998, 2). Therefore, specialized recruitment of African American families came under attack as such practices were assumed to be promoting race matching. In some states such as Texas, workers can lose their jobs if they delay or deny a placement for the purposes of race matching (McRoy, Oglesby & Grape 1997). However, these policies, presumed to promote transracial adoptions, seem to be implemented primarily for minority children. It is important to note that transracial placements of white children are still quite rare.

Laws and policies such as MEPA and IEPA tend to create more barriers for workers who desire to recruit for families in communities most like the communities from which the children have come. Similarly, these policies may serve as barriers to African American families adopting, as recruitment programs have been curtailed and workers can no longer advocate for an African American family for a particular African American child.

African Americans Who Foster and/or Adopt

According to the Child Welfare League of America, African American families can be found for infants, preschoolers, and school-age African American children (Sullivan 1994). Moreover, when income, age, and family composition are controlled, African American families adopt at four times the rate of white families (Mason & Williams 1985). There is relatively limited literature on characteristics of African Americans who foster and adopt. The majority of those who have adopted are middle-class, and 27 percent of the African American population is middle-class (Davis 1993). Sixty-five percent of these have at minimum some college. They are equally likely to identify with the mainstream culture as the African American culture (Davis 1993; Jones 1996), although other African Americans often accuse them of identifying too much with the dominant white culture.

Similarly, according to a study of seven adoption social workers from Medina Agency in Seattle, Washington (Jones 1996), most adoptive African American prospects they worked with were two-parent families with at least one biological child. Many were professionals and were at least in their thirties. However, there are increasing numbers of single women who want children, usually older children. Important to note, these single parents often have at least a high school education with the added feature of strong family support. Other research (Rosenthal, Groze & Curiel 1990) has revealed that although white adoptive families were often two-parent, minority families were both single-parent and two-parent.

Motivation to adopt varies, but in one study of 53 African American adoptive families who collectively worked with twenty different agencies, Hairston and Williams (1989) found that 70 percent desired to give a child a permanent home and 50 percent were infertile. In addition, 21 percent chose to adopt because they wanted to have a larger family and 14 percent wanted to provide companionship for another child. Eighty percent of these families cited recruitment and 84 percent cited the orientation/intake meeting as being instrumental in their decision to pursue adoption. Additionally, a study by Hollingsworth (2000) found that formal adoption seeking was highly correlated to parent-centered motivations (as compared with altruistic motivations) such as infertility, "wanting children of a particular sex, wanting more children or wanting a companion for an existing biological child or children" (Hollingsworth 2000, 3).

According to reports from the Medina, a Washington agency, response to advertisements for African American adoptive families has been very good (Jones 1996). It should be noted that the agency is located in an African American area of the city, and the location assists in their success along with their use of advertisements. However, the agency has found that some who respond to ads for adoption may not truly be committed to adoption but feel they have a duty to help children. These families often drop out of the process once they start to experience difficulties with completing paperwork and other requirements.

Adoption: An Africentric Perspective

It is evident that traditional Eurocentric approaches are successful in placing white children, but are not as successful in adoption practice with African American families. The Africentric perspective, according to Oyebade (1990), calls for a collective approach that emphasizes family strengths, interconnectedness, and interdependence of living things expressed in collective identity

(Turner 1991). In adoption practice, this approach calls for hiring culturally competent staff and locating offices in the African American community.

Revamping the process to be socially and culturally sensitive will increase the likelihood of successful adoptive placements of African American children with African American families. For example, the current adoption screening process has evolved from that which was initially set up to serve white middle- and upper-class families, and it reflects the cultural values of the creators. With the current screening process and lack of African American social workers, it appears that those who successfully navigate the process have a bicultural worldview (Davis 1993; Jones 1996). This view is defined as one that allows African Americans to be a part of the mainstream without sacrificing their African American identity. However, it is essential to be able to offer to families services that have an Africentric worldview as well and that take into consideration the strengths of African American families (English 1991).

Agencies should ensure that their staff's language, attitudes, and communication styles match those of the target community. Staff should be able to view and assess African American families through the lens of African American cultural values instead of through the traditionally white, middle-class lens. Having staff available who are culturally competent and supportive of prospective African American families encourages families to work with the agency through the entire adoption process. Agencies who are able to consider and embrace the values of the African American community in the formation of their recruitment and training processes have more success in recruiting adoptive African American families. Data are sparse on specific recruitment and training variables impacting African American adoptions.

Innovative programs that have focused on working within African American communities have had unparalleled success in placing African American children with adoptive families. However, the need for adoptive homes for African American children remains at overwhelming levels. Most of these children are still in the custody of state agencies that do not have mechanisms in place to work collaboratively with African American communities.

Recruitment is an art, and targeting African American adoptive and foster parents requires more effort. Given that many families have stated an interest in adopting, efforts need to be made to help them with the first step. Between 1973 and 1995, 9.9 million women considered adoption, "16 percent had taken steps towards adoption, and 31 percent of these had actually adopted a child" (National Center for Health Statistics 1999).

For both African American adoptive and foster parents, recruitment efforts can be successfully centered on the role of spirituality in their lives. Because the church belief promotes valuing children, it is a natural resource for appealing for help from African American families. However, special recruitment efforts outside of church need to be undertaken (Brissett-Chapman 1997).

Prior to the implementation of the Multiethnic Placement Act, agencies recruited African American families by creating specialized, well-funded recruitment units designed specifically to recruit and process minority families. One necessary aspect of creating such a unit may be reducing worker caseload in order to effectively reach the target population. Workers in these special recruitment units should be familiar with cultural practices and values in the target population. Bicultural/bilingual workers preferably would be responsible for contacting, matching, and placing families with available children (McRoy, Oglesby & Grape 1997). In order to create and maintain such a unit today and be in compliance with the Multiethnic Placement Act and Interethnic Provisions (discussed earlier), agencies must open up their recruitment and services to all families regardless of race. They can target specific communities, but must be open to working with all ethnic groups who respond to the recruitment effort and consider all eligible families for the available children. Moreover, the majority of white families are seeking to adopt infants of any race, and not the older minority children lingering in the system.

In addition to a specialized recruiting unit, agencies may establish an office in the target community and away from the central agency headquarters. This office may be identified by a different name from that of the main agency. Distancing this office from the main agency helps foster trust and ownership in the target community. Placing the office in an already established community organization (e.g., a church or recreation center) can also help establish positive community attitudes about the office (McRoy, Oglesby & Grape 1997). New or expanding adoption agencies may want to form partnerships with state agencies. Partnerships can give agencies access to public funds as well as connect families with children in the care of public agencies outside of their geographic jurisdiction.

Retention of African American Families

Once families are recruited, efforts must be made to retain them and keep them interested in adoption. Once potential adopters make the initial call to request information on adoption, they expect to be contacted relatively quickly. Jones (1996) found that although all of the families had seen advertisements about the need for African American adoptive parents, they all agreed that they were made to feel as if African American families were really not needed. The initial contact with the agency sets the stage for the relationship between the social worker and potential adoptive parents (Jones 1996).

The challenge of retaining African American families throughout the adoption process is a continuing concern. Traditionally, adoption workers have viewed families who withdrew without completing the adoption as being unfit or unready parents. However, as the effort toward recruiting African American families has increased, the question has been raised as to whether withdrawn families were really unfit or unready or were repelled by some aspect or practice of the agency. Families sometimes withdraw from the process because of their concern for privacy and respect from others. Personal questions such as those found on adoption applications are often met with mistrust. For example, Jones (1996) found that some families viewed some questions on the application as irrelevant. Noted especially was a question that asked the number of times the couple had sex every week.

During the adoption process, the social worker is often the greatest support available for the prospective parents. The social worker plays the role of advocate, educator, supporter, facilitator, and child protector. Overall, adoption workers view themselves as helping families to see if adoption is for them and if they are truly ready to adopt a child (Jones 1996).

For the average adoption worker, the process may seem to progress status quo, but for the African American adoptive parents, problems can be perceived at every corner. The adoption screening system has been set up with criteria that often exclude many would-be African American adoptive families (Everett, Chipungu & Leashore 1991). Examples of culturally biased processes abound in the literature. For example, one woman was turned down by other agencies for adoption once the agencies learned she had two previous marriages. She was always asked if she had been to counseling; this reflects the belief that formal counseling is the only way to get better (Jones 1996). The real issues should have been the stability of her current marriage and whether she would be a good parent. Another example is an agency having certain expectations of how potential adoptive parents should have educated themselves on adoption (Jones 1996). These types of subtle displays of cultural values screen out potentially good candidates for adoption.

Financial issues should be considered when involving African American families in the adoption process. A sliding scale fee could increase the number of African American families who would consider adoption (McRoy, Oglesby & Grape 1997). African Americans are disproportionately represented among the poor, who might be willing to adopt if resources were available to assist them (Billingsley 1992). Also, the cost of the adoption in addition to the expense of household needs for a child is prohibitive for some families. Agency workers should consider adoption subsidies in their recruitment and retention efforts. These subsidies may make adoption an option for some low-income families, including foster parents.

African American Adoption Recruitment: Best Practices

In order to glean additional information on best practices in reaching African American families, the author interviewed sixteen adoption agency personnel representing twelve programs, with seven of these specializing in African American adoptions. Eight of these programs were located in Texas including three specializing in minority adoptions. Agency staff responded to a series of questions on recruitment strategies for African American families. Agencies reported that their specialized African American recruitment efforts were motivated by a goal of creating an established, trusting relationship with the community. The most effective ways to achieve this goal were to partner with organizations in the community, particularly churches. Many agencies report that if ministers believe in the mission of the agency to recruit African American families, they can provide the agency with an inroad to the congregation. Other social and civic organizations in the African American community such as fraternities, sororities, clubs, Urban League, and so on also were identified as resources with which to partner with agencies.

Once an agency has established a positive reputation for itself within the community, word of mouth is a highly effective recruitment tool. Agencies report that previous adoptive parents have referred many families for adoptions. Advertising through the media is another tool used by agencies. Hanging posters in local grocery stores, commercials on popular radio shows, and giving presentations in civic organizations are three ways of making the community aware of the need for adoptive parents. Other suggestions made by agencies in the study were as follows: involve African American community leaders, have a children's artwork gala, get a famous spokesperson, advertise heavily, and hire more African American workers.

Once families have begun the adoption process, agencies stress that staff must provide them with avenues for ongoing support. Several agencies created mentoring programs with previous and prospective adoptive parents. Mentors keep in constant contact with prospective families and, along with staff, are available to answer questions or address concerns.

It is essential to have culturally competent staff members. Familiarizing staff with the cultural practices and values of the community gives the agency a basis from which to devise recruitment and retention techniques that meet the needs of African American families. Agencies reported that African American staff make some families feel more trusting of the agency motives and more comfortable with giving personal information to staff. The following section presents an example of a particularly successful African American adoption program located in rural Shelbyville, Texas.

Bennett Chapel: A Case Study of a Successful African American Adoption Recruitment Program

Since June 1998, African American families in a small Deep East Texas (Shelby County) community, known to prior generations as Possum Trot, Texas, and now known as New Harmony, have been adopting special needs African American children in record numbers. Rev. W. C. initiated these adoptions, and Donna Martin, who pastors at Bennett Chapel Family Outreach, have personally adopted five children and are in the process of adopting two other children. Since their adoptions, a total of seventy children have been placed with fifty families from Bennett Chapel. Their adoption feat came to the attention of the media. Rev. Martin, his wife, and other adoptive parents in the community were featured on the *Oprah Winfrey Show* and *48 Hours*, in articles in the *Houston Chronicle*, *Texas Monthly*, and *Essence* magazine, and in *Reader's Digest*. The Martins were selected for a national *Essence* award in 1999 and have since received numerous other recognitions.

Most of the African American adoptive families in this rural community come from large families of origin, have raised birth children, and are middle-aged and relatively low-income "empty nesters" or "almost empty nesters," according to media accounts. The majority of the children are school-aged. As Rev. Martin stated in one news report, "You start looking at all the kids are going through and you think, maybe I can help" (Henderson 1999). In Texas, in 1999, there were a total of 1,011 African American children needing adoptive placement and, according to state Children's Protective Services officials, "until the gates of Shelby County opened, their prospects were dim" (Henderson 1999).

As one social worker remarked in the same media account of this successful African American adoption program,

> We've never come across any single group that would adopt this many kids. CPS workers refer to the placement of children with Bennett Chapel families as "an experiment which has led to a surplus of African American families waiting to adopt CPS children." This is a community in which the state agency has moved beyond stereotypically, rigid boundaries to overcome barriers and facilitate adoptions by low-income, rural families. For example, CPS workers from the state initially asked the church families inquiring about adoption to travel about thirty miles to participate in adoptive parent training. When they objected, the workers indicated that if the church could gather ten families, the workers would come to the church to offer the training. When the workers arrived, twenty families seeking to adopt were present (A1).

These families not only provide evidence that African American families are available and will adopt, but also demonstrate a unique partnership between a state agency and an African American church that has defined its ministry as adoption. These families truly epitomize the Africentric belief that children are highly valued by and are the concern of the entire community (Harvey & Rauch 1997). The project also demonstrates one of the strengths of African American families and communities: the African American church. In this case, a pastor and his wife modeled adoption for the congregation and initiated the "Saving a Generation" ministry at the church.

Conclusions

Due to discriminatory child welfare practices, lengthy stays in the child welfare system, and low rates of adoption, there is an overabundance of African American children in the child welfare system. The disproportionate numbers of legally free African American children point to the great need for African American adoptive parents. The long-standing prejudices and misconceptions on both sides of the adoption process (staff and families) can impose staggering barriers to successful recruitment in African American communities. Other historical barriers to the recruitment and retention of African Americans as prospective adoptive parents have included underutilization of community resources, discriminatory fees, and underappreciation of the impact of informal adoption and kinship care. Addressing the causes of the problem should lead to an increase in the availability of prospective African American families for African American children. Specific innovations could include ethnically and culturally sensitive and diverse staff who respect the adoptive patterns of African Americans.

Thousands of African American children are awaiting permanent homes to a large extent because African American families have not been effectively recruited and retained. Unless child welfare agencies change their approaches to serving these families, they will fail another generation of children living in the nation's child welfare system.

NOTE

The author wishes to thank Jonathan Hardy (Casey Family Programs), Cheryle Yarbrough, and Latonia Parham for their assistance with the research used in this manuscript.

REFERENCES

Adoption Assistance and Child Welfare Act of 1980, 42 U.S.C. 42, sec. 620. Public Law 96-272.

Adoption and Safe Families Act of 1997. Public Law No. 105-89, III Stat. 2115.

AFCARS Report. April 2001. "Adoption and Foster Care Analysis and Reporting System." Retrieved 2/25/02 from www.acf.dhhs.gov/programs/cb/publications/afcars/apr2001 .htm.

Altstein, H., & R. G. McRoy. 2000. *Does Family Preservation Serve a Child's Best Interests?* Washington, DC: Georgetown University Press.

Barth, R. P. 1997. "Effects of Age and Race on the Odds of Adoption Versus Remaining in Long Term Out-of-Home Care." *Child Welfare* 76/2:285–308.

Billingsley, A. 1992. *Climbing Jacob's Ladder*. New York: Simon & Schuster.

Billingsley, A., & J. M. Giovannoni. 1972. *Children of the Storm*. New York: Harcourt Brace Jovanovich.

Brissett-Chapman, S. 1997. "Child Protection Risk Assessment and African American Children: Cultural Ramifications for Families and Communities." *Child Welfare* 76/1: 45–63.

Brown, A. W., & B. Bailey-Etta. 1997. "An Out-of-Home Care System in Crisis: Implications for African American Children in the Child Welfare System." *Child Welfare* 76/1:65–83.

Child Welfare League of America. 1955. *National Adoption Survey*. New York: Child Welfare League of America.

———. January 1998. "Family Foster Care Fact Sheet." Retrieved from www.cwla.org/cwla/fostercr/familyfcfacts98.html.

Courtney, M. E., R. P., Barth, J. D. Berrick & D. Brooks. 1996. "Race and Child Welfare Services: Past Research and Future Directions." *Child Welfare* 75/2:99–137.

Danzy, J., & S. M. Jackson. 1997. "Family Preservation and Support Services: A Missed Opportunity for Kinship Care." *Child Welfare League of America* 75/1:31–44.

Davis, R. A. 1993. *The Black Family in a Changing Black Community*. New York: Garland Publishing.

English, R. A. 1991. "Diversity of World View among African American Families." In *Child Welfare: An Africentric Perspective*, edited by J. Everett, S. Chipungu & B. Leashore, 19–35. New Brunswick, NJ: Rutgers University Press.

Everett, J. E., S. P. Chipungu & B. R. Leashore. 1991. *Child Welfare: An Africentric Perspective*. New Brunswick, NJ: Rutgers University Press.

Grape, H. 2000. Personal communication.

Hairston, C. F., & V. G. Williams. 1989. "Black Adoptive Parents: How They View Adoption Agency Practices." *Social Casework* 70/9:534–538.

Harvey, A., & J. Rauch. 1997. "A Comprehensive Afrocentric Rites of Passage Program for Black Male Adolescents." *Health and Social Work* 22/1:30–37.

Henderson, J. October 19, 1999. "Pining for Homes: Small East Texas Church Becomes Hub for Adoptions." *Houston Chronicle*, A1.

Hill, R. 1972. *The Strengths of Black Families*. New York: National Urban League.

———. 1993. *Research on the African-American Family*. Westport, CT: Auburn House.

Hill, R. B. 1997. *The Strengths of African American Families: Twenty-Five Years Later*. Washington, DC: R & B Publishers.

Hill, S. A. 1998. *African American Children: Socialization and Development in Families*. Thousand Oaks, CA: Sage Publications.

Hollinger, J. H. 1998. *A Guide to the Multi-Ethnic Placement Act of 1994 as Amended by the Interethnic Adoption Provisions of 1996*. American Bar Association Center on Children and the Law. Retrieved from www.acf.dhhs.gov/programs/cb/special/mepagui.htm.

Hollingsworth, L. D. 1998. "Promoting Same-Race Adoption for Children of Color." *Social Work* 43/2:104–116.

———. 2000. "Who Seeks to Adopt a Child? Findings from the National Survey of Family Growth 1995." *Adoption Quarterly* 3/3:1–23.

Interethnic Placement Act Amendments of 1996. Public Law 104-188.

Jackson-White, G., C. D. Dozier, J. T. Oliver & L. B. Gordner. 1997. "Why African American Adoption Agencies Succeed: A New Perspective on Self-Help." *Child Welfare* 76/1: 239–254.

Jeter, H. R. 1963. *Children, Problems, and Services in Child Welfare Programs*. Children's Bureau Publication no. 403-1963. Washington, DC: U.S. Department of Health, Education, and Welfare.

Jones, M. 1992. "Adoption Agencies: Can They Service African Americans?" *Crisis* 8:26–28.

Jones, T. C. 1996. *Adoption Decision-Making in the African-American Community.* Ph.D. diss., *Dissertation Abstracts International* 57/09:4132.

Kossoudji, S. 1997. "Race and Adoption in Michigan." In *Adoption Policy and Special Needs Children,* edited by R. J. Avery, 51–57. Westport, CT: Auburn House.

Lakin, D., & L. Whitfield. 1997. "Adoption Recruitment: Meeting the Needs of Waiting Children." In *Adoption Policy and Special Needs Children,* edited by R. Avery, 107–126. Westport, CT: Auburn House.

Maas, H. S., & R. E. Engler Jr. 1959. *Children in Need of Parents.* New York: Columbia University Press.

Mason, J., & C. Williams. 1985. "The Adoption of Minority Children: Issues in Developing Law and Policy." In *Adoption of Children with Special Needs: Issues in Law and Policy,* edited by J. Mason & C. Williams, 81–93. Washington, DC: American Bar Association.

McRoy, R. G., Z. Ogelsby & H. Grape. 1997. "Achieving Same Race Placements for African American Children: Culturally Sensitive Approaches." *Child Welfare* 76/1:85–104.

Mont, D. April 1993. *Race and Gender Differences in the Adoption of Special Needs Children.* Unpublished manuscript available from the author, Department of Consumer Economics and Housing, Cornell University, Ithaca, NY 14853.

Morgernstern, J. September 13, 1971. "The New Face of Adoption." *Newsweek,* 67–72.

Mosher, W. D., & C. A. Bachrach. 1996. "Understanding U.S. Fertility: Continuity and Change in the National Survey of Family Growth, 1988–1995." *Family Planning Perspectives* 28/1:4–7.

Multiethnic Placement Act of 1994. Public Law 103-382, 20. Retrieved from www.acf.dhhs.gov/programs/cb/policy/pi9523a.htm.

National Association of Black Social Workers. 1994. *Position Statement: Preserving African American Families.* Detroit, MI: National Association of Black Social Workers.

National Center for Health Statistics. 1999. "Persons Seeking to Adopt." Retrieved from http://www.calib.com/naic/adptsear/adoption/research/stats/seeking.htm.

North American Council on Adoptable Children. 1991. Barriers to Same Race Placement. St. Paul, MN: North American Council on Adoptable Children.

———. 1993. *NACAC Policy Statement on Race and Adoption.* St. Paul, MN: North American Council on Adoptable Children.

O'Hare, W. June 2001. *Child Population: First Data from the 2000 Census.* Baltimore: Annie E. Casey Foundation and Population Reference Bureau.

Oyebade, B. 1990. "African Studies and the Afrocentric Paradigm: A Critique." *Journal of Black Studies* 21/2:233–238.

Rodriguez, P., & A. Meyer. 1990. "Minority Adoptions and Agency Practices." *Social Work* 35:528–531.

Rosenthal, J. A., & V. Groze. September 1990. "Special Needs Adoption: A Study of Intact Families." *Social Service Review* 64:475–505.

Rosenthal, J. A., V. Groze & H. Curiel. 1990. "Race, Social Class, and Special Needs Adoption." *Social Work* 35/6:529–532.

Sandven, K., & M. D. Resnick. 1990. "Informal Adoption among Black Adolescent Mothers." *American Journal of Orthopsychiatry* 60/2:210–224.

Simon, R., H. Altstein & M. Melli. 1994. *The Case for Transracial Adoption.* Washington, DC: American University Press.

Stack, C. 1974. *All Our Kin: Strategies for Survival in a Black Community.* New York: Harper & Row.

Sullivan, A. 1994. "On Transracial Adoption." *Children's Voice* 3/3:4–6.

Turner, R. 1997. "Affirming Consciousness: The Africentric Perspective." In *Child Welfare: An*

Africentric Perspective, edited by J. Everett, S. Chipungu & B. Leashore, 36–57. New Brunswick, NJ: Rutgers University Press.

USDHHS. 1999. *Blending Perspectives and Building Common Ground: A Report to Congress on Substance Abuse and Child Protection.* Washington, DC: U.S. Government Printing Office.

Washington, V. 1987. "Community Involvement in Recruiting Adoptive Homes for Black Children." *Child Welfare League of America* 66/1:57–68.

Williams, C. 1997. "Expanding the Options in the Quest for Permanence." In *Child Welfare: An Africentric Perspective*, edited by J. E. Everett, S. P. Chipungu & B. R. Leashore, 266–290. New Brunswick, NJ: Rutgers University Press.

Yoest, C. 1990. "Points of Light: Informal Adoption in the Black Community." *Children Today* 19/5:8–12.

Conclusion

Still Within Our Power

Given the elevation of the public discourse on the overrepresentation of children of color involved in our nation's child welfare system, we assert that it remains within our power to not only correct the inequities in the child welfare system, but to create and develop social welfare policies and practices that will support and strengthen African American families and other families as well. In view of the many and varied technological and other advances that our nation has made, we are strongly of the opinion that advances can be made in strengthening and supporting families and children so that child abuse and neglect can be prevented and, when it occurs, appropriate and effective services are delivered.

As in our first book (Everett, Chipungu & Leashore 1997), we challenge policy makers, practitioners, and educators to address the "race issue" as they deliberate policy alternatives. Twelve years later, this issue is only beginning to be considered in what we consider a more serious and comprehensive fashion. As in the first book, we recommend in this one that deliberations be inclusive of an Africentric perspective. Failure to do so, as seen twelve years later, only escalates the social and economic costs for our country, and more important, increases the damage to our children and their families.

As we asserted twelve years ago, elevation of race as a factor in policy development, at the least, can educate the public about the historical and cultural tradition of self-help among African American families and communities. We further asserted that the results could include narrow policy directives as with those that protect the interests and well-being of Native American families and children, and/or more responsive, flexible, and humane policy directives. These directives can lead to more culturally competent and effective child welfare practices, including more effective preventive services provided at the community or neighborhood level.

The problem of child abuse and neglect, especially among African American families, as described by Okundaye, Lawrence-Webb and Thornton in chapter 9, is intertwined with many interrelated problems such as substance abuse, homelessness, HIV/AIDS, mental and physical health problems, poverty, racism, and sexism. In response, it is clear that integrative services are needed—services that can be designed so that all families and children benefit. Equally or perhaps more important, political action still remains necessary to achieve social and economic justice and social equality for African American communities, families, and children (e.g., adequate health care, employment, education, affordable housing). Kinship care policies and practices that strengthen and support families and children are needed and should, when possible, include both the child's paternal and maternal family, as suggested in the Johnson and Bryant chapter (chapter 8).

Twelve years ago, we indicated that definitions of child abuse and neglect should be refined—especially neglect—and that litigation against arbitrary applications should be encouraged. Indeed, the latter continues to be on the rise with many jurisdictions sanctioned by the courts to reform their child welfare systems. Likewise, we indicated that some policies should be changed or eliminated, as should unwarranted and harmful intervention, disruptive and stigmatizing approaches, and wasteful investigation of unfounded reports. In the meantime, too many families and children continue to be harmed.

The integration of an Africentric perspective in child welfare policies and practices continues to be needed. Various needs can be effectively addressed with the development of creative services that involve families and communities in serious and meaningful ways. Assessing these needs should be conducted using culturally sensitive and competent approaches, such as the ecological Africentric model proposed by Beckett and Lee. Services should be evaluated and research should be continuously conducted. And as Courtney et al. note: "The failure or unwillingness to at least acknowledge the relationships among race, child welfare services, and child welfare outcomes may only serve to invite uninformed speculation about the reasons for these relationships. Whenever methodologically possible, child welfare researchers should include race as an explanatory factor in research designs and consider their theoretical justification for doing so (i.e., why does the researcher think that race might play a role?)" (Courtney et al. 1996, 127).

Greater knowledge about which intervention models work well for particular problems, families, and children, under what circumstances, and for what length of time are extremely vital for ensuring the safety and health of African American children.

The delivery of child welfare services has significantly changed since the historic passage of the Adoption Assistance and Child Welfare Act of 1980. Greater emphasis is placed on achieving permanency for children through reunification, adoption, legal guardianship, or family preservation. Priority is given to the option of reunification in most states; however, the feasibility of adoption has increased, especially for young children, because subsidies are fairly common and less time consuming than locating relative placements. Legal guardianship is less common because only a few states have passed laws permitting its use. Some are developing initiatives that would provide legal guardianship with or without subsidy to relative placements.

Community-based service models, community partnerships, the increasing use of kinship placement, and family group decision-making models are increasingly being adopted by state and private agencies. Community-based child protection gained prominence even as the Adoption and Safe Families Act (ASFA) was winding its way into law. The values of community-based child welfare practice build upon common concepts and shared values. These values presume that children require a safe and stable family and that the community should support the family in caring for children; that the community has the responsibility to intervene when a child is at risk of harm; that family support services should be nearby and responsive to the linguistic, cultural, and religious needs of the family; that services should be based on strengths as well as the needs of an individual family; that partnerships within the community require open communication and the sharing of information, decisions, and resources by the public child welfare agency; and that the continuity of relationships, supports, and services will provide security to children who must be separated from their families (Barth, Goodhand & Dickinson 1994, 10).

While these approaches are indeed having some effect, the cry for more accountability and declines in state and federal funding for preventive services may significantly minimize any of the positive gains achieved through these approaches. There is little question that in order to prevent the removal of children from their homes, more community supports are needed such as family support programs. Moreover, treatment for substance abuse, mental health disorders, and health services should be easier to access and receive than is currently possible. Presently, when child welfare workers refer families for these types of services, they must contend with cumbersome or lengthy waiting lists, complications in determining eligibility and funding, and/or a mismatch between family problems and service programs. Stronger alliances or collaborations are needed between child welfare agencies and treatment facilities for substance abuse, domestic violence, and mental health problems.

The framework for examining "structural discrimination" provided by Hill in chapter 2 allows us to analyze "the disparate adverse consequences of societal trends and institutional policies on racial minorities that may not have been explicitly designed to have racially discriminatory effects" (Hill 1990, 89). Given the historical analysis of African American children in child welfare provided by Everett in the introductory chapter, one can conclude that African American children have been overrepresented in the child welfare system for the past half century, not just the 1990s. Certain social policies have contributed to this pattern, such as the Flemming Ruling and Title IV-E, which had the manifest functions of expanding services to poor children, but resulted in the latent function of expanding out-of-home placements in order to obtain federal reimbursements. Irrespective of the stated goals and objectives of child welfare policies, they have had disparate adverse consequences for African American children and families. Still, changes are needed in federal and state policies and child welfare practices to reduce these negative effects.

For example, IEPA should be amended to allow the consideration of race in the placement and adoption of African American children or revert to the original MEPA legislation. Passage of this legislation does not appear to have increased the number of adoptions of African American children significantly. In fact, it could be argued that its passage constitutes yet another obstacle in achieving permanence for these children. ASFA timelines need to be made more flexible for birth parents undergoing substance abuse treatment, job training, and domestic violence. Current AFCARS statistics indicate that it takes longer than eighteen months to achieve reunification, adoption, or legal guardianship. Federal rules need to be changed to allow for subsidized legal guardianship and subsidized adoption by relatives of children in foster care. While the increasing use of relative placements ensures a child's safety, the hardships placed on many relatives who are elderly, in poor health, and without financial security is a tremendous burden, especially since the motivation for using relative placements is simply to reduce the number of children in state custody. Shifting the burden is not enough. Providing subsidies to relatives to achieve permanency is as necessary as providing subsidies to strangers who adopt African American children. The Title IV-E administrative rules should allow financial bonuses for states that increase reunification rates. Such incentives are needed to increase the rates of reunification among African American families.

States also need to make changes. Some states have shorter timelines than ASFA requires. States also have the option of allowing for subsidized legal guardianship and subsidized adoption by relatives. States are in a much better position to implement requirements for cultural competence and the increased use of family group conferencing to allow extended family members to make the best decision regarding their related dependent children.

Child welfare practices need to be changed to reduce workers' discriminatory decision making at each phase of the child welfare system—from the initial investigations by CPS, provision of services to reduce placement, decision to remove and place, provision of services to reunify, to decisions to terminate parental rights and place a child for adoption or legal guardianship with relatives as the first preference. Every effort must also be made to carefully screen potential foster homes and relative homes to ensure the safety and protection of children. These and other actions, as was true twelve years ago, still remain within our power. If not us, who? If not now, when?

REFERENCES

Barth, R. P., J. Goodhand & N. S. Dickinson. 1994. "Reconciling Competing Values in the Delivery of Child Welfare Services under ASFA, MEPA, and Community-Based Child Protection." 1999 Child Welfare Training Symposium, "Changing Paradigms of Child Welfare Practice: Responding to Opportunities and Challenges." USDHHS, Administration for Children and Families, Administration on Children, Youth, and Families, Children's Bureau, June 1999.

Courtney, M. E., R. Barth, J. Berrick, D. Brooks, B. Needell & L. Park. 1996. "Race and Child Welfare Services: Past Research and Future Directions." *Child Welfare* 75/2:99–137.

Everett, J., S. Chipungu & B. Leashore, 1997. *Child Welfare: An Africentric Perspective.* New Brunswick, NJ: Rutgers University Press.

Hill, R. 1990. "Economic Forces, Structural Discrimination, and Black Family Instability." In *Black Families*, edited by H. Cheatham & J. Stewart, 87–105. New Brunswick, NJ: Transaction Publishers.

CONTRIBUTORS

JOYCE O. BECKETT, PhD, is professor of social work at the School of Social Work at Virginia Commonwealth University in Richmond, Virginia. She has written numerous articles, book chapters, and monographs. Her areas of research and interest include aging, mental health, intervention with oppressed populations, employment, and women and work.

VAUGHN D. BRYANT is assistant director of the Expanded Advising Program, UAC Stanford University, Palo Alto, California. He holds an MA in marital therapy from Northwestern University, Evanston, Illinois, and has been family therapist in the Oak Park/River Forest (IL) School District.

ALMA J. CARTEN, DSW, ACSW, is currently an associate professor at the Shirley M. Ehrenkranz School of Social Work, New York University, teaching in the social welfare policies and human behavior curricula sequences. She has conducted research and published on family preservation programs, maternal substance abuse, child survivors of the HIV/AIDS epidemic, independent living services for adolescents, and dimensions of abuse and neglect among Caribbean families.

SANDRA P. CHIPUNGU, PhD, is an associate professor at Howard University School of Social Work. Her current research focuses on child welfare, foster care, kinship care, evaluation of services to substance-using pregnant and postpartum women, high-risk youth, children of substance-abusing parents, and peer TA.

JAMES R. DUMPSON, PhD, CSW, ACSW, is currently visiting professor at the Graduate School of Social Service, Fordham University, where the James R. Dumpson Chair in Family and Child Welfare was established, and is dean emeritus of the school. From 1959 to 1965 he was commissioner of welfare for the city of New York, having been appointed by Mayor Robert F. Wagner. At the request of Mayor Abraham D. Beame, in 1975, he again worked for the city in the dual role of administrator of Human Resources Administration and commissioner of Social Services. He is a past president of the Council of Social Work Education, which accredits all graduate and undergraduate programs of social work in the

United States. In April 2000, he was enstooled as Nana Bonsu Abadio I by the minister of culture, Nana Akuoku Sarapong, of the Republic of Ghana, where the James R. Dumpson Library is being built in Agogo, Ashanti.

JOYCE E. EVERETT, PhD, is a full professor and co-director of the doctoral program at Smith College School for Social Work in Northampton, Massachusetts. Her research and publications focus on foster care, family support programs, working-class African American families, and the pedagogy of diversity.

MARIAN S. HARRIS, PhD, is an assistant professor at the School of Social Work, University of Washington, Tacoma. She is a faculty associate at the Chapin Hall Center for Children, University of Chicago, and an adjunct professor and research advisor at the Smith College School for Social Work. She is the co-investigator for a three-year research project (Individual and Social Protective Factors for Children in Informal Kinship Care) funded by the Children's Bureau of the U.S. Department of Health and Human Services.

GINA HIJJAWI is a doctoral student in community psychology at the University of Virginia. Her research focuses on father involvement in low-income families.

ROBERT B. HILL, PhD, is senior researcher at Westat, a research firm in Rockville, Maryland. Previously, he was director of the Institute for Urban Research at Morgan State University and director of research at the National Urban League. He is vice chair of the Census Bureau's Advisory Committee for the African American Population. His research interests are the strengths of families of color and the impact of public policies on African American and low-income families.

WALDO E. JOHNSON JR., PhD, is assistant professor at the School of Social Service Administration, University of Chicago, where he teaches social welfare policy and human behavior in the social environment (in the MA program), and research methods (in the MA and PhD programs). A family researcher, Dr. Johnson's substantive research focuses on male involvement in adolescent pregnancy, nonresident fathers in fragile families, and the physical and psychosocial health statuses of African American males. As a research methodologist, he is interested in the use of qualitative research methods in guiding policy and practice research.

CLAUDIA LAWRENCE-WEBB, DSW, is an assistant professor at the University of Maryland Baltimore County. She is also an affiliate faculty member in the Women's Studies Program and a member of the faculty of the UMBC Graduate School.

BOGART R. LEASHORE, PhD, is former dean and professor emeritus of the Hunter College School of Social Work in New York City. He has lectured and published extensively on child welfare, social services and African American families, and African American males. His child welfare interests include family reunification and legal guardianship, and he has served on the Accountability Panel (formerly the Child Fatality Panel) of the Administration on Children's Services in New York City. While at Hunter, he was principal investigator for the National Resource Center for Foster Care and Permanency Planning.

NICOLE LYNN LEE, MSW, is a doctoral candidate at Virginia Commonwealth University in Richmond. Her areas of research include intersectionality and its relevance to oppressed populations, mental health interventions for African Americans, and art and movement therapies.

MAXWELL C. MANNING, PhD, is an assistant professor at Howard University School of Social Work. During his professional career, Dr. Manning has worked primarily in the public mental health system, supervising the delivery of mental health, substance abuse, and HIV prevention services. He received his MSW from State University of New York at Stony Brook, and his PhD from New York University. He has a certificate from the Philadelphia Family Therapy Training Center, and additional postgraduate training in individual treatment from Hunter College, City University of New York, in New York City.

RUTH G. MCROY, PhD, holds the Ruby Lee Piester Centennial Professorship in Services to Children and Families and is the associate dean for research and director of the Center for Social Work Research at the School of Social Work, University of Texas, Austin. She also holds a joint appointment in the UT Center for African and African American Studies and is a member of the UT Academy of Distinguished Professors.

CRYSTAL S. MILLS, PhD, is currently professor at Eastern Michigan University, Social Work Department. She has also served as adjunct faculty at the Union Institute. She has been a pivotal force in bringing the need for culturally competent service delivery to the academic community. Her career has spanned over twenty years and includes the development of Ohana Inc., an agency that provides shelter and support services for homeless women and their children.

CARMEN P. MOTEN, MPH, PhD, is a behavioral scientist in the Division of Services and Intervention Research at the National Institute of Mental Health, National Institutes of Health, Bethesda, Maryland, and lecturer at Howard University, Washington DC. She has conducted research on women and domestic violence, sociocultural issues and mental health, and children and family mental health issues.

JOSHUA N. OKUNDAYE, PhD, is an assistant professor at the University of Maryland, Baltimore County. His research and publications are in the areas of addiction, HIV/AIDS, and spirituality and kinship care. Dr. Okundaye is a licensed clinical social worker with extensive experience in providing services to adolescents and their families.

JACQUELINE MARIE SMITH, PhD, is an associate professor of social work at Howard University. She has served on technical panels for national studies on foster care and African American Catholics, as a policy analyst for the Office of the Assistant Secretary of Policy, Planning, and Evaluation at HHS, and a visiting scholar at Chapin Hall at the University of Chicago. Her recent publications include "Foster Care Children with Disabilities" in the *Journal of Health and Social Policy*.

PAMELA L. THORNTON, MSW, is an adjunct professor at the University of Maryland, Baltimore County, where she currently teaches Information Technology in Social Work. Ms. Smith is also a doctoral student at the University of Maryland, Baltimore, where she is investigating adaptive coping strategies of African American foster care children and parents.

DEBRA P. USHER, MPA, is currently the chief operations officer for the Metropolitan Girl Scout Council of Southeastern Michigan in Detroit, Michigan. She has extensive history in the delivery of child welfare and family services. Her career spans over twenty years and includes tenure as the deputy director of Community Service Programs in Washington, DC, and the director of Strong Families/Safe Children for the Wayne County Family Independence Agency.

MELVIN N. WILSON is professor of psychology at the University of Virginia, Charlottesville. His academic, research, and training activities focus on understanding contextual processes and outcome in African American families. Besides research with young, low-income, unwed, and nonresident fathers, he is interested in developing prevention and intervention protocols aimed at fostering parent-child communication and helping young men meeting family responsibilities.

LAKEESHA N. WOODS is a doctoral student in clinical psychology at the University of Virginia. Her current research pertains to cultural influences on youth development, and her clinical interests are in youth and families, and forensic psychology.

INDEX

stringent suitable home requirements and, 48
Child Welfare Act (1989), 215
Child Welfare League of America, 258, 264
child welfare system: abuse investigations, 2; adoption priorities in, 110; Africentric perspective and, 77, 214–222; barriers to service in, 199; budgetary constraints, 2; challenges for African American families, 135–139; child maltreatment concerns of, 134; child rescue philosophy in, 3; choices for African American children in, 110; costs of, 78; cultural insensitivity in, 72; culturally relevant services in, 139; decision-making process and, 64–66; discrimination in, 257; disproportionality in, 38*fig*, 57; dominant American values in, 135, 136; Eurocentric perspective on, 226; flaws in, 2; impact of concept of nuclear family on, 8, 135, 138; institutional racism in, 6; interest in family dysfunction, 226; invisibility of African American children in, 4; mental health services and, 62, 243–245; not intended for services for African Americans, 61; overrepresentation in foster care due to class status, 58; overrepresentation of African American children in, 12; placement monitoring, 2; policy changes in, 80–84; professionals in, 137; racial bias in, 12; service delivery issues, 257–259; services to European immigrants, 61; treatment of unwed fathers, 176; variances in involvement with, 37
Chipungu, S., 6, 69–70, 77–86, 134, 135
Chrenoff, R., 243
civil rights, 48
Civil Rights Act (1964): Title VI, 60
Clinton, B., 83, 233
Close, M., 1
Coale, A., 16
Cohen, P., 152
Collectivism, 205
Colletta, N., 126
Collins, P., 159
Colorado: Family-to-Family initiative in, 234
community: African American, 216–217; care, 217; child care in, 158; development, 4; ethnic, 5; family preservation and, 225–239; improvement, 99; informal adoptions in, 259–261; kinship groups in, 227; needs, 94; neighborhood-based services, 225–239; power, 105; resources, 217; self-help values in, 146; service organizations in, 157; social welfare agencies in, 61; support systems in, 157
consciousness raising, 99
Cook, J., 230
coping: capabilities, 146; skills, 105; strategies, 6
Corcoran, M., 50
Courtney, M., 58, 93, 135, 257
Cowger, C., 102, 103
Crampton, D., 221, 222
credit unions, 61

Creighton, C., 126
critical analysis, 99–100
cross-cultural perspectives, 95
Crosson-Tower, C., 160
Crumbley, J., 162, 164
cultural: beliefs, 72, 148; competence, 85, 89, 217; differences, 136, 203; diversity, 218; insensitivity, 72, 93, 262; knowledge, 220; norms, 220; perspective, 5; values, 72
Curran, L., 48
Curry, L., 61
Curtis, P., 62, 73

Dalaker, J., 32
Danziger, S., 130, 171
Danzy, J., 94, 217
Daskal, J., 202
Davis, L., 97, 135
Day, D., 58, 59, 60, 61, 73
day care, 60
decision-making: Africentric perspective, 214–222; family group, 214, 217, 218, 220–222; family leadership in, 219; foster care and, 64–66; racism and, 64–66; structures of, 218; victimization in, 135, 136
delinquency, 4, 37, 63–64, 132
Demo, D., 147
Denby, R., 93
depression, 132, 150, 244
desegregation, 48
development: cognitive, 149
Devore, W., 163
discrimination: employment and, 130; by sectarian adoption agencies, 5; structural, 8, 12, 59; unintentional, 59
diversity theory, 1, 3, 5, 57, 60, 61, 95
divorce, 124, 130, 324
Dodson, J., 1, 3, 5, 57, 60, 61, 95
Dore, M., 200
Downs, A., 58
Downs, S., 162
Dressel, P., 216
DuBois, W.E.B., 3, 157
Dubowitz, H., 162
Dumpson, J., 7, 225–239
Dye, J., 128

Early, T., 102, 103
ecological perspective, 6, 94–98, 114–117*tab*, 203–206; connectedness and, 94; eco-maps and, 96, 97; general systems theory and, 94, 95; genograms and, 96; neighborhood-based model and, 232–233; subsystems in, 206; system boundaries in, 206; system interconnections, 206; systems of separate but interrelated members in, 206
eco-maps, 96, 97, 219
Edelstein, S., 207
Edna McConnel Clark Foundation, 233, 234
Ehrle, J., 69–70
Elizabethan Poor Laws (1601), 230
Ellison, C., 146, 147
Ellwood, D., 48